TIME FOR TEA:

Victorian Tea-Time Treats
and
Decadent Desserts

Moira Allen, Editor

A Victorian Voices Publication

Also available from VictorianVoices.net:

A Victorian Christmas Treasury

Bits About Animals:
A Treasury of Victorian Animal Anecdotes

Graveyard Humor:
Quaint and Curious Inscriptions and Epitaphs

Needle-Crafts from a Victorian Workbasket

Visit http://www.victorianvoices.net/books/index.shtml for details
and ordering info

Victorian Times
A free monthly e-journal of Victoriana!

Visit http://www.victorianvoices.net/VT/index.shtml to subscribe,
download back issues, read excerpts, or access the print edition

Contents

Victorian Cookery for the Modern Cook

Afternoon tea is a lovely tradition—one that is as honored in Britain today as it was in Victorian times. In America, tea-shops, afternoon teas and special "Victorian" teas are growing in popularity (and in price!). On either side of the pond, you're likely to find tea dainties much like those that graced the Victorian table.

Small wonder that Victorian women's magazines sought to meet the growing demand amongst their readers to provide both new treats and old favorites for the beloved afternoon tea. Just as magazines today fill their pages with mouthwatering temptations, so did Victorian publications. The recipes in this collection are drawn from two popular Victorian women's magazines: *The Girl's Own Paper* (from 1881-1902), and *Cassell's Family Magazine* (1875-1895)[1].

Living as we do in an age of microwaves, crock-pots, and fast foods, our first reaction to some of the instructions in a Victorian recipe might be "Huh? How's that again?" The recipes in this volume come from a day when there were no shortcuts. If you wished to make a cake, you started with flour and eggs; if you wished to create a dish with fruit, chances were good that you might have plucked that same fruit (or at least asked your gardener to do it) from your own kitchen garden. City dwellers might have purchased their ingredients from a grocer (or several grocers—one for "dry goods" such as flour and sugar, a "greengrocer" for fruits and vegetables, a butcher for meats and fish), but picking up a package of cake mix was not an option.

So here are some tips on understanding the underlying principles of these recipes, and how to adapt them for modern cooking techniques! (I've also provided a **Glossary of Victorian Cooking Terms** on page 119 to help explain a few of the less common terms and ingredients you may encounter in this book.)

What's for Pudding?

First, let's have a quick discussion of terms. This book offers a host of recipes for "puddings." If you're a British reader, this will be familiar territory. If you're an American, however, the first thing you need to know is that the British meaning of the word "pudding" is very different from the American dessert of the same name.

What we call "pudding" in America, the British would call a "custard." The American pudding is generally a soft, creamy concoction of milk and eggs: custard pudding, chocolate pudding, banana pudding, etc. In Britain, these would come under the category of "custards and creams."

A British pudding is a far more solid bit of fare. Most Americans are familiar only with one type of British-style pudding: The famous (or infamous) Christmas plum pudding. American versions of this holiday treat are often so overloaded with fruits and flavorings that the plum pudding has taken on nearly as

---

[1] Both magazines ran well into the 20th century, but these were the best years for "Victorian tea recipes." For *The Girl's Own Paper,* 1902 marks the end of its "Victorian" period, while *Cassell's Family Magazine* began moving away from women's topics such as food and fashion in 1896.

unhappy a reputation as Christmas fruit cake. If you loathe plum pudding, don't worry; this book offers plenty of delicious recipes that will make you forget all about it!

Another type of pudding many Americans may be familiar with is "Boston brown bread." Yes, technically, it's a steamed pudding. A can of Boston brown bread, available at any grocer's, will give you a fair idea of what to expect from a typical Victorian pudding dessert. (Ironically, the one recipe for "Boston Brown Bread" in this collection is for a bread, not a pudding!)

As I said, a British pudding is solid, not creamy. It's not quite a cake; it tends to be a bit heavier and much moister and smoother in texture. Puddings could be sweet or savory (though this cookbook, of course, focuses on the sweet varieties). British and Victorian puddings begin with flour and eggs and suet or lard. Traditionally, they are steamed. In Victorian days, a pudding steamer was an essential utensil in every kitchen; today, they're a bit harder to find. But while it's certainly possible to buy a genuine pudding steamer, you can achieve the same results much more easily and cheaply with a large, covered kettle and a smaller bowl or even a coffee can!

I won't even attempt to explain how to steam a pudding today. There are several excellent sites online that do a far better job at this than I ever could, including numerous YouTube demonstrations. Here are two to get you started:

How to Steam a Pudding
http://www.bbcgoodfood.com/technique/how-steam-pudding

Steamed Puddings
http://www.cooksinfo.com/steamed-puddings

Modern British usage can add to the confusion over the question of "what is a pudding?" because, today, the term is synonymous with "dessert." Where in America we might ask "What's for dessert?", in Britain the question would more likely be "What's for pudding?" The answer might be ice cream or cake or any other sweet dish. (By the way, the word "sweets" can also mean "desserts," rather than simply candy, as is the more common American usage.) The reason lies in the class system: "Dessert" is a term long associated with the pricey dainties of the upper classes, while "pudding" was a treat commonly enjoyed by everyday folks. The word "dessert" is considered overly posh (or American). Hence, "pudding" may mean "dessert," but doesn't always in fact mean *pudding!*

Speaking of Desserts, Let's Talk of Tea...

While a pudding may be a dessert, and dessert may be pudding, a pudding is actually unlikely to be served as a tea-time treat. This is because it is, actually, in American terms, a *dessert*. It's most likely to be served after the main meal of the day or the final meal of the day. And here's where things can continue to get confusing for Americans.

The term "tea," as used for a meal, can be confusing even in Britain. Americans associate the term with a dainty, elegant gathering—often something that we can obtain only at very high prices in very posh restaurants. There are afternoon teas, cream teas, high teas, and just "tea."

The tea-time recipes in this book would have been intended, generally, for an "afternoon tea." This is a light snack (or not so light) that is generally credited to Anna Maria Russell, the 7th Duchess of Bedford and Lady of the Bedchamber (and lifelong friend) to Queen Victoria. Allegedly, the duchess felt a bit peckish around 5 p.m. and established a habit of having tea and a light snack served, and the habit became fashionable.

If, as an American visitor to England, you hold any hopes of getting a "late lunch" in that country, dream on. From about 3-5 p.m., all you will be able to find in most restaurants is "tea." Today, this means *tea*, of course—and a selection of sweet snacks, such as cake, cookies ("biscuits"), tea-cakes, muffins, and scones. Occasionally you might also find savory finger-sandwiches, but most often, you'll find sweets.

This is not, as some suppose, "high" tea. Afternoon tea is "low" tea—because it was originally served on "low" tables. "Low tea" is served in the parlor, not at the dining table—in America, it might be served in the living room, perhaps, around a coffee table. "High tea" is actually a full meal—often the last meal of the day, or a meal preceding a very late "supper." It is served in the kitchen or dining room on the "high" table, i.e., the table where meals are customarily served. A pudding might indeed be served to finish a "high tea."

A "cream tea" was once most commonly found in Devonshire, as it consisted of tea and scones and jam and clotted Devonshire cream. Now, one can often find "cream teas" advertised in tea rooms throughout Britain. A tip to the newcomer: The Devonshire cream goes on your scone, *not* in your tea!

Many of the recipes in this book are appropriate for an afternoon or "low" tea. Any sort of cake, muffin, scone, "biscuit" (the British word for "cookie"), or bread such as certain types of buns, Sally Lunns, etc. would be quite at home on the Victorian tea table. A low tea was also likely to include savories, such as small sandwiches and the sorts of nibbles that Americans would refer to as "appetizers."

Cooking, Victorian Style

Another element of confusion that the reader may encounter in attempting to follow the recipes in this book are the lack of standard measurements. Such measurements *did* exist in Victorian times—the teaspoon, which originated as an apothecary measure of one drachm or ¼ of a tablespoon, had already evolved in the 1700's to its present measure of a third of a tablespoon. However, one gains the impression that devices such as measuring cups and measuring spoons were *not* standard equipment in a Victorian kitchen. Hence, you're more likely to be told to measure out a bit of something "the size of your thumb" or "the size of your fist."

By 1900, the idea of using standardized measures in recipes was only just becoming fashionable. In article from *The Girl's Own Paper* on page 44, from that year, the author notes that readers were beginning to ask for standard measures by volume such as teaspoons and tablespoons, rather than weight, because many households could not afford to keep a good set of weights for the kitchen.

I suspect that one reason the recipes in Victorian magazines don't trouble themselves with standard measures is that, at least prior to 1900, they were written *by* people who knew how to cook, *for* people who knew how to cook. As you probably already know in your own kitchen, the more experienced a cook you are, the less concerned you are with precise measurements. You know just how much moisture needs to be added to a certain amount of flour to make it workable—and this may not be precisely the same amount every time. You probably *do* use "a pinch of this and a lump of that." So, I suspect, did the authors of these recipes—most of whom were well-known cooks and recipe-writers in their day.

Knowing how to cook was an essential part of Victorian life. Today, with mixes and microwaves and frozen foods, one can survive quite well without ever really learning how to "cook from scratch." Not so in the 1800's. Whether one did one's own cooking, or employed a cook, meals had to be prepared from the most basic, raw ingredients every day. Hence, these recipes were written for a reader who could be expected to know not only how to make it work, but how to adapt a recipe depending on how many people actually needed to be served.

Even so, the instructions in these pages are sufficiently detailed to enable the modern reader to apply them in the modern kitchen. Often, too, one is able to take helpful shortcuts; instead of letting your "double cream" stand on the milk for at least 24 hours in a cool place, today you have only to pick up a carton of "extra thick" cream for the task. Nor, if you wish to cook something with apples, need you rely upon "dried apple chips from America." Isinglass, thankfully, has been replaced (even by Victorian times) with plain gelatin.

Another issue that may give the modern reader cause to pause and scratch one's head is oven temperatures. A Victorian cook had various means of regulating the temperature of the stove or oven over (or within) which she cooked—but setting a number on a dial was *not* one of them! Cooking temperatures were typically governed by the type of fuel. Though gas stoves made their first appearance around 1850, most kitchen stoves burned wood or coal. One adjusted the temperature by the type or quantity of fuel used (some woods burn "hotter" than others) or by the location on the stove where one actually placed an item. The nearer the firebox, the hotter—so if you wished to bring something to a boil, you would place it directly over the firebox, whereas if you wished something to simmer or stew slowly, you'd move it to the back or side of the stove, as far away from the flames as possible.

Hence, cooking instructions aren't going to tell you to bake for 30 minutes at 375°. They'll advise, instead, to cook in a "slow" oven or a "hot" oven. Here's a handy chart provided by the National Commerce Department[2] to help interpret such instructions:

Cool Oven	200°F	90°C
Very Slow Oven	250°F	120°C
Slow Oven	300-325°F	150-160°C
Moderately Slow	325-350°F	160-180°C
Moderate Oven	350-375°F	180-190°C
Moderately Hot	375-400°F	190-200°C
Hot Oven	400-450°F	200-230°C
Very Hot Oven	450-500°F	230-260°C
Fast Oven	450-500°F	230-260°C

Finally, it's worth noting that Victorian recipes could rarely be called "health-conscious" or "heart-friendly" or any of the other terms we use today to designate food that is supposed to be *good* for you. Basic ingredients were often *rich* ingredients: Eggs, butter, sugar, lard, suet, and so on. But oddly enough, this didn't seem to lead to scores of obese Victorians. Though Victorian ladies might never have heard the term "portion control," they practiced it; it was considered unladylike to be "greedy" at the tea-table, so a diner was unlikely to load up a plate with goodies and "dig in." Their approach was to enjoy, not to overindulge.

With that in mind, bon appetit!

---

[2] From https://en.wikipedia.org/wiki/Oven_temperatures

The Girl's Own Paper

One of my favorite Victorian magazines—indeed, the one that got me hooked in Victorian magazines in general—is *The Girl's Own Paper*. This began in 1880 and continued, in one form or another, well into the 1950's. It began as a weekly paper, with a bound collection for the year being issued each October. (The collection was usually known as *The Girl's Own Annual*, so either title is correct.)

The original intent of *The Girl's Own Paper*, as expressed by its original editor Charles Peters, was "to foster and develop that which was highest and noblest in the girlhood and womanhood of England.... putting the best things first, and banishing the worthless from his pages." The magazine was published by the Religious Tract Society—and so, not surprisingly, it provided a great many articles, stories and poems of a strong moral and religious nature.

However, unlike many religious magazines of its day, *The Girl's Own Paper*, went far beyond that. It is the most varied Victorian "women's" magazine I've seen. Besides articles of an obviously feminine interest—covering such topics as fashion, cooking, and housekeeping—*The Girl's Own Paper* covered a wide range of general interest topics, including history, archaeology, science, government and law. In earlier years, such articles might take on a somewhat condescending tone (e.g., "A chat on government for girls,") but in later years the magazine clearly accepted that women had minds and weren't afraid to use them. The magazine was also of interest in its coverage of emerging issues for women, such as education, work—and whether women ought to be permitted to ride bicycles!

The Girl's Own Paper was packed with cooking features. Many of its "Useful Hints" filler sections were simply collections of recipes. It offered articles that served as "cooking classes" for the less experienced cook, as well as more advanced recipes. Its most prolific cooking contributors were, respectively, Phillis (later "Phyllis") Browne and Lucy Helen Yates. I can find little information on Phillis Browne, but a contemporary review of one of her cookbooks ranks her alongside the famous Mrs. Beeton (whose book on cooking and household management is still reprinted today)—so evidently she was considered a leading cookery author in her day. Phillis Browne also contributed many articles to *Cassell's Family Magazine* (from which recipes will be found in Part II of this book); however, her articles there focused more on household issues than on cooking.

Lucy Helen Yates also wrote several cookery books, as well as books on money and finance. She began writing for *The Girl's Own Paper* in 1892. Her articles often provided specific recipes for the month or season, drawing upon what would be available in the market for that time of year.

Cooking articles in *The Girl's Own Paper* were generally presented (like most of the articles in that magazine) in a friendly, helpful, often chatty tone. This makes them particularly helpful to today's cook, who may need a friendly hand to guide them through some of the intricacies of Victorian cooking!

CREAMS.

HERE is so much room for variety in this branch of cookery that the difficulty is to know where to begin. However, the best thing we can do is to speak of general rules of universal application, and urge the members of our class to try the various combinations which are suggested for themselves, and if possible to invent one or two on their own account.

It will be remembered that when we were speaking of the quantity of gelatine used in making jelly we came to the conclusion that an ounce of good gelatine would be needed to set a pint and a half of liquid, exclusive of the wine and brandy, that is to say, an ounce of good gelatine was considered sufficient for about a pint and three-quarters of liquid. In making creams, however, we have to remember that the materials used have a little more consistency than those employed in making jelly, and therefore rather less gelatine is needed. Consequently we may calculate on being able to make a quart of cream with an ounce of gelatine, and occasionally a still smaller portion of stiffening is necessary.

Of course the gelatine must be soaked for an hour, or longer if possible, in as much milk as will barely cover it. When it has absorbed all the liquid, and has swelled considerably, it should be turned into a small stewpan and stirred over the fire until it has entirely dissolved. It must then be allowed to cool before it is mixed with the other ingredients.

In very rich creams cream only, pleasantly flavoured, is used. Thus made, however, cream is expensive, and some people would consider it a little sickly. It is very usual, therefore, to use half cream and half milk, and to enrich the milk by making a custard of it with eggs. To make the custard we beat in a basin the yolks of three and the white of one egg. Well strain these, and mix them with half a pint of milk. We pour the mixture into a jug, set this in a saucepan of hot water over the fire, and stir the contents of the jug until the custard is thick enough to coat the spoon, when we take it up. We must be careful not to boil our custard too long, or it will curdle. What is wanted is that it should be thick, as thick as the double cream, but perfectly smooth. Before the cream is added to the custard it should be well whipped, by which means it will not only be made lighter, but it will expand and occupy more room. Here I must say a word about the method of whipping cream. For one thing we must have "double" cream, that is, cream which is very thick, in consequence of its having stood twenty-four hours on the milk. The cream should be put into a cool place until it is wanted; indeed, if it has to stand a little while before being used, the vessel containing it should be put into another one which has cold water in it, and the cream should be left uncovered. When the custard and gelatine are almost cool, we put the cream into a large bowl and whisk it lightly and regularly with an ordinary egg-whisk until, though still smooth, it begins to stiffen. The great thing

in doing this is to stop in plenty of time. If we keep on only half a minute too long our cream will be spoilt, because it will crack or "turn," as it is called. We may know when it is sufficiently whisked by its hanging to the spoon when the latter is lifted up. We shall find that the cream after it is whipped occupies very nearly twice as much room as it did originally. If we liked, instead of using half a pint of whipped cream we could use a quarter of a pint, to which the whites of two eggs beaten to froth had been added. White of egg is often added to cream which is to be whipped, and the object of the addition is chiefly to increase the quantity. We should always remember to whisk cream in a cool place. It is much more difficult to whip in summer time than it is in winter. If, notwithstanding all our care, it should turn slightly, a spoonful of something cold, milk or water, should be put with it.

We may now flavour the custard with an ounce of white sugar, half a teaspoonful of essence of vanilla, two tablespoonfuls of brandy, if this is allowed. Brandy is frequently omitted, but it is a very great improvement to a cream of this kind, for vanilla and brandy always go well together. If the custard be cool we stir the whipped cream lightly into it, and turn the whole into a mould, which has, of course, been first scalded with boiling water, then rinsed out with cold water, and left wet.

As this cream may serve as a sort of model for an indefinite number of creams, I will give the recipe once more, briefly and altogether, so that there may be no mistake. Soak an ounce of gelatine in as much milk as will barely cover it. Make a custard with half a pint of milk, the yolks of three and the white of one egg. Add a tablespoonful of white sugar, half a teaspoonful of essence of vanilla, and two tablespoonfuls of brandy. When the custard is cool stir in lightly half a pint of cream, which has been whipped to a froth. Pour the mixture into a mould, and put it on ice or in a cool place till set.

If we wished to make a fruit cream we should observe still the same proportions and follow the same method, but we should substitute fruit pulp for the custard. This fruit pulp may be made either with fresh fruit, with jam, or with tinned fruit. Fresh juicy fruit, such as raspberries or strawberries, should be picked, then have a little white sugar sprinkled over them to make the juice flow freely. It should then be rubbed through a hair sieve, to make the pulp. A pint of fresh fruit will be sufficient for half a pint of cream.

Hard fruit should be slightly stewed before it is used, or it will not go through the sieve easily. Sometimes it is sufficient to chop the fruit small, or pound it before passing it through the sieve. A very delicious cream may be made in this way with tinned pine-apple.

When preserved fruit is used, two good tablespoonfuls of jam should be stewed with water, and the juice should be strained off. A little lemon juice may be added to jam, but it is not required for fresh fruit. A very pretty effect may be produced by moulding jelly and cream together, or by mixing creams of different colours. Thus, a mould may be filled to the depth of an inch with clear colourless jelly garnished with three or four large green grapes. When this is slightly set the mould may be filled with strawberry cream. Another effective dish may be made by filling a mould with alternate layers of half an inch thick chocolate cream and custard cream. Pink and white layers may be substituted for the brown and white by colouring half the custard cream with cochineal. To make chocolate cream, dissolve four ounces of chocolate in a pint and a half of milk and boil for ten minutes, flavour with vanilla and

add sugar to taste. Dissolve a third of an ounce of gelatine in a little milk; add this when cool. This cream is very good moulded by itself, and served with custard.

Sometimes jellies and creams are put into a mould which is fitted with a cylinder inside. Clear jelly is put into the outer portion of the mould, and when this has set the inner cylinder is taken out and the centre is filled with cream. Cylinder moulds are rather expensive, but a cheap substitute may be made with a plain round mould and a gallipot, or a circular mould and a small basin. When these are used the small mould is placed inside the other until the outer portion of jelly is set. It is then removed and the vacant space is filled with cream.

Blanc-mange, or, as it means literally, white food, ought, strictly speaking, to be always flavoured with almonds. It is, however, very usually flavoured with laurel leaves, cinnamon, lemon, or essence. It may be made with calves' feet stock, gelatine, cornflour, or arrowroot, and is generally named after the ingredient of which it is composed; thus we have cornflour blanc-mange, ground rice blanc-mange, arrowroot blanc-mange, &c. When gelatine is used, proceed as follows:— Soak an ounce of gelatine in as much milk as will cover it, blanch and pound half an ounce of sweet almonds and four or five bitter ones, and moisten them every now and then with a few drops of water to keep them from turning to oil. Put with the paste rather less than a quart of new milk, and turn it into a saucepan with the soaked gelatine and a little sugar. Stir the mixture over the fire until the gelatine is dissolved, and strain it through a napkin into a jug, and when it is almost cold mould it, and be careful to pour it off slowly and gently for fear any sediment still remains at the bottom. If the flavour is liked, a larger quantity of almonds may be used, but flavouring of any kind is like sugar. Some people like an abundance, and others are satisfied with a mere suspicion. A cook, however, should study the taste of those for whom she labours. If she satisfy them, and is able to lay the flattering unction to her soul that they have reason to be satisfied, she may disregard theories.

Cream alone, or cream and milk, is sometimes used when a very rich blanc-mange is wanted. When this is introduced, the blanc-mange should first be made with milk, and the cream should be added afterwards unboiled.

Blanc-mange made with cornflour is very easily prepared. Take four even tablespoonfuls of cornflour, which has been mixed to a smooth paste with a little cold milk, pour gradually on it a quart of boiling milk, which has been sweetened pleasantly, and flavoured either with lemon, cinnamon, or essence; stir it well to keep it from getting into lumps, put it back into the saucepan and boil it for two or three minutes, or till it leaves the side of the saucepan with the spoon, stirring it briskly all the time. Pour it into a damp mould, and when cold and set, turn it upon a glass dish and serve it with stewed fruit. For the sake of appearance blanc-mange can, if liked, be coloured with a little cochineal, or a little bright-coloured jelly may be set at the bottom of the mould before the blanc-mange is poured in. Cornflour blanc-mange is very wholesome and inexpensive, and when it is put on a bright clear glass dish, and pleasantly flavoured, and served with a good *compote* of fruit, it is a preparation by no means to be despised.

PHILLIS BROWNE.

TEA-CAKES AND ROLLS FOR BREAKFAST AND TEA.

"TELL me where is fancy bread?"

"At the baker's."

Right. I, however, should like fancy bread to be at home also, and therefore I want us to talk for a little while about how to make one or two very simple and inexpensive sorts thereof for daily use.

Nothing adds more to the appearance or elegance of a breakfast or tea-table than a variety of breads. Yet what a rarity it is to see anything but hot rolls from the baker's and hot buttered toast. Fortunately brown bread is much more common than it used to be, and brown bread, as we all know, is very nourishing and wholesome. Was it not Thackeray who said that an epicure was one who never tired of brown bread and fresh butter? Yet even brown bread would be more thoroughly appreciated if it were alternated occasionally with something else. Very few people now-a-days can eat a good breakfast. If you know of anyone who has a hearty appetite first thing in the morning and can eat a good meal before commencing his daily work, congratulate him; there is not much the matter with his liver. But if you come to think of it, you will discover that such individuals are very scarce. As a rule, people drink a cup of coffee or tea and only pretend to eat at breakfast, and then when the morning is half over they feel faint and sick, and are not half so energetic as they would have been if only they had had a good meal first thing in the morning.

One of the chief objects aimed at by the model modern housekeeper is to provide little appetising delicacies which shall render breakfast irresistible. Now we believe that the girls of our class aspire to be model housekeepers; some day let them try the effect of a little variety in the bread department. They have almost exhausted their resources in other directions. Take a new departure and see what can be done with a judicious course of old-fashioned Yorkshire tea-cake, milk rolls, scones, Vienna bread, and similar delicacies. I shall be very much astonished if this action on their part does not call forth the enthusiasm of those whom it is intended to please, and I quite expect that my friends will tire of making the appetising little novelties before fathers and brothers tire of eating them.

Hot buttered toast is the usual resource of those who seek variety in the way of bread, but like every article which has been saturated with fatty matter it is most indigestible, so also are hot muffins and pikelets. I never see these without thinking that stewed flannel petticoats would be almost as digestible; I shall not, therefore, say anything in recommendation of them. But simple fancy breads cannot be harmful; they are so delicious, and so easily made, too, that they are in the reach of all who are making little experiments in the cookery department.

For, understand, I am speaking now of home-made fancy bread and rolls; I am not advising you to send round to the baker's and get a specimen of his wares, but to try and make them yourself.

It is astonishing how frightened even clever cooks are to make anything into the composition of which yeast enters. This is not at all to be wondered at, because there have been so many failures made with yeast. Still it is scarcely possible to fail if strict attention be devoted to the directions here given. It will be noticed that I have recommended the use of German yeast. This is because German yeast is generally more easily obtained than brewer's yeast, besides which the latter is apt to be bitter. In large towns German yeast can be procured fresh every day. In country places brewer's yeast is more usually employed, and the brewer's cart is eagerly looked for by those who want the requisite supply of the article.

Our first experiment shall be made with what is called Vienna bread. Do you all know what Vienna bread is, I wonder? Have you ever, when travelling abroad, or making purchases in a good baker's shop, noticed some small, light, soft bread baked in the shape of horns or horse-shoes. You never see these horns very long, for they are sure to be sold off quickly. I cannot imagine why bakers do not sell Vienna bread more frequently than they do, for it is always appreciated. Yet you cannot buy it without specially ordering it, even in the outskirts of London. However we are going to be independent of the bakers.

Procure an ounce of German yeast fresh and dry. Choose a bowl that will hold about six pounds of flour, and put into it one pound of Vienna flour and one pound of best biscuit flour. (You know what Vienna flour is; it is flour which has been made very fine and white by being passed through silken sieves. It is used for making puff-paste and superior cakes.) Mix the flour and a pinch of salt, then rub in two ounces of fresh butter. Dissolve the German yeast by mixing with it a spoonful of sugar, then add very gradually a pint of lukewarm milk and two well-beaten eggs. Lukewarm milk — that is, milk which is neither cold nor hot — may be produced by mixing one part of boiling liquid with two parts of cold. Mix the liquid with the flour and knead it till it is smooth and lithe. Score it across the top with a knife, cover the bowl with a clean towel, and leave it in a warm place to rise.

This putting the dough to rise is the point where so many cooks fail, and yet people who are accustomed to use yeast seem to know exactly what is necessary. The bowl must be put in a warm place, but not too warm, and it must not be placed in a draught. If it is made too warm the dough will rise quickly and form a sort of spongy mass which will not answer our purpose at all. If kept too cold it will not rise sufficiently. In summer time it may be put further from the fire than in winter. Let it rise till it feels very light and lithe when touched with the fingers, and is more than twice its original bulk. It is rather unsafe to say how long dough should rise, because a good deal depends upon the quality of the yeast, the place in which it stands, the time of year, and also the method of mixing. When sufficiently risen, turn it upon a baking board and roll it out as you would pastry into pieces about seven inches square and a quarter of an inch thick. Cut the square across from corner to corner; this will give you four triangular pieces for each square. Roll each one of these lightly, beginning at the wide side, put them on a buttered baking tin, with the side uppermost where the point of pastry is, and draw the two ends of the roll towards each other to make a sort of crescent. Let the rolls rise again till they look light, brush them over with beaten egg or milk, and bake in a quick oven. The bread is most excellent when eaten cold.

Yorkshire tea-cakes are also delicious preparations. A true Yorkshireman would tell you that, compared with the sally-lunn of the London shops, they were as "moonlight unto sunlight or as water unto wine." They may be easily made as follows:—

Yorkshire Tea-cakes.—Rub six ounces of butter into two pounds of flour, adding a pinch of salt. Dissolve rather less than an ounce of fresh German yeast in half a pint of lukewarm water, put the flour into a bowl which will hold three times its quantity, scoop a hole in the centre, leaving flour to cover the bottom of the bowl, and pour the dissolved yeast into the hole. Draw flour down from the sides and mix it with the liquor to make a smooth batter. Sprinkle a little flour over the top, cover the bowl with a cloth, and leave it in a warm place till bubbles begin to rise through the flour. Beat two eggs and mix them with half a teacupful of milk, add lukewarm milk, and knead well till the dough is smooth and elastic. Cover the bowl again, and let the dough rise till it is quite light. Divide this quantity into ten pieces, roll these till they are about the size of an ordinary saucer, put them on a baking tin and let them rise for a few minutes, prick them with a fork, and bake in a quick oven. When wanted, split them in halves, toast them, butter them, and serve them hot; or split them, butter them, and serve them cold.

Much as we may enjoy teacakes, sally-lunns are not to be despised, and they will doubtless find advocates among true-born cockneys.

Sally-lunns.—Put a pound and a half of flour into a bowl and mix a pinch of salt with it. Put three-quarters of a pint of milk into a stew-pan with four ounces of butter, and let it remain till the butter is melted. The milk should not be much more than lukewarm. Dissolve the yeast with a little sugar, add the milk gradually, and stir both into the flour and also two well-beaten eggs. When quite smooth, divide the dough into four parts, place each of these in a well-greased tin, cover them over, and let them rise till they are about three times their original size. Bake in a quick oven. Sally-lunns are, it is well known, split into three portions before being toasted and buttered.

Milk-rolls with Yeast.—Mix a pinch of salt with two pounds of flour in a bowl. Make a hole in the centre and put in an ounce of German yeast which, with half an ounce of baking powder, has been dissolved in half a pint of lukewarm milk. Work in flour from the sides to make the sponge; sprinkle flour over the top and let the sponge prove or rise till bubbles break through the surface. Add gradually another pint of lukewarm milk and work the dough till it is smooth and elastic. With your hand form the paste into small balls or ovals the size of walnuts, put them on a baking sheet, cover them over, and leave them in a warm place to rise. When they feel light and springy brush them over with milk and put them in a quick oven to bake. This dough may be made into twists, rings, fingers, or plaits instead of rolls. These are the only recipes I will give for making rolls with yeast. I must, however, impress one or two points upon my friends. One is that when yeast is used every thing should be warm. The bowl even may be warmed with advantage, the flour should be perfectly dry, and the liquid should be lukewarm, but not hot. If hot milk is used the bread will be heavy. Another point to be noted is that the dough should not be allowed to get chilled. If it is, it will either rise very slowly or refuse to rise altogether.

Milk-rolls made with Baking Powder.— People who are afraid of yeast may make very good rolls with baking powder. Rub two ounces of butter into half a pound of flour, add a little salt and a teaspoonful of baking powder, and, gradually milk to make a stiff dough. Roll the pastry lightly into small oval shapes and bake quickly in a brisk oven. The more quickly rolls are made with baking powder, and the less they are handled, the better they will be. When half baked, the roll may be brushed over with milk. This is a very easy way of making hot rolls for breakfast where hot bread is not objected to. Plain bread also is excellent and wholesome made with baking powder, and of course it is very easily made. You need only to mix a teaspoonful of baking powder and a pinch of salt with a pound of flour, work it into a firm but not over stiff dough, make it up into small loaves, and bake immediately in a brisk oven. It will be baked in about half-an-hour.

Sometimes in summer housekeepers are annoyed to find that, notwithstanding all their care, the milk will go sour. When people are economically disposed it is a great annoyance to have to waste anything; therefore I give the following recipe, as it shows how milk may be not only utilised but really turned to very good purpose :—

Scones made with Sour Milk.—Mix a pinch of salt, a heaped teaspoonful of carbonate of soda, and the same of cream of tartar, with a pound and a half of flour. Add a pint of sour milk to make a light paste, knead the dough, lightly roll it till it is the third of an inch thick, divide it into rounds about six inches in diameter, cut these across twice to form triangular pieces, put the scones on a floured tin and bake in a quick oven. Scones may also be made with baking powder (a dessertspoonful), a pound of flour, a pinch of salt, and four ounces of butter. Make into a rather stiff paste with milk, and bake as before.

I have so often said that practice only will teach this and that in cookery, that I feel almost ashamed to repeat the remark; nevertheless this is especially true with regard to fancy breads, particularly those which are made with yeast. A little experience will enable a girl to make delicious rolls and cakes almost in the dark, while an inexperienced person with the most exact directions for her guidance will make some ridiculous mistake or other, and so throw away all her trouble. Therefore I wish to say to my friends, do not be discouraged if at first you don't succeed, but try again. Remember good Eliza Cook's words,

"Pay goodly heed, all ye who read,
　And beware of saying 'I can't;'
'Tis a cowardly word, and apt to lead
　To idleness, folly, and want."
PHILLIS BROWNE.

APPLES, AND WHAT TO DO WITH THEM.

IT is expected that apples will be very plentiful this year, plentiful and consequently cheap. Let us hope that the expectation will be realised. Apples are delicious and wholesome; they can be prepared in a hundred different ways; they keep well, and last long; they are universally popular, and they possess many most excellent qualities. We are speaking within the mark when we say that the apple is the most useful fruit we possess.

I have heard it said that there are 1,500 varieties of named apples. I cannot answer for the truth of this statement, but I willingly acknowledge that apples are of all sorts and sizes, tastes and flavours. There are apples sweet and apples sour, apples juicy and apples dry, apples soft and apples hard, apples mellow and apples rough, apples large and apples diminutive. The true connoisseur in apples generally judges of an apple by its smell; if this is good, appearance is for him a comparatively minor consideration.

For a long time apples have been largely imported from America, and now they are sent to us from New Zealand and Australia. I had some apples given to me a few months ago which came from Sydney, and they were excellent both in quality and flavour. It is said that this year we shall not need to have apples from anywhere; we shall have quite enough at home. This is good news, yet I confess that, when the time comes for them, I hope we shall have Newtown pippins. In my opinion no apples are to be compared with Newtown pippins. For years English gardeners have been trying to reproduce this apple, and they have grown something very nearly equal to it, but possessing not quite the same delicious flavour. The worst of Newtown pippins is that they are not good keeping apples, and on this account fruit dealers are chary of purchasing them, because unless sold off quickly there is sure to be loss connected with them. People who are very fond of apples would find it a good plan to buy one or more barrels of Newtown pippins, according to their requirements, as soon as they come into the market, and then use them straight away. Apples are very much cheaper bought in quantities thus, and, if care be taken of them, they will prove very serviceable. Where there is room for storage, this plan is to be recommended also for English apples, care being taken always to buy sound fruit of a kind which keeps well. For the use of my own family I have bought Blenheim oranges and Flanders pippins, and these two varieties have with me kept all through the winter, and been good to the last.

Apples which are to be stored for winter use should be picked from the tree carefully, they should not be thrown about, and they should be handled as little as possible. Those which are sent from a distance should be unpacked as soon as may be, and they should be wiped carefully with a soft cloth, because moisture will cause them to decay sooner than anything. They should be examined carefully before being put away, and those which show signs of decay should be put aside for immediate use. This process of looking over the fruit should be repeated regularly at intervals, say of a week, for decomposition quickly communicates itself from one apple to another. A little straw should then be spread on the floor or shelf, and the apples should be put in rows side by side, and they should not be allowed to touch. The room or outhouse in which the fruit is kept should be cool, dry, and airy.

Delicious as apples undoubtedly are, they are not so delicious that they cannot be improved by additional flavour. Old-fashioned cooks are accustomed to put one or two cloves with apples, in cooking them. I have sometimes had apple pie, in which the taste and the aroma of the cloves overpowered that of the apples. Grated lemon rind is also employed for the same purpose, as are also cinnamon, grated nutmeg, and in all cases sugar, and, whenever it can be obtained, cream.

Individual taste must, of course, determine what flavour is to be used; therefore, in giving recipes later, I will not repeat this information in each case. May I, however, suggest to those who have not tried the combination, that apricots or quinces, and apples, should be put together. A great epicure once said that quinces, though of little value in themselves, improved an apple pie beyond the power of words to describe. *One* quince is sufficient for a moderate-sized apple pie.

Dried apples or chips are imported in large quantities from America, and, though there is a great difference in their quality, good dried apples are both excellent and economical. They need to be soaked all night in cold water, and then stewed gently in the same water till soft, before being used. Sugar should not be put with them until they have been stewed for some time. As it is difficult to judge the quality of dried apples by their appearances, *intending* purchasers should be careful to procure them of a respectable dealer. Inferior dried apples are a great delusion.

I will now give a few recipes for the preparation of apples, and I shall make no mention of apple pie, the ordinary boiled apple pudding, apple dumpling, apple tart, apple sauce, apple fool, or baked apples, because I should think that by this time the girls of our cookery class know as much about these preparations as I do.

Compôte of Apples.—Cut four good sized apples into quarters, then peel them, and throw them at once into water with lemon juice. (It saves time to quarter apples before peeling them, and it preserves their colour to throw them into water to which lemon juice has been added.) Make a little very thin syrup with loaf sugar and water. Boil this till clear, put in the apple quarters, and simmer them very gently till they are soft, without breaking. Take them up and put them aside to cool. Add more sugar to the syrup, and boil it again till it is very thick. Arrange the apples in a circle, colour the syrup either with a few drops of saffron water or a little cochineal or red jelly, and serve cold. A pennyworth of saffron may be bought of the chemist, and a portion of this should be soaked in a tablespoonful of boiling water, until the liquid is a deep orange colour. A very pretty compôte may be made by peeling, coring, and stewing the apples whole, and putting a little red jam in the centre of each when dishing them. This dish may be further ornamented by putting little strips of angelica or of marmalade on the top of each apple.

Apple Fritters.—Make a little frying batter by mixing smoothly four ounces of flour with two dessertspoonfuls of salad oil, and a gill of lukewarm water. This batter may be made thus far before it is wanted. About ten minutes before it is used, stir in lightly the whites of two eggs which have been beaten to a froth. Choose three or more large, firm apples. Peel them and cut them across the core in rounds as thin as a shilling, and stamp out the core. Make some dripping hot in a stewpan. As soon as it is still and a blue smoke begins to rise from it, take up the apple rings one by one by means of a skewer put into the centre hole, dip them into the batter to cover them completely, and drop them into the fat. Three or four fritters, as many as the pan will hold without their touching, may be fried at one time. Have ready a sheet of kitchen paper on a plate. When the fritters are lightly browned on one side, turn them quickly on the other; when this side also is coloured, they are done. Put them on the paper to drain, and keep hot, till all the fritters are cooked. Arrange them in a dish, sift white sugar over them, and serve. Some cooks use apple chips in making apple fritters. When this is done, they must be soaked well and stewed a little before being fried, or they will be hard.

Apple Charlotte.—Take a plain round mould, about five inches deep; butter this inside. Cut some thin, stale bread into strips for the sides, and a round for the bottom of the mould; melt some butter, dip the pieces of bread into this, and line the mould so that there are no vacant places, thus making a bread mould within the other mould. This is most easily made (by people who have not had experience in making a Charlotte Russe) by making the strips of bread overlap each other. Stew some apples to make a pulp, which must be firm and well sweetened, mellowed with butter, and flavoured with lemon juice. Very little, if any, water must be used; but it is impossible to lay down an exact rule, because the nature of the apple must determine the quantity. Fill the mould with the pulp, lay a piece of buttered bread on the top, put a plate, or cover, with a weight to keep the fruit in its place, and bake in an oven for about three-quarters of an hour, till the bread is deeply browned; turn out carefully, and serve with cream or sifted sugar. A simple variety of this dish, known under the name of Brown Betty, is made by filling a buttered dish with alternate layers of apples and breadcrumbs, intermixed with butter and sugar, and flavoured with lemon-peel or nutmeg. Breadcrumbs should form the uppermost layer, a little melted butter be poured over all, and the pudding baked till well browned.

Apple Cheesecakes.—Peel some apples and grate them to the core; take equal weights of grated apple, castor sugar and butter, and flavour with a little grated lemon-rind; melt the butter, add the other ingredients, and mix thoroughly, then add one egg for each quarter pound of pulp; line cheesecake tins in the usual way, half fill them with the mixture, and bake.

Apple Gâteau.—Soak half an ounce of gelatine in water, to cover it; peel, core, and slice two pounds of good baking apples; put them into a stewpan, with water to cover them, and let them simmer till quite soft; drain off the water and beat the apples till smooth, or press them through a sieve, and add a little grated lemon-rind and sugar to that; put the water which was drained off into a saucepan, and add the gelatine. When this is dissolved, stir in the apple pulp, first allowing it to cool, mix all thoroughly; pour into a damp mould, turn out when cold, and serve with cream and sugar. If liked, one or two tablespoonfuls of cream can be put with the apple pulp, which may then have a pint of good custard poured round it.

Apple Custard Tartlet.—Peel, core, and quarter some good baking apples to fill a quart basin, and stew them with very little water till quite soft, being careful not to let them burn. Add a flavouring of lemon or cinnamon, sugar to taste, a good slice of fresh butter, and an ounce of flour. Beat the flour till smooth, and stir the mixture over the fire for a few minutes to cook it. When the apple pulp is cool add, one at a time, two well-beaten eggs. Line large tartlet tins with pastry, spread the apple custard on them, garnish with pastry leaves or twists, and bake in a good oven. Serve hot or cold.

Apple Custard.—Stew some apples to a firm pulp, as in the last recipe; sweeten, and flavour. Put the fruit into a glass dish; when quite cold pour some thick custard over, garnish with angelica or strips of lemon-rind, and serve with sponge fingers. If liked, the apple pulp can be put into a pie-dish, custard can be poured over, and then gently baked, or the apple pulp can be laid on sponge biscuits which have been spread with apricot marmalade, and soaked in syrup.

Apples and Tapioca (a simple wholesome dish for the nursery).—Soak overnight two tablespoonfuls of tapioca, then stew it gently in the same water till it is clear. It must not be over thick. Peel, core, and quarter six large apples, and stew them in the oven, or steam them till they are slightly softened. Put the apples in a pie-dish, sprinkle sugar over them, sweeten and flavour the tapioca, pour it over the fruit, and bake gently till tender. If liked, the tapioca can be coloured with cochineal, or sago may be used instead of tapioca.

A refreshing drink for invalids is *Apple Water*, made by pouring a pint of boiling water upon three juicy apples (which have been peeled, cored, and sliced) and a little lemon-rind; then sweetening to taste. When the liquid is cold it may be strained, and is then ready for use.

A peculiar, but by no means disagreeable, pickle or relish to eat with cold meat may be made by mixing some apple grated with its bulk in finely-chopped onion, to which are added a little red chili cut up small, salt, and vinegar to moisten the whole.

PHILLIS BROWNE.

USEFUL HINTS.

JENNY'S APPLE PUDDING.—INGREDIENTS.—Three eggs, four or five large apples, three ounces of bread finely grated, three ounces of currants carefully washed and dried, about three ounces of sugar, a pinch of salt, and a little nutmeg. Mix all well together, and if too stiff add a little milk. Put the mixture into a buttered basin and tie it over with a cloth. Boil for two hours, serve plainly, or with sweet sauce made with corn flour.

RHUBARB WINE—8 lbs. rhubarb to 1 gallon of water, 1 lemon, 3 lbs. loaf sugar, bruise the rhubarb, mix with the water, and let it stand four or five days. Strain it, stir in the sugar and sliced lemon. Bottle in old champagne bottles. It becomes a very brisk wine, effervescing like champagne, and has the recommendation of being both pleasant to the taste and thoroughly wholesome.

RHUBARB PUDDING.—Well butter a rather deep dish and fill with alternate layers of rhubarb, peeled and cut into inch long pieces, and thin bread and butter; put brown sugar and grated rind of lemon with the rhubarb to sweeten and flavour. The top and bottom layers should be rhubarb, and a few little bits of butter should be put on the top, and half a cupful of water poured in before the dish is put into the oven. Bake thoroughly. If eaten cold it may be turned out into a glass dish and garnished round with a little whipped cream or white of eggs whisked to a froth, like snow. The tinned apples used instead of rhubarb and in the same manner make very nice puddings. Tinned peaches and pears stewed and served with a rice mould, are excellent, especially when fresh fruit is scarce and dear.

BUTTERSCOTCH. — 1lb. of the coarsest brown sugar, ¼lb. fresh butter, and half a teaspoonful of vinegar to make it crisp. Put the ingredients in a lined saucepan, and let it boil gently for twenty minutes or half-an-hour, stirring it the whole time, or it will burn. Then, when it is finished—you can tell if it be so by taking a little of the butterscotch and putting it into cold water, and if it is done it will be crisp—pour the butterscotch into a buttered dish and let it remain until cool.

RECIPE FOR BLANC-MANGE.—To a pint of milk add three table-spoonfuls of hominy, with a little salt; boil gently until it thickens, when add about ⅓ pint more milk; boil until sufficiently thick, add sugar and flavouring to taste. Pour into a mould and serve cold, with jam or stewed fruit.

SOME FOREIGN SWEET DISHES, AND HOW TO MAKE THEM.

FRIED RICE.

Prepare rice and milk with a little salt, as for a rice pudding, and cook till firm. Then sprinkle a wooden board with flour, spread on it the rice about the thickness of a finger, sift over it flour, and then lightly roll with a rolling-pin so that the rice is quite even. When it is cold cut it into squares, and fry a golden colour. As soon as they are done sprinkle with sugar, and serve hot or cold, with a spoonful of apricot jam on each, or with a cream sauce handed in a sauce-boat.

CLARET SHAPE.

Stew five ounces of sago in three-quarters of a pint of claret until the sago becomes quite transparent, add to this, when done, as much wine, sugar, and rum as is liked for flavouring, and cook these together until the mixture begins to get thick; then pour into a mould and let it stand all night in a cool place. Turn out on a dish and serve with whipped cream round it.

"AUFLAUF" OF JELLY.

Take a quarter of a pound of good jelly—the remains of a shape will do—and two ounces of sifted sugar; beat them well together for half an hour. Take the whites of nine eggs, beat them till stiff, stir into the jelly lightly, and immediately put into a silver or china dish and bake in the oven (which must not be too hot) for nearly half an hour, until it becomes a nice golden colour. One can tell best that the "Auflauf" is done if, when the dish is held a little on one side, it does not run out, but remains firm.

ITALIAN CREAM CHEESE.

One and a half pints of thick sweet cream, three lemons, of which the rind must be rubbed on sugar, as much sugar as is liked, and the juice of the lemons pressed through a cloth, and four tablespoonfuls of rum. Whisk altogether in a basin until it is firm, then spread a piece of muslin in the colander, and pour the mixture in, spread it quite even with a spoon, and stand for a night in a cool place. The colander must be stood on a plate to catch the liquid that will drop from the cheese, and before serving the cheese it must be carefully turned out of the colander on to a flat plate.

FANCY PASTRY, AND HOW TO MAKE IT.

By PHILLIS BROWNE, Author of "The Girl's Own Cookery Book," &c.

ALL amateur cooks are fond of making pastry, and quite reasonably, for pastry making is very interesting work, and when successfully done is sure to obtain credit for the maker. As everyone knows, however, it requires practice and a light, cool hand. Some months ago I gave in THE GIRL'S OWN PAPER minute directions for making the different sorts of pastry. I have no doubt the girls of our class have profited by the lesson, and have for a long time been adepts in the art of pastry making, and accustomed to make beefsteak pies, apple tarts, gooseberry turnovers, &c., to their own exceeding satisfaction and that of their friends.

It is not always, however, that one wants a pie or a tart. It is often a convenience to have on hand small articles of pastry suitable for serving at luncheon or breakfast, or supplying an elegant little addition to the tea-table. Supposing, for instance, that we are homely people, with not too much money to spend, and a friend drops in unexpectedly to tea : how much better the tea-table looks if we can put on it one or two pretty little inexpensive fancy dishes which have cost very little more than the trouble of preparing them, and which yet make all the difference between an elegant, tasteful, inviting repast and a solid, homely, sternly-economical one. If we have to get these little extras from the confectioner, we seem, both to ourselves and our guests, to have made quite a fuss. Our guests recognise the confectioner's pastry at a glance, and they think that we are making strangers of them, while for our part we are unpleasantly con-scious that we have gone into unusual expense, because trifles which cost only a penny a piece are expensive when we have not got the money to spare for them. Yet if these trifles were made of the little pieces of pastry which were left over when we were making pies, they would cost us comparatively nothing. Or supposing a child has to take refreshment to school, or the father of the family, unable to get a proper midday meal, is accustomed to take something in his pocket to "put him on," as the saying is, until he reaches home again—how weary both father and child become of the inevitable sandwich. Far be it from me to say anything in disparagement of well-made sandwiches. I am quite aware that they can be varied to any extent and made to be most appetising. Yet it does not follow that an occasional change from them will not be acceptable, and it would be so easy to supply this out of the trimmings left over after making pies and tarts.

With regard to these same trimmings, it is astonishing how much more some cooks will make of them than others. It very rarely happens in making pies that the exact quan-tity of pastry is made, and that no scraps are left over. Yet on these same scraps some cooks will bestow trouble and make half a dozen pretty little tartlets, which will furnish an inviting dish; others will toss them into the fire and be done with them, while the large majority will roll them out into one irregular piece, put them into the oven, and then leave them to burn. It is the cooks who are not afraid of trouble who make the most of odds and ends, and one reason why we are glad that so many girls are now interested in cookery is that they are generally not averse to bestowing pains on what they do. To these girls I now address myself, hoping, if I can, to supply a few ideas which may be use-ful in preparing the small extras and inex-pensive trifles of which mention has been made. I suppose that everyone knows as much as I do about ordinary jam tartlets and patties, therefore I will say nothing of them, but try rather to give suggestions for something different.

Open Fruit Tarts may be made as follows : Roll out a piece of pastry a quarter of an inch thick, and stamp it into a round shape with a saucer or a saucepan lid whatever size may be wished. Make a border by moisten-ing the edge of the round and sticking upon it a roll of pastry, which roll may be pinched with the fingers to make it thinner at the top than it is at the bottom, the paste outside being afterwards pressed. Prick one or two holes in the round to make it keep flat, then bake it. When cold, fill the centre with any kind of fruit which has been boiled till soft without being broken in a syrup of sugar and water, and pour over all the cold syrup which has been boiled longer than the fruit to make it thick. The pieces of fruit should be ar-ranged neatly in a single layer, not piled one upon the other. Apples cut into quarters, small fruit and plums cut into halves, with the stones turned out, are very good served in this way. If liked, an open tart of this sort may be made of firm pastry by rolling the paste to a flat round and turning up the edge, or roll-ing the edge by turning the paste over, then baking it, and filling it when cold with sections of bright-coloured red jam and yellow marma-lade or apricot jam. A superior tart also may be prepared by spreading jam upon the round of pastry, then piling whipped cream on the top, and scoring a pattern on the cream, or sprinkling chopped pistachios and chopped cherries upon it.

Cream Tartlets.—Mix a teaspoonful of flour and a quarter of a pint of cream (or of cream and milk, or of milk alone) till quite smooth. Turn the mixture into a small saucepan, and stir it over the fire without stopping till it is thick and the flour is quite cooked. Turn it into a basin, and put with it a piece of butter the size of a walnut, some sugar to sweeten it agreeably, a little grated lemon rind, the beaten yolk of one egg or more, and two macaroons, or six ratafias, which have been crushed to powder with a rolling-pin. Put the basin containing the mixture into a sauce-pan of boiling water over the fire and stir it again, keeping the water boiling round it till the egg is cooked. Line *some small* tartlet tins with the rolled-out trimmings of pastry, fill with the preparation, and bake in a good oven. If liked, these tartlets may be still further enriched by placing lightly on the top of each, before putting the tartlets in the oven, a little knob of icing which has been made by mixing the white of one egg with a tablespoon-ful of icing sugar.

Pastry Fingers.—Roll the pastry out thinly, and cut it into fingers about an inch wide and three inches long. Spread a little jam or marmalade on one half of these, and press the remaining halves on the top to make a sort of jam sandwich. Bake these lightly in a well-heated oven. A minute or two before they are done brush them over with white of egg, and sprinkle on the top crushed loaf sugar, and either almonds or pistachios which have been blanched and roughly chopped. Put them back into the oven till the glazing is set, and pile them crosswise on a dish.

Fruit Custard Tartlets.—Line some small tartlet tins with pastry which has been rolled out very thin. Dissolve a tablespoonful of red or black currant, or any other fruit jelly, and mix with it three spoonfuls of beaten egg. Fill the pans with the custard, and bake in a quick oven till the pastry is done.

Fruit Rissolettes.—M. Soyer recommends that tartlets should be made as follows :—Roll out as many scraps of pastry as there may be into two thin large pieces of equal size. Upon one of these pieces lay at equal distances, about an inch apart, little knobs of firm jam. Moisten the pastry round each knob with water or white of egg, then lay the other piece of pastry on the top, and with a small round cutter press the pastry lightly close to the jam. With another cutter a size larger cut the tartlets out, lay them on a buttered baking sheet, brush them with white of egg, and bake. This is a quick way of making a number of small tartlets all at once. Round ring cutters are to be bought, both plain and fluted, in boxes containing a dozen each for a moderate sum—two and sixpence, if I remember rightly—and they are very convenient for stamping out trifles of this sort. The appearance of these rissolettes will be still further improved if, after being egged over, a little round of pastry the size of a shilling is laid on the top of each, then egged over again. When the tartlets are almost baked, take them out of the oven, sift white sugar over them, and put them back to glaze. Before serving them put a knob of bright-coloured jelly upon the smaller ring.

For a homely dish made from the remnants of pastry, the following is to be recommended :—Grease a plate or oval dish, and line it with pastry. Fill the centre with a single layer of fresh lemons, which have been very thinly sliced, after having been peeled and freed entirely from the white pith and the pips. Sprinkle castor sugar over the fruit, pour a little golden syrup on the top. Moisten the edge of the tart, lay the cover on, and fasten it down securely, to keep the juice in ; pinch or otherwise ornament the edge, and bake in a good oven.

Lemon Cheesecakes are perhaps too well known to need description, but they are so good that I give the recipe. Put the strained juice and grated rind of one large fresh lemon into a saucepan, with the yolk of an egg, two tablespoonfuls of sugar, and a slice of butter the size of an egg. Stir the mixture without ceasing until the ingredients are thoroughly blended, and it begins to thicken. These quantities make a small portion only, but they can be relatively increased if liked. A large open cheesecake, made with this mixture, may have one or two very thin slices of candied citron laid on the top.

Turnovers of all sorts are always approved. The pastry should be rolled out thinly, and stamped into a round shape with a saucer. A little jam or stewed fruit is then placed on one half of the pastry, and the other half is turned quite over, the edges being first moistened to make them adhere. Sometimes thin slices of cheese, with pepper, salt, mustard, and a few drops of vinegar, are put inside turnovers for the sake of variety.

I must not turn away from speaking of the small trifles which may be made of pastry, without reminding my friends that, if there should happen to be a little cold meat of any sort in the house, very excellent Cornish pasties may be prepared, especially if there are also a few cold boiled potatoes in the larder. There should be about equal quantities of meat and vegetable. If there are no cold vegetables, they must be boiled specially for the purpose. Cornish pasties are prepared as follows :—Cut both meat and vegetables quite small (the potatoes are best when passed through a wire sieve), and with each pound of meat put half a small onion, which has been chopped as finely as possible, and plenty of salt and pepper. If approved, other additions may be made such as chopped

apple and chopped boiled turnip ; but, whatever these are, it is better that they should be well chopped. A by no means despicable Cornish pasty may be made of flaked dressed fish and potatoes. Roll out the trimmings of pastry to the thickness of a quarter of an inch, then stamp it out in rounds with a saucer. Wet the edges all round, put a little of the savoury mixture in the middle, bring the edges to the top by doubling the paste up, and press them together with the thumb and finger to make a frill. Put them on a greased baking sheet, and bake in a good oven till the pasty is done, then take them out, brush them over with yolk of egg or with a little milk, put them again in the oven to brown, and they are ready. I believe these pasties, as actually made in Cornwall, are much larger, and square, instead of round ; but the idea is the same.

I daresay cooks who think themselves very clever will be very scornful as they read this recipe. They will say these pasties are made of nothing but cold meat and cold potatoes, they are not worth thinking about. I assure the girls of our class they are worth a good deal. Make them carefully and take pains with them, and fathers and brothers will be sure to enjoy them, and will say, "What good pasties those were you made the other day. When shall we have some more ?" Only remember, that the various ingredients, and especially the onion, must be finely chopped. If this is put in slices or large dice, or if too much is used, it will be too strong, but if it is chopped till it is as fine as dust, and then mixed in, it will give a good flavour, and that is all.

Sausage Rolls are also very excellent. Boil the sausages for five minutes in water. (This preliminary boiling is necessary, because the sausages would not be sufficiently cooked if they were allowed only as much time as was required for baking the crust.) Take them up, drain them, skin them, cut them in half, and let them cool. Roll out the pastry to the thickness of a quarter of an inch, and cut it into pieces, four inches one way three inches the other. Lay half a sausage in each, wet the edges of the pastry, roll it round the meat, and press the ends securely. Bake in a good oven, and five minutes before the rolls are taken out, brush them over with egg or milk. When baked, let them stand upright leaning against something till cool.

Sometimes trifles of pastry are wanted, specially when there are no scraps to be utilised. If required at short notice, Victoria sandwiches will be found both excellent and convenient, for if the oven is hot they can be made and baked in half an hour, and can be used either for tea or as a substitute for a pudding. Use two eggs as weights, and take the same weight of sugar, butter, and flour. Cream the butter and sugar together, that is, beat them with the back of a spoon till the mixture looks thin and has the appearance of cream ; then add the eggs, and gradually the flour, beating well between every addition. Put the mixture into a greased pudding tin, and bake in a good oven. The preparation should be about half an inch thick, and should rise well in the oven. When the cake is cold cut it in half; spread jam on one piece, lay the other on the top ; press the two together, and cut the sandwiches into fingers. Pile crosswise on a glass dish ; sift white sugar over, and serve. If this mixture is considered too rich and costly, an economical variation may be made by creaming four ounces of dripping, or half butter and half dripping, with four ounces of sugar, then adding two eggs well beaten, half a pound of flour, and half a teaspoonful of baking powder.

Genoese Pastry.—(Light and wholesome. Used for Swiss roll, jam sandwiches, trifle, or

to be eaten cold.) Genoese pastry is often cut into fancy shapes, and iced or ornamented as fancy dictates. To make it, melt six ounces of butter, and with a portion of it grease a saucepan or shallow cake tin about ten inches in diameter, line the pan with paper, and grease this also. Melt the butter, and keep it in a liquid state till wanted, but do not let it be hot. Pass six ounces of Vienna flour through a wire sieve to be sure it is free from lumps. Put half a pound of castor sugar into a basin, and break seven eggs in, one at a time. Set the basin over a saucepan of boiling water, draw it back, do not let it boil underneath, whip the mixture vigorously for twenty minutes, and work in at the same time grated lemon rind, or any suitable flavouring, till it is frothed and very light. Lift the basin away from the hot water, add the butter gradually, stirring all the time, then add the flour, stirring it lightly. Pour the mixture on the buttered paper, and bake in a hot oven until the pastry feels firm in the centre, then turn it top side down on a towel, spread jam over it, and roll it by raising one end of the towel, or letting the pastry turn over and over. Some cooks prefer to take the pastry out when half baked, spread jam on it, roll it over and over, and put it again in the oven. If the pastry is not to be used for Swiss roll, it may, of course, be simply turned out, have the paper torn from it while still warm, and used as required. A simple way of making Swiss roll is to mix the eggs as Victoria sandwiches are mixed, taking any number of eggs according to the quantity of pastry needed, and using them as weights for the sugar, butter, flour, and castor sugar. When the ingredients are worked together the mixture may be poured upon a well-greased paper on a baking sheet spread to the thickness of a quarter of an inch, and baked in the oven, as already directed. A cheap Swiss roll pudding for family use may be made with six ounces of butter, six ounces of sugar, eight ounces of flour, three eggs, and a teaspoonful of baking powder. Pour the mixture on a greased paper, bake ten minutes, spread jam over, roll and bake till done ; sift white sugar over, and serve.

There is still another sort of pastry which, before I leave the subject, I should like to mention, because it is so much liked by many people. It is the pastry used for

Petits Choux, or Spanish cakes, which are elegant little trifles usually made up in the form of balls, and either served plain or opened at the side for the insertion of a little whipped cream and preserve, or decorated in some way to give them an attractive, glossy appearance. The following is the recipe for making these delicious cakes:—Put half a pint of water and two ounces of butter in a stewpan, and stir in when boiling five ounces of flour which has been passed through a sieve, and two ounces of castor sugar. Beat very well over the fire with a wooden spoon till the mixture leaves the sides of the saucepan quite clean, and has the appearance of a soft, compact paste. Work in a few drops of any flavouring essence which may be chosen, then add, off the fire and one at a time, three eggs. If the paste should be stiff, another egg or the yolk only may be beaten in. Butter a baking sheet and lay the pastry on it in small round balls the size of a pigeon's egg. They may be shaped with two spoons and smoothed with a knife dipped in hot water. When arranged, dust the cakes with castor sugar and bake in a slow, steady oven for one hour. When finished they ought to be quite crisp and hard, and are very usually brushed over with caramel and then sprinkled over with desiccated cocoanut or chopped pistachio kernels. The caramel is made by boiling a quarter of a pound of sugar in a gill of water for about five minutes. When the syrup is stringy it is ready for use.

s cold sweets are always welcome during the hot summer days, I shall give recipes for some in due hopes that some may be new to my readers. New puddings are usually welcome, as one tires sooner of them than anything else, and so one longs for more variety.

Apple Souflée.—Butter the *outside* of a pudding dish, and cover it with "short crust," made of six ounces of fine flour, three ounces of butter, two teaspoonfuls of sifted sugar, the yolk of one egg, beaten light; rub the butter, sugar, and flour together, and add egg and enough water to mix to a paste; roll out into a sheet the size of the dish, cut the edges neatly, and bake to a pale brown in a steady oven. In the meantime pare and core a pound and a half of apples, add a quarter of a pound of sugar, the grated rind and strained juice of half a lemon; stew till soft, then stir in half a dozen ratifia biscuits and one penny sponge cake crumbled down, the yolks of two eggs well whisked, and a very little water; stir well over the fire a few minutes to cook the eggs, then pour into your paste dish (which has been gently slipped off the mould), and make the apples smooth on the top; whip the whites of three eggs stiff with a tablespoonful of castor sugar, spread evenly over the apples, dust some sugar over the icing, ornament round the edge with ratifia biscuits, and put the souflée into a nearly cold oven just to *slightly* brown the icing.

Chocolate Pudding.—Soak a third of an ounce of gelatine in a little milk. Dissolve four ounces of vanilla chocolate in a pint and a half of milk, and boil in a clean pan for ten minutes, stirring all the time; flavour with a very little vanilla essence, and sugar to taste; put into a jug to cool. Put the soaked gelatine in a pan and dissolve it; let it also cool, then add it to the chocolate and mix well. Pour, when almost cold, into a mould previously wet with water. When set, turn out and serve with whipped cream round it. This pudding should be made the day before it is required. If liked, a cup of strong coffee can be used in place of chocolate, and is very refreshing.

Chocolate Solid.—Make a custard (as directed below in "Pineapple Sponge"), and to it add three ounces of chocolate boiled in a quarter of a pint of milk. When cool, add a very little essence of vanilla, and pour all into a wet mould to set.

Devonshire Junket.—Put one quart of lukewarm sweet milk (the richer the better) into a punch bowl, or a crystal one, add sugar to taste, and a few drops of brandy or any flavouring, and a dessertspoonful of rennet. Leave it in a cool place to "set" or "curd," when it will be ready. Send to table in the bowl, with little lumps of whipped cream on the top, and serve with cream.

Haycocks.—Beat three eggs very light; beat their weight in sugar and butter to a cream; add same weight in flour gradually, and lastly, beat in the eggs and a little of any flavouring; half fill buttered dariole tins with the mixture, and bake in a quick oven. When cold, scoop out a little hollow on the top of each and fill with whipped cream and a few pistachio nuts chopped and sprinkled on the top, or else fill with any preserve and sprinkle almonds or cocoanut on the top. They can also be served simply glazed over with any preserve, such as apricot, and a thin custard poured round them in the dish.

Italian Cream.—To one pint of good rich milk add enough fine sugar to sweeten it, the *thin* rind of a lemon, an inch of cinnamon stick, and three quarters of an ounce of isinglass; put all into an enamelled pan and stir till it boils and the isinglass is dissolved. Beat in a large basin the yolks of six eggs till very light, strain over them the boiling milk, etc., stirring well all the time and till the mixture is nearly cold, then add a desert-spoonful of lemon juice; pour into a wet mould, and when quite set turn out.

Kendal Puddings.—Rub the rind of a lemon on to six or eight lumps of loaf sugar, pound and add them to one pint of milk in a pan and let it boil; mix to a smooth batter two large tablespoonfuls of ground rice with a little milk, add the boiling milk on to the rice, stir well, adding more sugar if required, and also half an ounce of butter. Stir over the fire till the mixture thickens, and let it boil a little. Have ready some little cups or tins well buttered, fill with the rice, and set in a cool place till quite cold. Turn them out on a dish and garnish the top of each with a little piece of bright-coloured jelly. Pour round them a good thick cold custard sauce.

Coffee Mousse.—Make a teacupful of strong coffee, using a quarter of a pound to the cup of water. When strained add to it an ounce of sugar and the yolks of two well-beaten eggs. Put into a tin gallipot, place it in a pan of boiling water, and let the water boil round it till the coffee thickens, and which must be constantly stirred. Let it get perfectly cold. Whip one pint of thick cream stiff, add the coffee by degrees so that it is smooth and thick, and serve in old china cups or coloured glasses. It is only fair to say that as a rule *coffee* sweets and creams are only liked by a few, as it is an acquired taste, and therefore they are not always appreciated as they should be.

Moonshine.—Dissolve three quarters of an ounce of isinglass in a pint of boiling water, add half a pound of loaf sugar, the thin rind of two lemons, boil for ten minutes; then strain it; while hot add the juice of the two lemons, strained, and when the mixture is nearly cold whisk it till it looks like snow. Put into a wet mould, and turn it out next day.

Gâteau.—Take a fresh Madeira cake, cut off the top to make it even, then cut the cake into slices half an inch thick; on the lower slice spread some marmalade, place a slice on the cake, on top spread it with raspberry jam, then cake, then some apricot jam, and so on till all is together; glaze outside with marmalade, and serve with cream or custard.

Orange Fool.—Juice of four oranges, three well-beaten eggs, one pint of cream, a little cinnamon, nutmeg, and sugar to taste. Set it on the fire to thicken till it is like melted butter, but do not allow it to boil; then pour it into a glass dish and serve when cold.

Pineapple Sponge.—To three yolks and one white of egg, beaten, put a pint and a half of milk which has been boiled with an ounce and a half of gelatine and three ounces of sugar; return all to the fire in a jug set in a pan of water, to thicken; add to it a small tin of grated pineapple, and pour into a wet mould to set. Turn out the next day.

Queen Pudding.—Take half a pint of bread or stale cake crumbs, one pint of milk, yolks of two eggs, two ounces of sugar, an ounce of butter, and a little essence of lemon. Mix all in a pudding dish and bake for an hour. Put a thin layer of jam on the top; beat up the whites of the two eggs to a stiff froth with a little lemon juice and two ounces of fine sugar; lay it over the jam, and return to the oven for a few minutes to brown lightly. Serve cold.

Quaking Custard.—Three cups of milk, the yolks of four eggs (reserve the whites for meringue), half a packet of gelatine, six tablespoonfuls of sugar; vanilla or lemon essence to taste. Soak the gelatine in a cup of the cold milk for two hours, then heat the rest of the milk to boiling, add the gelatine, and over the fire stir till quite dissolved. Take off, let it stand five minutes before adding the yolks and sugar. Heat slowly until it thickens—say seven or eight minutes—stirring constantly. When nearly cold add the flavouring; pour into a wet mould, and leave till set. Turn out. Have the whites beaten up to a stiff froth with three tablespoonfuls of fine sugar and the juice of a lemon. Heap round the custard in the glass dish.

Raspberry Gâteau.—Take a round sponge cake a pound in weight, cut into slices, and over each slice, commencing with the lower one, pour a syrup of the fruit while hot, made of half a pound each of currants and raspberries boiled with six ounces of sugar. Pour the fruit over along with their juice. Whip half a pint of cream till thick, sweeten, cover the cake with it roughly dropped from a spoon; colour a little of it pink with juice, and put a dot of it between each spoonful.

Russian Pudding.—One quart of claret, three quarters of a pound of loaf sugar, the juice of one lemon, one ounce of isinglass, a breakfastcupful of damson jam, and a small glass of brandy. Soak the isinglass with the claret, brandy, and sugar, then put in the jam and stir all over the fire. Let it boil for a few minutes, then strain it into a wet casserole mould. Fill the centre with whipped cream when the pudding is set and turned out.

Rhubarb Cheesecake.—Stew a bunch of rhubarb till soft, beat well with a fork, drain all the liquor away, add the juice and grated rind of two lemons, sweeten to taste, add a little nutmeg and three well-beaten eggs. Pour all into a paste-lined dish and bake three quarters of an hour in a moderate oven; turn out and serve cold with cream.

Snowballs.—Boil a teacupful of rice with a pint and a half of milk, flavour with chopped almonds, and add sugar to taste. When the rice is tender beat it well till smooth; pour into wet cups, and when the rice is cold turn out on a glass dish and garnish with jelly.

Cornflour Meringue.—Five eggs, one quart of milk, three quarters of a cup of sugar, four teaspoonfuls of cornflour, half a cup of jelly or jam. Heat the milk to boiling, and stir in the cornflour previously wet in a little milk; boil for a few minutes, stirring well; remove from the fire, and while hot add the beaten yolks, sugar, and vanilla essence, lemon, or almond. Pour into a buttered dish and bake fifteen minutes. Beat the whites of eggs stiffly with the jelly or jam, add a little flavouring, draw the pudding to door of oven, quickly spread on the meringue, and bake covered for five minutes; remove the cover and brown slightly. When cold, serve with fine sugar over the top.

Fig Compote.—Take one dozen large figs, cut into halves or quarters, put them into a saucepan with a sixpenny packet of gelatine, two ounces of fine sugar, and enough water to quite cover them; let them simmer *slowly* for two hours; then pour into a wet mould. When quite set, turn out, and serve with spoonfuls of whipped cream round. Prunes can also be done this way, using half a pound of prunes (stoned) to the packet of gelatine.

Lemon Mould.—Steep the thinly-pared rind of eight lemons in one pint of water for twelve hours; strain, and dissolve in the water three quarters of a pound of castor sugar, add the juice of the lemons and whites of seven eggs beaten very stiff, and the yolk of one. Boil this over a slow fire, stirring well till as thick as double cream. Pour into the glass dish and use cold.

Lemon Pudding.—Half a pound of butter, one pound of sugar, six eggs (whites and yolks separately), the juice of one lemon, the grated rind of two, one nutmeg. Cream butter and sugar, beat in the yolks, lemon, and spice; stir in the stiffly-beaten whites last. Bake in a paste-lined dish, and eat when cold.

Lemon Pudding.—One cup of sugar, four eggs, two tablespoonfuls of cornflour, two lemons, the juice of both and grated rind of one, one pint of milk, and a tablespoonful of butter. Heat the milk to boiling, and stir in the "wet-up" cornflour; boil five minutes, keep stirring; while hot, mix in the butter and set away to cool. Beat the yolks light, add the sugar, and mix well before putting in the lemon juice and rind. Beat to a stiff cream, add gradually to the cold cornflour, and when *quite* cold stir smooth; put into a buttered dish and bake. Eat cold.

Semolina Cream.—Soak an ounce of semolina in a gill of cold milk for an hour, then boil it until soft in three gills of milk. Stir this into the contents of a large tin of Nelson's blanc-mange dissolved in a pint of milk; flavour to taste; put into a wet mould and stand till set.

Italian Cream.—Take three quarters of an ounce of Nelson's gelatine and soak it in half a pint of cold water; boil the thin rind of a lemon in a pint of cream, add the juice of the lemon and three spoonfuls of raspberry syrup to the gelatine; pour hot cream on the above ingredients, stirring gently. Sweeten to taste; add a few drops of cochineal, whisk till thick, and pour into a wet mould.

There are also many varieties of cornflour shapes, for which directions are given on the packets, so that I need not take up space to repeat.

Apricot Compote.—Take a stale Madeira cake, cut off the top, and from the centre cut a large piece, leaving a wall of cake all round of two inches thick. Stew a tin of preserved apricots with a teacupful of sugar for a little while. Fill up the centre of the cake, put on the top slice again, and pour over enough of the hot syrup to soak the cake. When cold, pour either a thick custard over it or else spoonfuls of thick cream whipped up stiff with a little sugar and essence of vanilla.

A very good summer pudding you will find the following to be, though it is served hot. The lemon flavouring makes it very refreshing.

Lemon Pudding.—Wet with a very little cold water two good tablespoonfuls of cornflour, then pour over it, stirring well, as much *boiling* water to make it to the consistency of thick starch; add five or six spoonfuls of sugar, the juice and grated rind of two lemons, and the yolks of two eggs, beaten well. Bake in oven ten minutes, spread the two egg whites beaten up with a little sugar, and very slightly brown in the oven.

A very good mould can be made in much the same way, making the starch very thick, adding sugar, lemon, and one egg yolk and white, returning all to the pan and allowing it to cook for a little while, then pouring it into a wet mould. Let it get cold, then turn out. I have no doubt that amongst the foregoing recipes each one will find something new, and I can confidently assure you that they are all very good. Many of them are suitable for use at garden parties and all such outdoor entertainments.

"CONSTANCE."

CHEAP AND PRETTY SWEETS.

IN most households it will be often found a great convenience when we have sweets to have them cold. As a general rule, it will also **be found much easier** to make cold dishes look pretty than hot. This applies to all dishes, but particularly to sweets. If we attempt to ornament hot dishes composed of meat, as a rule the decorations will be found expensive. Cockscombs and truffles, button mushrooms and ornamental slices of red tongue dipped in glaze, undoubtedly will make dishes look very pretty; but we should have to pay a very pretty figure for doing so. There are many kinds of dishes that may be called sweets that can be made, which combine the three following essentials in the every-day cooking of middle-class families. They can be made cheap, wholesome, and pretty.

A very economical, but at the same time a really elegant dish, can be made out of a single orange, a tablespoonful of cornflour, and some white sugar.

First choose a good-sized ripe orange—and the darker the colour the better. Take a dozen lumps of sugar and rub them on the outside of the orange—so as to get off the colour that is. When the orange has been rubbed all over, it will look a great deal paler. Next place six of these lumps in a very small saucepan, such as an egg saucepan, and dissolve them in about a wineglassful of water; add some more lump sugar till you get a thick syrup when hot; this will of course crystallise when cold. Next take the orange and peel it carefully, so as to avoid breaking the thin inside skin; now divide the orange into its natural divisions. To do this it is best to pull the orange in half with the fingers, and then gradually separate these little divisions from one another by pulling them apart from the centre. If this is done carefully, you will find that you do not lose any of the juice. We cannot say for certain what number of pieces will be obtained, as oranges vary. We recollect, however, that of the last two oranges experimented on, one contained eleven pieces and the other nine. Now dip these pieces of orange one by one in the syrup, so that a certain quantity of syrup will adhere to each piece of orange, and place the pieces on a plate. Sometimes it will be found advisable to drop a little of the syrup, when it begins to cool and gets thicker, on the edge of each piece of orange, which, when cold, of course has the appearance of being crystallised. We next take the remaining lumps of sugar that have been rubbed on the outside of the orange and dissolve them in the syrup, to which some water can now be added. We now take a small round basin—one holding about a pint—a little more or a little less is of no consequence. We must, however, add sufficient water to what is left of the syrup to about fill the basin.

We will, however, suppose the basin to hold exactly a pint. Take a piece of butter and smear the inside of the basin with this butter, so as to make it slightly greasy. Now take another rather larger basin, and put in it a brimming tablespoonful of cornflour, and moisten this with a wineglassful of cold water; stir it up, and mix it till it is quite smooth.

Now bring one pint of diluted syrup to the boil—it is best to taste it to see if it is sufficiently flavoured with the orange and sufficiently sweet. Pour this pint of boiling, sweetened, and orange-flavoured water on the cornflour. Be careful to stir the cornflour before pouring it on, and keep stirring it, as when you mix cornflour with cold water, however carefully you may mix it, it will settle at the bottom in a cake if left to itself even for a few minutes. Keep stirring the cornflour with a spoon in the left hand while you pour the boiling liquid in with the right. Of course it will thicken into a very light yellow-looking jelly. Now pour this into the buttered pint basin, and put it by till it is quite cold. By this time the little pieces of orange will also have got quite cold, and will look like crystallised orange, which indeed they are.

Next take a round glass dish, and having eased the cornflour by pulling it away from the basin all round the edge, turn it out on to a glass dish. Then take the pieces of orange and place them round the edge on the glass dish with the thin part touching the bottom of the pudding.

The dish looks very pretty as it is, but can be made to look still prettier by means of a little green angelica, a quarter of a pound of which can be bought for fourpence.

It is a great mistake to think that a small sum of money spent on ornamenting sweets is necessarily extravagant, and housekeepers are too apt to regard any novelty or innovation as unnecessary extravagance. The same persons who will spend threepence or fourpence a week in parsley to ornament cold meat do not consider it extravagant, because they and their mothers before them have been in the habit of using it. Angelica keeps good for months, and four pennyworth will probably last as long for ornamenting sweets as four shillings' worth of parsley, bought at different times, would last in ornamenting cold meat; and, in addition, we eat the angelica, but look at the parsley, which, we trust, is afterwards used for flavouring soups and gravies.

Cut four little strips of angelica about an inch long, and pointed at each end, and make a star on the top of the cornflour pudding. A little piece of lump sugar can be placed in the middle of the star, coloured a light yellow by means of the orange peel. A little piece of angelica can also be placed on each division of the orange round the base of the pudding.

This dish is extremely pretty in appearance. The pale yellow and bright green contrast very favourably, and we do not think the dish could be improved in appearance by introducing any ornament of a brighter colour; but, of course, a preserved cherry might be placed in the centre of the star, and the pudding itself could be sprinkled over by a small teaspoonful of hundreds and thousands, which are also used for ornamental purposes.

As a rule tinned apricots, though undoubtedly very delicious and very pretty in appearance, are rather expensive when served by themselves.

A very economical dish, however, can be made out of a small tin of apricots, which can be utilised so as to give pleasure to a dozen children. The dish that we are going to describe can be called Imitation Poached Eggs.

First of all we must take half a pint of milk, boil it, sweeten it, and flavour it with a few drops of essence of almonds, and pour this boiling milk on rather a small tablespoonful of cornflour, as we want to make it rather thick. While it is still liquid, pour a tablespoonful of this mixture into a dozen saucers—teacup saucers are better than breakfastcup.

Next we must have by us a plain stale cake without any currants. A cake that has been baked in a square tin about four inches square would be best. Cut this cake into slices, each slice being about the size we have named, four inches square, and toast these slices a light brown. Place each slice with the brown side uppermost on a small pudding-plate. Next open a small tin of apricots, pour the syrup into a basin, and place the half apricots on a dish to drain. Taste the syrup to see if it is very sweet, and, if necessary, add a little sugar, as tinned apricots vary very much in sweetness. Pour a little of the syrup on to each slice of toasted cake, so that it soaks into the cake without running on to the plate. The twelve slices will probably soak up the whole of the syrup.

Next, by means of a very thin knife we must loosen the cornflour settled in the saucers, so that it will turn out. It is best turned out on to a slice such as we use for fried eggs. Place a round of cornflour with the convex side uppermost in the middle of each piece of cake. You can slide off the cornflour from the slice on to the middle of the cake with a knife. Next place half an apricot—each half must be dry and free from any syrup running off it—on the centre of each white round of cornflour. You now have a dozen poached eggs apparently; indeed, in the distance everybody would feel certain that they were real genuine poached eggs. If you like you can give one or two grates of a nutmeg over each " poached egg," which looks, of course, like pepper. It is a very pleasant and agreeable surprise to little children, besides being an exceedingly nice dish to eat.

Of course these twelve poached eggs could be all placed in one dish, but then it requires a very large dish for the purpose; and after the cake has been soaked in the syrup, it is very apt to break in being moved from a dish on to a plate, unless an egg-slice be used instead of a tablespoon for the purpose.

If, in making the above, you should have any stale pieces of cake left over, suppose even they are broken into fragments, you can use them up to make what we will call orange pudding. Suppose, however, you have no cake, the pudding we are going to describe can be made equally well, though perhaps not quite so nice, from small crusts of stale bread, though each piece should not be bigger than the top of the thumb down to the first joint.

We must commence as we did in our first receipt by rubbing some lumps of sugar on the outside of an orange, and as we only want the outside of the orange, and not the inside, it is quite possible to make one orange do for the two dishes; and in the case of having a children's party, when both dishes might be made at the same time, it would be as well to bear this fact in mind.

First of all we must make some syrup by dissolving the sugar that has been rubbed on the outside of the orange and a little more sugar added to it by pouring some boiling water on to the sugar and stirring it up. Now soak the pieces of stale cake or the stale crusts of bread in this syrup, and then place them on a plate to drain. Next take four eggs and separate the whites from the yolks of two, and put by the two whites in a basin. These have to be whipped up to a froth by-and-by with some powdered sugar. Take a pint of milk and boil it, and when it has boiled, sweeten it with the remainder of the syrup and the syrup that has drained off from the pieces of stale cake or crusts of bread. Beat up the four yolks and two whites very thoroughly, and gradually add the hot sweetened milk. Pour this mixed egg and milk into a pie-dish, add the soaked cake or crusts of bread, and place the pie-dish in the oven and bake till it sets. When it is quite set, take it out and let it get cold. When it is quite cold, spread a layer of orange marmalade on the top so as to cover the whole of it.

Now take the two whites in a basin, and with a fork beat them to a froth, and gradually add nearly a teacupful of powdered sugar. The sugar must be very finely powdered indeed, and it is far safest to buy the sugar powdered, and not attempt to make the powdered sugar at home. Now pile up this thick white froth on the top of the marmalade and edge of the pie-dish, taking care that the whole of the edge is completely covered. If you take pains in whipping the white of the eggs to a froth, you will be able to make a sufficient quantity to cover the whole of the dish an inch deep. Now place the dish once more in the oven, which must be very slack, as we do not wish the white to turn colour. In a very short time this white foam will swell and set firm. Then take it out of the oven and let it get cold.

The top of this white froth can now be ornamented in various ways. You can, if you like, use up the remainder of the orange—if one was used for this pudding only—and place these divisions of the orange round the edge of the dish, and you can place little leaves of green angelica between each piece of orange, the green and yellow on the white having a very pretty appearance. One piece of orange can be placed in the centre of the dish, upright, like the crescent on the Turkish flag; but if the remainder of the orange has been used for the cornflour pudding described in our first receipt, you can ornament the dish in other ways. Perhaps the prettiest ornament of all is to sprinkle some hundreds and thousands over the top.

These pretty little sweets known as hundreds and thousands can be bought at twopence an ounce, and if used solely for ornamenting purposes, one ounce will be sufficient to ornament a very large number of dishes like the ones we have just described.

For instance, suppose you have a dish of stewed pippins—a teaspoonful or less of this white froth can be placed in the middle of each pippin, and a very tiny pinch of hundreds and thousands placed on the top of each; in fact, a saltspoonful would be sufficient to ornament a dozen pippins. The expense is almost *nil*, but what a difference in the appearance.

Another very cheap and pretty dish can be made with apples and cornflour.

Take six or eight large apples, and try and get them as much as possible the same size. Peel them carefully and scoop out the cores. For this purpose a scoop like that used by cheesemongers for tasting cheese will be found very convenient, or you can use an ordinary silver or bone marrow spoon. Put these apples in a tin with a little sugar and water, and two or three strips of lemon peel. White sugar must be used for the purpose. Bake these apples in the oven gently till they are tender, and baste them from time to time with the syrup in the tin. Do not let the apples get discoloured, as this would have the effect of browning the syrup, and we want to have the syrup as clear and bright as possible, though we shall not be able to have it perfectly bright.

When the apples are cooked sufficiently to be eaten with a spoon, take the tin out of the oven, and with an egg-slice move the apples on to a dish to get cold. Now pour off the syrup—which of course is flavoured with apple—from the tin into a small saucepan. Rince out the tin with a little warm water, and add this to the syrup. If we have right apples we shall want about a pint of sweetened water. Add a few drops of cochineal to the syrup till it is a bright red. When the apples are quite cold we must let the syrup boil, and pour it on to a tablespoonful of cornflour in a basin previously mixed with a little cold water, as we did before, of course remembering to stir the cornflour while we pour the boiling syrup. We shall now have a pint of cloudy

red jelly. Wait till it begins to cool, and then with a spoon pour the jelly over the apples. We first fill up the hole in the centre of the apples where the cores have been removed. We then, taking only a spoonful of cornflour jelly at a time, gradually cover the apples with red jelly. This requires some little time and patience. It is best to put a little on at first, and then when that has got cold, add a little more. This is a very pretty-looking dish.

You can, if you like, ornament each apple by cutting out little green leaves of angelica and placing them on the top.

When the dish is quite cold, in autumn you can place some real green apple leaves round the base, just as we place strawberry leaves round the dish of strawberries, or mulberry leaves round a dish of mulberries. Indeed, in ornamenting every kind of fruit no decoration is so pretty or so suitable as the leaves of the tree from which the fruit was gathered.

In the summer and autumn, when fruit is cheap, ripe, and plentiful—and it is only at such a time that fruit is really in its prime—we can make a great variety of cheap and pretty sweets with the assistance of a tablespoonful of cornflour and a little sugar.

For instance, suppose blackberries are in season. The advantage of using blackberries is that, generally speaking, they cost nothing beyond a morning's pleasure for the children of the family. The disadvantage of blackberries is undoubtedly the pips.

Suppose we have a quart of ripe blackberries. Pick out two or three dozen of the largest and best, and place the remainder in a small saucepan with a little water and sugar. The amount of sugar is a matter of taste, but you should bear in mind that in making blackberry jam a pound of fruit only requires half a pound of sugar. Add a little water to the blackberries in the saucepan, and let them stew gently till they are perfectly soft and tender. Now strain them through a hair sieve, pressing them with a wooden spoon.

After we have drained off the juice we can put the blackberries back in the saucepan and add a little more water, stirring them up and pressing them against the sides of the saucepan, and then drain them through the hair sieve again, rubbing them with a wooden spoon, and scraping the pulp from the bottom of the sieve and adding it to the juice. When we have got a pint of juice, we must boil it and pour the boiling juice on to a tablespoonful of cornflour as before. Let it get cold in the basin, and then turn it out on to a dish. A round glass dish does very well, or if we use a silver dish, we must place a piece of ornamental paper at the bottom.

Now ornament the dish by placing one ripe blackberry on the top, of course picking out the best one for the purpose, and surround it with a few fresh blackberry leaves. Place the remainder of the blackberries round the dish touching the mould, with a green leaf under each blackberry. This looks very pretty on a silver dish with an ornamental piece of paper, and the cost is almost *nil*.

A number of similar dishes can be made from other kinds of fruit; for instance, ripe mulberries can be treated in exactly a similar manner; so can black and red currants, only bear in mind that in ornamenting the dish you must pick the smallest leaves for the purpose.

Ripe gooseberries make a delicious sweet, but, strange to say, ripe gooseberries require more sugar than early green gooseberries, though of course the latter would not be suitable for the purpose.

Should you try the experiment with ripe raspberries, which resemble blackberries with regard to pips, bear in mind that you cannot get a good colour without adding some ripe red currants to them.

FRUIT SALADS.

By LUCY HELEN YATES, Lecturer on The Cookery of Vegetables and Fruits to the Horticultural Exhibition Committee.

WITH the hot days before us, and the promise of a plentiful supply of fruits, we are generally on the look-out for new and dainty ways of serving these most acceptable gifts of our generous Mother Earth.

Fruit tarts, fruit puddings, stewed fruit, even fruit compôtes, we are all well acquainted with; but I wonder how many of our girls know how to make a fruit salad?

Perhaps the favoured few, who have had the good fortune to make acquaintance with Parisian and Viennese restaurants, may have tasted with wondering admiration the strange compound set before them; but I doubt whether they dared to attempt an imitation of it at home, although we may meet with occasional recipes for it in some few cookery books —none too reliable, I must confess.

Now, give me your attention, dear girls, while I tell you exactly how to make and serve this most delicious of delicacies.

First, I must tell you, you cannot make it of any fruit, or of fruit in any condition. It must be good and sound, perfectly ripe, and very dry. This last requisite, you will remember, is needful for the success of any salad, fruit or vegetable.

Gooseberries will not make a salad; nor will plums, apples, or pears.

Too much soft fruit, like ripe currants, may mar its success.

Now let us see what will do best.

Strawberries and raspberries, with a few stoned cherries, and a small proportion of very fine red or white currants, will make a splendid salad, as they accord well together.

Then pineapples, bananas, apricots, peaches, nectarines, all combine perfectly; while oranges, lemons, melons, with a small admixture of candied cherries, greengages, and chestnuts, make an excellent fruit salad about Christmas-time.

Take first the strawberries and other soft fruits, as these most nearly concern us at the present moment.

Let the fruit be very much "morning gathered," if you have not the good luck to be able to gather it yourself. Strawberries and raspberries must be very dry and free from dust. To ensure this, when you pick off the hulls, brush each one over lightly with a camel's-hair brush. The cherries should be stoned; you will easily do this with practice. Black cherries are preferable to "white hearts" for use in a salad. They are more tender.

Choose the finest bunches of currants, and pick them off the stems without bruising them.

A deep crystal dish, round or oval in shape, is to be preferred to the salad-bowl for a fruit salad, even though the latter may be a crystal one.

Arrange the fruit, not in layers of each kind, but in mixed layers, and keep it in pyramid shape. When you have sufficient fruit make your " dressing."

For this you will need a tumblerful of some sweet red wine—Rousillon or a sweet port. First take a tumblerful of water and about a dozen lumps of sugar. Set these over the fire in an enamelled saucepan. Let this boil for five minutes, then set aside to cool. Stir in the wine and a tablespoonful of some good liqueur, like Prunelle, which has the flavour of nuts. Let this mixture be quite cold before pouring it over the fruit; indeed, you had better make it early in the morning if intending to use the salad for lunch.

Pour it very gently over all, being careful to cover all the fruit, and let it slowly filter through.

If you want to make this dish very handsome, beat up the white of one egg with its equal in powdered sugar, till a stiff froth. Take small portions of this with a teaspoon, and place about the pyramid of fruit, like snow. Arrange a bed of cool ivy leaves on another dish, and set your crystal dish on this. Serve with a silver spoon and fork, taking care to give a little of the "dressing" with each helping.

Pare the pineapple and the bananas, and slice them evenly, but not too thinly. The apricots and peaches must be skinned, and the stones cracked to get at the kernels. Pound these latter in a mortar with a little sugar, and sprinkle the powder amongst the other fruit. Arrange it also in pyramidal form. The dressing for this salad would be made in the same way, only as the colour of the fruit is yellow, so the wine must be the same—a sweet white wine, sherry, or Frontignan, and a glass of Maraschino. You may put "snow" about this salad too if you wish.

In making the winter salad, you will need to pare both oranges and lemons. One lemon to half a dozen oranges is about the right proportion. Grate a little of the rind of both fruits, as the flavour of the peel is very choice. The late melons have a very fine scent. Pare a quarter of one small melon, scrape away all the seedy part, and slice it very thinly. The candied fruit should be split in half, and arranged among the other with regard to its colouring. For this salad you would make the same syrup; but a raisin or ginger wine would be most suitable.

Perhaps some of my readers who are teetotallers will take objection to the wine. I am sorry to say you cannot produce the same effect without it. I have never tried whether the "champagne cider" and other teetotal beverages could be made to answer the purpose; but I am afraid they would not. Better far would it be to use cream and sugar, as do those good people who object to oil in a lettuce salad.

CAKES FOR AFTERNOON TEA.

THE accompanying article has been written in accordance with a request sent to the author by a reader of the GIRL'S OWN PAPER. It is hoped that the information given will be useful.

Probably there is no kind of cookery which is so interesting as is cake making to individuals who take up the business from a natural liking for it rather than from necessity. Of course we all know that very excellent cakes can be bought at the confectioner's at a very reasonable price, but bought cake stands on quite a different footing from home-made cake. Again and again it occurs that cake offered to visitors in a house is refused as a matter of course; but if a hostess says to a guest, "Will you not taste this cake; it was made at home by my daughter?" the cake disappears at once. Not long ago a lady, who had the reputation of being quite a philosopher in a small way, was heard to remark, "I make it one of the principles of my life never to refuse home-made cake when I have the chance of getting it," and she helped herself as she spoke to a good slice of the product. There are a good many people who follow the same principle; and this being the case, there is little fear that cakes made at home will fall into disfavour.

Cakes are of many sorts; and one reason why so many people fail in making cakes is, that they think that the rule, dear to their hearts, which holds good for one sort, applies to all sorts; and the probability is that it does nothing of the kind. Thus, some people will say, "The way to make a cake properly is to beat it thoroughly." This is the case undoubtedly with cakes raised with eggs, but it is not invariably true. Others will say, "When cakes are heavy we may be sure that they have been mixed too moist." Certainly plain cakes are very frequently made heavy by being too moist; but it is not the invariable rule; for according to the difference of method is the degree of consistency required. Others, again, will say, "You can never use too many eggs for cakes; the more eggs there are, the lighter the cake." It does not follow at all. The eggs used must be in due proportion to the butter used. "Eggs bind as well as lighten."

Taking these variations into consideration, can we wonder that individuals who make one kind of cake very well indeed, do not always succeed with another kind? The fact is, that there is no direction in which it is so necessary that the operator should exercise judgment and discretion as in the making of cakes. Also, there is no direction in which the experience which comes from practice tells more powerfully. This experience enables the operator to tell at once when anything is wrong, and how it is wrong; and the best recipe that ever was written cannot do that for us. Thus we come back to the old rule—those who wish to learn how to make cakes must make them.

Another point of importance is, that the materials used must be of the best quality, and carefully prepared. This goes so much without saying, that perhaps it is scarcely necessary to say it; and readers of the GIRL'S OWN PAPER know quite well that the best and finest sifted flour and white sugar should be used for cakes, that butter should be fresh and sweet, currants and raisins and all ingredients perfectly dry, and eggs quite fresh. Nevertheless, cakes are so constantly spoilt for want of attention to these details, that one must mention them.

With regard, then, to the different sorts of cake. These may be divided broadly into three classes:—Class 1. Those that are raised with yeast. Class 2. Those which are raised with chemicals—that is, baking-powder and its equivalents, soda and cream of tartar, egg powders, and similar compounds. Class 3. Those which are raised with eggs, which eggs may be either beaten when cold, or beaten over the fire.

With regard to the 1st Class. It is probable that all girls who have experimented in cookery at all know how to make cake with yeast. Of this sort of cake, therefore, nothing will be said here, especially as there is so much to be said of the other kinds of cakes.

Class 2.—Cakes raised with Chemicals.— A good many people have a great scorn for cakes made with baking-powder, etc. Some of these cakes are, however, very good, and they are said to be wholesome and digestible. An advantage belonging to them is, that they are not so likely to be spoilt if made by inexperienced cooks, as are cakes raised either with yeast or eggs. In all cakes made with chemicals the idea is the same—an alkali is mixed with an acid; thus an effervescence is produced, and the bubbles raise the cake. Understanding this idea, we see how necessary it is that cakes raised with chemicals should be put into the oven immediately after the chemicals are set to work. If they are not, the air bubbles go down, and their power is gone. By all means, therefore, when we are making a cake with chemicals, we should be most particular not to mix the same until the oven is ready, and until we know that the cake can be baked at once. When cakes made thus are a failure, the reason almost invariably is, either that the cake has not been baked instantly, or that the oven has not been hot enough. The easiest way of introducing baking-powder is to mix it with the flour in the first instance. If, however, the cake cannot be made at once, the powder should be left till last.

The various chemicals used in raising cakes amount on the whole to very much the same thing, and it is generally safe to substitute one for the other, so long as we know the strength. Thus, with good baking-powders we generally calculate that a teaspoonful of powder is needed for each pound of material, and that half a teaspoonful of cream of tartar and a quarter of a teaspoonful of carbonate of soda are equivalent to a teaspoonful of baking-powder. The danger associated with the use of soda, however, is, that it varies so much in purity, and if one gets even a little too much of it, the taste is at once evident. Too much baking-powder also makes cakes coarse, open, and crumbly.

In making cakes, the employment of sour—not rancid—milk helps to make cakes light. It is to be remembered, however, that sour milk and fresh milk should not be used together. Also, if sour milk is used, soda also should be used, instead of baking-powder.

In the majority of cakes raised with baking-powder, eggs are also used; but not in numbers sufficient to dispense with powder. Sometimes the butter is creamed—that is, beaten with a spoon or with the hand until it looks like cream; sometimes it is rubbed into the flour. When rubbed in, the cake is firmer and more solid; when creamed, the cake is light and somewhat spongy. The difference in method produces a difference of result.

Here are recipes for cakes raised with baking-powder and its equivalents, and eggs.

Sultana Cake.—Rub a quarter of a pound of butter (or two ounces of butter and two ounces of clarified dripping) into ten ounces of flour. Add two teaspoonfuls of baking-powder, two ounces of castor sugar, one ounce of finely-shred candied peel, four ounces of sultana raisins, and the grated rind of a lemon. Mix the dry ingredients thoroughly. Beat the yolks of two eggs with half a gill of milk, and stir into the flour, etc. Have the whites ready whisked to a stiff froth, add them lightly, turn into a well-greased mould, and bake for about an hour and a half in a good oven.

Seed Cake.—Follow the same recipe, but use a teaspoonful of caraway seeds instead of the raisins and the candied peel.

Walnut Cake.—Use a gill measure for a cup. Put a cupful of white sugar and half a cup of butter into a basin, and beat them together till they look like cream. Add gradually two cupfuls of flour which have been mixed with two teaspoonfuls of baking-powder, twenty-five drops of essence of vanilla, and half a pint of peeled walnuts or hazel nuts cut small. Have ready whisked, and introduce last of all, the whites of four eggs which have been whisked till firm. Bake in a shallow tin. This cake can be covered with fondant icing, and half the nuts can be sprinkled over the icing before it hardens.

Lemon Cake.—Follow the same recipe, but flavour with grated lemon rind and an ounce of finely-shred citron.

Cocoa-Nut Cake.—Follow the same recipe, but use three teaspoonfuls of desiccated cocoanut instead of the chopped nuts.

One, Two, Three, Four Cake. — The Americans are very fond of a cake called sometimes by this name and sometimes Cup Cake. In American books we are always coming upon it, and it is much approved in this country also. Like the two recipes already given, it can be followed for a number of cakes by simply varying the flavour. The formula is—One cup of butter, two cups of sugar, three cups of flour, four eggs, two teaspoonfuls of baking-powder, and a cupful and a half of milk. The method is—Beat the sugar and butter to cream; add the yolks of the eggs and the milk; then the flour mixed with the baking-powder, and last, the whites of the eggs whisked till firm. The flavours (chopped nuts, dried or candied fruits, spices, etc.), should be put in after the cake is made. Made plain, and baked in shallow tins, this cake can have fruit jelly put between two layers, and then it becomes Jelly Cake.

Feather Cake is another cake well-known in American homes, and there are individuals who declare that it went over from England with the *Mayflower*. The formula is—One tablespoonful of butter, one cupful of sugar, one cupful and a half of flour, half a cupful of milk, two eggs, and a teaspoonful of baking-powder. Beat butter and sugar together and a little milk; add flour and baking-powder a little at a time; lastly, the eggs, beaten very well. Bake in a hot oven.

Lemon Feather Cake.—Follow the above recipe, and flavour with the grated rind of a lemon. Cakes flavoured with lemon rind keep well.

Orange Feather Cake.—Flavour with the grated rind of an orange instead of a lemon, and introduce orange juice in place of part of the milk.

Family Cake is very similar. Cream together three ounces of butter and a quarter of a pound of sugar. Add two eggs, three quarters of a pint of flour mixed with a small teaspoonful of baking-powder, and six tablespoonfuls of milk. Flavour with nutmeg, currants, raisins, or almonds.

Chocolate Cake.—Beat half a pound of butter and four ounces of castor sugar to cream. Add two ounces of ground rice, four ounces of flour mixed with two ounces of baking-powder, the yolks of six eggs well beaten, and half a pound of chocolate, grated and dissolved in two tablespoonfuls of water. Last of all introduce the whites of the eggs beaten till stiff. Pour into a greased tin, and bake in a moderate oven about an hour and a half.

Ginger-bread.—Put half a pound of treacle, six ounces of brown sugar, and six ounces of butter into a saucepan to get hot. Add *off the fire* (because the soda will make the liquid rise) half an ounce of soda. Have ready, thoroughly mixed, a pound and a quarter of sifted flour, two ounces of blanched and chopped almonds, three quarters of an ounce of grated ginger. Beat the two mixtures well together, and squeeze in last of all the juice of a lemon. Bake in a shallow tin (never in an ordinary cake tin) in a slow oven. When half done, brush over with milk and sugar.

Class 3.—The third class of cake is raised with eggs only, and here success depends chiefly upon correct beating, mixing, and baking. A great many people think cakes of this sort are exceedingly extravagant. They are less so, however, than at first sight appears. For one thing, a cake made without yeast or baking-powder keeps well. A first class pound cake, for instance, if left with the greased paper used in baking still round it to keep in the flavour, and if stored in a dry tin with a well fitting lid, will keep good for weeks. For another thing, good cake is much more satisfying than plain cake—no one could possibly eat very much at once. Besides, we have to remember, that after all cake is an extra; and having decided to make it, we might as well take a little pains with it, and make it worth having. The difference in money cost between plain cake and "better" cake is not very much; the chief difference is in the time and labour bestowed upon the making. Of the superiority of the one over the other there is no question.

Fine cake is of two sorts—the cake that is good because it is rich, and the cake that is good because it is light. Of the first, Pound Cake, of the second, Sponge Cake, may be taken as the type.

The *Pound Cake*, as its name implies, is made with a pound weight of each of the chief ingredients; that is, a pound of white sugar, a pound of flour, a pound of butter, eight eggs, a pinch of salt, and some flavouring. The flavouring may consist of either the rind of two oranges or two lemons, or half a pound of currants or sultanas (with either of which may be used a little chopped candied peel and grated nutmeg), or three quarters of a pound of almonds blanched and chopped, dried, warmed, and floured. Eight eggs, it should be understood, when they are large, are equivalent to a pound of flour; if small, ten eggs would be needed. It is, however, most important that the eggs should be fresh; no amount of beating will make stale eggs satisfactory. In warm weather the eggs may be laid in cold water for a few minutes before beating, and the addition of a pinch of salt will help the whites to froth. All the ingredients must be brought together, weighed, and made ready before the mixing commences. The eggs must have the yolks separated from the whites, and the latter must be whisked with a pinch of salt till firm. The butter must be put into a cloth and have the water squeezed from it. The cake is best mixed in an earthenware bowl. Beat the butter till it looks like cream. (If the cake is made in winter, when butter is hard, it may be warmed a little to soften it, but never so much so as to oil it.) Add the sugar gradually, and beat between every addition. Next add the yolks of eggs one at a time, and a tablespoonful of brandy or a little sherry, and a few drops of rose-water if approved. Beat again, and be sure that every egg yolk is thoroughly incorporated before another is added. Now put in the flour and, last of all, the whites of eggs. If the batter should become too stiff, a little of the whisked whites must be put in between, and the mixture must be well beaten. For pound cake, however, the batter should be stiff. The bulk of the whites, however, should for a plain pound cake be thrown in last of all, and they should be mixed in thoroughly and no more. When fruit or almonds are used these ingredients should be introduced after the whites, and lightly stirred in just enough to mix—no more.

One word should be said about the movement in beating a cake. Not *stirring* but *beating* is required; therefore the hand or spoon should go, not round and round the bowl, but the batter should be brought up from the bowl with every stroke, the aim being to drive air into the cells. The air thus introduced will expand as it gets hot, and the cake will be made light thereby. Towards the last the motion may be slower, but it should be always upward.

Thus far a pound cake, though requiring care, is not difficult to make. The majority of cakes of this sort that are spoilt, are spoilt in the baking. The oven, then, must be very moderate and very steady. Nearly or quite two hours will be required for baking a pound cake; if it has to be turned in the oven, it must be touched gently, and not shaken; when a straw or knitting-needle put into it can be drawn out quite clean it is done. It should be left in the tin for awhile after being taken from the oven, otherwise it may break. When turned out it should be put sideways on a sieve till cold, so that the steam may thoroughly escape. The hoop or tin in which it is baked should be thoroughly greased in every part, and well lined with greased paper. When the cake is first put in the oven it is a good plan to put a cap of brown paper on the top, to prevent its becoming over brown. A crack at the top or an uneven surface is a sign of imperfect baking.

Sponge Cake is generally considered very difficult to make, but individuals who have had practice in making it generally think it quite easy. It is true that it requires well beating, and consequently it needs a strong arm. For my own part, I may as well confess, that where arm ache is likely to ensue, I do not think it is worth while to make sponge cakes at home. They are very useful cakes because they enter into the composition of so many sweet dishes; but they can be bought at the confectioners for very little more than the cost of the material; and the cakes thus bought have not cost an arm ache, for they have been beaten by machinery. Nevertheless, though we may not desire to make them regularly, it is just as well to be able to make them, and therefore girls may be glad of the following directions:

Prepare the cake mould and have the oven ready before beginning to mix. A sponge cake requires a moderate, steady oven, and the heat must not be increased after the cake is put in. M. Gouffé, who is a great authority on matters of this kind, says that the oven for sponge cake should be a "dark yellow paper temperature," which means, that when a piece of white paper is put in a baking tin in the oven it very soon becomes dark yellow. If it were to be black or nearly so the oven would be too hot.

The condition of the tins or moulds also is a point of very great importance for all cakes, but especially for sponge cakes. Many a cake, excellent in everything else, has been spoilt because the part that touched the tin has been unpleasant in taste. Girls should be more particular about the material they use for greasing the tins even than they are about the material used for shortening. In making plain cakes it is sometimes allowable to use dripping in the place of butter; but dripping alone should never be used for greasing the tins; the sweetest butter is needed for this purpose, and preferable even to butter is clarified butter and fat. This is M. Gouffé's way of preparing the same for greasing moulds.

Pick one pound of veal suet, chop it very fine, and put it to melt in a large stewpan over a slow fire. Stir the fat occasionally with a wooden spoon, and when it is quite clear take the stewpan off the fire; add one pound of butter, cut into pieces, and stir with a skimmer until it is melted. Be careful that the fat does not boil over. When the butter and fat have become quite clear, and attained a slight yellow tinge, strain, and put by for use.

If butter is used for greasing moulds it should have the water squeezed from it before being applied to this purpose. When the moulds are to be used for sponge cakes and light cakes, make them hot, pour a little melted fat into them, and turn them round and about so that the fat shall run over every part of the inside

surface; then drain. When the butter has drained off, and before it is cold, strew fine sugar over the inside of the moulds, and knock them about so that the sugar shall cover all the butter. This sugaring must be quickly done. The moulds for rich cakes should be lined with paper, two or three thicknesses of paper being put in the bottom.

There is a general rule for making sponge cakes, which can be easily remembered. To make them we want any number of eggs, their weight in sugar, and half their weight in flour, with any flavourings that may be liked. Beat the yolks of the eggs and the flavouring essences together; add the sugar and flour, and lastly the whites of the eggs whisked till firm. The cakes may be flavoured with rose or vanilla extracts, with a little nutmeg or a little brandy, with grated lemon or grated orange rind. The addition of a little lemon juice makes them not quite so dry. They may be baked in moulds of any size, which moulds should not be more than half filled, and finely sifted sugar should be dredged thinly but evenly over the top of the batter. A band of kitchen paper two inches broad should be fastened round the top of the mould to allow for rising, and the oven door should not be opened until the cake has had time to rise and set firm. When baked, the cake should be the colour of ripe corn; and if there is any fear that it will become too dark, it should be placed when half baked in a tin containing salt or sand. It is enough when the blade of a small knife comes out free from dampness, and should be left in the tin for a short time before being turned out.

There are two methods of operations in making cake with egg: in one the ingredients are beaten cold, as already described; in the other, they are beaten over hot water. The process is more difficult than the ordinary one, but the result is excellent. Cakes thus made are very light and good. We talk, however, of a strong arm being needed for beating sponge cakes; decidedly a strong arm is needed for this process. The finest sponge cakes are made in this way.

Sponge cakes are, however, well known, and they can be made according to the old method. It will therefore, perhaps, be most useful if a recipe for *Mocha Cake* be given, Mocha cake being a very superior product, highly approved by those who know it. Get a good sized basin large enough to afford room for thorough beating—a basin which will hold three quarts will be about right. Procure also a stewpan in which this basin can stand. Put water into the stewpan and bring it to the boil. Put two ounces of castor sugar into the basin, break four eggs therein one at a time, stand the basin over the boiling water, draw the pan back, and whisk lightly and steadily till the batter froths up and is light and thick. While the batter is being beaten the water should be kept just below boiling point, and the beating will have to be kept up for twenty minutes. Take the basin off the fire and stir in four ounces of fine flour. Mix thoroughly, pour into a cake tin, and bake in a good oven.

To make Coffee Icing for this Cake.—Beat to a cream four ounces of sugar and two ounces of butter. Strain, in a drop at a time beating well between every addition—as much strong clear coffee as will make a stiff paste. Put this on the cake when it is quite cold with an icing tube, and dry in a cool oven.

Chou Paste, for making *Duchesse Loaves, Éclairs, etc.*—Put half a pint of water, two ounces of butter, and two ounces of castor sugar into a stewpan. When it boils draw the pan back, and mix in thoroughly five ounces of fine flour. Beat the whole well over the fire for some minutes (here the strength of arm comes in), until the ingredients form a smooth, compact paste, leaving the sides of the saucepan easily. If it has caught at the bottom of the

pan at all it must be put into another pan before the eggs are introduced. Let the mixture cool a little, add any flavouring essence that may be preferred, and three whole eggs, one at a time, and let one be thoroughly incorporated before another is added. The paste should be of such a consistency that it will fall of its own weight out of a spoon, but not so soft that it will spread. If the paste is too stiff, another yolk may be added.

Petits Choux.—Make paste as above. Put the mixture into a forcing bag with a plain tin pipe in the end, rather large in the opening. Butter a baking tin, and press the mixture on it in small pieces about the size of a pigeon's egg, and cut off each piece with a knife. Leave room between the pieces, because the cakes swell very much. Smooth them, then dust them with castor sugar, and bake in a slow, steady oven. They ought to be crisp and hard when baked, and of a light brown colour. They may be served plain, or they may be filled inside with whipped cream, fruit cream, or with delicate jam. If liked, they can be brushed over with beaten egg before baking, and just before they are done fine sugar can be sifted over them, and they can be put back in the oven till this is melted. Sometimes the choux after baking are dipped in caramel, then gently rolled in roughly chopped pistachios mixed with an equal proportion of lump sugar chopped small. The caramel is made by boiling a quarter of a pound of sugar in a gill of water for five minutes till it is stringy. It is to be noted that the choux should not be dipped in caramel till they are cold, and that they should not be filled with cream till they are cold. The incision is usually made in the side.

Éclairs are made by forcing choux paste out of the bag in lengths three inches long and three quarters of an inch wide. They should be brushed over with egg, and baked of a bright yellow colour. When cold they should be filled with whipped cream flavoured with vanilla, and glazed with coffee icing. To make the icing for this purpose, make half a gill of very strong coffee, mix it with about half a pound of icing sugar to a stiffish paste, and stir over the fire till warm. Have the éclairs by the side of the pan, pour the icing over them one by one, covering them evenly, and let them dry. If the icing should get cold before they are all done, add a few drops of water and warm again. Cakes of this description are excellent when they are a success. They are, however, difficult to make, and skilled cooks occasionally fail with them—a too hot oven soon ruins them.

It will perhaps be well if we conclude with a few general hints about cakes, which are useful to be remembered.

1. All cakes made without baking-powder or its equivalents, soda and cream of tartar, require a much slower oven than those made with them.

2. Cakes made with chemicals or with yeast dry quickly.

3. Cakes made with much butter need careful and long baking.

4. Cakes made with chemicals should be baked as soon as mixed.

5. To warm butter before beating gives cakes a "short" taste.

6. Cakes should never be moved or shaken in the oven after they have risen before they are firm. Very rich cakes especially need to be very gently handled when taken from the oven.

7. Cakes need to soak a few minutes even after a skewer comes from them dry.

8. When taken from the tin, cakes should be stood wrong way up on a sieve, to let the steam escape.

9. Cakes keep best if left with the paper in which they were baked still round them.

PHYLLIS BROWNE.

STRAWBERRIES.

By PHYLLIS BROWNE.

THE American philosopher, Emerson, once said, "The plum at its best is the fruit of Paradise." One wonders if, when he made this remark, Emerson remembered that there were such things as strawberries. He must have done, for he was a very enthusiastic gardener, and very much given to cultivating fruits. Indeed, his biographer tells us that he failed completely with pears; so much so that a certain Horticultural Society once sent a deputation to inspect his orchard in order that they might discover "what soil it was which produced such poor specimens of such fine varieties." Maybe the sage was as unsuccessful with his strawberries as with his pears, and this was the reason why he was not as enthusiastic about them as he was about plums.

Whether Emerson appreciated strawberries or not, there are few girls who do not approve of them. When the scarlet berries appear, peeping between the stalks for those who have gardens, or resting in their baskets at the greengrocer's for those who have none, girls find themselves longing to taste the same, and congratulate themselves that good things have their season. This is the time of year when the sight of strawberries may soon be expected to awaken this longing; and whether our prospects with regard to them are good or bad, of one thing we may be quite sure—that they will not be with us long. Very shortly after we have discovered that they are in full season, and reasonable in price, we shall discover also that they have begun to "go off," and then for twelve months they will be seen no more. The period during which we can enjoy them freely will have to be counted by days; therefore we shall show our wisdom by making the most of them while we have them.

A clever housekeeper once said: "I am often told that I must take things as they come; but I find it much more difficult to part with them when they go." If we wish to part with strawberries when they go with equanimity, we must prepare to use them reasonably, enjoy them to the extent of our possibilities, convert them into dainty dishes while we have the opportunity, preserve them carefully, and do our duty by them fully, and so "seize their day," as Horace says. To do this, however, we ought in plenty of time to get to know all about them, and collect together the recipes for dishes into which they will advantageously enter. By way of helping girls to do this, it is proposed to take up here the subject of strawberries, and to give as much information about them as possible. Thus, girls will be in a position to "take strawberries" when they come, and to benefit by them to the full.

The strawberry as we have it is a comparatively modern product. Until the early part of the seventeenth century the only strawberry grown in England was the wild strawberry of the woods, and this, though pretty to look at and sweet to taste, was too small to be of value. It is true that for some time before this the French had found out how to cultivate strawberries so as to increase their size, and there was a certain wood near Paris which was so noted for the fruit, that people used to come thither from all parts to buy them. The fruit thus purchased was, however, necessarily costly, and not until English gardeners gave attention to strawberries did they come within the reach of all classes. Now they are so well cared for, that every year sees them improved, while the number of varieties is very large.

Strawberries and Cream.—When strawberries are at their best, of a good sort, freshly gathered, fully ripe and not over ripe, they ought to be eaten as they are. Even cream and sugar are not worthy to be put with them, and the experienced epicure would prefer to eat them without any addition, while to cook them would be simple desecration. When a little short of being perfect, they should be mixed with cream and sugar; indeed, it is probable that under all circumstances the majority of strawberry lovers would say that strawberries and cream was an almost perfect combination of flavours.

There are two or three ways of serving a dish so well known as strawberries and cream. Some content themselves with piling the fruit on a dish covered with leaves, and sending sweet cream and sifted sugar with it to table separately. Then the guests prepare their own food. They pick off the hulls, bruise the berries with a fork, add sugar and cream to suit their individual taste, and proceed to enjoy themselves. The method is homely, but it is not elegant. The discarded hulls make the table look untidy, and those who are not accustomed to work of this kind get out of patience with it. Girls might at least hull the fruit before they place it before their friends, and doing this would give them an opportunity to pick out and lay aside berries that are not quite sound. Attention to this one detail would be a great improvement.

For a really superior dish of strawberries and cream, proceed as follows: Procure ripe, sound, freshly-gathered red strawberries, and do not touch them until a short time before they are wanted. They will spoil with keeping. Hull them and discard all imperfect berries, then bruise them lightly with a silver fork, and sweeten them to taste. The quantity of sugar needed will, of course, depend upon the quality of the fruit. Probably from three to four tablespoonfuls of sugar will be sufficient for a pint of berries. Now pour over them about a quarter of a pint of cream, and toss them lightly with two forks to incorporate them with the cream; then cover the surface with cream that has been whipped until it is firm and frothy. In laying on the cream, the aim should be to coat the fruit entirely, so that the preparation looks quite white. When the spoon is put into it to serve it, the red berries will show themselves, and the preparation will have a most inviting appearance. It will be the sort of dainty to which the gentleman referred who, when imploring the girl named Curly Locks to be his, told her that she—

"Should not wash dishes, nor yet feed the swine,
But sit on a cushion and sew a fine seam,
And feast upon strawberries, sugar, and cream"—

a very inviting prospect, truly.

It is perhaps scarcely necessary to say that cream which is to be whipped thus must be "double cream," that is, it must have stood twenty-four hours instead of twelve, and it must be whisked in a cool place until it thickens, and no longer. It will not take many minutes to thicken, but if worked too long it will curdle. The objection to preparing strawberries and cream in the way referred to is that so much cream is needed. Altogether (that is, including the cream in which the berries are tossed and the cream used for whipping), about three quarters of a pint would be required for each pound of strawberries. To whip cream, however, increases its bulk, and this increase may therefore be calculated upon.

Next to strawberries and cream the preparation which will most naturally occur to girls who want to make the most of the fruit while it is in season, is strawberry jam. Now, truth before all things; so I may as well confess that, to my mind, this simple jam is one of the most difficult jams to make satisfactorily, and one of the worst to keep. Probably, on reading this remark, individuals accustomed to make strawberry jam will say, "Difficult! not at all! We have made strawberry jam year after year, and it has been enjoyed, and has kept well enough." Doubtless this was the case, and we think we know exactly what this jam was like, and how it was made. The fruit was hulled, and boiled down alone for awhile, after which sugar was added in the proportion of three quarters of a pound of sugar to a pound of fruit, and it was boiled again until it set when a little was put upon a plate. Whilst it was being made the fragrance sent forth by this jam was most inviting; indeed, it was the best part about the business—it conveyed a promise which would never be fulfilled. When this jam was brought out after being kept for awhile, it would be pure, unadulterated, and wholesome. It would be enjoyed by the children, and by individuals who like sweets of any sort, and it would be excellent for puddings and tarts. Most probably, however, the majority of grown-up folks who tasted it once would say, "No, thank you," next time it came round, for it would only have a suggestion of the true flavour of the fruit; and should the season be unfavourable, so that any of the jam went mouldy, the strawberry jam would be the first to go. If, in order to make sure of the jam keeping, a pound of sugar were put with a pound of fruit, the jam would be so luscious that it would be almost sickly. Jam of this sort can scarcely be called satisfactory.

What we wish to do, of course, is to make jam that will keep and will yet retain the refreshing flavour of the fruit. Here are two or three special recipes for strawberry jam, and it is hoped that girls who feel inclined to experiment in this direction, will choose the one which looks most inviting, try it, and see if they do not like the jam thus produced better than that made in former years.

Strawberry Jam No. 1.—Hull the fruit, and with a silver knife cut each berry into two. (When the berries are divided, the sugar penetrates more readily to the heart of the fruit, and this helps the jam to keep.) Allow equal weights of sugar and fruit. Boil the fruit gently for about half an hour, add the sugar, and boil again until the jam will set. Now add some red currant jelly—a pound pot of jelly for each three pounds of strawberries will be about right. Boil again until the jelly is melted and incorporated; it will lessen the lusciousness of the jam.

No. 2.—Choose red, ripe, fine strawberries. Allow equal weights of sugar and fruit, and crush the sugar to powder. Put fruit and sugar in layers, and leave it for twenty-four or even forty-eight hours to draw out the juice. Drain off the syrup, and boil it separately till it thickens; then put in the berries, and boil well for about twenty minutes. (Jam made according to this recipe is excellent, but too luscious. One feels that the red currant jelly would be an improvement. It looks pretty, however. The berries remain whole, and are suitable for garnishing, and the syrup is valuable for making creams and puddings.)

No. 3 (Francatelli's way).—Allow equal weights of fruit and sugar, and add a quart of red currant juice for each six lbs. of strawberries. Hull the strawberries and draw off the juice before beginning to boil. Put the sugar into the pan with a cupful of water for each pound, stir until dissolved but not after, and boil until large globules cover the surface of the syrup. Now put in the fruit and the juice and boil sharply, stirring gently for about twenty minutes. Take up a spoonful of the jam and pour it back quickly. If as it slides down into the pan the last portion hangs in drapes or wide drops on the edge of the spoon, the jam is ready. If it does not present this appearance, it must be boiled a little longer.

No. 4 (Miss Parloa's way).—There is at the present time in America a very clever lady named Miss Parloa, who, within the last few months, made public the fact that for years she had been experimenting trying to find out a way of making strawberry jam which satisfied her. At length she tasted some strawberry jam which she considered delicious. The summer before last she tried a good many ways, but jam made as this was she liked best of all. This is the method of procedure.

Sun-cooked Strawberry Jam.—Do not commence operations unless the weather is very fine and settled. Pick over the strawberries, and put them in the preserving kettle with their weight in granulated sugar. Stir them gently to keep from burning until the mixture begins to boil, and counting from this time boil ten minutes. Pour the jam into wide shallow platters so that it shall be two inches deep, and set these in the sun on a table before a sunny window or on a sunny lawn for ten hours. (The original recipe said twenty-four hours, but it was found that ten hours was enough.) Put into jars and tie down in the usual way. Jam thus made will be very rich, but it will retain the flavour of the fruit. It will have plenty of syrup, and if carefully stirred the berries will be whole.

So much for the strawberry jam.

We now come to the various ways of cooking strawberries. One of the simplest is—

Strawberry Tapioca Pudding.—Soak a cupful of crushed tapioca or of large sago in a pint of cold water for two or three hours, or, better still, set it to soak overnight. Put it into a porridge pan or double saucepan, and set it by the side of the stove until quite clear. Stir it occasionally to keep it from forming in lumps. When done stir into it a good pinch of salt, a squeeze of lemon juice, and a cupful of white sugar. Then add off the fire a pint of ripe strawberries which have been hulled. If too thick, a little strawberry or red currant juice, or even more water, will be needed. Serve quite cold with whipped cream or milk. A mixture of strawberries and raspberries, or strawberries and red currants, makes a very good pudding of this sort, and, indeed, of every sort. Sometimes cream alone is stirred last thing into the tapioca, and the pudding is garnished with strawberries.

Strawberry Cream.—Set an ounce of gelatine to soak in a gill of cold water. Hull a pound of strawberries, sprinkle over them three tablespoonfuls of castor sugar (it will help to draw out the juice), bruise them, and let them stand awhile; then rub them through a fine sieve. Put with the *purée* thus produced the juice of a lemon. Whip half a pint of cream till stiff, and mix it with the *purée*. Melt the gelatine in a saucepan. When cool add it to the other ingredients and turn into a damp mould when it is beginning to form. Of course the appearance of this cream would be improved if it were either garnished with berries or if a little clear jelly were employed to decorate the mould.

Strawberry Jelly.—Soak an ounce of gelatine in a quarter of a pint of cold water. Hull a pound of strawberries, sprinkle six ounces of white sugar over them, and bruise them well. Put them with the gelatine, the juice of a lemon, half a pint of water, and the crushed shells and whites of two eggs. Whisk the ingredients over the fire till they rise in the pan; draw the latter back, and let it stand for awhile; pour through a jelly bag or cloth, and mould. This jelly should not be put into a metal mould, or it may become discoloured. If an earthenware mould is not at hand, a cup or pudding basin will answer the purpose.

When time and trouble are to be considered, there is an easier way of making strawberry jelly. Hull and sugar the fruit, and steam it to draw out the juice. Strain it, put it with gelatine and water into a saucepan, and boil for about ten minutes. Mould when nearly firm.

In summer time an ounce of gelatine may be trusted to set a pint and a quarter of liquid.

Jellied Strawberries.—Hull some ripe, fresh, sound, dry strawberries. Make a little clear lemon jelly in the ordinary way, but rather stiff than otherwise. Pour a little when beginning to firm into a damp mould or moulds (a soup plate or even half a dozen cups will answer the purpose if there is nothing else at hand). Place the strawberries upon the jelly so that they do not touch each other, then carefully cover with more jelly, and repeat till the mould is full. Turn out when set, and garnish with whipped cream.

Strawberry Charlotte.—Take a cupful of any ordinary sweet jelly (a small quantity left from another dish would answer excellently for the purpose provided it is fairly firm when set). When it begins to thicken, dip into it one by one some fine ripe strawberries cut in halves, and arrange these, the cut side downwards, round the inside of a mould with straight sides which has been soaked in cold water, and left damp. If the mould is quite cold, the jelly will quickly set and the fruit will adhere. Make some strawberry cream according to the recipe already given, and when it is so far set that it retains the form of a

spoon when a little is taken up and put back, place it gently in the lined mould. This sweet when turned out will look very pretty if the lining is tastefully arranged; and if the cream is well made it will taste delicious.

Strawberry Trifle.—This is a very delicious sweet, but it is to be avoided by teetotallers. Hull fresh strawberries (and if a few raspberries can be added all the better), bruise them slightly, sweeten them, and pour over brandy and sherry to moisten them well, in the proportion of four tablespoonfuls of sherry to one of brandy. Soak for an hour, then pile sponge fingers which have been dipped in a little hot syrup for a moment on the top, and cover with whipped cream, half of which may be made pink with a little cochineal and half left white. Authorities say that a trifle made with strawberries, oranges, and bananas, is specially delicious.

Strawberry Shortcake is an American preparation. If we were to visit the States during the hot weather, and were to be entertained by friends clever in cookery, or to go into a good restaurant, we should have an opportunity of partaking of a dish which looked like sublimated strawberries and cream—pink, white, and yellow. This would be shortcake; and when we became more intimately acquainted with it, we should discover that it consisted of layers of " biscuit dough " (which we should call Genoese pastry or the pastry used in making Swiss roll), with crushed and sweetened strawberries between the layers, and either whipped cream or creamy sauce poured over all. The shortcake is eaten both hot and cold, although most people prefer it cold. When served hot, the cake must be torn open with two forks, or cut while warm, not hot, with a very sharp knife which has been warmed and is held perpendicularly, to avoid making the cake heavy. It should also be buttered while hot. A peculiarity of this shortcake is, that almost every housekeeper who has been brought up to value it has a special recipe for it, and despises every other; just as English housekeepers think their own recipes for mince pies are superior to all others. Strawberry shortcake is particularly good for high tea.

Perhaps girls would like to try this celebrated dish. I therefore give a choice of recipes. Both come from America. No. 1 is Miss Parloa's recipe. No. 2 is the genuine old-fashioned shortened cake as made by a lady named Mrs. Keeler, who says that shortcake thus made is " dear to many hearts."

No. 1.—There will be required for this cake one quart of flour, three eggs, half a cupful of butter, three gills of milk, one cupful of granulated sugar, three heaping tablespoonfuls of powdered sugar, three heaping tablespoonfuls of baking-powder, half a teaspoonful of salt, and three pints of hulled strawberries. Mix the salt, baking-powder, and one tablespoonful of the granulated sugar, and rub the mixture through a sieve. Now rub the butter into the prepared flour, beat the yolks of the eggs well, and add the milk to them. Stir this mixture into the dry ingredients, and when a smooth dough is formed, divide it into four parts; spread these in four buttered jelly cake-tins (a dripping-tin will answer the purpose, and the dough should be about half an inch thick), and bake in a hot oven for ten minutes. While the cake is baking, crush the hulled strawberries with the rest of the sugar, beat the whites of the eggs to a stiff, dry froth, and beat into them the powdered sugar. When the cakes are done, place two on large plates, and spread one quarter of the crushed strawberries on each. Place the remaining cakes upon the first two, and cover them with the remainder of the fruit. Spread the white of egg and sugar over, and set the cakes in the oven for four or five minutes. Serve at once. If a richer cake is desired, mix half a cupful instead of a spoonful of sugar with the flour, and butter the cakes before spreading the berries on them.

No. 2.—Make a dough with one quart of flour well sifted (to make it quite free from lumps), and three teaspoonfuls of baking-powder. Rub in three tablespoonfuls of butter or lard till it feels like coarse sand, and add milk, or milk and water, to make a dough as soft as can be *rolled out*. If lard is used, add a little salt, and in all cases be careful to handle as little as possible after adding the milk. Roll to about half an inch thick, and bake in a dripping-tin in one large cake. Bake in a hot oven for about ten minutes. When done the cake should have risen considerably. While warm cut into three-inch squares with a warmed knife, split each square in half, and butter the inside. Put the crust side down, and cover the top with berries which have been well crushed and sweetened. Cover with the other half, putting the crust side next the berries and the soft inside on the top. Cover this also with a liberal supply of crushed berries, allowing some to run over the sides. When ready to serve, moisten the cake with a little sweetened cream or milk, and heap over each portion either whipped cream, custard, or a sauce made as follows: Beat to a cream a cupful of powdered sugar and one tablespoonful of butter. Add one whole egg, which has been thoroughly whisked, white and yolk first separately, then together. Now add to the mixture, a little at a time, half a cupful of milk, and beat again between every addition.

It is to be noted that two cakes about the size of a pudding-plate could be made of the quantities given. Also that the milk which has gone sour (a mischance very likely to occur at the time of year when strawberries are ripe), is excellent for making shortcake. When it is employed a smaller quantity of baking-powder will be needed. When strawberries are not to be had the same sort of cake may be made of raspberries, red currants, tinned peaches, and other furits.

Milk Puddings with Strawberries.—When strawberries are abundant, a pleasant change from the ordinary milk puddings may be made by covering them with a *méringue* of strawberries. Rice pudding, sago pudding, tapioca pudding, corn-flour pudding, etc., may all be treated thus. Make the pudding in the usual way, using the yolks of eggs only, and bake. Have ready a good quantity of strawberries—that is, about a pound for a pudding made with a pint of milk. Hull the fruit, crush it, sweeten it, and spread it on the pudding. Beat the unused whites of eggs to a stiff froth, mix a tablespoonful or so of powdered sugar with them, and spread the *méringue* neatly over the fruit. Set in a cool oven to set the egg.

Strawberry Tarts not to be despised may be made by lining patty pans with good pastry, and filling them with ripe strawberries which have been hulled, sweetened, and tossed in beaten egg.

Strawberries and Orange Juice.—We think that strawberries and cream go well together, but it is an interesting fact that the Spaniards approve quite as much of another combination —strawberries and orange juice, maintaining that here art has improved nature. Girls who would like to pronounce an opinion upon the case might easily do so, for oranges remain with us in these days for a month or two after strawberries have appeared. To prepare them we need only to hull the strawberries, and pour over them the strained orange juice to moisten them, then let them stand for an hour.

Strawberry Fool.—When strawberries are too much crushed to be fit to send to table, they may be converted into strawberry fool with advantage. Hull them, squeeze over them the juice of a lemon and sprinkle sugar over them. Let them stand for an hour, then rub them through a sieve and mix with the pulp a cupful of milk. Pile whipped cream on the top, and serve with sponge fingers.

Compôte of Strawberries is suited for individuals who desire something especially dainty. Here is a superlative recipe. Hull the berries and put them into a bowl, pour syrup over them to cover them (made by boiling a pound of loaf sugar with a cupful of water to a clear syrup) and let them stand for an hour. Drain off the syrup, and add a wineglassful of red currant juice to each pint thereof, and boil down to half the quantity. Put the strawberries in a glass dish, strain the syrup over them and serve with sponge fingers. If it is to be had, a small glassful of Maraschino will improve this *compôte*.

So much for the recipes. It is to be hoped now that girls will feel that they will be at no loss when strawberries appear for ways to deal with them. One word, however, yet remains to be said on the medicinal value of strawberries. With regard to most of the good things of this world, which come within our reach, we have to acknowledge, that though they may be pleasant to the sight they are not good for food; good, that is, in the sense of being wholesome; and, indeed, the more delicious they are the more probable is it that they will be indigestible. But with strawberries it is not so. At any rate, we have the authority of Dr. Abercrombie, the celebrated physician, for saying they are of value. Here are the great Scotchman's own words: "Physicians concur in placing strawberries in their small catalogue of pleasant remedies. They dissolve the tartarous incrustations of the teeth. They promote perspiration. Persons afflicted with the gout have found relief from using them; so have patients in cases of the stone; and Hoffmann states that he has known consumptive people cured by them." Dr. Abercrombie lived a hundred years ago. We do not know that modern physicians would endorse what he says here. But if one-half of this statement is correct, we see at once that it is our duty to eat strawberries. Not merely because we like them, but because they will do us good, must we resolve to make the most of them. When duty and inclination go hand in hand, what can we desire more?

ALL ABOUT ORANGES.

"Oh, that I were an orange tree—
    That busy plant!
Then should I ever laden be,
    And never want
Some fruit for Him that dresseth me."

 o wrote good George Herbert more than two hundred and fifty years ago, and we can easily understand the ground of his wish. Orange trees are indeed, under favourable circumstances, exceedingly prolific. Some live to a great age, and they bear fruit from fifty to eighty years. One which was planted at Versailles, near Paris, lived more than four hundred years, and there are orange trees growing at Cordova, in Spain, which are said to be more than six hundred years old. A good tree will produce a large quantity of fruit; and as many as a thousand oranges have been know to grow on one tree. There is no wonder that the poet said an orange tree was "a busy plant."

Oranges are amongst the most delicious of fruits. They are exceedingly wholesome, and are enjoyed by the sick and the hale. It is well for us that we have them in such abundance, for we should sorely miss them if we were deprived of them. Large as the demand for them has been of late years, it is steadily growing, and some idea of the quantity imported may be gained from the fact that a fruit-broker of whom enquiries were made a few months ago said that during the previous year there were 453,000 cases of oranges shipped to England from Valencia alone, and that each case weighed over a hundredweight, and contained from 400 to 700 oranges. That is to say, that averaging them all round at 500, there were imported from Valencia alone 226,500,000 oranges, weighing about 32,000 tons. After hearing this, no one can say that oranges in England are not appreciated.

When oranges are ripe, sweet, and sound, it is scarcely possible to do better with them than eat them *au naturel*. The individuals who care for the fruit most are generally most averse to cooking it. This is a mistake, for in many forms it is most excellent when cooked. For the benefit, therefore, of those who feel disposed to experiment in this direction, it is proposed to give a few suggestions for dainty dishes, into the composition of which the orange may be allowed to enter. Girls acquainted with these dishes would be able to introduce a most agreeable variety into the daily fare of the household.

Before, however, speaking of oranges in cookery, it will be well to say a word or two about the choice of oranges, and the best way of buying the fruit.

Within the last few years oranges have been obtainable in England very nearly all the year round. Until a very recent date, however, they were in season only from November till May or June, so that during the autumn months we had to do without them. Every year, however, the fruit appears earlier and stays later, so that it may almost be said that oranges are always with us. Two or three years ago it was hoped that Australian oranges would be available during the autumn months; but we cannot congratulate ourselves that the orange trade between England and Australia is as yet thoroughly developed, because the cost of freightage is so heavy, and this makes a difficulty. Even the most enthusiastic lover of the juicy fruit does not care to pay three-pence or fourpence each for oranges when plums, pears, and blackberries are to be had in perfection, especially if the said costly treasure is not quite up to the mark, creating the impression that it is past date, and has lived through the prime of its life. If, however, Australian oranges are not always quite what one would wish them to be, it is to be remembered that they have been brought from a very long distance, and that their importation can scarcely be said to have passed as yet beyond the experimental stage. Fruit merchants say that when the difficulties have been surmounted there is a great future before Australian oranges, and that they will arrive here in excellent condition if only they are properly packed. It is to be hoped that this prediction will be fulfilled.

Of the oranges which come to us from parts nearer home, probably the best of all are the *St. Michael's*. This variety comes chiefly from the Azores, and not many years ago it used to be thought that no other orange was worth mentioning by the side of it. Of late it has somewhat gone out of fashion, and dealers tell us that of the five islands of the Azores which used to supply us, only one now sends it; the trees therein have ceased to bear, and have not been renewed. "Why have they not been renewed?" girls will perhaps ask. The answer is that other varieties are preferred by orange buyers. The fact is that St. Michael's oranges do not keep well; also they are not handsome, and the public of to-day is very eager for what looks beautiful. Curiously enough the more speckled and battered a St. Michael's orange looks—so long as it is sound—the more likely it is to be sweet and juicy. This orange is light-coloured, and has a thin, smooth rind, and it usually comes to market packed in the long, dried leaves of Indian corn, whereas Valencia oranges and other Spanish sorts come wrapped in thin paper. If, therefore, girls see at the greengrocers cases of light-coloured oranges, with long, thin, dried leaves about them, it will be fairly safe to conclude that the oranges contained therein are real St. Michael's.

For two or three years *Valencia* oranges have held the market. They are very excellent, very juicy, and very good; they are generally to be had in perfection towards the end of January. *Jaffa* oranges are a recent importation; they are most excellent, large, juicy, substantial, and delicious. Heretofore the chief objection to them has been their price; but they are getting cheaper. The small *Tangerine* oranges are usually approved as a dessert dish. They are excellent for decorative cookery, because they can be freed so entirely from the white pith. The skin of these oranges has a delightful fragrance; and one of the most delicious ice creams of which we have any knowledge is made of cream flavoured with the rind of Tangerines. Maltese oranges are quite unlike all others. The pulp is streaked with red, and is very soft and juicy, and there is a sweet bitterness in the taste which is quite confined to this variety. It is said that Maltese oranges owe their peculiarity to the fact that they have been grafted on the pomegranate tree. *Seville* oranges are of course not fit to eat, being very bitter. They are used for making marmalade, wine, and bitters. They generally come in towards the end of February, and are at their best during March. Girls who think of making marmalade should not defer the business over long.

Now let me give a few recipes for dishes made of oranges. First in popularity comes—

Orange Marmalade.—This preparation is known and approved all over the civilised world. It is understood to be the pet dainty of the people of Scotland, and Scottish housekeepers are particularly expert in making it. The great Thomas Carlyle spoke eloquently in its praise, and said that it was "a delicious confection, pure as liquid amber," in taste and look most poetically delicate." Students and men of letters are almost invariably partial to it; and it is so wholesome, so excellent, and so satisfactory, that it would scarcely be possible to speak extravagantly in its praise. There are in existence scores of recipes for making it, and many of these are very good; indeed, the majority of proved recipes are good, and the difference between marmalades made by one and by another is as the difference between tweedledum and tweedledee. The objection usually brought against them is that they are very troublesome, and girls who have made marmalade once or twice, and who have other work on hand, feel tempted, when March comes round, to shirk the business, and buy their marmalade of the grocer.

Now there is no denying that much of the marmalade offered for sale is very pure and good; still, there is a charm about home-made produce which commercial products can never boast. Girls, therefore, who have become a little out of patience with the elaborate methods usually followed, are recommended to try the following recipe. The marmalade made from it is most delicious, and also very economical, and the method easy indeed. Marmalade made thus with lump sugar at threepence per pound cost me twopence three-farthings per pound.

Recipe.—Slice six Seville and one sweet orange. Cut the fruit into very fine strips and remove nothing but the pips. Put pulp, fruit, and everything into three quarts of water, and leave for twenty-four hours. Turn into a preserving pan and simmer for two hours; at the end of this time add five pounds of white sugar and boil for one hour, or longer if necessary. When the marmalade is quite clear it is done, but the thing is to boil it enough. Stir all the time after the sugar is put in.

Orange Jelly is a very pleasant change from marmalade. Take three pounds bitter oranges, three pounds sweet oranges, and six lemons. To each pound of fruit allow three pints of water. Cut the fruit in round slices, and boil the pips and all until the liquor is reduced to one half. Strain through a jelly-bag, and to every pint of juice put a pound and a half of lump sugar. Boil about an hour, until the preparation jellies. This confection is more easily made than the last, because one does not need to stand over it at all. Yet it is most excellent.

Orange Pudding.—There are three or four ways of making the dish which is served with this name.

No. 1.—Take three ounces of stale cake-crumbs (ratafias or stale sponge-biscuits will do; cake with currants in it is not suitable). Rub them through a sieve and put with them two ounces of sugar, the grated rind of two oranges, and the juice of three. Pour on half a pint of milk, the yolks of three and the whisked white of one egg. Line a pie-dish with a little good pastry, pour in the mixture, and bake till set and a light brown colour.

No. 2.—Boil the rind of a Seville orange till a pin will pierce it easily, then pound it to paste in a mortar. Put with it a quarter of a pound of fine breadcrumbs which have been passed through a sieve, the strained juice of the fruit, a piece of butter the size of half an egg, a teacupful of white sugar, and the beaten yolks of two eggs. Whisk the whites of the eggs separately till they are firm, and just before the pudding is to be cooked dash them lightly in. Turn the preparation into a buttered mould, put a piece of buttered paper on the top, and steam it for an hour, or till firm in the centre. Let it stand a few minutes before turning it out.

No. 3.—Peel and cut three or four oranges into thin slices, free them entirely from the white pith (which, if left, will swell and quite spoil the pudding), lay them in a pie-dish, and sprinkle white sugar thickly over them. Boil a pint of milk, mix a tablespoonful of flour smoothly with a little cold milk, add it to the boiling milk, and stir till thick. Add also two tablespoonfuls of sugar and the yolks of three eggs well beaten. Pour the preparation over the sliced oranges, bake it in the oven, and serve hot or cold.

An *Orange Sauce* for any of these puddings may be made by soaking thin orange rind in syrup till the latter is pleasantly flavoured, adding orange juice, and thickening the preparation with arrowroot.

Francatelli's Orange Pudding (very rich).—Put the strained juice of ten oranges and the rind of three rubbed on lumps of sugar into a basin with six ounces of bruised ratafias, six ounces of sugar, a pint of cream, ten yolks of eggs, and six whites whipped. Add a pinch of salt and a little grated nutmeg. Work these ingredients together for five minutes with a whisk, and then pour the mixture into a pie-dish already furnished with a thin border of puff-paste round the rim of the dish and reaching half way to the bottom. Shake some bruised ratafias over the surface, set the pudding in a baking-tin, and bake for about half an hour, till it is a light fawn colour.

This recipe, it is very evident, is the original of which recipe No. 1 is a humble modification. Francatelli's pudding is intended for people who can use cream and eggs galore; it would be regarded as most extravagant by ordinary individuals.

Orange Soufflée.—Girls who have succeeded in making soufflées know that they are not costly, and are both elegant and good. The chief points to be careful about with regard to them is, first, to cook the sauce very well, to whisk the egg-whites very stiffly, and to steam the pudding very gently and regularly. Prepare a quart tin mould with straight sides by greasing it well, and by twining a broad band of double paper, greased, round the outside, to make the sides of the mould several inches deeper. The paper must be fastened securely with twine, and must be close to the top of the tin, not low down, or the water would touch it. Put the thin rind of a small Seville orange into a basin with half a pint of milk, and set in a warm place till pleasantly and rather strongly flavoured. Melt an ounce of butter in a stewpan over the fire, stir in two dessertspoonfuls of flour and one dessertspoonful of arrowroot; mix and cook thoroughly, then add gradually the flavoured milk, with sugar to sweeten the preparation. Stir the mixture with a wooden spoon till it boils and thickens. When it leaves the sides of the stewpan quite clean it is enough. Draw it from the fire, let it cool a little, then drop into it (still off the fire) one by one the yolks of three eggs. Just before it is to be cooked whisk the whites of four eggs to a firm froth, stir these lightly into the batter, taking care not to break down the foam, and lay a piece of greased paper on the top to keep out the moisture from the steam. Place the tin in a deep saucepan with boiling water to reach half way up the sides, and steam steadily and gently for three quarters of an hour. When the soufflée is very light, and feels firm to the touch when pressed in the centre, it must be turned out carefully and served on the instant.

Orange Cream is an excellent and easily-made sweet. Soak an ounce of gelatine in a gill of milk. Put the thin rind of two or three oranges (without any of the white pith) in three quarters of a pint of milk, and sweeten with four ounces of loaf sugar. Boil and strain over the soaked gelatine, stirring well the while. Let the milk get cold; then mix with it half a pint of orange juice and the juice of one lemon. Mould when the cream is beginning to get firm. Of course this cream will be all the richer if cream, or a portion of cream, be used instead of milk. In this case the cream should be whipped stiffly before being added to the other ingredients. A pleasant change may be made by adding egg yolks to the milk, and thus converting it into custard. This will give it the yellow tinge which suggests oranges.

Orange Jelly for immediate use is of course simply jelly flavoured with orange juice. It is easily made because it does not need to be clarified. It makes variety to introduce sections of orange into the jelly, instead of having it quite plain. The oranges should be freed entirely from pith, and cut into small pieces with a sharp knife. They should then be stirred into the jelly just as it is beginning to set. If put in while the jelly is liquid they would sink to the bottom; and what is wanted is that they should permeate the mass.

Chartreuse of Oranges is a most elegant and tasty preparation. Line the inside of a plain round mould with straight sides with sections of Tangerine oranges by dipping the sections into jelly just ready to firm, and fixing them on the tin. If the mould has been rinsed in cold water and left damp, the sections will attach themselves instantly. When the lining is firm fill the mould with orange cream, made as above, or made by whipping half a pint of double cream, sweetening it with two ounces of sugar, flavouring it with the juice of three oranges, and adding to it a tablespoonful of gelatine dissolved in a little milk.

Orange Tarts.—Line a shallow dish or tartlet tin with pastry, spread some orange paste upon it, and bake till the pastry is done. To make the mixture put the grated rind and strained juice of three oranges upon the beaten yolks of three eggs, and add an ounce of butter and a quarter of a pound of sugar, or less if the oranges are sweet. Mix the ingredients thoroughly, and put them in a small stewpan; keep stirring one way till the paste is as thick as honey.

Orange Compôte.—Divide oranges into sections; free them from pith, and boil them for a few minutes in thin syrup flavoured with orange juice. Drain them and boil the syrup till thick. When cold lay the orange sections in a compôte dish; sprinkle desiccated cocoanut over them, and also a little of the syrup. Repeat until the ingredients are used. If the employment of alcoholic beverages is approved, a little sherry or brandy may be added to the syrup.

Orange Fritters.—Sections of orange freed from pith and fried in batter constitute a most excellent and elegant dish for the pudding course. Probably girls know well how to make these, so it is not necessary to give the recipe in full. Good batter may be made with a quarter of a pound of flour, a pinch of salt, two tablespoonfuls of salad oil, a gill of luke-warm water, and the whites of two eggs whisked to a firm froth and dashed lightly in last thing. The batter will be all the lighter if made some hours before it is wanted. It is to be noted that oil used instead of milk makes the batter crisp instead of leathery. If liked, three tablespoonfuls of oil might be used instead of two—then the whites of the eggs could be omitted altogether. Batter thus made would be too rich for everyone.

Orange Jelly set in Orange Peel.—Gouffé's

Recipe.—Oranges thus prepared look very pretty when they are a success; and they are not as difficult to make as one would imagine. Girls with clever fingers, who would bestow a little pains upon them, could make them well enough. Choose some even-sized oranges, and with an inch plain cutter make a hole in the top of each. Remove the inside of the oranges carefully and completely, partly with a fruit knife and partly with the fingers, and be very careful not to tear the rind. When the skins are clear put them into cold water to soak for awhile; then drain and dry them. Afterwards set them on pounded ice, and fill them with orange jelly. When the jelly is firmly set cut each orange in four pieces, and arrange them on a graduated stand with laurel leaves between the pieces. They will look better if the jelly with which the skins are filled is of different colours. Sometimes the orange rinds are cut into the shape of baskets with handles, and the jelly, instead of being set in the baskets, is set separately, then coarsely chopped and set in last thing. The handle of the basket should be marked evenly across the stalk end of the fruit, and should be about half an inch thick. If the peel should be broken at all when cleaning it for the jelly, the hole can be stopped with a little butter, which can be removed when the jelly is set. If the rind has become thin, a little butter may be run over the inside to make it bold. The pulp can be most easily detached after the basket is cut out.

Rice Balls with Orange.—Wash a teacupful of rice in one or two waters; drain it, and cook it slowly in a pint and a half of milk, with five or six almonds, till the rice is quite tender and has absorbed the liquid. Beat it vigorously for three or four minutes to make it smooth, sweeten it with sifted sugar, and pack it tightly into small cups which have been rinsed in cold water and left wet. Cut the thin rind of an orange into neat shreds. Boil these in half a pint of water till soft. Take them out, and put into the water three ounces of white sugar, and boil to a clear thick syrup. Turn out the rice. Pour the syrup over the balls, and baste them with it in order to glaze them; sprinkle the cut rinds over them, and serve with cream.

Orange Marmalade Pudding.—Take six ounces of fine breadcrumbs, a pinch of salt, six ounces of finely-shred suet, two ounces of flour, two tablespoonfuls of sugar, six ounces of orange marmalade, half a teaspoonful of baking-powder, and two eggs. Put the mixture into a greased mould, lay a buttered paper

over the top, and steam for four hours. Serve with sweet sauce.

Orange Baked Custard.—Take the very thin rind of a Tangerine orange (if this is not to be had, an ordinary orange may be used), boil it till tender, pound it to a paste, and mix with it a tablespoonful of brandy. Beat the yolks of four eggs in a basin, and pour on them a pint of boiling milk; stir well. Add two tablespoonfuls of sugar, a little salt, and the orange paste. Turn into a buttered dish or mould; set this in a tin containing warm water, and bake in a moderate oven till the custard is firm in the centre. Do not move it or shake it in any way. When cooked lift it out as gently as possible, and let it remain till cold. If necessary, put more water into the tin in which the pudding stands, but be very careful not to shake the pudding itself. Standing in water thus will ensure moderate cooking, and will make the pudding firm and smooth throughout without the holes which spoil the appearance of baked custard. When the pudding is quite cold turn it out carefully; pour orange syrup round it, and garnish with whipped cream. Orange custard may be converted into a very excellent sweet by turning the custard upon a layer of orange jelly, made according to the directions for the second of the jellies. (The first jelly is intended for storing.) The layer of jelly should be a little larger than the custard pudding, and should be stiff enough to support it. The orange sauce is made by boiling a quarter of a pound of sugar with a gill of water, adding three tablespoonfuls of orange juice and the rind of the orange, which has been boiled till tender and cut into thin strips. If four eggs are considered extravagant in making this dish (and eggs, be it remembered, are always dear when oranges are in season), two whole eggs may be used instead of four yolks. The eggs must, however, be fresh; and it is to be noted that though, when this number of eggs is used, the custard will taste good, it will not look as rich, and it will need to bake more than twice as long as if the larger number of eggs were employed. As, however, it is to be served cold, this does not signify. The custard can be put in the oven and left till firm; and if baked in water, it will be smooth and even throughout.

Such are a few of the recipes for dishes of which oranges are the distinguishing feature. It is to be hoped that girls who make them will succeed with them, and will enjoy them.

PHYLLIS BROWNE.

"CARAMEL AND CRÊMES."

TELLING OF THE POSSIBILITIES OF SUGAR-BOILING.

By the Author of "We Wives."

THERE is no doubt candy-making will always exercise a fascinating influence over young folk. The very idea of "pulling" barley sugar into ringlets with well-oiled fingers makes one's mouth water! But, if once we have started on the enticing path of confectionery, we shall never rest satisfied with such elementary work. Caramel sugar, with its "thready, bubbly, snappy, and smooth stages, is easy enough to manipulate." At least our club found it so. They loved to test the caramel with finger and thumb until the "little thread" had been boiled into its stronger form. Above all, they

liked the sugar "snap" of a properly prepared syrup. I have told you how to prepare this sugar candy in a previous paper. To-day I would fain initiate my readers into the mysteries of fondant or French creams.

Can anything be more delicate than the soft creams one buy sat every first-class confectioner's? Fondants pink, fondants white, fondants with a chocolate cap, fondants with green frills. Yet the basis of this large number of sweets is practically the same. Those who can make it can exercise their ingenuity without limit.

Over a clear fire stir together (in an enamelled saucepan) one pound of best loaf sugar and a small cupful of cold water. When melted, mixed, and beginning to boil, leave severely alone for ten minutes. It will not burn. Now dip an ivory bodkin or skewer into the mixture and see what comes from its point. If a drop forms boil a minute or so longer. If a long, silky hair adheres, remove from the fire at once without shaking and leave until cool.

When a finger can be dipped into the mixture without being burnt, turn it into a bowl and beat briskly with a spoon until you have a white thick cream on hand. Then knead the paste as if you were making bread dough. When worked enough—and mind no time is lost at this stage—it becomes a soft, smooth paste. It will not be rough at all or "grainy" unless the *crème* has been allowed to get too cold before being beaten, or if it has been shaken whilst still hot. If either of these misfortunes are met with, return the caramel to the saucepan and begin all over again. The sugar will not be spoilt unless burnt, however often it may be reboiled. Of course it lessens in quantity.

This soft paste is our "fondant," and will be the foundation for all our efforts in this line. We can flavour it with essence of coffee or melted chocolate, drop it on buttered paper, and we have fondants of that name and colour, or we can add raspberry syrup to make raspberry *crèmes*, or some spinach water and we have green fondant.

Even the very writing about this kind of confectionery recalls the joy of working up the smooth balls into sweetmeats of various hues. I can see the cherrywood walls of a prairie home shining in the glow of the stove; I can see the candy club busy at work with tucked-up sleeves and puckered brows; I can see the triumphant wave of wooden spoons and feel the old "crinkly" touch of palms and fingers, and, as memory calls up all this, I hear a murmur of many voices directing me to tell my readers about our "cream nuts." I hasten to obey.

For these "American walnuts" we need some specially prepared kernels. The shells are carefully cracked, and their contents divided in halves. Then into a cushion of fondant each walnut piece is softly pressed, the two parts brought together and left to dry.

"Sioux filberts" were only nuts of that name rolled in fondant. In order to have them perfectly round and smooth, fingers had occasionally to be dipped in water. But, as this expedient sometimes resulted in re-ducing the *sucré* to liquid, it was not often resorted to.

Perhaps the simplicity of fondant-making may be a revelation to many people. The possibilities of sugar-boiling can only be believed in after direct experiment. Our candy club grew so proficient in this branch of confectionery that we treated many things in this way. Almonds, brazil nuts, cranberries—ah! how good is cranberry caramel!—all made acquaintance with our soft sugar cushions. The initial stage was the only difficult one. After it what a vista of possibilities was opened up.

But, before going further, I must give an idea of quantities. Well, one pound of sugar and one cup of water will make enough fondants to cream two pounds of husked walnuts.

Of course our club was not content with "American nuts"; they also joyed in making "clear cobs" as they were called. Ordinary candy-sugar was required for these. When the threads hung thick to the point of the fork or skewer, half a teacupful of vinegar was thrown in or the juice of a lemon, and the candy boiled quickly until it "snapped." Into it now we dipped our nut kernels by means of big darning needles! When coated evenly we laid them on a greased slab to dry. The nuts could be seen reposing coyly behind a clear veil of icing. Hence their name.

Cocoanut Caramel was another sweetmeat we were fond of indulging in. Also *Cocoanut Fondant*; for both of these receipts, the nut needs to be broken in pieces two or three days before use, as it is too oily to bear the heat of an oven, and all nuts used in this kind of confectionery must be as dry as possible. For the cocoanut caramel the "desiccated" preparation may be used successfully. To every pound of boiled candy or caramel allow four ounces of the grated white rind. Stir in well whilst the sugar is boiling, and do not leave for an instant until it is ready to take off the fire, as this nut is very apt to burn.

For cocoanut fondant the nut must be broken irregularly in pieces about half an inch square, rolled in the soft pasty cream, and allowed to dry on buttered tins.

Nougat was the last and crowning achievement of our candy club. You see we had no Buzzard or Noblett to supply us with any such delicacies. We were driven to make sweetmeats ourselves, or do without them!

Though Sir Walter Scott has said that "Nougat should be left to the confectioner," we—the members of the club aforesaid—did not fear to rush in where such an "angel" of a cook even feared to tread. And we succeeded—mostly, generally, nearly always! Sometimes we failed. We are but human—even in America. But we did not grumble over spilt milk, and the redskins are fond of sweet things! even if burnt.

Nougat we always made after the stove was "redded" up with cabbage stalks and slack. Pine knots formed too quick a fire for the delicate operation. On a slow range we put an enamelled saucepan filled with half a pound of superfine sifted sugar; it was put on dry, not a drop of water allowed, when it melted we threw in a similar quantity of blanched almonds and a handful of bitter ones. These had been thoroughly dried in the oven and chopped into rough dice. Very quickly we stirred altogether, and turned out the paste on to a dish previously well-buttered. We worked it a little, then rolled it flat—either with oiled palms or a greasy rolling pin. Sometimes we put a little spinach water into the confection. More frequently we left it curdy and white.

Cut into slips or squares, this nougat was put away in stoppered bottles. For it was our company candy, and too highly prized to be indulged in often.

With a bit of poetical advice I will close—

"Make your transparent sweetmeats truly nice, With Indian sugar and Arabian spice, And let your various creams enriched be With swelling fruit just ravish'd from the tree."—*Dr. King.*

SOME AUSTRIAN RECIPES.

Vanilla Sugar.—Vanilla sugar so often finds a place in Austrian cookery that a recipe for it must preface the following directions for making some very delicious dishes often enjoyed in that country. The pod of vanilla bean can be had at most grocers, and the flavouring it gives is most delicate and preferable to any of the liquid essences. Take a piece of this vanilla bean and some sifted sugar and pound the two together until quite fine. You must judge of the quantity of both vanilla and sugar by adding the latter gradually until on tasting it, it is well-flavoured with vanilla. Pass this through a sieve and keep it in a tin. When required for use add it to other fine sugar according to taste.

Vanilla Crescents.—Ingredients: Eight ounces of best flour, six ounces of fresh butter, three ounces of peeled almonds chopped very finely indeed, and two yolks of egg. Mix all this up with a knife on your pastry board, and then roll it out with a rolling pin. Cut the paste thus formed into small pieces and form them into little crescents about two or three inches long and as thick as your thumb—if you have a small hand. Bake in a very moderate oven, and remember that they must not brown. Cover with finest vanilla sugar powdered thickly over them. These biscuits, if properly made, should be very light and extremely brittle. They keep good and fresh if placed in an air-tight tin.

Lemon Soufflé.—The Austrian recipe for the above is as follows:—

Ingredients: Five tablespoonfuls of sifted sugar, five yolks of egg, the flavour of one rind of a lemon, and the juice of one lemon. This should all be stirred for half an hour, and then a hard snow-like mixture should be added, made of the five whites of egg whipped until quite consistent. Bake about fifteen minutes in a brisk oven, in an ordinary pie-dish in which the mixture has been heaped up. Serve immediately it is done.

Apricot Soufflé.—Take five tablespoonfuls of apricot jam, passed through a sieve. Two spoonfuls of fine sifted sugar. Stir this up well for half an hour. Make a stiff snow of five whites of egg, and add very lightly to the above. Heap this up lightly in any pie or soufflé-dish, and ornament with some sliced almonds on the top. Bake from fifteen to twenty minutes in a brisk oven. Serve immediately it is cooked.

Chestnut Cream.—Boil some large chestnuts, peel them and pass them through a sieve. Mix with a little cream and vanilla sugar to taste. Heap part of this paste in the middle of a dish. With a fancy forcing bag make part of it into balls the size of a chestnut, and glaze these balls with sugar. Surround the centre heap with whipped cream, flavoured with vanilla sugar, on which the glazed chestnuts are to be laid.

Chocolate Pudding.—Dissolve three ounces of the best chocolate in half a pint of single cream which is on the fire. Let this get cold and then gradually mix it with two spoonfuls of flour and two ounces of white sugar. This should be done while the mixture is on the fire until it is of the consistence of a thick batter. Let this cool in one basin, and in another stir well two ounces of fresh butter with five yolks of egg; then add the cold batter and mix it up well. Next beat up five whites of egg until they are in a stiff froth, and add slowly but lightly to the aforenamed mixture. Bake this in a soufflé dish for about twenty to twenty-five minutes. The same mixture can be made with essence of coffee instead of the chocolate.

LEMON DROPS.—Grate the peel of three good sized lemons, add to it half a pound of castor sugar, one tablespoonful of fine flour, and beat well into it the whites of two eggs. Butter some kitchen paper and drop the mixture from a teaspoon into it and bake in a moderate oven on a tin sheet.

SULTANA DROP CAKES.—Mix one pound of dry flour with half a pound of butter; after you have rubbed it well in, add a quarter of a pound of castor sugar, half a pound of sultanas well-washed and dried, one egg and two table-spoonfuls of orange flower water, and one tablespoonful of sherry or brandy; drop on a baking sheet well floured.

GHERKIN PICKLE.—Cut some nice young gherkins or small cucumbers, spread them on a dish and sprinkle the ordinary cooking-salt over them, and let them lie in the salt for seven or eight days. Drain them quite free from salt and put them in a stone jar, covering them with boiling vinegar. Set the jar near the fire and cover over the gherkins plenty of nice fresh vine leaves, and leave them for an hour or so, and, if they do not become a pretty good colour, pour the vinegar back again and boil, and cover them each time with fresh vine leaves; after the second time they will become a nice spring green. Tie it up with parchment or use a good cork, and keep it in a dry place.

AFTERNOON-TEA DAINTIES.

By the Author of "Summer Puddings," "Scotch Scones," etc.

NOW when the general exodus from town has begun and country "house-parties" are in full swing, where one of the pleasantest meals of the day, afternoon tea, requires catering for to make it as appetising as possible (to men tired with a day's shooting or maybe fishing, as well as to women), perhaps some hints and recipes for sandwiches, cakes and scones, may be welcome to the hostess. Afternoon tea can be made substantial enough for men by the addition of nice sandwiches, and a variety of these can be readily made.

Sardine Sandwiches.—Take some sardines, carefully extracting the bone and draining off any superfluous oil; pound them in a mortar with a drop or two of vinegar and a dash of pepper. Spread this paste between thinly-cut buttered brown bread. See that the edges of the sandwiches are nicely trimmed. Always use a very sharp knife and see that the bread is not too new. For those who like anchovy, another way is to pound a dozen sardines, one anchovy one ounce of butter, some mustard, cress and capers together, add a dash of cayenne, a drop of vinegar and spread between brown bread and butter.

Jelly Sandwich.—A quarter of a pound of butter, half a pound of fine sugar, three-quarters of a pound of flour, three eggs, three-quarters of a teacupful of milk and a heaped teaspoonful of baking powder. Beat the butter and sugar to a cream, put in the eggs, one by one, beating between each, then add the milk, flour and powder. Spread on well-buttered jelly cake tins and bake ten minutes in a good oven. When half cool, spread between either jam or lemon preserve, lay together, press gently, and with a sharp knife cut into neat pieces, and ice on top or not as desired. Plain icing is most suitable, made with icing sugar and water. The lemon preserve is made by stirring in a pan two ounces of butter, half a pound of fine sugar, three eggs, beaten, the juice and grated rind of two small lemons; let it boil slowly a minute or two, turn into a jelly mould and use when cold. This preserve keeps some little time, and delicious lemon cheese-cakes are made, by lining tartlet tins with puff paste or short crust, putting a spoonful of the preserve in the centre and baking till the crust is ready.

Lincoln Sandwich.—Chop some sardines very fine, add some grated or chopped ham; mix with a little bit of butter, chopped pickles, mustard and pepper to taste, and place between white bread and butter.

Salmon Sandwiches are made of potted salmon (home made for preference) spread between white bread and butter.

Then there are so many "potted meats" to be had in small tins, such as the excellent "Strasbourg," "potted game," "chicken and ham" and "pâté de foie gras," that innumerable changes can be rung. Then if there are any scraps of cold meat, chicken or ham in the larder too small for other use, they can be utilised by being pounded or passed through a mincing machine, seasoned to taste, and made into dainty sandwiches, either white or brown bread ones.

Hard-boiled eggs, finely chopped, and cress, make together very nice "bites"; also cress alone, well washed and picked and used with brown bread and lettuces, washed in well salted water, rolled in thinly-cut, well-buttered white bread, are very dainty and much relished.

And now having given, I hope, a large enough selection of the more solid part of the tea, let me pass on to the cakes, etc., which are none the less relished by the sterner sex, and many of whom have a "sneaking regard" for the "sweets of life!"

Hot tea-cakes are or should be always a feature of "five o'clock tea," and so I will give a few of the best of them.

Athole Teacakes.—Rub into half a pound of flour a quarter of a pound of butter, add one ounce of sugar, a pinch of salt, and a heaped teaspoonful of baking-powder. Beat up one egg, and add it, with as much milk as will make a nice firm paste, to the dry ingredients. Work on the board a very little and roll out half an inch thick, cut into round cakes and bake on a floured tin in a very quick oven for ten minutes; split and butter while hot, and serve at once. These are also good cold with butter.

Brown Scones.—Three cups of wheaten flour, one cup of white, three cups of milk, two tablespoonfuls of lard or butter, a little sugar, a pinch of salt, two teaspoonfuls of cream of tartar and one of baking soda. Mix all dry ingredients together, rub in the butter and mix to a paste with the milk; roll out quickly, cut into small round scones, and bake on a flat tin. Eaten either hot or cold, split open and buttered.

Drop Scones.—Two cups of flour put into a basin with two tablespoonfuls of fine sugar, one teaspoonful of cream of tartar, half a teaspoonful of soda; mix well with a wooden spoon, then into the centre break one egg and add enough butter-milk to make a moderately thick batter; beat it briskly for a minute, then let it stand till the "girdle" is quite hot, grease it well, then drop the batter in small spoonfuls, as round as you can keep them;

when brown, slip a knife under them and turn quickly. Butter and place them in "twos" and keep in the oven till all are ready; serve hot. Practice will enable you to judge of the right thickness to make the batter, you can easily add a little more milk should the first scone seem too thick; they should just spread a little, when dropped on the girdle, which should be buttered between each lot of scones, to prevent them sticking.

Soda Scones are very good and have the advantage of being just as good the "second day" cold and well buttered as freshly made. One pound of flour, a teaspoonful of salt, one heaped teaspoonful of cream of tartar, half the quantity of soda, stir all together, then add, mixing with a knife, enough butter-milk to make a soft lithe dough.

Work on the board a little, then roll out quickly, cut into round or three-cornered scones and bake on a clean girdle, turning when a pale brown. A few minutes in the oven after they are taken from the girdle ensures them being thoroughly well baked. A sweet milk variety of them can be made by adding to the above quantities of flour, soda and tartar, a spoonful of fine sugar, two ounces of butter rubbed in, and enough sweet milk to make rather a firmer dough. These can either be baked on a girdle or else on floured tins in the oven. Now I shall pass on to the sweet cakes and biscuits.

Genoa Cakes.—Beat six ounces of sugar, with the same quantity of butter to a cream, add three eggs, beating well between each, then sift in six ounces of flour and one heaped teaspoonful of baking powder; beat a very little, just sufficient to mix well, and put into a well-buttered, shallow, square tin, and at once place in a good oven to bake for about ten or fifteen minutes; take out when ready, lay on sieve to cool, then cut into cakes any size you like. Make chocolate icing by mixing equal quantities (say four ounces) of icing sugar and grated chocolate, add a few drops of vanilla, and about one to one and a half tablespoonfuls of warm water; beat smooth, hold to the fire a minute, then with the blade of a knife wetted in boiling water, spread each cake evenly with the icing and set in a warm place to firm. You can vary the icing by using the icing sugar plain and adding any flavouring, or else colour it pink; a great many changes can be made and gives scope for ingenuity, while icing can be ornamented with chocolate or the pink, and *vice versâ*.

Tuscane Cakes.—Beat together three ounces of butter and half a pound of desiccated cocoanut, add three ounces of castor sugar, same of *crème de riz*; beat together for five minutes, then break in three eggs and a few drops of essence of vanilla. Butter some small tartlet tins, dust them inside with sugar, and put small spoonfuls of the mixture in and bake in a moderate oven for fifteen or twenty minutes. These are delicious little morsels.

Mock Crab.—A quarter of a pound of cheese, grated, a yolk of one hard-boiled egg, a little cayenne pepper, a little salt, half a mustard-spoonful of mustard, a little vinegar, and a table-spoonful of salad oil ; mix to a paste well, then spread between brown biscuits.

Anchovy Toasts are simply thin slices of fried toast spread with a thin layer of anchovy paste, sprinkled with grated yolk of hard-boiled egg, and are delicious.

Cheese Sandwich.—Chop very finely one hard-boiled egg, add to it in a mortar a quarter of a pound of grated cheese, a good dash of pepper, half a teaspoonful of mustard, a pinch of sugar ; melt a bit of butter the size of a pigeon's egg, add it with a spoonful of vinegar, mix to a paste and spread between two buttered water biscuits or bread as preferred.

Doughnuts.—Half a cup of butter, one cup of fine sugar, two eggs, half a cup of sour milk or cream, half a teaspoonful of soda dissolved in a little hot water, a little ground nutmeg and cinnamon, and enough flour to roll out to a soft dough. Cut or roll into balls or twists and fry in boiling lard to a golden brown.

Paris Buns.—Ten ounces of flour, four ounces of fine sugar, one teaspoonful of cream of tartar, and half a teaspoonful of soda, two ounces of butter, and one egg. Beat butter and sugar to a cream, add egg well beaten and mixed with a cupful of buttermilk. Lightly stir in flour, tartar, etc., and bake in a quick oven. Enough for ten buns.

Lemon Cakes.—Rub into three quarters of a pound of flour three ounces each of lard and butter ; add six ounces of sifted sugar, the grated rind of one lemon, and a large tea-spoonful of baking powder ; mix into a moderately stiff paste with two well-beaten eggs ; divide into small pieces roughly, lay on a buttered tin and bake for twenty minutes in a brisk oven.

Ginger Cakes.—Rub five ounces of butter into one pound of flour, add three quarters of a pound of coarse sugar, and a quarter of an ounce of ground ginger. Beat one egg up in a bowl, add to the flour and put in half a pound of treacle and mix well together. Make into cakes the size of a large marble, and bake in a slow oven.

Lemon Biscuits.—Rub three ounces of butter into half a pound of flour ; add seven ounces of castor sugar, a very little baking powder, and moisten with two well-beaten eggs and a teaspoonful of lemon essence. Work to a paste, roll out, and cut into round biscuits. Bake to a pale brown in a moderate oven.

Shrimp Sandwich.—Mix to a paste as many hard-boiled egg yolks as you require, with their weight in butter, add shrimp essence to taste, a little mustard, pepper and cayenne to taste, and put between slices of fried bread.

Queensland Cakes.—Take one pound of desiccated cocoa-nut (or ground almonds) and two pounds of castor sugar. Beat seven eggs till very light, then stir in sugar and almonds. Blanch one pound of almonds, split them, add to the mixture and a dash of flour to make a stiff paste. Take little heaps of the mixture, lay on wafer paper and place on baking tins ; bake in a very cool oven to a pale brown.

I daresay I have now given as many recipes as will give the required variety, and all of them are easily made, so that any ordinary cook could follow the directions successfully.

ANGELS' FOOD.

By DORA DE BLAQUIÈRE.

CAKE—or, perhaps, as it would be better called, the sweetmeat —known to-day under the name of "angels' food," is by no means of modern origin. Indeed, the basis of the mixture may be found as far back as the days of Queen Elizabeth, when a very light, porous kind of sweetmeat was made, in a rather more clumsy mode of manufacture, under the name of "angelic sweetmeat." The foundation of all "angel" cakes is much the same, the chief distinction between them consisting in the number of eggs used, which varies from eight to one dozen. Nor need the housekeeper, who is anxious to make the attempt to manufacture "angel cake" of any kind, be deterred by the seeming expense, for there are plenty of good eggs to be obtained, hailing from "foreign parts"—from Normandy, Brittany, or Holland—at the comparatively small price of thirteen a shilling, or in the summer time even less.

The first recipe I shall give is quite a new one, and hails from America ; it is called "angels' food" : — 1½ cups of pulverised (castor) sugar ; 1 cupful of flour ; 1 teaspoonful of cream of tartar ; the whites of ten eggs beaten to a stiff froth.

The newest English-American recipe I can find differs but little from it, and is as follows :—The whites of eleven eggs which have been kept in a very cool place, or upon ice, before they are used ; one tumbler and a half of castor sugar ; three-fourths of a tumbler of flour ; one level teaspoonful of cream of tartar, and one teaspoonful of flavouring—almond,

lemon, or vanilla, whichever is preferred—lemon being the best, I think, of all.

The following instructions for making should be strictly followed :—The ingredients should be all carefully gathered together before their blending, that they may be all to hand conveniently. Mix the cream of tartar and the flour together and sift the mixture several times, adding a small pinch of salt. Beat the eggs (whites only) to a very stiff froth, and add the sugar to it very quickly and quietly ; then, when these are well mixed, put in the flour in the same manner, sprinkling both through your fingers and being careful to avoid any lumps of either. One of the secrets of making "angel cake" is the method of mixing it. You do not exactly either beat it or stir it, but you lift it up and down with your fork from the bottom of the tin ; and if the first cake should turn out either tough or sticky, you will know that your mixing has been too violent, and with your next you must be more gentle. Put your cake into a clean, bright cake-tin (and some good authorities will tell you on no account to butter it) ; the oven should be a cool one, or, at least very moderate, and you may bake for forty-five minutes. Wait a quarter of an hour before you look at it, and be careful not to keep the oven-door open too long. You can try the cake with a straw to see if it be done. Many people cool this cake off by leaving the oven-door open and allowing it to remain for a time, and then taking it out and standing it upon the table to cool off. Before putting it into the oven you should sprinkle the top lightly with powdered sugar, but not so much sugar should be used as would make the cake fall in baking it.

Amongst the varieties of angels' food which are indulged in in America, are "angel surprise cake," "almond angel cake," "angel custards," and angels' cake made with peaches, bananas, and pineapples. The first named "surprise cake" is made with a freshly-made angel's cake, which for this purpose should

be baked in a round tin, and left in the tin until it be quite cold. When turned out, the first thing to do is to cut off the top, about half an inch thick, then take a sharp knife and cut round the inside of the cake, about half an inch from the crust, or the outer wall of the cake, and so take out the soft white centre. Then to whip a pint of fresh cream into a stiff froth and flavour with vanilla or lemon ; pour it into the hollow cake and smooth it over the top so that you can replace the lid, and make it look as if it were quite undisturbed. This, of course, constitutes the "surprise" when cut. Many people add candied fruit or almonds to the cream.

"Almond angel cake" is also a delicious confection made in much the same manner as the preceding, except that the cake is cut in layers, and the whipped cream is mixed with half a pound of almonds, blanched, and cut in small pieces. The cream is then put in between the layers, and the top is cut open, so as to allow the cream to be the top layer ; and some of the almonds, cut into long and thin pieces, are stuck into it ; so as to make it look "porcupiny." "Angel custards" are made in rather a different manner, for the angel batter must be baked in muffin rings, and, as usual, the cakes when baked must be left to get perfectly cold before being turned out. Then the top must be cut off each cake, and some of the inside taken off, which you must replace with a custard, which you may make as rich, or as simple, as you please. The following is a cheap and good recipe for a custard, which you may use with angel cake, or in any other way. Take the yolks of two eggs, a tumbler of milk, and four lumps of sugar. Simmer till thick, stirring the mixture carefully to prevent burning. Add a few drops of vanilla flavouring, and pour into a clean jug. Stir till cold.

I have left the preparation of "angel fruit cakes" until the last. They are nearly all made in the same way, namely, the angel batter, instead of being baked in only one cake, is baked in layers in the small round tins to be purchased at any tinsmith's, made for that purpose. They must not be very brown nor burnt. The lower layer of all must be spread with whipped, sweetened, and flavoured cream, and then you should cover this with a layer of bananas, peeled, and daintily sliced. Then put on another layer of cake, and repeat the addition of cream, and the sliced bananas. There are generally three layers of cake used, the top layer being completely covered up with the whipped cream.

Angel peach and pineapple cakes are made in the same manner, and both can be made of the preserved or canned fruits instead of the fresh, and so are suitable for winter as well as for summer use.

And no account of angels' food would be quite complete unless it were supplemented by a mention and a recipe for "angel water," called in French *Eau d'Ange*. This is of very ancient use in England, and is often spoken of during the time of the plague. It was also called "Portugal water," and was in great repute at one time for its healing properties. Simple "angel water" is made of the flowering tops of the myrtle only, distilled with water; but there are three or four kinds of aromatic waters, under the same name, that contain many more ingredients, and are known under the various names of "distilled musk" and "boiled angel water." In a very old cookery-book in my possession there are at least half a dozen recipes for "angel water." A simple one, that could be made at home, was—1 pint of orange-flower water, 1 pint of rose-water, and ½ pint of "myrtle-water;" to these put ¼ ounce of essence of musk, and 1 ounce of essence of ambergris; shake the whole together. This recipe is marked "to be made in small quantities only, soon spoiled, either by heat or cold."

I find a recipe for distilled "angel water" is made thus :— Gum benzoine (crushed small), 4 ounces ; liquid styrax, 2 ounces ; cloves (bruised), ½ ounce ; Calamus aromaticus (bruised), ¼ ounce ; cinnamon (bruised), ¼ ounce ; coriander-seed (bruised), 1 drachm ; water, 7 pints ; distil ½ gallon.

We have left off the home manufacture of all these fragrant waters, which used to form a great part of the duties of our ancestresses. The "still-room maid" retains her name, but has other duties to perform, and the recipes are shut up in mouldy and unused books. But I am sure much of the beauty of our lives went out with these old avocations and fashions; and in order to regain something lost we shall have to make our tastes more simple, and go back to that almost forgotten love of the country, its quiet and peace, away from the hurried and unrestful life of the great city.

AFTERNOON TEA-CAKES.

DAINTY cakes are always a welcome addition to afternoon tea, more especially if home-made, and so I venture to give a few recipes for some delicious and easily made cakes.

LEMON CAKES.

Into three quarters of a pound of flour rub three ounces each of lard and butter, add six ounces of castor sugar, the grated rind of one lemon, and a teaspoonful of baking powder. Mix into a moderately stiff paste with two well-beaten eggs; divide into small rough pieces, place on a buttered tin, and bake in a brisk oven for twenty minutes. When done, and while hot, sift castor sugar over them.

COCOA-NUT CAKES.

Into half a pound of flour mix a quarter of a pound of ground rice, then rub in three ounces each of butter and lard, add six ounces of castor sugar, one teacupful of desiccated cocoa-nut, and a dessertspoonful of baking powder. Whip the whites of two eggs to a stiff froth, mix in, add a little milk if not moist enough, and bake the same as above in a moderate oven.

COCOA-NUT CAKES, NO. 2.

One cocoa-nut skinned and grated, the milk of same, an equal quantity of water, a pound and a half of castor sugar, and the whites of three eggs. Dissolve one pound of the sugar in the milk and water, and stew till it becomes a "ropy" syrup; turn out on to a buttered dish. Have the whites beaten to a very stiff froth with the remaining half a pound of sugar whipped into it. Mix this with the nut, and then little by little—beating the while—the boiled syrup when it is a little cooled. Drop the mixture in tablespoonfuls on to buttered papers. Bake in a very moderate oven, and do not let them brown at all.

SPONGE FINGERS.

Beat two eggs very light with a quarter of a pound of castor sugar; sift in gently two ounces of fine flour and the grated rind and juice of half a small lemon. Drop on buttered papers in long fingers, not too near each other. The oven should be very quick, and the "fingers" a delicate brown. When you drop the mixture, if it inclines to run, beat the mixture a little longer *hard*. These are very nice dipped in chocolate icing.

COCOA CONES.

One pound of powdered sugar, half a pound of grated nut, five egg whites, one teaspoonful of best arrowroot. Whip eggs stiffly, adding sugar as you go on until it will stand alone, then beat in nut and arrowroot. Mould the mixture with your hands into small cones, and set them on buttered paper two inches apart. Bake in a very moderate oven.

DROP CAKES.

Put a quarter of a pound of butter into a basin; beat to a cream; add half a teaspoonful of baking powder, and work in gradually half a pound of flour; add a quarter of a pound of currants, two ounces of sugar, two ounces of mixed peel (finely shred), and grated rind of a lemon. Beat one egg well, mix it with a gill of milk, and stir into dry ingredients. It should be stiff. Drop in knobs the size of a walnut on baking sheet dusted with flour, and bake in a brisk oven. Place cakes on tin an inch and a half apart.

HUNTING NUTS.

Rub five ounces of butter into one pound of flour; add three quarters of a pound of very coarse sugar and a quarter of an ounce of ground ginger. Break an egg into a bowl, and mix all together with half a pound of treacle. Make the nuts the size of a marble, and bake on buttered tin in a slow oven.

OSWEGO CAKE.

Quarter of a pound of corn-flour, two ounces of butter, two ounces of fine sugar, one teaspoonful of baking powder. Beat sugar and butter to a cream, add eggs (two) one at a time, then corn-flour and powder. Bake in a rather shallow tin, buttered, in a moderate oven.

QUEEN CAKES.

Beat two ounces of butter to a cream; beat two eggs well; add half a pound of fine sugar to the butter, and a little of the beaten egg, and one tablespoonful of milk. Beat in half a pound of fine flour, another tablespoonful of milk, the grated rind of a lemon, or a few drops of any essence, and pour in the rest of the egg by degrees. Roll out to about as thick as a penny, cut into round cakes, lay on buttered tins dusted with flour, and bake to a pale brown for about fifteen minutes in a well-heated oven. Lay on a sieve to cool.

ALMOND CROQUETTES.

Whisk a batter of half a pound of castor sugar and six eggs ; add six ounces of ground almonds, grated part of lemon rind, and sift in half a pound of fine flour. Place in small, well-buttered tins, and bake in good oven.

INVALID CAKE.

Three ounces of flour, two ounces of butter, two ounces of castor sugar, two eggs, quarter of a teaspoonful of baking powder, grated rind of half a lemon. Beat butter and sugar in a basin to a cream, add one egg and half the flour ; beat well, then add the second egg and remainder of flour, lemon rind, and lastly the powder. Beat well a minute or two, then pour into a small round tin, well buttered, and dusted with sugar, and bake in good oven. While still warm pour over an icing made with half a pound of icing sugar, moistened with a tablespoonful and a half of water and a few drops of essence of lemon. Beat it free from lumps, heat before the fire for a few minutes, then pour over cake, and ornament with a few dried cherries on top.

GÉNOISE CAKES.

Beat a quarter of a pound of fresh butter to a white cream with a wooden spoon, add to it four ounces of powdered loaf sugar, and beat till light and white ; then add one egg and beat smooth, then add three more eggs, singly, and always beating between each. Lastly, mix in lightly a quarter of a pound of fine flour, and as soon as you have beaten it smooth pour out on a well-buttered plate and put into the oven *at once*. Bake till done (in about ten or fifteen minutes) and turn out, underside up, on a sieve to cool. Spread on half the cake some apricot jam, place the other half of cake on top, and with a sharp knife cut into neat squares or diamonds. Ice over top with the icing flavoured with vanilla.

GERMAN BISCUITS.

One pound of flour, half a pound of butter, half a pound of fine sugar, one egg, and a good pinch of baking-powder. Rub dry ingredients together, and mix to a paste with the egg well whisked ; roll out thin and cut into round cakes. Moderate oven to bake them a pale brown. Put in pairs with jam between and icing on top. "CONSTANCE."

A PAGE OF PUDDINGS,

The Queen of Puddings.—One teacupful of fine white sugar, two teacupfuls of dry breadcrumbs, a tablespoonful of fresh butter, a pint of boiling milk, pinch of salt, and the beaten yolks of three eggs. The grated rind of a fresh lemon should be added to the first-named ingredients, to the which are put first the boiling milk, and, when cool, the yolks of the eggs. Mix well and pour into a shallow buttered fireproof china dish, or an enamelled pie-dish, bake in moderate oven until set firm and a pale brown colour. Spread over the surface a little choice preserve without stones, and heap upon that a *méringue* of the whites of the eggs beaten with a tablespoonful of sugar and same of cream. Return to the oven to slightly colour the top, then remove at once. Good either hot or cold.

Lemon Méringue Pudding.—A quart of boiling milk poured over two teacupfuls of fine breadcrumbs, when well soaked add two ounces of castor sugar, the grated rind of a fresh lemon, two ounces of butter, and lastly the yolks of four eggs with the juice of half the lemon. Bake in gentle oven to a pale brown colour, then cover with a *méringue* sweetened and flavoured with the remaining lemon-juice. This also is good to eat cold.

Orange pudding may be made in the same way.

Newark Pudding.—One cupful of breadcrumbs soaked in a pint of milk, a tablespoonful of ground rice, a quarter of a pound of raisins, the stones removed and cut in two, a few drops of vanilla or almond essence, two tablespoonfuls of melted butter, a pinch of salt and half a teaspoonful of carbonate of soda. Separate the yolks and whites of two eggs; add the yolks to the other ingredients first, then lastly stir in lightly the whites; pour the mixture into a buttered dish and bake in gentle oven one hour.

Winter Raspberry Pudding (most delicious).—Two ounces of butter, two eggs, a pound pot of raspberry jam, half a pound of breadcrumbs, a quarter of a pound of brown sugar. Beat the butter and eggs separately, to the butter add the sugar and jam, then the eggs.

Butter a plain mould, sprinkle crumbs all around it and a layer at the bottom, then put in a layer of mixture, then more crumbs and more mixture, until the mould is full. Cover with a buttered paper and bake from three-quarters to one hour in moderate oven. Serve with sweet wine or cream sauce.

Apple Custard Pudding, for eating cold.—Pare, core and slice up four or five good cooking apples, add a little water to them and cook until they will beat up smoothly; sweeten well and flavour. Put them into a buttered pie-dish and carefully pour on the top half a pint of custard made from half a packet of custard powder (sweetened), grate a little nutmeg over, and let the pudding stand in a cool place.

Marmalade Pudding.—Half a pound each of breadcrumbs, beef suet (chopped) and sugar, six ounces of marmalade added. The whole well worked together with three or four well beaten eggs (no other moisture). Boil in a mould for two hours. Best made over-night.

Curates' Puddings.—Put into a saucepan one pint of milk, a few lumps of sugar and a bit of lemon rind, let it nearly boil, remove to cool. Whisk three eggs light, beat into them three spoonfuls of flour, add the sweetened milk by degrees, beat to a smooth batter. Pour into cups, only half filling them, and bake.

Cocoanut Pudding.—Half a pint of milk, quarter of a pound of cocoanut, two tablespoonfuls of cake-crumbs or fine breadcrumbs, two ounces of castor sugar, two ounces of butter, three eggs, one teaspoonful of vanilla.

Simmer the cocoanut in the milk in a saucepan, cream the butter and sugar together. Beat up the eggs, yolks and whites separately. When the cocoanut is tender take the saucepan from the fire and stir into it the butter and sugar. Add the yolks of eggs and vanilla, stirring well; and lastly the whites whipped to a stiff froth; stir lightly and thoroughly and pour into a buttered pie-dish and bake half an hour.

Fig Pudding (superior).—Half a pound of fine grated breadcrumbs, half a pound of good figs cut small, quarter of a pound of beef suet chopped fine, quarter of a pound of moist sugar, two ounces of candied peel shred fine, one ounce of sweet almonds or a little of the essence, half a nutmeg grated.

Mix the dry ingredients well together with a pinch of salt, then moisten the whole with two well whisked eggs and, if wished, a glass of sherry or light wine.

Butter a plain mould or basin, and pour in the mixture, cover the top with a thin paper, tie a cloth tightly over and boil for three hours. Turn out and serve with sweet sauce.

Exeter Pudding (choice).—Make a mixture of the following ingredients—six tablespoonfuls of fine bread-crumbs, two tablespoonfuls of fine sago, three tablespoonfuls of finely chopped suet and three tablespoonfuls of soft sugar. Beat two eggs well, adding half a cup of milk and a little lemon flavouring. Pour over the dry ingredients and mix thoroughly.

Now butter a pudding mould and put in a layer of sponge rusks at the bottom, cover these with a layer of the mixture, next another layer of rusks. On these spread a layer of delicate jam, then a layer of mixture, and so proceed until the mould is full; the top layer must be one of mixture. Bake in the oven for forty minutes or steam for an hour and a half. Serve with sauce made by boiling two or three tablespoonfuls of jam with a little water and straining it.

Nice Chocolate Pudding.—Take a quarter of a pound of stale sponge cakes or rusks in crumbs, two ounces of sugar, three ounces of butter and a quarter of a pound of mild chocolate, three eggs and three quarters of a pint of milk. Rub the butter and sugar to a cream, add the egg yolks well beaten, dissolve the chocolate in the milk and stir altogether, lastly stir in the whites well beaten to a froth. Bake in a deep round tin or steam in a mould about one hour.

Ginger-Bread Pudding.—Excellent for cold weather. Rub together in a basin eight ounces of breadcrumbs and four ounces of flour with six ounces of suet, one teaspoonful of baking-powder, and one teaspoonful each of ground ginger and mixed spice, also half a teaspoonful of salt. Warm well six ounces of treacle. Beat up one egg with a quarter of a pint of milk and stir well into the warm treacle. Pour over the dry ingredients and mix all well together. Pour into a greased mould leaving a little room to swell. Boil steadily for three hours. A few chopped figs or dates can be added to this pudding by way of change.

Swiss Apple Pudding.—Ingredients: Half a dozen large baking apples and half a pound of finely grated breadcrumbs. Butter a pie-dish and cover the bottom with a layer of crumbs, then a layer of sliced apples; sprinkle over these a large spoonful of moist sugar and a little grated nutmeg and lemon rind. Fill the dish with these alternate layers, letting crumbs form the upper and lower layers. Place little pieces of butter here and there over the top of the pudding, or, if liked, a sprinkling of fine suet crumbs, which is better for children. Pour into the dish half a cupful of water and bake gently in a moderate oven until the apples are tender; about half an hour.

Raisin Pudding.—Into one pound of flour rub a teaspoonful of baking-powder and a pinch of salt. Grate the rind of a fresh lemon into it, and add eight ounces of finely shred beef suet, also half a pound of good raisins stoned and cut small. A little spice may be added to flavour if liked. Work into a rather stiff paste with an egg and a cupful of milk.

Butter a plain mould and three parts fill it with the mixture, tie over it a buttered paper and steam the pudding for four hours. Serve with a sauce made by mixing one ounce of cornflour with half a pint of water, one ounce of butter, three ounces of sugar, the grated rind and juice of a lemon. Boil to a cream.

Pembleton Pudding.—Take equal quantities (a teacupful) of breadcrumbs, chopped suet, raisins, currants, sugar, a little shred lemon peel and pinch of salt. Mix with two beaten eggs and a little milk. Bake in well-buttered pie-dish until well set. Make a custard with two more eggs, half a pint of milk sweetened and flavoured, and pour on the top, baking until the custard is firm.

ALMOND PUDDING.

Half a pound of almonds blanched and finely pounded, five ounces of sifted sugar, the rind of a lemon finely chopped, and the yolks of eight eggs. Mix these ingredients well together, and then add the whites of the eggs (which should have been previously whipped till quite stiff), then stir in lightly. Pour into a buttered mould, and bake like a custard. Turn out before serving, and pour round it at the last minute the following cream sauce:—

LEMON CREAM.

Quarter of a pound of sugar rubbed on one lemon, half a cupful of lemon juice, one wine-glassful of water, and three eggs, the latter to be well beaten. Cook in a lined saucepan on the fire, beating it all the time. When it begins to get frothy and thick it is done.

ALMOND BALLS.

Half a pound of almonds blanched and well pounded, six ounces of sifted sugar, the finely-chopped rind of one lemon. Mix these ingredients well together with three eggs, and add flour until the mixture is stiff enough to form into balls the size of small apples, then fry them a golden brown. When done insert small slips of candied lemon peel to resemble an apple-stalk in each one, and serve with the above lemon cream placed in a sauce-boat, the balls to be arranged in a glass dish.

APPLES IN CREAM.

Pare and core as many apples as will make a nice sized dish, stew them with water and sugar until the liquid is nearly all boiled away, and the apples are transparent, but not so soft as to lose their shape, then arrange them in a glass dish. Make a cream of three-quarters of a pint of cream, which cook in a lined pan until it nearly boils, then stir in three well-beaten eggs, three ounces of blanched and pounded almonds, and three ounces of sifted sugar; keep stirring until it begins to boil, then take it off quickly, and when both the apples and cream are nearly cold pour the latter over the apples, strew with sifted sugar, and before serving pass a red-hot salamander over the top until a pretty glaze is formed.

CREAM AND SPONGE CAKE.

Three-quarters of a pint of cream and four yolks of eggs, well beaten together, with the rind of a lemon rubbed on a piece of sugar. When mixed, put on the fire in a lined pan, and keep stirring until the cream begins to boil. Cut three or four stale sponge cakes in four pieces, and arrange in a glass dish, and pour the cream over them. Then beat up the four whites of the eggs till quite stiff, add a little sifted sugar, and when the cream is cold pile up the beaten whites on the top, sift sugar over it, and colour with a red-hot salamander.

PISTACHE PUDDING.

Butter a mould and line it with puff paste—a pie-dish will do as well. Then take a teacupful of blanched and pounded pistachio nuts, six whole eggs well beaten, and three-quarters of a pint of cream. Beat all these ingredients well together and pour into the mould. Cover with thin puff paste, press the edges well together, and bake the same time as a custard. Turn out on to a dish before serving; either a cream or rum sauce is best with this pudding.

FLOAT KUCHLI.

Half a pound of flour, four ounces of butter, two ounces of sifted sugar, two tablespoonfuls of sour cream, and two yolks of eggs. To be all well mixed and kneaded together. Put on one side for two or three hours, then roll out, cut into fingers about five inches long and one and a half inches wide, and fry well in hot fat. Serve piled up in a glass dish, to eat with creams or stewed fruit.

SUGAR NUTS.

Four ounces of sifted sugar, half a pound of flour, three well-beaten eggs, and a piece of butter the size of a walnut, and any flavouring that is liked. Mix well together, and knead well. Then form into balls about the size of a walnut and fry in very hot fat. Serve piled up on a cloth, with white sugar sifted over them.

"SOME EASTERN SWEETS."

By the Author of "We Wives."

 IN order to redeem the promise made in a recent number of THE GIRL'S OWN PAPER (January, 1896), I have been culling from my ancient shagreen cookery-book some recipes for Indian sweets. They are all old tried friends, and may be depended on. Any which take only foreign produce as a *pièce de résistance* (as, for example, pineapple snow) I have purposely omitted. Any which are very expensive to make I have also excluded.

It is a favourite maxim of mine, that if one can afford costly dishes, one can afford a professed cook to prepare them. The following recipes are plain, economical, and simple. They can be prepared by anyone of ordinary skill in the culinary department. As such they ought just to suit the many budding housewives who rejoice in this magazine.

Cocoanut Pudding.—As this hard, brown, string-covered nut can be as easily procured in the United Kingdom as in the tropics, we will begin with this recipe. For sixpence you can buy a large one. Break in good-sized pieces, and take off a thin brown skin covering the white lining. Grate and mix the flakes with three ounces of loaf-sugar and half an ounce of lemon dust. (The latter is only the yellow rind of a lemon finely grated and sifted.) Moisten with two well-beaten eggs and amalgamate the whole with some milk. Having lined a deep tin with puff paste (half a pound of butter or lard to three-quarters of a pound of flour makes sufficiently rich pastry for this), fill it with the cocoanut mixture. When baked a light brown, slip on to a dish and serve.

This might almost be called "cocoanut cheese-cake," as the tart should present an appearance like the lemon-cheese at a confectioner's.

Leechée Cream.—Take one pint of fresh milk and bring to the boil. When bubbling sweeten with loaf-sugar and season with vanilla essence according to taste. Then add two well-beaten eggs. Now mix one tablespoonful of cornflour to a cream with a very little cold water. When quite smooth pour into the milk mixture, and stir thoroughly and carefully till it comes to the boil. Boil for one minute only. Have ready a glass dish with two tablespoonfuls of strawberry-jam layered at the bottom. When cooled a little, otherwise woe betide your cut crystal! pour the cream over it, and decorate the top with tiny ratafias or a pile of freshly-scraped cocoanut. (Desiccated does just as well, I may remark *en passant*. A half-pound tin can be bought for fivepence at any store.) Serve cold.

Pears in Jelly.—We are all, perhaps, somewhat tired of the monotonous stewed fruits. How seldom one sees pears served in any way but swimming in a cochineal sea after being inhumanly butchered in twain! The same fruit coyly veiled in jelly! Ah, what a welcome sight!

Six stewing pears, two ounces of sugar, two ounces of butter, a pint of water, half an ounce of gelatine. That is what we need. First we soak our sheet of gelatine (much cheaper this than the packets of prepared stuff), and stew our pears until they are soft. Of course we have peeled them first! and sweetened the stew-water. When quite tender we turn them into the basin containing the gelatine in solution, and stir a little. Then very carefully, so as not to break the fruit, we lift each pear and place them side by side round a well-buttered mould, filling the centre with the liquid syrup. Don't look at the mixture if you are afraid of the result until it is "set." Then you will find a crimson jelly ready to be turned out. At regular intervals therein repose the luscious pears! Serve cold with a little whipped cream, and earn the gratitude of your friends!

Cocoanut Cake.—In order to have this cake in perfection one must have gathered the nut from beneath its feathery fronds oneself. But everyone does not live in India, and for us "at home" the same thing can be bought in a desiccated form. Not as good as the fresh, sweet, creamy, fragrant thing, but sufficiently good for all practical purposes.

We must begin by working four ounces of butter to a cream, and adding to it a quarter of a pound of sifted sugar, the yolks of two eggs, half a grated cocoanut, or three table-spoonfuls of the same in its desiccated form, and, lastly, half a pound of dried flour in which one teaspoonful of baking-powder has been incorporated. Keep to the order in which the ingredients are named. Mix all well together, and beat in enough milk to moisten sufficiently. Bake a light brown in a well-buttered tin.

Whilst this is cooking whisk the two egg-whites you have left over until stiff. This is best done with the blade of a knife on a soup-plate. Get someone else then to add slowly half a pound of icing-sugar, whilst you keep on whisking. This should be like a thick, smooth cream when spread on the cool cake. Wet the knife in water, and you will easily make quite a professional appearance *re* icing. When smooth sprinkle some cocoanut thickly on the wet surface, and put in the oven to set. Take care it does not colour, otherwise the snowy appearance of your cake will be destroyed.

Indian Fritters.—These are a pretty addition to a luncheon-table, when any visitor elects to arrive unexpectedly. They should be as light as dough-nuts, of a light-brown colour, and crisp as a cracker. Some bright-looking preserve should be selected as an accompaniment. Put three tablespoonfuls of flour into a bowl and pour on enough boiling water to make a stiff paste. Stir carefully as you do so, and beat out any lumps with the back of a wooden spoon. Have ready the yolks of four eggs and the whites of two broken into a basin, but not whisked. When they are in the paste-mixture, you must beat and stir well together. Fry in boiling lard or butter (I need not repeat directions as to when fat is at a proper heat), dropping in a tablespoonful of batter at a time only. Each should look like a puffy ball.

Serve on a dish with a spoonful of peach or guava jelly between each fritter.

Plantain Fritters.—As this fruit can be bought in any city for a penny apiece, we need not go to the East to enjoy this delicacy. Strip the yellow, sausagey-looking thing from its thick outer skin, beginning to pare from tip to root. Divide exactly in two. Brush them slightly with yolk of an egg, dust with flour, and fry in boiling butter.

This must be eaten hot, and served piled up in a pyramid with sugar sifted over. My readers will find this as pleasant a way of preparing this luscious fruit as the complicated one recommended by Mrs. Beeton. Its simplicity will recommend it, I am sure, to many amateur cooks.

Lemon Honey.—Perhaps there is no word in our English language more calculated to excite a pleasing thirst than that of "lemon." In order to understand the longing aright one must have basked in an oriental city for a certain time. No wonder that Eastern philosophers have attributed wonderful powers to this much-esteemed fruit. Virgil spoke of it as an antidote to poison. Pliny, whilst rejecting it as unfit for human food on account of its acidity, lays stress on its being a useful medicine. Athenæus, a Latin writer, has left on record that two Arabians stung by adders felt no ill-effects therefrom, because they partook freely of this species of citron. Anyhow, in India we like to keep a store of the following lemon honey, not because we are in the habit of being bitten by snakes, but because guests come uninvited into our bungalows and need feasting. This honey will keep for months if sealed up in stone jars, which is a great recommendation. After mixing together in an enamelled saucepan one pound of crushed loaf sugar, the yolks of four or six eggs, the whites of three, and three ounces of butter, we strain to it the juice of four lemons, and grate into it the rind of two.

Over a very slow fire we put the mixture, and stir quietly until it thickens and clears like honey. At once we take it off, put into bottles or gallipots, and seal down quickly. The above quantity only costs, on an average, one shilling, and numberless patty-pan cases can be filled from it.

With *Cream Toffee* this list of Eastern sweets must close. I do not want to trench on the domain of any cookery-book published.

Instead of using equal quantities of butter and sugar as in ordinary toffee, make this delicious sweetmeat with equal quantities of thick fresh cream and sugar. Necessity, perhaps, caused this change. As everyone knows, butter for the breakfast-table of an Anglo-Indian is painfully produced by shaking a glass bottle! Cream was so much simpler to get at, and some enterprising cook made toffee therewith. Result? Well, you just try it, and you will not need to be told how vastly inferior is the ordinary butter-scotch!

After making, pour the soft mass on to a well-buttered soup-plate, and leave to cool. Cut into dice, and put away in a tin or glass. It will keep well for many months, unless our boys get at it!

SOME RECIPES FROM AN OLD HOUSEKEEPER'S BOOK.

Tansey Pudding.—Take a large teacupful of fine bread-crumbs, throw them into a pint of boiling milk, put in a saucepan over a cool fire, and let them simmer a few minutes; then add six ounces of good butter, stir until quite melted, remove from the stove, add four well-beaten eggs. Have ready the juice of a few tansey leaves mixed with a little spinach juice, to make it green, mix all well together, sweeten to your taste with pounded white sugar. Border a pie dish with puff paste, put in the mixture and bake in moderate oven.

Carrot Pudding.—Pound and sift four ounces of biscuits, beat with six ounces of butter to a cream, add the red part of five or six carrots that have been boiled and rubbed through a sieve, four eggs, a gill of cream, two ounces of chopped almonds, and sugar to taste. Put in a buttered basin with buttered paper and cloth over the top, and steam for three hours.

Sanders.—Mince very finely half a pound of any kind of meat or poultry (raw or cooked), with a small onion, a piece of lemon peel, and a boned anchovy; add four ounces of fine bread-crumbs, salt, a very little cayenne, and some nutmeg. Put two ounces of butter in a saucepan, when melted, add the mince, etc., stir over the fire to mix well, then stir in the yolks of two eggs and remove from fire at once. If the eggs are large, sometimes one is enough. Make into cakes, dip them in white of egg, roll in bread-crumbs, fry in boiling fat and serve.

Potato Pudding.—Mash half a pound of boiled potatoes with a fork, add six ounces of butter, four ounces of pounded loaf sugar, one ounce of chopped almonds with three bitter almonds, and four eggs; beat the whole for half an hour. Bake or steam with buttered paper over the top. If baked, it should be served directly it is taken from the oven.

German Puffs.—Two eggs, two ounces of flour, two ounces of butter, a gill of milk, a little nutmeg and salt. Beat the butter to cream, add the flour, then the eggs and other ingredients, beat for ten minutes; butter some dariole tins or cups, half fill with the mixture, bake half an hour and serve.

Boiled Ground Rice Pudding.—Boil five ounces of ground rice in a pint of milk, with a quarter of a pound of butter; when the rice is cooked, add a quarter of a pound of white sugar, with which a large lemon has been grated, and half a nutmeg grated, add four eggs beaten up with two tablespoonfuls of milk, stir for a minute over a slow fire to mix well, then put in buttered basin, cover, and boil for an hour and a quarter. Serve with sauce or preserve.

Cheese Pudding.—Grate half a pound of mild rich cheese, add two beaten eggs and two tablespoonfuls of sifted bread-crumbs, put in a saucepan, add sufficient milk to moisten, stir over a slow fire until cooked, then put in a buttered dish and brown the top. Pepper and salt can be added if desired.

Duke of Buckingham's Pudding.—Half a pound of finely chopped suet, a quarter of a pound of raisins weighed after they are stoned, a quarter of a pound of flour, two teaspoonfuls of sugar, two eggs, a little nutmeg and ginger, mix well; put in buttered basin, tie down close, boil for five hours at least. Serve with white sauce, or with wine and powdered sugar.

Muffins.—To one pound of flour put half a pint of warm milk, in which you have melted one ounce of butter, add one egg, and a large tablespoonful of fresh barm. Let the dough rise two or three hours. Make your bakestone very hot, rub it with a little butter wrapped in a linen rag, put a spoonful of butter on the stone; when done one side, turn it and cook the other. This is the instruction in the original receipt. I find a tile on my oven sheet answers very well for baking muffins in the oven.

Crumpets.—Two recipes for making them. Take a pint of warm milk and water and a large dessertspoonful of yeast, beat in as much flour as will make a batter, rather thicker than for a batter pudding, beat it well, let it stand to rise two or three hours, and proceed as for muffins.

Second recipe.—Boil a pint of new milk, stir in a piece of butter half the size of a walnut, let it stand until new milk warm, then add to it two eggs, and a dessertspoonful of barm; shake in, beating all the time, flour enough to make it a thick batter, let stand an hour to rise. Proceed as for muffins.

SOME USEFUL RECIPES

SOME LITTLE-KNOWN SWEETS ON OLD METHODS.

Lemon Pudding (an old recipe).—Ingredients: A quarter of a pound of sugar, a noggin of cream (a noggin is a small cup), a quarter of a pound of butter, a quarter of a pound of almonds, the rinds of three lemons grated, the juice of two squeezed lemons, and a little nutmeg; the yolks of ten eggs, with the whites of four beaten separately. Melt the butter with the cream, and let it cool. The almonds must be pounded in a mortar with the rinds of the lemons. Mix all well together. Put paste round your dish. Half-an-hour will bake it.

College Puddings.—Ingredients (after an old recipe): Half a pound of flour, half a pound of currants, half a pound of suet; the yolks of four eggs, the whites of two eggs; a little salt and sugar. Make this into small rolls, fry them in butter, and make a sauce of cordial, sugar, and butter.

Larkin Pudding.—Ingredients: One pound of flour, one pound of raisins, one pound of suet, half a pound of currants, two ounces of chopped apples, two ounces of grated potato, two ounces of grated carrots, two ounces of lemon-peel. Boil the above, when well mixed, for four hours.

Bakewell Pudding.—Line a tin with puff-paste, and put a layer of raspberry jam, and fill it up with the following ingredients:—Half a pound of clarified butter, half a pound of powdered sugar, eight eggs, but only two whites well beaten, the rind of two lemons grated very fine. Mix all well, and bake in a moderate oven.

Vermicelli Pudding.—A quarter of a pound of vermicelli boiled in a pint of milk, with cinnamon and bay leaf, till it is tender. Then add half a pint of cream, a quarter of a pound of powdered white sugar, a quarter of a pound of melted butter, the yolks of six eggs well beaten up. Lay a puff-paste round the edge of the dish, and bake it three-quarters of an hour.

Graham Pudding.—Boil one pint of cream, and mix with it the yolks of twelve eggs, and some powdered sugar. Pass it through a sieve, and put it in a mould. Place the mould in a stewpan with some water, cover it and close it, and let it simmer half an hour. Then whip the whites of eggs to a froth, cover the pudding with them; sift plenty of powdered sugar over it, and brown it with the salamander.

Queen's Pudding.—Line a dish with paste, spread a layer of raspberry jam, then take a quarter of a pound of melted butter, a quarter of a pound of flour, a quarter of a pound of powdered sugar, three eggs (yolks and whites well beaten separately), and a few sweet almonds pounded. Mix all well together, beating it until quite light, and pour it on the dish and bake it.

Watkin Pudding. — Ingredients : Six ounces of suet chopped fine, six ounces of grated bread, six ounces of sugar, three eggs, two tablespoonfuls of orange marmalade well mixed. Butter a mould or basin and boil for four hours.

The sauce for above.—Squeeze half a lemon, add sugar, and a quarter of a pint of water.

Iced Vanilla Pudding.—Whip the whites of three eggs to a good strong froth, then make a rich, well-flavoured custard, and when it is cold add the whipped whites and put it in a mould, into which drop dried fruit cut small, and fasten the top of the mould tightly down, and put it in ice for four or five hours. If you do not wish it to be iced, add isinglass to the custard in the proportion of half an ounce to a pint.

Fig Pudding.—Take one pound of figs, shred fine, half a pound of suet, chopped small, six ounces of bread-crumbs, half a nutmeg, and the yellow rind of a lemon, grated off, three eggs, well beaten, and sufficient milk to make it of a perfect consistence. Mix and boil in a cloth or buttered mould.

Irish Sally Luns.—Ingredients: One pound of flour, two eggs, two ounces of melted butter, two spoonfuls of barm. Mix all this with as much warm milk as will make it into a thick batter. Let it remain twelve hours mixed, and when you are going to put it into the oven, work it a little. An hour will bake it.

Irish Potato Cake.—To one pound of fresh butter well beaten up, add one pound of potato flour well dried, one pound of loaf sugar, grated, the yolks of twelve eggs, and the whites of six to be whisked separately, the strings picked out. Then take some grated lemon peel and caraway seeds. The butter is to be beaten while the other ingredients are added, but the seeds are only to be mixed just before putting it into the oven.

Tea Cakes.—Take half a pound of butter, melt it gently and mix with it half a pound of finely powdered white sugar. Add one pound of flour and roll it to a thin paste. Cut this into small shapes—the top of a wine-glass will do this—and bake them for a few minutes, but they must be carefully watched. Beat up the white of an egg and lay it over them with a feather, and then gently sprinkle a little fine sugar. If properly made they will eat very short and crisp.

Lemon Cake.—Ingredients :—The yolks of twenty-four eggs, the whites of twelve eggs, one pound of powdered sugar. The grated rinds of two or three large lemons and the juice of one. One pound of flour, two ounces of sweet almonds, half an ounce of bitter well pounded. Mix well and bake until of a light brown.

Soda Bread.—Take of dressed flour three pounds, bicarbonate of soda nine drachms, hydrochloric acid eleven and a quarter fluid drachms, water twenty-five fluid ounces. Mix soda and flour thoroughly by shaking the soda from a small sieve over the flour with one hand while they are stirred together by the other, and then passing the mixture through the sieve. Next pour the acid into the water and diffuse it by stirring with a stick. Then mix the flour and water so prepared as speedily as possible with a wooden spoon or spatula.

TASTY DISHES.

Brown Bread Savoury.—Grate a sufficient amount of Parmesan cheese and whip together with cream, say sixpennyworth of the latter, and two ounces of cheese. Whip until quite stiff, adding a pinch of white pepper and a sprinkling of salt. Spread the mixture between thin slices of brown bread and butter, cut into squares and serve as soon as ready.

Horseradish Sauce, for hot roast beef or mutton.—Scrape about two ounces of horse-radish, and stir it into half a pint of cream made boiling hot, add an ounce of fine white bread-crumbs, a little milk, a pinch of cayenne, same of salt, and just before taking to table stir in the juice of half a fresh lemon.

Eggs and Mushroom Sauce.—Boil some new-laid eggs until they are quite hard, remove the shells without breaking them, and keep the eggs hot. Cover them with a thick brown gravy, made by stewing half a pound of dark mushrooms in a little butter, and when thoroughly done rub them through a sieve, stir in a teacupful of melted butter, season highly, add a spoonful of sharp sauce, a few drops of soy, and boil altogether for a moment.

A Delicious Dish of Tomatoes.—Take out the core from some large tomatoes, sprinkle them with pepper and salt and lay them in a baking-tin with a little butter; cook them in the oven for ten minutes. When done, lift each tomato on to a separate piece of toast just its size, and lay a poached egg on the top. For a more truly vegetarian taste, or to make a perfect luncheon-dish of these, a tin of preserved peas might be made hot, and the contents put as a bed for the tomatoes to rest on.

HOUSEHOLD BREAD.

Ingredients.—Three pounds and a half of flour (household), about one pint and a quarter of warm water, one dessertspoonful and a half of salt, one ounce of dry yeast, one ounce of moist sugar.

Method.—Put the flour and salt in an earthenware pan, and mix well together; put the pan to warm; work the yeast to a cream with the sugar, and add to it a gill and a half of the warm water. Make a well in the flour and mix in the yeast and water, so that there is a soft batter in the middle of the flour; sprinkle flour over this, lay a cloth over the pan and put it in a warm place for fifteen minutes to set the sponge; then stir in the rest of the water; flour the board and knead the dough for about twenty minutes until very elastic; replace it in the pan with a deep cross scored on the top to help it to rise, cover up and put in a warm place to rise one hour and a half. Make into loaves and bake; the oven should be very hot at first and moderate for the rest of the time. A quartern loaf will take nearly two hours to cook. If the water used is hot instead of warm, the yeast will be killed and will not act.

GINGERBREAD.

Ingredients.—One pound of flour, six ounces of golden syrup, four ounces of brown sugar, four ounces of dripping, one ounce of ground ginger, two teaspoonfuls of carbonate of soda, one teaspoonful of mixed spice, two-thirds of a gill of milk.

Method.—Put the flour, sugar, ginger and spice in a basin and mix well together; put the treacle, milk, soda and dripping in a saucepan and melt over the fire; pour the contents of the saucepan into the contents of the basin, mix well, beat for five minutes, pour in a greased tin and bake in a moderate oven.

SCONES.

Ingredients.—One pound of flour, two ounces of dripping, three ounces of sugar, half an ounce of cream of tartar, one teaspoonful of carbonate of soda, milk to mix, a few sultanas (floured and picked).

Method.—Mix the tartar and the soda well with the flour in a basin, rub in the dripping, add the sugar and sultanas, mix with milk rather more soft than for pastry, roll into two thick rounds, cut each into six equal pieces, lay on a floured tin, brush over the top with milk and bake in a good oven twenty minutes. Plain scones can be made by leaving out the sultanas and the sugar. These scones are best made with milk that is slightly sour.

PLUM CAKE.

Ingredients.—One pound of flour, six ounces of dripping, six ounces of brown sugar, six ounces of sultanas (floured and picked), four ounces of currants (washed and dried), one teaspoonful of baking powder, two eggs, one gill and a half of milk.

Method.—Put the dripping in a basin and work it to a cream with a wooden spoon; mix the flour with the baking powder and stir it into the dripping; stir in the currants, sultanas and sugar, and last of all the eggs beaten up with the milk. Put in a well-greased cake tin, and stand the tin on a thickly-sanded baking sheet. Bake in a hot oven for an hour and then in a cooler oven for another half an hour.

SEED CAKE.

Method.—Make like plum cake, using an ounce of caraway seeds for the sultanas and currants, and a little less milk.

UNFERMENTED BREAD.

Ingredients.—One pound of flour, one tablespoonful of baking powder, milk and water to mix, one teaspoonful of salt.

Method.—Mix together to a soft dough; make into six rolls, brush with milk and bake in a sharp oven fifteen minutes.

POTATO CAKE.

Ingredients.—Three-quarters of a pound of mashed potatoes, half a pound of flour, two ounces of butter, one teaspoonful of salt, one small teaspoonful of baking-powder, one egg, half a gill of lukewarm milk.

Method.—Melt the butter, and mix it with the mashed potatoes, mix in the flour and baking powder, add egg well beaten and the lukewarm milk. Flour the board, roll into a thick round, lay on a floured and greased tin, and bake in a good oven about three-quarters of an hour.

ROCK CAKES.

Ingredients.—Half a pound of flour, two ounces of currants (washed and dried), two ounces of sultanas, two ounces of dripping, two ounces of brown sugar, one ounce of candied peel, one teaspoonful of ground ginger, one teaspoonful of baking powder, one egg, a little milk.

Method.—Mix the flour and baking powder in a basin, rub in the dripping, add the currants and the sultanas, sugar, peel and ginger, mix very stiffly with egg and milk; pile in little rough heaps on a greased tin with two forks and bake in a good oven ten minutes.

CITRON BUNS.

Ingredients.—Half a pound of flour, two ounces of margarine, two ounces of brown sugar, one teaspoonful of baking powder, one egg, a little milk, three ounces of citron.

Method.—Mix the flour with the baking powder, rub in the margarine with the tips of the fingers, add the sugar; cut eight good-sized pieces of the citron peel and chop the rest small; mix the chopped citron with the other ingredients, and then add the egg beaten with a little milk. Mix rather wet; divide into eight, lay on a greased tin, lay a piece of citron on each cake and bake for fifteen minutes in a good oven.

SHORTBREAD.

Ingredients.—One pound of flour, three-quarters of a pound of butter, half a pound of castor sugar.

Method.—Rub six ounces of the butter into the flour and sugar, melt the rest and mix it in; work a little with the hands to form a dough; roll into two thick rounds and pinch them round the edge with the fingers to ornament them. Prick over the top with a fork or a biscuit pricker; put two or three large pieces of candied peel on each and bake about half an hour in a moderate oven.

RICE CAKES.

Ingredients.—Three ounces of ground rice, two ounces of flour, three ounces of butter, three ounces of castor sugar, two eggs, vanilla.

Method.—Beat the butter to a cream with a wooden spoon, add the sugar and cream to that; stir in the ground rice with the flour by degrees; add the eggs well beaten and the flavouring; fill greased patty pans and bake in a moderate oven fifteen minutes.

ALMOND CAKES.

Ingredients.—Eight ounces of flour, four ounces of butter, five ounces of castor sugar, four eggs, three ounces of almonds, half a pound of icing sugar, a little almond flavouring, a little water.

Method.—Beat the butter to a cream with a wooden spoon, stir in the sugar, beat in the eggs one by one, putting a little flour with each to prevent its curdling, stir in the rest of the flour after the eggs are beaten in, lastly the almonds blanched and chopped. Brush some little cake moulds with clarified butter and dust them with mixed castor sugar and flour; fill these three-parts full with the cake mixture and bake in a good oven a pale brown, turn out on to a sieve, and when cold ice as follows.

Icing.—Sift half a pound of icing sugar and mix it very smoothly with a little cold water and enough almond essence to flavour it until it is just thick enough to coat the cakes, pour over and let it set. Put a crystallised cherry on each, and arrange strips of blanched almonds to ornament.

CHOCOLATE CAKE.

Ingredients.—Half a pound of flour, quarter of a pound of grated chocolate, three ounces of butter, six ounces of castor sugar, four eggs, one small teaspoonful of baking powder, vanilla flavouring, a little browning.

For the Icing.—Half a pound of icing sugar, three ounces of chocolate, a little water and browning.

Method.—Beat the butter to a cream, add the castor sugar and the grated chocolate; beat the eggs in one at a time, putting a little flour with each; add the flour, the vanilla flavouring and a little browning. Have ready a cake tin brushed out with clarified butter and lined with buttered paper; put in the mixture, which should three parts fill it, and bake in a good oven about one hour and a half.

For the Icing.—Melt three ounces of chocolate; mix the icing sugar with about four tablespoonfuls of warm water and stir in the melted chocolate; work well with a wooden spoon and pour over the cake when it is cold.

ROSCOMMON LOAF.

Ingredients.—One pound of wholemeal flour, quarter of a pound of household flour, one ounce and a half of butter or dripping, half a teaspoonful of carbonate of soda, one teaspoonful of salt, sour milk to mix.

Method.—Mix the flour, salt and soda well in a basin, rub in the dripping, mix to a rather soft dough with the sour milk; make into a flat loaf, score across with a knife, and bake in a good oven one hour and a half.

CHOCOLATE DATES.

HAVE you ever tasted chocolate dates? If so, these directions will be almost needless to you, for I fancy that you will not have stopped at a taste, but will have tried and found out a way to manufacture them for yourself. But so far as I know, these dates are, as yet, quite a home-made sweet, and they are so delicious and so wholesome that they ought to be more widely known. Here then is the recipe. Any sort of dates and any sort of chocolate may be used, but the best results are got from the best materials in confectionery even more than in other work. Take then a pound of Tunis dates, either bought in the familiar oblong boxes or by the pound. Leave out any which are not perfectly ripe; the soapy taste of one of these paler, firmer dates is enough to disgust anyone with dates for ever. Wipe the others very gently with a damp cloth (dates are not gathered by the Dutch!), slit them lengthwise with a silver knife, but only so far as to enable you to extract the kernel without bruising the fruit. Then prepare the chocolate. Grate a quarter of a pound of best French chocolate, add an equal weight of fresh icing sugar, two tablespoonfuls of boiling water, and mix in a small brass or earthenware saucepan over the fire until quite smooth, only it must *not* boil; last of all add a few drops of vanilla.

Then put your small saucepan inside a larger one half filled with boiling water, just to keep the chocolate fluid until all the dates are filled. Take up a little of the mixture in a teaspoon, press open the date, and pour it neatly in. There must be no smears or threads of chocolate if your confectionery is to look dainty. When about a dozen are filled, gently press the sides together, and the chocolate should just show a shiny brown ridge in the middle of the date. Place on a board in a cool place to harden; they may be packed up next day.

Almost as nice as chocolate dates are nougat dates. The foundation for the nougat is the same as for American candies: the white of one egg and an equal quantity of cold water to half a pound of sifted icing sugar, all mixed perfectly smoothly together. Then chop equal quantities of blanched walnuts, almonds, Brazils, and hazel nuts together, mix with the sugar in the proportion of two thirds of nut to one of the sugar mixture, and leave until next day in the cellar. By that time the nougat will be firm enough to form into kernels by gently rolling between the hands; if it sticks, your hands are too warm. It is best to do this part of the work in the cellar. Having stoned and first wiped your dates, put in the nougat kernels, gently pressing the sides together; they will harden in a short time, and very pretty they look packed alternately with the chocolate dates in fancy boxes. Tunis dates do not keep good much longer than two months, the grocer tells me; we have never been able to keep them half that time to try! Of course, you can use the commoner dates, which are very good to eat, but hardly so nice to look at as the others, because on account of their more sugary consistency it is impossible to fill them so neatly as the moister Tunis dates. Tafilat dates are somehow too dry and solid to combine well either with nuts or chocolate.

AFTERNOON TEA-CAKES AND SANDWICHES.

By DORA DE BLAQUIÈRE.

TEN years ago one would probably have enumerated muffins and crumpets, and given them the first place amongst tea-cakes, whether for what is called "high teas," or the lighter meal of a late introduction, which has risen into such world-wide fame, that the French have adopted it as a new word, and call it "five o'clocker." Here it is brought up as a matter of course every day, and is one of the usual afternoon entertainments, cheap, and at times rather dull. In Canada and America, it does not seem to have been so universally adopted, probably because high teas are the rule, and will never, I fancy, be ousted, the late dinner being nearly an impossibility in that region of few servants and surpassing difficulty in getting them. In the large cities and towns it is rather different; but even in these the afternoon tea seems still an entertainment for visitors, not a rule of the house. In New York I was introduced to the afternoon tea-table minus a teapot, and graced only with a handsome tea-kettle and spirit lamp, which was very boiling indeed. Instead of the teapot, a tea-infuser was used. This, as many of my readers may know, is an article in metal, of about the size of a very small egg, perforated with small holes, and having a chain and ring attached for holding it. It is filled with tea, and then dropped into a cup, which is then filled with boiling water, and you keep it in till your tea be as strong as you require it. Then it is passed on to another cup, and so on, till it be thought to be exhausted, and it is then replenished. But if the cups should be small ones, the amount of tea put in at first will usually go round, and be enough for half a dozen cups. Of course there is a great advantage in this modern method of tea-making, for you have what the medical men recommend, i.e., five-minute tea, and, consequently, you are quite safe from all injurious consequences. I prefer, however, the old-fashioned style; but for anyone who wants a cup of tea early or late, in a hurry, the tea-infuser is extremely helpful, and as such I have used it many times. In illness it is extremely useful; for the kettle is nearly always at hand in the invalid's room, when cold enough to require a fire, and no equipage is required.

I have begun by saying that muffins and crumpets would have formed part of the feast, but, strange to say, both these ancient and excellent articles of luxury seem to have gone out of fashion for the afternoon tea-table. I cannot, in fact, recall having seen them for the last few years. Their place has been taken by a score of things. By sandwiches, for instance, a concession to the many who nowadays do not eat sweets of any kind. An immense amount of small fancy cakes, and biscuits, made of almond paste, cream, chocolate, and sugar; and last, but not least, thin bread and butter, brown or white, which puts in an appearance on all occasions.

Hot buttered toast, in many houses buttered scones, or some form of tea-cake, such as Sally Lunn, is always seen; and it is generally the master of the house who wants such unwholesome things, or the boys at home from school. Sally Lunn, of Bath notoriety, never seems to lose her influence over her votaries; but her rivals, the muffins and crumpets, are no longer seen at fashionable teas. Two things have sent them out of date, I think. No one wants to soil their gloves, nor to take them off; and I don't think either of them are so nice as they once were; I know in the North of England they are twice as good as they are in the south, and much bigger. Many people would probably tell you also that the modern digestion is not the same as that of the last century, nor even when our sailor King was reigning.

In Scotland, or in a Scotch-English domicile, you will find, oh, such cakes; and if you never heard of "the land o' cakes" before, you will be a devout believer in its beauties to the end of your days. The Scotch scone is, of all cakes, when well made, and made at home, the best of all; even cold it preserves its supremacy. Next to them come potato-cakes, and that wonderful thing known in Yorkshire as fat rascals. The following is a Scotch recipe, tested and tried, i.e., One pound of flour, two ounces of butter, one egg, one teaspoonful and a half of baking powder. Mix all together with a cup of cold milk, having first rubbed the baking powder into the flour, and make into tiny cakes, the size of a penny; bake in a very quick oven and split, then butter and serve very hot. This is a small tea-cake that can be made and served in a few minutes, and there need be no difficulty in having them for afternoon tea at any time.

What is known in our English cookery-books as Benton tea-cake, is as follows. One pound of flour, four ounces of butter, and enough milk to make a paste; roll out very thin, and bake either on a hot hearth-stone or on an oven plate. Now this, which is a very old recipe, is evidently a kind of mother of all quickly-made tea-cakes, and is called granny cake in some parts of Canada and in Ireland; but the invention of baking powder has improved it. The Canadian recipe is very good, and has lost the butter. One teacup of milk, two cups of flour, two teaspoonfuls of baking powder, and a pinch of salt. Mix, roll into one flat round cake, and cook in a clean frying-pan. When done on one side turn the other up, cut into quarters, and serve very hot. This cake requires much butter.

The following has been sent me as the correct recipe for "fat rascals," but I cannot say if quite correct. Take two pounds of flour, mix in four ounces of butter and a pint of milk, three spoonfuls of yeast, and two eggs. Beat all well together and let it rise; then knead it and make into cakes; let them rise on tins before baking, which do in a slow oven. Split while hot and butter. This is done very profusely in Yorkshire.

A simple Scotch scone is taken from a good source, and is as follows. One pound of flour, a quarter of a pound of butter, a quarter of a teaspoonful of soda, and the same of tartaric acid and a little salt. Mix with milk, roll out to the thickness of half an inch, cut into large rounds, and score with a knife into quarters, so that they can be broken easily when done. They require a hot oven, and to be baked for about twenty minutes. Nearly every cookery-book contains a recipe for scones, and when once made, you will quite understand how to manage so as to have good ones in future.

Now I suppose no notice of possible tea-cakes would be complete without a recipe for the famous American shortcake. This is another quickly-made cake, and is quite possible for afternoon teas. One quart of flour, two tablespoonfuls of butter, two cups of sweet milk, two teaspoonfuls of good baking powder. Mix well, roll out, cut into small round cakes and bake quickly. Split and butter, and serve very hot. Of course, these quantities need not be used, but the above is an American recipe, and I have not changed it in any way. It would be a simple matter to take half only.

Whigs are a kind of bun, but the modern dictionary gives the name as applied to them as obsolete. For all that there are people in country places in the north who still call them "whigs." They are made as follows: Take half a pint of warm milk to three quarters of a pound of fine flour, and mix into it two or three spoonfuls of yeast. Cover it up and set before the fire to rise for an hour; then work into the paste four ounces of butter and the same of sugar, knead it into flat whigs, i.e., cakes, with as little flour as possible, and bake in a quick oven. Split and butter while quite hot. They are also good cold, and instead of the yeast two teaspoonfuls of baking powder may be used.

I do not advise anyone to attempt hot tea-cakes for a large party; they are only suitable for a home party, or when a few very favoured visitors are expected who are likely to be coming out of the winter's cold to feel the hot cakes a treat. Sunday is a favourite day to have them; especially in houses where a late supper is the order of the day, in order to arrange for the evening church-going; then, indeed, the hot tea-cake is a treat and a special luxury.

Now, so far as the fashionable afternoon tea is concerned, it must be considered a very light and airy meal. The usual cakes are those purchased at some confectioner's, who, for the moment, manufactures the fashionable cake. Some three or four years ago there was a perfect rage for the angel cake, a frothy and slight concoction of extreme sweetness. Just now the cakes most in vogue are those made from almond paste, as I have said, the general price of these is from 2s. 6d. to 3s. per pound at a first-class confectioner's. Then there are bon-bons of all kinds served at dessert in tiny silver dishes: good chocolates seeming the most popular. Other cakes, such as cherry cake with almond icing; Dundee and pound cakes are liked, the latter being rather a revival from ancient days, and too often, alas, a failure because the maker has not been sufficiently generous to purchase the very best of butter. But when good, nothing in the way of a cake can surpass it. I am always so sorry for myself when some one has been married, and I am obliged to eat wedding-cake at an afternoon tea. If there is a horrid and disgusting mixture, it is a modern wedding-cake.

The question of sandwiches is an all-engrossing one, I notice, at some afternoon teas, where they are made much of in the *menu* of the feast. But for all that, the first craze for them has worn off in a great degree, and they require to be very nice indeed, or especially appetising to make anyone take them, and the differences of opinion about sandwiches is remarkable. One person will consider them made of cucumber delicious, while a second will be equally determined to think them disgusting. They are often spoilt by being made of undressed cucumbers, which is a great mistake, as they should be always dressed with pepper, salt, vinegar and oil, or else with a salad dressing, before being introduced to the bread and butter they are intended to re-organise. Lately I have tasted some cucumber sandwiches with hard-boiled egg in them, which I think is a great mistake; but the greatest blunder of all is to chop the cucumber up finely and then use it for sandwiches. Of all our fruits and vegetables this is the one

most intolerant of the touch of a knife, and nothing can exceed its quickness in "taking a taste." I am certain that chopped-up messes are never successful in sandwiches. Anything, however, that can be pounded and made into paste is both suitable and palatable.

Curry, chutnee, and Parmesan, or any other rather delicate cheese sandwiches, including those delicious American ones made of toasted cheese, are all, or any of them suitable for winter; but even while I am writing of them, I must beg of you to be dainty and delicate in the use of all these ingredients, which are a little overpowering. There are several forms of curry sandwiches, curried-egg-paste, curried fish, or a fine paste made of chicken and curry, even curry powder rubbed into a little butter is said to make a good sandwich. The eggs are hard-boiled, and then rubbed smooth with curry and butter, just as you would proceed to make Indian eggs; and they would be regularly curried and then placed on the bread and butter in the nicest flakes you could make.

Chutnee is also used with hard-boiled eggs and cold meat; or the Lahore chutnee may be used alone, but must be minced, as the pieces are large of which it is composed. For those who do not mind hot things, a hotter chutnee may be liked, and a good Madras would be enjoyed. I have tasted pickle sandwiches made both of Indian pickle, and picca-lilly; and though I did not care for them myself, many people would.

Anchovies were, and are a very favourite thing for sandwiches, and so are sardines and lobsters. The former are generally used with watercress, and are well boned, and soaked in milk and water before using them; they are also pounded with hard-boiled egg, and sometimes I have used a good anchovy paste, which I have thought better flavoured than the anchovies, either whole or pounded. Lobster must be pounded in a marble mortar, with a little butter, red pepper, and salt; and I have had some very good fresh shrimp sandwiches, though I should think they would be quite as good made from some shrimp paste. The same may be said of those made of game, for delicious fresh potted game can be had, and so can potted meat, chicken and tongue, as well as cheese; and these, if made at home by a good cook, would be sure to be appetising.

I am always afraid in writing of sardine sandwiches, or indeed of sardines in any way, to go through the ordeal of cooking, lest sufficient care should not be taken in wiping them, and making them quite free from oil. Lately they have not been so good, and this is in consequence of the oil used, which, I feel quite sure, is not olive, but cottonseed oil, which, in consequence of its greater cheapness, is sold everywhere as "salad oil." I am told that in asking for oil in the shops, you should always be very distinct in asking for "olive," not "salad oil." Olive oil can always be purchased at a chemist's; and I remember that some years ago, an old Italian friend of mine would either purchase it at the chemist's by the gallon, or go to a real Italian ware-house, as he was sure to get it fresh, and quite recently made. Sardines must be wiped, boned, and laid in lemon juice, and a very little water, for an hour before using. Then drain and place them in the bread and butter. They may be served with lemon-juice and cayenne, with a mayonnaise sauce, or with a tomato sauce very much seasoned, made hot and poured over them. When cold, make the sandwiches. Parmesan cheese had better be purchased in powder, sold in bottles, as it gives far less trouble. It can then be mixed in any proportion that may be liked, with hard-boiled eggs, and pounded into a paste.

The sandwiches which I have the most enjoyed in the winter myself, have been of *pâte de foie gras*, or *caviar*; but it must be

remembered that these two ingredients are not universally popular, also that *caviar* must never be touched by a steel knife, but spread with a silver one; and a little lemon and cayenne pepper added. The *pâte de foie gras* is bought in tins or jars, and can be used as it is, being excellent at all times with bread and butter.

A new sandwich to me was one made of very thinly-sliced sausages. They were purchased at a real German shop in London where the Deutscher *delicatessen* are sold; and the sausage in question had been boiled, after buying, and had been served hot at table, and much enjoyed. I daresay that every one who has been in Germany has tasted it in this manner. Those who dislike the flavour of onion, garlic, or herbs, must be careful in buying German sausages.

The old proverb, "There is nothing new under the sun," is constantly brought to one's mind in daily life. The other day, looking over a cookery book of the latter part of the last century, I suddenly came upon a page devoted to sandwiches, and in it I found one or two quite novel ones. Beetroot sandwiches, for instance, are made as follows:—Take some slices of boiled beet-root; put vinegar over them and let them stand; drain them carefully free from vinegar, and put them in between bread and butter for sandwiches, adding a little made mustard to each. Slices of beetroot fried in butter are also said to make good sandwiches with mustard. The recipe for egg sandwiches is much as they are made now; but there are instructions how to make sandwiches of fried eggs, which seem likely to be nice. Beat up four eggs, season with pepper and salt, fry them in butter as for a pancake; and when cold cut in small slices and put between bread and butter. This is what is now called scrambled eggs without the usual stirring up they receive. Omelet sandwiches are made with four eggs well beaten, two tablespoons of water, adding a few bread-crumbs; season with pepper and salt, fry in small fritters of the size of a half-crown; and when these are cold, use them for sandwiches between bread and butter with mustard.

The best of these old recipes is, however, that for making them with good Cheshire cheese; but in these days of decadence, we shall probably find it difficult to discover a real Cheshire cheese, and may have to use the nearest substitute. Take two-thirds of grated Cheshire cheese, one-third of butter, a little good cream, and a small proportion of made mustard. Pound all together in a mortar till smooth and without lumps. Add a little cayenne pepper or any relish you may please, then spread over bread and butter—not too thickly—and press very well together to form sandwiches.

The origin of these omelet and egg-sandwiches is probably French; for cold omelet is constantly used in France, and it is very enjoyable indeed for salads, and eaten with meat. Fried with butter, it is also excellent. I hope it is needless to remark that the eggs should be as fresh as possible. I never write anything about eggs, but the story of a friend of mine is recalled to my mind, i.e.: Walking down a street in London the labels on the eggs attracted him. They began at New Laid, then Fresh; Cooking eggs; and finally, "Eggs!" only what these were he could not imagine.

Tomato has been used lately for sandwiches with or without the addition of Parmesan cheese dressing, mayonnaise or anchovy sauce; or the true American breakfast dressing of vinegar and sugar. I prefer that they should be left quite plain myself, with a little pepper and salt, and cut in the thinnest of slices; they are quite good enough to my taste.

All kinds of fruit sandwiches are very good, though but little used on this side of the water. Bananas, pineapple, and peaches are all excellent in sandwiches; so are strawberries cut into slices with sugar and liqueur. Almond icing and lemon cheesecake are also very good for sandwiches; the latter especially, which can be made at home without much difficulty and kept in the house for use whenever wanted. The following is an old recipe for making it: To half-a-pound of butter put one pound and three quarters of castor sugar, the yolks of eight eggs and the whites of six; the grated rind of four lemons and the juice of six. Simmer all together in a clean enamelled saucepan over a slow fire, stirring till it becomes as thick as cream; then store away in well-covered pots till wanted.

With these instructions for sweet sandwiches I shall leave this part of my subject, only delaying to implore my readers to be very careful to select the best of bread, and the better than best of butter. The latter is an ingredient not to be trifled with where sandwiches are concerned; and the former should also be thought of in time in order to secure a second day's tin loaf of the proper shape for sandwiches.

Brown bread should also be of the same age, and should not be of the crumbly sort. Mustard-and-cress, water-cress, and sardines, will all make nice brown-bread sandwiches; but cucumber will not answer, though most sweet things will be good. One of the most attractive of the brown-bread sandwiches is made with good fresh Devonshire cream. Of course, only the thickest part is used, and they must be made and served at once. I have often wondered whether that sour cream, which is served in France with fruit, would not be nice. Of course it would have to be slightly sugared before using it.

SWISS CAKES, AND HOW TO MAKE THEM.

THE following recipes I have translated from a Swiss cookery book, recommended to me by a Swiss lady. Many of them are peculiar to the Bernese Oberland.

ALMOND SUGAR-BREAD.

Take half pound sugar-dust, quarter pound almonds (sweet) blanched and finely chopped, the rind of a lemon finely chopped, the weight of three eggs in flour, and five eggs. The yolks of the eggs and the sugar must be well beaten together until they begin to get white, then add the lemon-peel and the juice of the lemon, then the whites of the eggs (beaten till stiff), and lastly the flour and the chopped almonds, stirred in very lightly, and the whole well mixed. Pour into a cake-tin which has been previously well buttered and sprinkled with sugar. Sift sugar over, and bake.

SWABIAN BREAD.

Put thirteen ounces of flour on a pasteboard, rub into it ten ounces of fresh butter, moisten with the white of one egg, and work them together; then add by degrees half pound sugar and half pound almonds, not blanched, the sugar and the almonds to be well pounded together before adding to the other ingredients, also half ounce pounded cinnamon and the rind of a lemon, with a little salt; work all together, and cut out into shapes with a cutter, brush over with the yolk of an egg, and bake on a floured tin.

LITTLE MACAROONS.

Quarter pound sifted sugar, quarter pound almonds (sweet) blanched and finely pounded, the rind of a lemon finely chopped, and the white of one egg beaten till stiff. Mix all together, and pour into little cakes; bake on a buttered paper.

TRONCHINES.

Three ounces sifted sugar, good weight, the finely chopped rind of a lemon, and the whites of three eggs beaten till stiff. Mix these together, and then stir in a good ounce and a half of flour. Spread this mixture on a buttered baking-tin, about the thickness of the back of a knife; when baked, while the cake is still hot, cut into small square pieces.

CHOCOLATE ROLLS.

Three ounces of sifted sugar, one and a half ounces good chocolate grated, the whites of two small eggs beaten till stiff; mix all well together, make into little heaps on buttered paper, and bake.

STEINERLI.

Take one pound of sifted sugar, one pound flour, and four eggs, the whites of which should be beaten a little; cinnamon according to taste, or the chopped rind of half a lemon; mix these ingredients together, roll out very thin, cut into shapes with a cutter, and bake on a floured tin; they should not be long in the oven, nor baked hard.

CHOCOLATE CAKE.

Quarter of a pound of chocolate grated, half a pound sugar pounded, with quarter of a pound blanched almonds, a little pounded vanilla or cinnamon; mix all together with the well-beaten whites of four eggs, then stir in a handful of flour; put the mixture into a well buttered mould; bake in a moderate oven, so that it is baked quite through.

EXCELLENT LITTLE CAKES.

Half a pound white sugar, half a pound blanched almonds. Half the almonds to be pounded, and the other half to be cut into strips; put the latter in a small saucepan with a very little water and the sugar, stir diligently over the fire until the sugar is melted and the almonds a little roasted; put this mixture in a bowl with the pounded almonds and the whites of three eggs well beaten, stir well together; then form into little cakes (flat) on a slightly buttered plate or dish, and bake till a golden brown. Great care must be taken that they do not burn.

FREEMASON BREAD.

Half a pound sifted sugar, and two whole eggs and two yolks to be beaten together for an hour; then stir in ten ounces of flour, and lastly one and a half ounces of lemon peel and one and a half ounces orange peel, and the rind of a lemon finely chopped or grated, together with a little pounded cinnamon, and, if liked, a little pounded clove. Make this mixture into little rolls as long and as thick as your finger; sprinkle a baking-tin with flour, and lay the fingers pretty far apart on it; make three little cuts across each with a knife, and bake in a slow oven.

SCHMELZBRÖDCHEN.

The whites of five eggs, the yolks of three eggs, the weight of four eggs in sifted sugar, the weight of two eggs in fresh butter, the weight of two eggs in flour, and the rind of a lemon grated or finely chopped. Beat the yolks of the eggs together with the sugar and lemon rind, until little bubbles appear on the surface, beat the whites till quite stiff, and stir in lightly, sift in the flour, and beat together; lastly add the butter a little melted. When well mixed, butter some small moulds, and fill them a little more than half full with the mixture, and bake a light brown.

TIRE-BOUCHONS.

The whites of three eggs beaten till quite stiff, two ounces of sugar, on which rub the rind of a lemon, two teaspoonfuls of red wine and three teaspoonfuls of ordinary white wine, and a tablespoonful of flour. First dissolve the sugar in the wine, then stir in the whites of the eggs well beaten, and lastly add the flour; when well mixed pour into a slightly buttered tin (flat), which ought to be large enough to allow of the mixture being quite thin; as soon as it is baked cut into long narrow strips, and while they are warm wind them round a stick, slip them off when cold.

L. STANTON.

"AFTERNOON TEA;" A CHAT OVER THE TEACUPS.

By AMY S. WOODS.

WITHIN the last twenty years the simple but most popular meal known by the name of "afternoon tea" has become a prominent feature in domestic and social life.

"Afternoon tea!" The very words suggest to our minds pleasant visions of cosy fireside tea and talk on winter afternoons, or lazy enjoyment of the "cup that cheers" under the welcome shade of some spreading tree in drowsy summer-time.

True, the institution of this meal has been much condemned of late. We are told that women drink far more tea than is good for them and are growing more nervous in consequence; while the sterner sex complain that the enjoyment of their dinner is spoiled by their previous indulgence in the dainties of the tea-table.

Nevertheless, I think even those who cavil most at the evil influence of tea and its accompanying delicacies would, in their hearts, be sorry to witness the abolition of a meal which has won the support of so large a section of English society, from royalty downwards.

To those who are weary of formal entertainments, it comes as a boon and a blessing, while to those whose love of social pleasures is larger than their purse it is even more welcome, as it enables them to entertain their friends more frequently, with but little of the cost and trouble which more elaborate social gatherings involve. And it is to this latter class of afternoon-tea devotees that I dedicate the following recipes and suggestions.

It is easy for dwellers in London or other large towns to obtain a nice variety of cakes and biscuits wherewith to grace their tea-tables; but those who live in country villages are less fortunate, and are sometimes sadly conscious of lack of variety in the cakes they can make or procure. I hope therefore that the recipes here given will be acceptable to all those who are willing to spend a little care and trouble in carrying them out. Most of them are capable of further variation, and clever heads and fingers will devise artistic and dainty decorations and ornamentations for themselves, the result of which will be that their cakes will be quite as beautiful to look upon, and probably more beautiful to eat than those supplied by a fashionable confectioner.

One thing must be remembered by all aspiring cake-makers, viz., that dainty cakes and biscuits require time, care, and patience in their production, and cakes that are hurriedly made are seldom satisfactory. Another point to be remembered is that afternoon tea is not a substantial meal, so that we must endeavour to have all our dishes as dainty and elegant as possible both in their composition and manner of serving.

We cannot perhaps all boast of silver or Sheraton tea-trays, or of Dresden or Worcester china; but a plain linen or small-patterned damask cloth embroidered with a large initial, and either prettily hemstitched or edged with Torchon lace, will hide all the deficiencies of our tea-tray, and now that such pretty Coalport china can be bought at such a reasonable price, no one need be without a charming tea-set.

In arranging the china and linen for afternoon tea, it will be well to remember that coloured china looks best upon a white cloth or upon a cream-coloured one embroidered in silks or flax threads to match the colours in the china, while for use with plain white or white-and-gold china a cloth of art linen, in plain blue, yellow or pink, with white embroidery is most suitable.

Nor need any hostess lament over her scarcity of small silver table appointments in the way of teapot and cream jugs and sugar basins, for a china teapot and hot-water jug and the sweet wee cream jugs and tiny basins now sold to match almost every stock pattern

AFTERNOON TEA.

of china, look quite as dainty and artistic as their more imposing silver brethren.

See that your bread-and-butter is delicately thin, and that it and your cakes and sandwiches are served upon dainty doyleys of fringed damask, and if you provide two small plates, one with brown and one with white bread-and-butter, they will be found more convenient to hand about than one large plate.

When there is only a small party, the use of a luncheon tray, with three divisions, will save trouble in handing cakes, etc., and, be it whispered, these same trays are also convenient when your stock of cake is low, as small pieces of cake which could not possibly attain to the dignity of the cake-basket, will make quite an imposing appearance if cut in slices and arranged in one division of the tray, with some biscuits in the second and some carefully-rolled bread-and-butter in the third.

No doubt all my readers are acquainted with the silver or electro-plated handles which are now sold for attaching to cake and bread-and-butter plates, and a very convenient invention too; but should your means preclude your indulgence in these luxuries, do not, I pray you, be inveigled into buying the substitutes made of a sort of millinery arrangement of wire, ribbon, and artificial flowers. They soon become shabby and tawdry, while even when they can boast of pristine freshness the idea of ribbon and artificial flowers in such close proximity to eatables is to my mind at once incongruous and inartistic.

In cutting bread-and-butter or sandwiches, a loaf at least twenty-four hours old should be used, as it is impossible to obtain a satisfactory result with new bread. Servants, it may be noted, are as a rule far too liberal with the butter, which they often leave in lumps in any holes there may be in the surface of the bread; and should the bread be cut as thin as it ought to be, the butter will probably work its way through to the other side with very unpleasantly greasy results.

And now for the recipes themselves, and as savoury sandwiches—and, indeed, sandwiches of every kind—are always favourites we will have a friendly chat concerning them before passing on to cakes and biscuits.

For the foundation of all sandwiches, we must use evenly cut, and not too liberally buttered, bread, and be very careful that our seasoning is generously used, but with discretion. To crunch a lump of salt in a sandwich is by no means a pleasant experience.

Cress Sandwiches, though always appreciated, are simplicity itself. Carefully wash and thoroughly dry the cress, arrange on slices of bread-and-butter, sprinkle with salt, and, after pressing the covering slices firmly down, cut into two-inch squares and pile on a doyley, garnishing with tiny bunches of cress.

Watercress Sandwiches are made in the same way, using only the leaves, which must be most carefully washed in salt and water. Most people consider the addition of a little mayonnaise sauce a great improvement, and the following will be found a simple but excellent way to make it:

Rub the yolk of a hard-boiled egg very smooth, adding a good pinch of salt, a grain or two of cayenne pepper, and a quarter of a teaspoonful of made mustard; then add alternately, and drop by drop, lest the sauce should curdle, one tablespoonful of vinegar and two of salad oil, and one tablespoonful of very thick cream. Use a wooden spoon for the mixing, and do not make the sauce too liquid or it will ooze through the sandwiches.

Chicken Sandwiches, made with a little finely pounded chicken with a layer of watercress or lettuce and a little mayonnaise, are excellent.

Cucumber Sandwiches are always welcome in hot weather. Soak the slices of cucumber in some well-seasoned vinegar for two or three hours before using, turning it frequently. Cut the bread round each slice of cucumber with a small round pastry-cutter and garnish with parsley. A little dab of mayonnaise in each sandwich is a great improvement.

Shrimp Sandwiches are delicious. From a pint of shrimps, pick out a few of the largest with which to garnish your sandwiches, shell the remainder and allow them to get thoroughly hot over the fire (but not to boil) in a quarter of a pound of fresh butter, or two ounces of butter and two tablespoonfuls of thick cream, and a discreet seasoning of salt and pepper. Pound the mixture in a mortar until perfectly smooth, and then spread upon either white or brown bread-and-butter, and cut the sandwiches into rounds. A dariole or tiny pudding-mould with a crimped edge answers capitally for the purpose. Pile upon a doyley and garnish with the shrimps upon some fresh parsley.

Crab or lobster paste prepared in the same way but with the addition of a little mustard and vinegar, and no cream, makes excellent sandwiches.

Anchovy Sandwiches are made in the same way, using a good brand of anchovy paste instead of the shrimp mixture. If you have plenty of eggs at command, the hard-boiled yolks of two, pounded to a paste with two ounces of butter and a tablespoonful of anchovy paste, will make a superior sandwich.

Egg Sandwiches are filled with the same paste of pounded eggs, well seasoned, but without the anchovy; another ounce of butter or two tablespoonfuls of cream is an improvement in this case.

So much for sandwiches; the eight varieties I have mentioned will serve as a foundation from which clever housekeepers will devise numerous other kinds. Almost any scraps of shell-fish, game, or poultry, can be pounded and used as I have described, and if the seasoning is all that it should be, and the sandwiches are delicately made and served, they will always find some appreciative mortals to enjoy them!

And now to turn our attention to the cakes and biscuits, which I hope my fair readers will make with their own dainty hands, and thus ensure success, even if it be evolved from early failures.

Before passing on to the actual recipes, will they accept six general hints as to successful cake-making?

Firstly (as I have said before)—Give yourself time, and do not hurry or slur over any part of the process.

Secondly—Be sure your oven is at the right temperature before you put in your cakes. A quick oven is best for buns and small cakes, and a tolerably quick one to raise large cakes, and then the heat must be lowered and kept at a regular temperature to bake them through. When a cake has risen, lay a sheet of buttered paper over the top to prevent it blackening. To ascertain if a cake is sufficiently baked, plunge a clean knife or skewer through the centre; if it comes out clean and dry the cake is baked, if sticky, it requires further baking.

Thirdly—Be very careful that your cake-tins or moulds are thoroughly clean and well greased. Line your plain tins with well-greased plain paper, not printed. The tins for small cakes such as queen cakes should be sprinkled with flour and castor sugar after they are buttered.

Fourthly—Use only the best flour, and see that it is well dried, sifted, and warmed before using. Clean currants and sultanas with flour on a sieve; this not only cleans them but prevents them from sinking in the cake.

Fifthly—Before commencing to mix your cake, be sure your tins are ready, and that you have round you all your ingredients weighed and prepared, so that you may not have to leave your cake unfinished while you fetch something you have forgotten. All cakes but those made with yeast should be baked directly the mixing is finished.

Sixthly—Do *not be disheartened if your* first attempt to make a new cake is a failure. We too often forget that success is frequently the outcome of many failures.

Before giving any recipes for fancy cakes, let me advise you to give the following recipes for " Sally Lunns " and " Tea Cakes made with yeast," a trial.

For the former, mix half a teaspoonful of salt in a pound of flour, and add *three table-spoonfuls* of sugar. Melt half an ounce of butter in half a pint of new milk, and when milk-warm pour it over half an ounce of German yeast. Add a well-beaten egg and a little grated nutmeg. Stir lightly into the flour with a wooden spoon, cover with a cloth and set it in a warm place to rise; then bake from fifteen to twenty minutes in a quick oven. Some well-greased hoops are best to use for baking Sally Lunns, and the cakes should be brushed over with some beaten egg before they are quite baked. To serve, split each one into three slices, toast a delicate brown, butter and cut each slice in two, place together and serve on a very hot plate.

For *Tea Cakes* take two pounds of flour, half a teaspoonful of salt, quarter of a pound of butter or lard, and three ounces of sugar, with a few currants or sultanas if liked. Mix half an ounce of German yeast with three-quarters of a pint of warm milk and one egg. Rub the butter into the flour, and add the other dry ingredients, mix in the liquid part and knead lightly, and then set to rise. When sufficiently light divide into round cakes, place on a baking-sheet and allow them to remain a few minutes longer to rise again before baking. They will require from a quarter to half an hour in a good oven. They may either be split open, buttered, and eaten while hot, or toasted in the same way as Sally Lunns. The great culinary authority, M. Soyer, recommends that after toasting cakes or hot buttered toast, each piece should be cut through separately and then placed together, as when the whole is divided at once the pressure needed to force the knife down to the plate, forces the butter into the lowest slice, which is often swimming in grease while the upper slices are comparatively dry.

And now we will turn our attention to a few cakes which I can cordially recommend. Let us take *Cherry Cake* to commence with. For this you will require six ounces of flour, three ounces of butter, three ounces of castor sugar, two eggs, the grated rind of half a lemon, two ounces of crystallised or glacé cherries and a teaspoonful of baking-powder. Slightly warm but do not oil the butter, beat it to a cream with the sugar and lemon, add the eggs, well beaten, then the flour and cherries (cut in halves), and lastly the baking-powder. Whisk thoroughly, pour into a paper-lined tin and bake from three-quarters to half an hour. Another plan is to bake the cake in a Yorkshire pudding tin, and when baked to cover the top with pink icing, made with the white of an egg beaten up till fairly liquid but not frothy, and mixed very smoothly with sufficient icing sugar to make a smooth paste. You will find the readiest way of doing this is to use a wooden spoon on a dinner-plate, holding the bowl of the spoon with the fingers; a little practice and patience are needed to make the icing perfectly smooth, but remember one lump spoils the appearance of the icing. Add a few drops of cochineal and a few drops of vanilla flavouring, and spread the icing evenly over the top of the cake with a paper knife or dessert knife; a steel one must not be used. Take off any drops that may run over the sides of the cake and divide it in two pieces while the icing is wet, then dry at the mouth of the oven.

For *Orange Cake* take the weight of three eggs in butter, sugar and flour, the grated rind and strained juice of an orange, or two, if small, and a teaspoonful of baking-powder. Make and bake the cake in exactly the same way as the preceding one, but if iced, use white icing, or colour it with a little grated orange-rind and juice, using orange-juice to flavour it.

Madeira Cake is made in the same way and with the same proportions, but the orange is of course omitted and some finely-sliced lemon or candied peel substituted as a flavouring, or a little essence of vanilla.

For various kinds of cake you cannot have a better foundation than by taking the weight of as many eggs as you wish to use, in flour, butter and sugar, and then adding the various flavourings and a teaspoonful, more or less, according to the number of eggs, of baking-powder.

Desiccated cocoanut makes a nice change if *Cocoanut Cake* is desired, or, if you do not mind the trouble of grating it, the fresh cocoanut is of course superior. After the cake is baked brush the top over with a little white of egg and scatter some of the cocoanut upon it.

Twelve delicious little *Rice Cakes* may be made by taking one egg and its weight in sugar and butter, half its weight in ground rice and half in wheaten flour. When mixing add the rice after the flour, and also a few drops of flavouring or the grated rind of half a lemon. Bake in small tins in a quick oven for ten minutes. If two or more eggs are used and the other ingredients increased in proportion an excellent cake can be made.

Almond Buns are also nice. For these take half a pound of flour, six ounces of butter, six ounces of castor sugar, four ounces of almonds blanched and chopped, and a teaspoonful of baking-powder. Mix together the butter, sugar, eggs and flour, add the almonds and baking-powder last, form into buns and bake on a buttered tin for twenty minutes.

Queen Cakes are always favourites but require careful making and the proper heart-shaped tins to bake them in. Prepare the tins as previously directed by buttering them very thoroughly and sprinkling with castor sugar and flour. Then take three eggs, their weight in fresh butter, sugar, flour, and currants, and the grated rind of a lemon. Cream the butter and sugar together, add the eggs, fruit, and a pinch of salt, then the flour and half a teaspoonful of baking-powder, and lastly a small wineglassful of good brandy. Whisk thoroughly, shake off any loose flour or sugar from the tins, fill them three parts full of the mixture and hit each one sharply on the table before putting in the oven. Bake for twenty minutes.

Genoese Pastry is also popular, but cannot be made in a hurry. Take half a pound of butter, half a pound of castor sugar, half a pound of flour, the yolks of two eggs and the yolks and whites of two more eggs, and half a teaspoonful of baking-powder. Mix thoroughly, spread evenly over sheets of buttered paper placed in Yorkshire pudding tins, smooth over with a knife dipped in boiling water, and bake twenty minutes in a moderate oven, but keep the cake a pale brown colour.

While it is baking prepare some icing as directed for cherry cake, using the two whites of egg left over from the cake. Divide into two portions on two plates, colouring one pink and leaving the other white; flavour the former with a little raspberry syrup, or juice from some jam, and the latter with vanilla, lemon, or a little maraschino liqueur. Dissolve half an ounce of grated chocolate with two tablespoonfuls of water and stir it over the fire till thoroughly smooth and liquid, adding two or three lumps of sugar. If you have not a forcing bag with which to ornament your icing, or if you are not an adept in the use of it, provide yourself with a few crystallised cherries, blanched almonds, chopped pistachio nuts, and pink and white comfits with which to decorate your cakes. How they shall be decorated I leave to your own artistic minds to decide—only reminding you that almonds, pistachio nuts or a neat pattern of pink and white icing, or a border of alternate pink and white comfits are most suitable for decorating chocolate icing, while cherries and pink sugar look best on white, and almonds and white sugar on pink. A very speedy and effective decoration is to sprinkle white grated cocoanut on your pink cakes, and a mixture of pink (coloured with cochineal) and pale green (coloured with spinach juice) on white icing, using a mixture of all three colours on the chocolate. The study of the cakes in some high-class confectioner's will help you here. When the cake is baked lift it by the paper on to a clean pastry-board, remove the paper, divide each slab of cake across, and then split it open. On one piece put raspberry jam and press the other half upon it while hot; on another marmalade, on the third apricot, and on the last strawberry or pineapple. Pour over the apricot cake your chocolate icing, and while still hot cut into strips about two and a half inches wide, and then cut again slantwise across the strips so as to form diamond-shaped pieces. Then place them at the mouth of the oven to dry, while you proceed in the same way with your other cakes. Be careful to use your pink icing with the red jam, and white with the yellow. When partially dry the decorations must be added, otherwise they will not adhere to the icing, and then the cakes must be again dried until the icing will not take the impression of the finger when pressed upon it.

Scotch Shortbread is a favourite with many people, though hardly to be commended to the notice of dyspeptic sufferers. The following recipe for it, given to me by a Scotchwoman, will be found a very good one.

One pound of flour, four ounces of ground rice, one pound and a quarter of butter, three-quarters of a pound of sugar, a little candied peel, and a pinch of salt. Beat the butter to a cream, add the sugar, and very gradually sift in the flour and rice; work with the hands till quite smooth and divide into six pieces. Put each piece on a sheet of paper and roll out to the thickness of half an inch, prick it all over, lay on it the pieces of candied peel, pinch the edges, and bake in a moderate oven from twenty minutes to half an hour.

Fancy Biscuits can be made at home, and will be found quite equal in taste and appearance to the more expensive kinds sold in the shops. Care must be taken that the oven is not too hot as they will not look well if they are browned; and the flour and sugar used for them must be very finely sifted and thoroughly dry. To make four varieties of these biscuits at once, take one pound of fresh butter and cream it with half a pound of castor sugar, and add two well-beaten eggs. When well whisked divide the mixture into four basins. Divide also a pound of fine flour into four parts. To the contents of the first basin add a quarter of a pound of flour and two tablespoonfuls of ground ginger. Mix well. Turn on to a floured board, roll out to the thickness of a quarter of an inch, cut out with a small pastry-cutter or the top of a wineglass, place a piece of candied peel or a preserved cherry on each, and bake on a sheet of buttered paper laid on a baking tin for about twenty minutes. Proceed in the same way with the second portion, but instead of the ginger add the grated rind and juice of an orange, and if needed, a tablespoonful more flour. To the third division add half a teaspoonful of vanilla flavouring, and ornament the top of each biscuit with a little pink and white icing after baking. If the biscuits are made stiff they will keep their shape well in the baking, and may be cut into various fancy patterns such as ivy leaves, stars, diamonds, etc. Ivy leaves with the veins put on in white or pink icing are very pretty. To the last basin add one ounce of finely-chopped almonds, and make the biscuits oval in form with two strips of blanched almonds on the top. Walnuts may be used instead of almonds, in which case I should make the biscuits in the shape of a half walnut shell with half a peeled walnut on the flat part. These would require to be made very stiff. Chocolate icing is very nice to put on vanilla biscuits.

And now space warns me that our chat over the tea-table must come to an end. I hope that the few simple recipes I have given will be found both good and economical. Too economical perhaps for some of my friends, but I would remind all who wish for richer cakes that in the many excellent cookery-books, both French and English, now published, they will find recipes which cannot fail to win their most cordial appreciation. Yet in all humility I venture to hope these few hints of mine may win a meed of fainter praise from those who, appreciating dainty cookery, have yet to study economy in their household management.

HOME-MADE BISCUITS IN SWITZERLAND.

 N almost every country it is the fashion to have some particular sweetmeat at Christmastide. In England we have the inevitable and indigestible mince-pie and plum-pudding, in France the *galettes*, the *sucre de pomme*, and various dainty *gâteaux*, in Italy the *panna montata* with its accompaniment of *cialdone*, and in Switzerland a host of very delicious and ornamental biscuits.

Now, just as it is the fashion in England for every member of the family to have a hand in the mince-pie making or give a stir to the Christmas-pudding, so in Switzerland is it considered the proud duty of every housewife to lay in her store of biscuits at Christmastide for the whole year round.

To those English girls who would like to supplement their mince-pies with an inexpensive and very tasty novelty, I send the following recipes of home-made Swiss biscuits:—

SCHENKELI.

Ingredients.—Three ounces of butter, eight ounces of sugar, four eggs, one pound of flour, lemon-peel or almonds.

Beat the eggs and sugar together for at least a quarter of an hour, then add a pinch of salt. Shred up the peel of half a lemon or almonds (three ounces) and add to the above mixture. Melt the butter in a pan and also add it to the above. Take the pound of flour and work it by degrees into the mass until a thick paste is made. Knead the paste well with the hands, cover it lightly with flour, then roll it with the hand until it is the thickness of a finger. Cut the rolls of paste into pieces of about four inches, and fry them in a pan of boiling fat, letting them swim in the fat until they have assumed a golden-brown colour.

These biscuits can keep for about three months, and are very good eaten with wine. This quantity should make about seventy biscuits.

A more economical schenkeli may be made by taking two eggs instead of four and replacing the butter with lard. A little milk may be added if the paste is too thick, and a pinch of baking-powder should be mixed with the flour.

KÜSSENS.

Ingredients.—Quarter of a pound of ground chocolate, quarter of a pound of ground sugar, four whites of eggs.

Beat up the whites of eggs with the chocolate and sugar until a reasonably thick paste is formed. Take a buttered paper and on to this drop teaspoonfuls of the mixture. Bake in a moderate oven for a quarter of an hour.

ROSINELI.

Ingredients.—One pound of flour, quarter of a pound of currants, half a pound of butter, four yolks of eggs, half a pound of moist sugar.

Moisten the flour with the warmed butter and the well-beaten yolks of the eggs. Add the currants and sugar. Drop the mixture from a spoon on to a white buttered-paper, leaving space between each to allow the biscuits to spread. Bake in a slow oven for a quarter of an hour.

FASTNACHTKÜCHLI.

Ingredients.—Six eggs, six spoonfuls of milk or cream, two spoonfuls of moist sugar, flour.

Mix the eggs, milk, and sugar together, with a pinch of salt. Beat well for about ten minutes. Pour in the flour little by little until a thick and rather dry paste is made. Work the paste well and then let it remain over-night in a covered pan. Then form from the paste little round balls about the size of a walnut. Roll these balls out until they are round and flat and as thin as possible. Fry in swimming, but not too hot, fat.

MAILANDERLI.

Ingredients.—Half a pound of flour, quarter of a pound of butter, six eggs, quarter of a pound of sugar.

Work the butter and sugar into the flour, and then add the rind of half a lemon finely shredded. Take two whole eggs and four yolks and a little milk (two teaspoonfuls), and work fast and well until the dough is smooth. Roll the dough to the thickness of a quarter of an inch. Cut with a knife into small squares or forms, smear over with the yellow of an egg, and bake in a hot oven for about a quarter of an hour.

BASLERBRAUNS.

Ingredients.—Half a pound of almonds, three-quarters of a pound of chocolate, four eggs.

Chop the almonds up very fine and add the ground-up chocolate. Take the whites of the eggs and beat them up into a snow with the above ingredients. Cover the kneading-board with white moist sugar. Spread the dough out to half an inch in thickness. Cut into forms. Butter the baking-tin well, lay the biscuits thereon, and bake in a hot oven.

KÜMMELS.

Ingredients.—One ounce of carraway seeds, one pound of flour, quarter of a pound of sugar, quarter of a pound of butter, three eggs.

Mix together the flour, sugar, and carraway seeds. Stir into this mixture the butter, well beaten, and the eggs, well whisked. Roll out the paste. Shape the biscuits in round forms by means of a knife or cutter. Brush them with milk. Bake in a moderate oven for about a quarter of an hour.

SANDKÜCHLEIN.

Ingredients.—Half a pound of butter, three yolks of eggs, one ounce of sugar, half a pound of flour.

Beat the butter, and then little by little stir in the three yolks of eggs, then by degrees the sugar, and lastly the flour. From this paste little round masses must be formed, smeared with egg-yolk, and baked in a hot oven.

REISKÜCHLI.

Ingredients.—Four eggs, half a pound of butter, half a pound of powdered sugar, one pound of rice flour.

Beat the butter well and then stir in the sugar and flour. Beat the eggs for about ten minutes, and moisten the above mixture with them. Roll out the paste and shape into round cakes. Bake in a slow oven for about a quarter of an hour.

ZUCKERBREZELN.

Ingredients.—Half a pound of flour, quarter of a pound of butter, quarter of a pound of sugar, one egg.

Mix the flour, butter, sugar, and egg together. Work well into a paste. Cut out in little forms, smear over with egg and moist sugar, and bake in a hot oven.

MACAROONLIES.

Ingredients.—Half a pound of almonds, three-quarters of a pound of moist sugar, four whites of eggs, one spoonful of flour.

Grind the almonds up finely. Add the sugar. Mix the above with the beaten whites of eggs and the flour. Work into a stiff paste. Take a sheet of paper, well buttered, and lay the mixture thereon in little round heaps. Leave it to rest over-night, and bake the following day in a moderate oven.

PFEFFERNÜSCHEN.

Ingredients.—Half a pound of sugar, four eggs, eight grammes of allspice, four grammes of cloves, lemon-peel, flour.

Stir up the sugar lightly with the four eggs and the allspice (or cinnamon), add the clove powder, the peel from half a lemon finely shredded, and as much flour as possible to make a good firm dough. Roll the dough out to the thickness of half an inch, cut into figures, lay on a well-buttered baking-tin, and bake until they are light golden.

ZIMMETKÜCHLEIN.

Ingredients.—Half a pound of flour, quarter of a pound of sugar, quarter of a pound of butter, fifteen grammes of cinnamon, sour cream or milk, three eggs.

Mix the flour, sugar, and cinnamon together. Add one whole egg, two yolks of eggs, and sufficient sour cream to make a firm dough. Roll out and form into round biscuits. Strew over with moist sugar and egg-yolk. Bake in a moderate oven.

ZUCKERSTANGEN.

Ingredients.—Half a pound of sugar, half a pound of butter, half a pound of flour, four yolks of eggs.

Mix the sugar, butter, flour, and eggs together, and work into a stiff paste. Roll out to the thickness of a finger. Cut into figures five inches long. Lay on a flour-covered baking-tin, and bake in a hot oven.

ZIMMETSTERNE.

Ingredients.—Six eggs, one pound of sugar, thirty grammes of cinnamon, lemon-rind, one pound of flour.

Stir the eggs and sugar together for at least half an hour. Add the cinnamon, the rind of a lemon finely shredded, and the flour. Work the mass well together, roll out the paste, and cut with a star-shaped cutter. Leave the biscuits to rest over-night, and in the morning lay on a buttered baking-sheet. Bake in a moderate oven.

GEDULDS BISQUIT.

Ingredients.—Five eggs, quarter of a pound of sugar, three ounces of flour.

Stir up together the five yolks of eggs and the quarter of a pound of sugar. Work the five whites of the eggs into a snow. Add the flour. Spread the mixture on to a baking-sheet and bake in a moderate oven.

BREMERBROT.

Ingredients.—Four eggs, half a pound of sugar, orange and lemon peel, quarter of a pound of almonds, half a pound of flour.

Stir up the sugar and eggs into a light mass, add the lemon-peel, orange-peel (half a lemon and half an orange), and almonds finely shredded, then stir in the flour by degrees until a paste is formed. Form with a spoon into little long rolls. Place on a flour-bestrewn baking-sheet. Bake until they are golden.

DIFFERENT WAYS OF MAKING AND SERVING FRENCH PASTRY AND CAKES.

As I write I have in my mind's eye the tempting-looking chocolate and coffee *éclairs* that most high-class confectioners display. But these high-class confectioners are not to be found in all towns, to say nothing of the numberless small country places where any variety of that species is unknown, and yet it is often here that hostesses are at a loss to find something a little out of the common with which to regale their guests at the small social functions in which most people find enjoyment. Chocolate *éclairs* are universal favourites with old and young, and yet they are seldom to be seen where the refreshments provided are home-made. Let no one say, " How absurd to try to make these delicacies from written instructions ! " a remark, I must own with regret, that I should not be surprised to hear, for truly in many of the recipes one reads the quantities are vague, and the length of time required for cooking often left to one's imagination, while whether the oven should be hot, cool or moderate, is a point apparently not worth consideration. I can only suppose that in these days of cookery schools and County Council classes scattered all over the country, writers think details are superfluous. And yet generally it is the details which make or mar not only the recipes, but many other things in life. Want of detail, then, shall not be laid to the charge of this paper, and if attention be paid to that, I feel sure I can promise my readers success.

Personally my experience is that French pastry is easier to manipulate than puff pastry, and it is a great deal more digestible and not any more expensive, though cheapness cannot be claimed for it ; but there are occasions when it is necessary to launch forth a little in the matter of expense.

Before giving the actual recipes I should like to say a little about weights and measures. My reason for doing so is this : a little time ago, in speaking to a friend with whom I was staying, about the usefulness of *reliable* recipes, she remarked, " I do wish that in giving quantities the American plan of measuring in cups and spoons was followed instead of always employing weights and scales, for it frequently happens that the latter are not available in houses of modest means," and she went on to say that her scales were far too cumbersome to weigh anything under pounds, and that as she often had to do her own cooking when anything special was required (for her *ménage* consisted of two inexperienced domestics), it was a great boon and a real help if cups and spoons replaced scales. " A word to the wise is sufficient," and I made a mental note that henceforth in writing cookery articles I would always give the equivalent for avoirdupois weight. I shall carry out my resolution by beginning the reform to-day. After this digression we will come back to the subject in hand.

French Pastry.—Five ounces (five table-spoonfuls not heaped up) of pastry flour, two ounces (two tablespoonfuls) of castor sugar, three ounces of butter (one ounce is a piece the size of a walnut), half a pint of water (one tumblerful), a quarter of a teaspoonful of salt, one teaspoonful of flavouring of any kind, three small eggs. Take a saucepan of the capacity of two pints, put in the water, butter, salt and sugar ; when boiling fast sift in the flour with one hand and stir vigorously with a wooden spoon with the other. Remove from the fire and heat well until the lumpy-looking mass becomes perfectly smooth ; when this is accomplished add the eggs one at a time (unbeaten). As each egg is added you will find the mixture again separates and has a lumpy appearance, but it will get smooth with beating and stirring. The lightness of the pastry depends entirely upon the beating, for it is in this process that the necessary air is beaten in. In passing I might say that we *stir* when we wish to mix, but we *beat* when a mixture depends upon the amount of air beaten in for its lightness. The flavouring goes in last, and then the pastry is ready to make up into any desired shape, the most popular being a roll. Take a dessertspoonful of the mixture and roll lightly with the hand on a floured board until you have a roll three and a half inches in length, and about two or two and a half inches in circumference. They should be free from cracks, and if made this size you will get at least fourteen *éclairs* from the amount of pastry I have given. Place on a slightly greased baking tin, and bake in a moderately hot oven until well risen and of a pale fawn colour. Twenty minutes is generally long enough for this ; afterwards they should be allowed to dry and become quite firm in a rather cooler heat for three-quarters of an hour. I must expatiate upon the baking, for it is so important. Many people can make, few can bake, and I think most will agree with me, that the latter needs far more experience than the former.

If the oven for French pastry be too cool at first, it will not rise properly ; and when it has risen be careful not to move it until the surface is firm to the touch ; if the cold air (which is much heavier than hot air) is allowed to fall upon it before being set, the weight of it will cause the pastry to fall irretrievably. Now we have the reason for never banging the oven door. Therefore a moderately hot oven for first twenty minutes, and a more gentle heat for rest of time. To be very exact, 350° F. to begin with, and 300° to finish. When cooked enough the pastry should be crisp and of a pale brown colour. Sift on to a sieve or place round a plate to allow the steam to escape from underneath, and when cold finish them off with whipped cream or custard inside and icing on the outside.

The rolls must be split open with a knife, a spoonful of cream or custard nicely flavoured inserted. If the cream is unobtainable make a custard as follows : One tablespoonful of cornflour, one cup of milk (half pint), one tablespoonful of sugar, two eggs beaten, flavouring. Mix the cornflour smoothly with the milk, add sugar and eggs. Stir over a gentle heat until quite thick. Turn on to a wetted plate and when cold, use. This is a very good substitute for cream and not much trouble to make.

Icing for coating.—Eight tablespoonfuls of icing sugar, two tablespoonfuls of coffee essence, four tablespoonfuls of water. Put coffee and water into a small saucepan and then stir in the sugar. Stir over the most gentle heat until the icing is smooth and thick enough to coat the back of the spoon. By coating the spoon I mean the icing should only just run off, for if too thin it looks poor and unfinished, and if too thick the pastry lacks the professional appearance it should have. The icing may be varied by using the juice of a lemon or orange instead of water and

coffee ; if chocolate icing be preferred, allow one ounce of chocolate, Fry's soluble is best, to half a small cup of water, boil until dissolved, and add sugar as before, flavour with vanilla, and use. Instead of making the *éclairs* into rolls, they look very pretty made in the shape of meringues. Tea-spoons must be used for shaping, and being smaller they will only take forty minutes to cook ; of course, the finishing off is the same.

Victoria Sandwiches.—These are most superior and, as far as I know, are only to be obtained at one well-known confectioner's in the West End. Make the pastry exactly as for *éclairs*, except that the sugar and flavouring are left out and a little more salt added. Make up into rolls and brush each over with a little beaten egg, bake until crisp. When cold, split open, have some mustard and cress washed scrupulously clean, place some inside each roll with a teaspoonful of good salad-dressing and a boned sardine. Serve daintily on a folded napkin garnished with parsley. Watercress, shred lettuce, or any other green-meat may replace the cress, while it is hardly necessary to remind my readers that any cooked fish, hard-boiled eggs, or finely-cut pieces of chicken will find as much favour as the sardine.

A very favourite sweet which one often meets with abroad and occasionally in England is a *Gâteau à la Princesse*. It is so pretty that I really must give the readers of the " G. O. P." the benefit of the recipe.

Gâteau à la Princesse.—Make some French pastry as directed for *éclairs* and drop it in rounds about the size of a halfpenny on to a greased baking-tin. If a forcing-bag and pipe are at hand, put a tablespoonful of the mixture into it and force it out sharply ; this will ensure the drops being of a uniform size. Do not have them too large. Bake for half an hour. The little cakes look much nicer if brushed with beaten egg before being cooked. Take a round of sponge cake (or short crust not rolled too thin) as large as a breakfast plate. Dip each cake into syrup (which I will give instructions for presently), and arrange in a circle on the flat round of cake. It must be done quickly and a strainer used for dipping the cakes into the syrup. This makes them adhere to the foundation besides giving a brilliant surface. Place two more rows on the top of this until you have formed a kind of wall with a well in the middle. Whip half a pint of thick cream flavour and sweeten to taste, pile it high in the middle and decorate with few dried fruits. Custard may be used instead of the cream ; whichever is employed it must be piled high to give a handsome appearance to the dish, which should be served on a round silver dish.

Syrup for coating. —Three-quarters of a pound (three teacupfuls) of loaf sugar, a quarter of a pint of water (one cup). Put sugar and water into a saucepan, and when dissolved boil briskly over the fire until on dropping a little into cold water it sets ; use *at once*, as it very soon goes sugary. When taken from the fire it is an excellent plan to plunge the saucepan into another utensil containing hot water. This prevents the syrup getting sugary or crystallising. Stir as little as possible for the same reason. While the sugar and water are boiling skim if needful ; it depends entirely upon the sugar whether there is little or much scum. Inferior sugar throws up a good deal ; cane sugar is the best to use.

There is another kind of pastry which is much more like cake both in appearance and texture. It is made with the following ingredients : Three large eggs, four table-spoonfuls of good flour, five tablespoonfuls of castor sugar, three tablespoonfuls of butter (melted), pinch of salt, flavouring. Put the eggs into a good-sized mixing-bowl, whisk in the sugar, place the basin over a pan of hot water and whisk until the mixture is quite thick and light in colour. It will take at least twenty minutes to get it the right consistency ; the heat from the water helps the eggs to thicken more quickly. The flour and butter go in alternately. They should not be stirred in but folded in with a few turns of the whisk. Have ready a small Yorkshire pudding tin greased and lined with unprinted paper. Pour the cake into this and bake in a moderate heat for about thirty minutes. Turn out upside down on to a sugared paper. Remember that, if the oven is not the right heat, this, like French pastry, will not rise

properly. It should be the colour of a sponge cake when finished and one and a half inches thick. It is much nicer for cutting up when stale, and does not get dry even if kept for longer than a week. This is a great advantage when one wishes to get forward with the making of the fancy cakes. The same advantage cannot be claimed for French pastry, which cannot be too fresh. To finish off the flat cake, cut with a sharp knife into small squares or diamonds, coat with chocolate, coffee or lemon-icing entirely so that the cakes are completely hidden beneath it ; on the top of some place half a blanched almond, on the rest a cherry or star of angelica, or anything that presents itself for decoration.

So far I have said nothing about the ingredients used, but as it is a matter of importance as far as the success of these

recipes is concerned, I will conclude with just a few hints worth remembering.

Flour.—This must be of good quality, and the tests by which you can distinguish superior from inferior flour are that a good flour is always perfectly dry and is of a yellowish tinge, smooth to the touch, free from all trace of grittiness, and lastly the smell should be pleasant.

Butter ought to be fresh, but if salt butter be employed, wash it in a basin of cold water first and dry in a floured cloth.

Eggs need not be touched upon, as very few people think of using a stale egg.

Icing Sugar.—This is best procured from a confectioner, and should not cost more than fourpence per pound, at the outside fivepence. This, like flour, should be perfectly smooth after passing through a sieve.

A. M. B.

FRUIT PUDDINGS.

By the Author of "Summer Puddings," "Savouries," etc.

So many people get tired of the ordinary way of serving fruit simply stewed or as a tart, that I hope the following collection of recipes of different and dainty ways of utilising fruit may be used to vary somewhat the monotony of a wholesome article of diet.

Apple Pudding.—Six apples peeled and cut up in pieces, one quince, half a teacupful of water, two tablespoonfuls of sugar, the rind of half a lemon, one teaspoonful of lemon juice and a piece of butter the size of an egg. Put all into an enamelled pan and stew to a soft pulp and rub through a sieve. If the apples have been cooked very soft and are free from lumps, then it is not necessary to put them through a sieve.

Into the pulp stir three eggs, well beaten, a quarter of a pound of stale bread or cake crumbs grated, a dash of nutmeg, and two tablespoonfuls of milk. Pour into a tin mould previously well buttered inside and dusted with crumbs and bake in a good oven for quite an hour, turn out and serve with fine sugar over the top.

Apple Soufflé.—Butter the outside of a pie-dish and cover with pastry made as follows—

Six ounces of flour, three ounces of butter, two teaspoonfuls of sugar, and the yolk of an egg. Rub butter, sugar, and flour together, then mix to a paste with the beaten yolk and a little water. Roll out in the usual way, cut to the size of your dish, cover, and put into a good oven to bake, and slip off, and then you

have a dish of paste. Meanwhile peel and core one and a half pounds of apples, and stew them with a quarter of a pound of sugar and juice and grated rind of half a lemon till quite soft ; then stir in half-a-dozen ratafia biscuits and a penny sponge cake crumbled down, the yolks of two eggs and a drop of water. Cook on the fire again for a minute or two, then pour into the pastry-dish and spread over the top the whites of the three eggs beaten to a stiff froth with a tablespoonful of sifted sugar, dust sugar on the top and ornament with ratafia biscuits and preserved cherries to taste, then place in a nearly cold oven to slightly brown.

Apple Fritters.—Make a batter of a pint of milk, two well-beaten eggs, and flour enough to make a thick batter. Pare, core, and chop up into small pieces six apples, mix into the batter and fry in spoonfuls in boiling lard deep enough to cover the fritters. Fritters can also be made by slicing pared and cored apples, dipping them into thick pancake batter and frying them in butter.

Apple Dumplings.—Six apples pared and cored, six ounces of dripping, one pound of flour, one teaspoonful of baking powder, one quarter of a teaspoonful of salt, two ounces of sugar.

Put flour, powder, and salt in a basin, rub in the dripping lightly, then make into a stiff paste with water. Divide into six pieces, roll out and place an apple on each, fill up cores with sugar and work paste round each apple till covered, brush over with milk, place on a greased tin and bake from half an hour to three-quarters.

Apple Meringue.—Stew six apples pared and cored till soft, then stir in a small piece of butter. When cold add a cup of grated bread-crumbs, the yolks of two eggs, a tip of salt, sugar to taste, and a small cup of milk. Butter a dinner plate, cover it with short crust or puff paste, make a fancy border, and bake till done. In the middle pour the apple batter, and heat up. Take the whites of the eggs, beat stiff with half a teacup of fine sugar

and a few drops of essence of lemon, pile on the top of apples to cover them, place in oven to set but not to brown. Sprinkle pink sugar over the top and serve hot or cold.

Apple Pudding (American).—One quart of milk, four eggs, three cupfuls of chopped apples, the juice of a lemon and half the grated rind, nutmeg to taste and a pinch of cinnamon, one quarter of a teaspoonful of carbonate of soda dissolved in a little vinegar, flour enough to make a stiff batter. Beat the yolks of the eggs very light, add the milk and seasoning, then the flour ; stir hard for five minutes, then beat in the apples, then the whites of the eggs beaten to a stiff froth, and lastly mix the soda well in. Bake in two square shallow tins, buttered, for one hour. Cover with a buttered paper when half done to prevent it hardening. Eaten hot with a sweet sauce.

Apple Meringue Pudding.—One pint of stewed apples, three eggs (yolks and whites beaten separately), a half cupful of fine sugar and one dessertspoonful of butter, one teaspoonful of nutmeg and cinnamon mixed, one teaspoonful of lemon juice. Add sugar, spices, butter and yolks to the apples while hot, pour into a buttered dish and bake for ten minutes. Cover while still in the oven with a meringue made of the stiffly-beaten whites, two tablespoonfuls of castor sugar and a little almond essence. Spread it smoothly and quickly, close the oven again and brown slightly. Eat cold with cream and sugar.

Apple Omelette.—Six apples, one table-spoonful of butter, nutmeg to taste, and a teaspoonful of rose-water.

Stew the apples as for sauce, beat them smooth while hot, adding the butter, sugar and nutmeg. When perfectly cold put in the yolks beaten well, then the rose-water, and lastly the whites whipped stiff ; pour into a warmed and buttered pie-dish. Bake in a moderate oven till delicately browned.

Brown Betty.—One cupful of bread-crumbs, two cups of sour chopped apples, half a cupful of sugar, a teaspoonful of cinnamon, and two tablespoonfuls of butter chopped into small bits.

Butter a deep pie-dish, put a layer of apples at the bottom, sprinkle with sugar, cinnamon and pieces of butter, then crumbs, then another layer of apples, sugar, and so on till the dish is full, having crumbs on the top. Cover closely and bake in a moderate oven for three-quarters of an hour, then uncover, sprinkle with a little sugar and brown quickly.

Apple Batter Pudding.—One pint of rich milk, two cups of flour, four eggs, a teaspoonful of salt, a quarter of a teaspoonful of soda dissolved in hot water.

Peel and core eight apples, and arrange them closely together in a pie-dish. Beat the above batter till light and pour it over the apples and bake for one hour in a good oven. Unless the apples are very sweet, the cores should be filled up with sugar.

Apples and Tapioca.—One teacupful of tapioca, six juicy sweet apples, a quart of water and some salt.

Soak the tapioca in three cups of lukewarm water in a pan, put the pan back on the range and let it just keep warm for several hours till the tapioca becomes a clear jelly. Peel, core, and pack the apples together in a dish, fill the centres with sugar, cover and steam in the oven, then put the tip of salt into the tapioca, and pour it over the apples, return to the oven and leave till quite cooked—about an hour. Serve with cream. If there is any objection to the appearance of the pudding, then a beaten white of egg can be spread over it just before removing from the oven.

German Apple Tart.—One and three-quarter pounds of apples, quarter of a pound of dates.

Peel, core, and cut the apples into small pieces, stone and quarter the dates, and put them in a pan with a very little water and stew till soft. Then stir in two tablespoonfuls of sugar, one ounce of butter, one teaspoonful of ground cinnamon, half a teaspoonful of ginger. Beat smooth, then turn out to cool.

Make a short crust of half a pound of flour, two ounces of castor sugar, one teaspoonful of cinnamon, a small teaspoonful of baking powder, and a quarter of a pound of butter. Rub all together and work into a dough with the yolk of one egg and half a teacup of milk. Divide the dough into three pieces, roll out for bottom and sides a little thicker than the piece for the top. Line tin, fill up with the apple mixture, smooth on top, then lay third piece of crust over it, pinching the edge to the side crust, then bake in a moderate oven for half an hour. Beat the white of egg to a stiff froth, sift in two ounces of castor sugar, a drop or two of lemon juice, and then spread evenly on top of the tart when nearly cool, and leave to set.

Apple Mould.—One and a half pounds of apples, pare, core, and cut in quarters, put in a pan with half a pound of sugar and four ounces of butter. Stew till soft, but keep the pieces whole, lift them on to a sieve and let the syrup run into a dish. Butter a pudding-dish, line it with thin fingers of bread, lay in the pieces of apple, cover with slices of bread, brush over with egg, pour over some syrup, and bake in a moderate oven for three-quarters of an hour. Turn out and serve with sauce.

Apple Charlotte.—One and a half pounds of apples, peel, core, and cut up, and put on to stew with very little water and three ounces of sugar. When soft rub through a sieve, then put back into the pan, add four ounces more sugar and simmer till thick, taking care not to let the pulp burn.

Cut some stale bread into fingers, dip into melted butter, and arrange them round a well-buttered pudding mould, lapping one edge over the other and pressing firmly down, cover the bottom with rounds of bread in the same way, shake in some bread-crumbs, fill up with the apples, place more rounds of bread on the top, put into the oven and bake for an hour. Turn on to a dish, let it stand a few minutes, then draw off the mould and dust sugar over. By allowing the mould to remain a little, there is less danger of it sticking.

Before leaving the recipes for apples, I would like to give an excellent way of stewing. Pare the apples, quarter them, take out the cores, and cut the quarters into thin slices, then put them into a pan, put sugar over them to taste, shake it down through the fruit, then put a piece of white paper over, tucking it well round the edges to keep in the steam, then put on the lid, and set the pan at the side of the fire and shake occasionally till it heats.

The steam generated by the moisture of the apples is quite enough to prevent burning, and if care is taken in shaking the pan well there is no fear of burning. Stew slowly till soft. By using no water, the flavour of the fruit is much finer and the apples become a clear jelly and are most delicious to taste.

Gooseberry Fool.—Take a quart of green gooseberries, put them, after topping and tailing them, into a pan with four ounces of loaf sugar and stew them as directed for the apples—without water. When soft, rub them through a sieve, and then stir into the purée half a pint of thick cream, stir all together, add more sugar if required, then when cold pour into a crystal dish. Garnish with whipped cream on the top.

Gooseberry Pudding.—One pint of nearly ripe gooseberries, six slices of stale bread toasted, one cupful of milk, half a cupful of sugar, and one tablespoonful of melted butter. Stew the gooseberries very slowly so as not to break them. Cut your bread to fit your pudding-dish, toast the pieces, then dip while hot into the milk, then spread with butter, and cover the bottom of the dish with some of the pieces; put next a layer of the cooked gooseberries, sprinkle with sugar, then put more toast, more fruit and sugar, and so on till the dish is full. Cover closely and steam in a moderate oven for half an hour. Turn out and pour a sauce over it or eat with cream.

Gooseberry Flummery.—Take six ounces of rice and wash it, then put it into a pan with two pints of milk, and let it cook slowly till it gets soft and thick, then add two ounces of sugar and stir well. Let it get cold, then butter or oil a mould and cover the inside with a layer of the rice about an inch thick, leaving the inside empty till the rice sets. Then fill up with gooseberries stewed thick and soft with sugar and no water, and let it stand till quite stiff and cold. Turn upside down carefully—just before serving a little time—and draw off the mould carefully so as not to break the rice. This can also be steamed after putting in the fruit and served hot with custard sauce.

Flummery of Currants.—Take two pints of red currants, squeeze them and take the juice, add a little raspberry juice, and add three-quarters of a pound of loaf sugar and six ounces of rice flour to it; cook all over the fire and stir continually. Boil for five minutes, then pour into a mould which has been dipped in cold water. Let it stand till cold and set, then turn out.

Raspberry Mould.—Have a mould—a plain one—or a small bowl lined with strips of stale bread, packing them closely together. Then have some raspberries stewed with enough sugar to sweeten them, pour into the mould, cover the top over with fingers of bread, seeing that the mould is quite full, put a plate or saucer on the top with a weight on it and set away till cold. Then turn out. This is all the better for being made the day before it is required so as to give it time to soak up all the juice into the bread; then it is a pretty pink shape. Any kind of fruit—juicy—can be used in this way, but raspberries or red currants are the nicest.

Lemon Pudding.—Take two tablespoonfuls of cornflour and wet it with a little cold water, then add boiling water to make a thick starch, add five spoonfuls of sugar, the juice and grated rind of two lemons and the yolks of two eggs well beaten. Pour into a dish and bake for ten minutes, then heap the stiffly-beaten whites on the top, dust with sugar and brown very lightly in the oven for a few minutes.

Compôte of Oranges.—Pare the rind of three large oranges, cut the fruit across into halves, removing the pips and white skin and pile the fruit in a glass dish. Boil the thin rind with half a pint of water and six ounces of loaf sugar, till the syrup is clear and thick, then strain it over the fruit. Garnish with little spoonfuls of whipped cream.

Pear Meringue.—Take a dozen and a half pears, peel them and put into a pan with sugar and a very little water and stew till tender, but avoid breaking them. Lift them carefully and arrange them neatly in a glass dish. Boil up the syrup with more sugar till thickish, add a drop or two of cochineal—pear syrup is always rather a dull colour without it—and pour over the fruit. Take the whites of three eggs and whip them very stiff, add six spoonfuls of castor sugar, spread roughly over the pears and brown slightly in the oven or with a salamander.

Rhubarb Cheesecake.—Stew a bunch of green rhubarb till soft, then beat it smooth with a fork, draining nearly all the syrup away. Add to the pulp the juice of two lemons, grated rind of one, a scrape of nutmeg—if liked—and sugar to taste, then add three well-beaten eggs. Have a pie-dish lined with pastry—or a deep plate will do—pour in the mixture and bake in a moderate oven for three-quarters of an hour. Serve cold.

Prune Pudding.—Half a pound of prunes. Stew till soft, then remove the stones and add sugar to taste, then the whites of four eggs beaten stiff, put into a dish and bake to a pale brown.

Orange Fool.—Juice of four sweet oranges, three eggs well beaten, one pint of cream, sugar to taste, and a very little cinnamon and nutmeg.

Put all into a pan and set it on the fire till the mixture is as thick as melted butter, keep stirring, but do not let it boil, then when a little cool pour into a glass dish. Serve cold.

Queen's Mould.—Skin and cut into small pieces enough young rhubarb to fill a quart measure, put into an enamelled pan with one and a quarter pounds of sugar, the grated rind and juice of half a lemon, and twelve almonds blanched and chopped; boil fast and skin and stir till all is a rich marmalade, then add half an ounce of gelatine dissolved in two table-spoonfuls of boiling water. Rub a mould with oil, pour in the rhubarb, and set aside to cool and set. Turn out and serve with cream.

Rhubarb Scone Pudding.—Make a plain paste of half a pound of flour, two ounces of butter, a dessertspoonful of castor sugar, a pinch of salt, one teaspoonful of cream of tartar, half a teaspoonful of baking soda. Rub all together, then add enough sweet milk to make a nice firm paste, roll out the size of a dinner plate, butter the plate, lay the paste on and ornament the edge, and bake in a moderate oven till done. Fill the middle with stewed rhubarb—any stewed fruit is good—cover with the whites of two eggs beaten stiff, dust the top thickly with castor sugar and return to the oven to let it get a pale brown.

CONSTANCE.

46

CAKE-DECORATING.

By LINA ORMAN COOPER, Author of "We Wives," etc.

No paper on cake-making and cake-baking can be considered complete until some directions with regard to icing the same are given. In the Summer Part I spoke about the former branch of this kind of confectionery. To-day I would tell how to beautify the home-made cakes we have prepared.

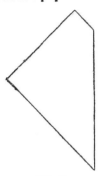

FIG. I.

We all know what a professional air hangs over a well-iced erection. But there is no reason why amateurs should not be equally successful.

There are two kinds of icing, called respectively, soft and royal. For both of them we require proper icing sugar, carefully and patiently sifted through a wire sieve or piece of muslin. This initial operation must on no account be neglected or hurried over. On the perfect smoothness of the sugar much of our success will depend. Roughly speaking, it takes one pound of sugar to ice the top of a pound cake properly. It is impossible to say exactly, but at least that amount must be ready beside us.

If we desire to decorate our cake with soft icing, we put some of this sugar into a bowl, add to it the juice of a quarter of a lemon and then as much boiling water as is required to make it "mushy." If too much is added, we can thicken with the reserve we have in hand; so never put all your sugar at first into the bowl.

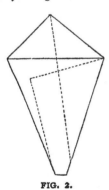

FIG. 2.

Take great care to beat this well; for thorough beating gives our icing that glossy and snowy look admired so much. When of a right consistency—something like cream—add whatever colouring is required. A squeeze of laundry blue ministers to its whiteness and is often necessary, though the lemon and beating may whiten it much. Sixpenny bottles of colouring liquids may be bought. If you prefer pink ice, a few drops of liquid carmine brings a blush to its cheek, or carmine mixed with yellow gives a salmon tinge, or bright green may be chosen. Whatever colour is selected must be added to the icing when the latter is liquid enough to run from the spoon. This soft mass can then be poured on to the cake, smoothed with a knife dipped in cold water, and set away to dry.

A variation of this icing is made with chocolate. For this we must put down three teaspoonfuls of grated chocolate to boil in a little water. It must be thoroughly smooth and melted before adding to the sugar. By this method we can regulate colour far better than by putting the dry powder with the dry sugar. It also ensures smoothness. A rule of thumb in this matter is about an ounce and a half of chocolate to three ounces of sugar. A

FIG. 3.

few drops of lemon-juice added to it helps to harden the same.

For royal icing no exact proportions can be given. Put one pound of well-rolled, finely-sifted sugar into the bowl and add some lemon-juice. Now pour right into it, without whisking, the whites of one or two eggs. Then, with the back of a wooden spoon incorporate together until all the sugar is converted into a quite stiff mass. Beat for at least a quarter of an hour if you want to have the icing really like satin.

When sufficiently stiff, sufficiently white, and sufficiently silvery, coat your cake over thickly and smoothly. Then come our last professional touches. We want to have stiff rosettes and crinkles and basket-work all over our cake. Or we want to put a name and date thereon. Well, for this part of the process confectioners use a kind of pump fitted with different sized nozzles. It costs about 12s. 6d. But we amateurs need not go to this expense unless we wish. A few sheets of stiff cooking paper—four can be bought for a penny—a case of different-sized noses, involving an outlay of a few pence more, and we can do all we wish.

Cut some paper, as per Fig. 1, with a blunt point and two sharp ones. Hold the blunt corner between your left finger and thumb and twist round until the two sharp points meet, and you have in your hand a conical-shaped bag (Fig. 2).

Insert one of your bought nozzles into the tiny opening at the tail, and you can manipulate your sugar at will. Rosettes are simply little dabs of icing forced into a lump.

Basket-work is represented with strands of sugar drawn from one point to another.

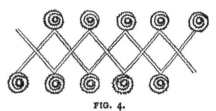

FIG. 4.

A row of waved icing top and bottom of this gives a nice finish, and the result would be as Fig. 5.

If the cake be covered with white icing, the roses may be pink and the trellis-work green, with a result infinitely pleasing to everyone. Or the icing can be chocolate with white basket and rosettes.

There is one very unprofessional method of icing which is nevertheless often successful and is very quickly done. For years I decorated my children's birthday cakes with it, to their satisfaction and delight. We lived in the country, so sometimes had to be satisfied with castor sugar. Beating up the whites of two eggs on a plate, with a pinch of salt, I used to add the sugar gradually until it no longer clung to the blade of my knife. Then I spread it smoothly over my cake, ornamenting it whilst wet with crystallised fruits—chopped cherries or rows of coloured sweeties. A few seconds in a cool oven "set" this perfectly, and the work was done. Of course, this way of icing was my own invention, like the white knights pudding, with a foundation of experience instead of blotting-paper.

Two things I must ask the printer to put in italics.

(1) *Be sure your icing sugar is passed through a sieve.*

(2) *Let your cakes be quite cold and very dry before attempting to decorate them, or dire will be the results.*

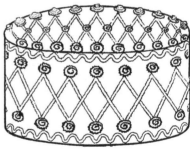

FIG. 5.

IN the present article I propose to have a little talk with girls about making sweeties. Yet I have no intention to discuss the making of toffee and similar delights. I am ambitious, and desire rather to deal with much more pretentious sweeties, such as marrons glacés and cream walnuts. These superior sweeties are not so very difficult to make if one knows how to set about the business; and if patience and care be bestowed upon them they are most excellent. Made at home, of the best materials, and eaten in reason, they are not unwholesome—indeed, marrons glacés are quite nourishing—yet they are so delicious that no one can help enjoying them. They are also particularly suited for presentation, and girls who can make them need never be at a loss what to provide as a Christmas, Easter, or birthday gift for friends or relatives who have a sweet tooth. If these dainties had to be bought they would cost a good deal, but made at home they would cost little money—only time and care. Therefore, it is well worth while to learn how to make them; and I am sure that girls who will pay attention and master the details of the process will be delighted with the result.

The making of sweeties, it will be understood, is not exactly cookery, and there are numbers of very able cooks who know nothing about it; also, it is not exactly confectionery, but it occupies a sort of borderland between the two. It is, however, most fascinating work; and as a girl said who not long ago experimented in it, "Boiling sugar is quite exciting—one never knows what is going to happen with it, and the twists and turns it takes are most unexpected. Yet when you do exactly as you are told things are sure to come right in the end, because the sweeties you spoil are almost as delicious as the sweeties that are a success, while one is at liberty to hand spoilt goods round for the benefit of the community." This is a very excellent statement of the case.

First, then, let us take marrons glacés, and it just occurs to me to say, "Do all girls know what marrons glacés are?" If, however, those who do not know will go to a high-class shop (the dainties are not sold by small dealers), and ask for marrons glacés they will have offered to them a number of dark-brown, shiny, queer-shaped balls, which look like chestnuts boiled and coated with varnish. That is exactly what they are, only the varnish is made of sugar, and the chestnuts are cooked; and their taste is most delicious. These marrons are suitable for private delectation, and for dessert. Placed on a fancy dish they constitute a most valuable addition to the dessert course. Yet the price usually asked for them is three shillings a pound, and there are not many in a pound!

Professional confectioners would probably regard with a little scorn humble individuals who proposed to dabble in the mysteries of sugar boiling with ordinary kitchen tools, and in a homely sort of way. They would say that it was necessary to have various utensils—a proper sugar boiler, a spatula, a saccharometer for testing the condition of the sugar, a marble slab, a drying closet, and so on. We propose, however, to dispense with these "necessaries." We shall attempt only sweeties which can be made with tools that are to be found in every kitchen. A saucepan will serve us as a sugar boiler, a tablespoon will do instead of a spatula, we shall let our common sense be a substitute for the saccharometer, and a pudding basin or greased plate will do for us in the place of a marble slab. Thus provided, we shall manage very well.

With regard to the saucepan. A correct sugar boiler is generally made of untinned copper. Francatelli, however, says that "a candying pan" should be made of block tin

measuring about fourteen inches by eight inches, and two inches deep; that the sides should be rather on the slant, with a small funnel-like tube in one of the angles or corners of the pan; and that if you require several of these pans for making any large quantity of candies, it becomes necessary to have the funnel-shaped tubes placed at different corners —on the right of one pan and the left corner of the other, so that when placed upon each other the excess of sugar may easily drain off. A pan of this description few people possess, but almost everyone has a block tin or a plain iron saucepan, and either will answer the purpose. An enamelled saucepan is not very suitable, it is so liable to burn; but perhaps the best of all (if we work with a closed stove) is an earthenware saucepan of the sort which are much more common than they used to be, and which dainty cooks always like because they can be so readily cleaned.

The sugar which we use must be of the very best: to attempt work of this sort with common sugar would be to court disaster. Therefore, we must have either the best lump sugar or the best granulated sugar. Icing sugar will not do at all. It is frequently made up with starchy matter, and this would entirely disturb our reckoning. Moreover, when the best loaf sugar is used for home-made candies, it is quite allowable to dispense with clarification, and this saves much trouble. To clarify sugar is to boil it with white of egg and water, and to keep removing the scum as it rises until it is quite pure. If, however, we get the best refined sugar, it is purified from the first, and it is scarcely likely that amateurs would improve it by trying to make it better.

When experimenting in work that is unusual, it is always wise to try our hand, in the first instance, with small quantities; then if we come to grief we do not have very much waste. Let us, therefore, suppose that we have collected the materials required for our experiment, viz., a block tin or a very clean iron saucepan, a pound of sugar, a jug of water, two pounds of fine sound chestnuts, a basin containing brown sugar, a few thin wooden skewers about eight inches long, and a good fresh lemon. How shall we proceed?

Make an incision in the outer skin only of the chestnuts, and boil them till they are tender, but not soft. At this early stage it is very easy to make a mistake. We want to keep the chestnuts whole, and if we boil them even a little bit too much, they break into small pieces. Yet if they are not boiled enough they will not taste as they should. We have to try them to see if they are ready. When they have their skins on it is, of course, not easy to ascertain their condition. Therefore many people roast instead of boiling the nuts. Roasted chestnuts do not smash so easily as boiled chestnuts. Others put them into boiling water, take off the outer skin, then boil them again until ready, after which the inner skin is removed. The best way, however, is to boil them till tender, then put them into cold water for a little while, and afterwards peel away both the inner and the outer skin. In any case, it has to be remembered that it is most desirable to keep the nuts whole, and that when cooked they readily fall to pieces. Therefore they should be taken up when under cooked rather than over cooked. They are sufficiently cooked when a knitting needle will pierce them easily. The time required depends on the size and quality of the chestnuts: it would not be safe to try to give information on this point, because nuts vary so much. The slit made in the skin before commencing proceedings will prevent bursting. Also, girls should be careful to procure the best

nuts. Inferior nuts have an internal division; the finest sorts are quite entire when shelled, and the difference is important.

The chestnuts being ready, our next point is the sugar. We put a pound of sugar and half a pint of water in the saucepan and set it on the fire. Until it is dissolved we may stir it; but after it has boiled we must on no account stir it, and we must move it about as little as possible. When it has boiled ten minutes we dip a fork into it. So long as the syrup, after it has run off, leaves only a drop of syrup behind, we let it continue to boil. In a minute or two, however, when we hold it in the air, there will be seen a long silvery hair. Now we say that the candy begins to "hair," and this is a term that is to be borne in mind. We now squeeze into it the juice of a lemon, or add about two tablespoonfuls of vinegar: watch it still more closely and let it boil rapidly for a minute or two. We have ready a cup of cold water, and keep dropping therein a morsel of the syrup. When it sets in the water like toffee, so that it leaves the finger clear, and so that a morsel tried with the teeth feels brittle, it has arrived at the degree of boiling known as the "crack" or the "snap," and is ready for our purpose.

What we now have to do is to dip our boiled chestnuts into the hot candy, and turn them over in it to coat them entirely, and dry them in the air. We shall have to be very quick in our movements, because, though the sugar is in good condition now, it will very quickly deteriorate. Now it is quite clear and bright, but it will very shortly begin to get thick and look white; then it will not do for our chestnuts. However, in order that we may make the most of it while it is right, we must have everything ready to our hand; the brown sugar in a bowl (we shall have to stick the skewers which hold the chestnuts in this, so that the syrup may dry without having the varnish spoilt), and the skewers with a chestnut stuck upon each laid by the side. We must put the pan containing the syrup either in a vessel containing boiling water, or in some situation where it will not cool readily, and if we can get a friend to come and help so that we may get as many chestnuts varnished as possible before the sugar cools, so much the better. The varnish is to be very thin, and there is to be no portion of the nut left untouched. We dip the nut upon the skewer in and out of the syrup, taking care to coat it entirely, and we let it remain on the skewer till it is dry. If we can so arrange matters that we can give the chestnuts a second coating they will look so much handsomer.

Expeditious though we may be, it is to be expected that before our task is complete the sugar will be unworkable. In this case we may put the saucepan on the fire and melt it. It cannot, however, be melted more than once, for it will get hard, and when remelted it will be very liable to burn. Therefore, what we have to do is to make all the haste we can in coating the chestnuts in the first instance. After a little practice we shall probably be dexterous enough to glacer all our chestnuts whole. While we are new to the business, however, we shall probably smash a few. Yet even under these circumstances we need not have waste. All we have to do is to boil up what syrup remains with a little cold water "to the ball"—that is, until a little dropped in water can be gathered up like a soft ball. Pour this boiling hot over the nuts and stir until cool; then turn upon a well-greased dish. Broken into knobly pieces this candy will be much appreciated by the young folks.

If we wished we might substitute another sort of nut for chestnuts in following the above method, and the result would in every case be satisfactory. Walnuts, filberts, hazelnuts, almonds, Brazil nuts, might all be glazed thus. They would not need to be boiled previously, as chestnuts do, but they would have to be dried, and in some cases peeled. Therefore they would need to be made ready two or three days before being used, and left exposed to the air. If glacé when newly taken out of the shell their oiliness would prevent success. Fruits also, such as oranges, greengages, plums, cherries, dates, and even red currants, may be treated thus, and would be a great delicacy. In short, if girls once manage to make marrons glacés properly they can make a dozen sweeties in the same way.

When making marrons glacés experienced cooks frequently put the chestnuts in liquid syrup after cooking them, and boil the syrup afresh every day for three or four days, so as to permeate them with the sugar before varnishing them. The method is superior undoubtedly; but it is much more troublesome and tedious, and when the other way is successfully managed, the result leaves very little to be desired. The repeated soaking in syrup is more necessary when the chestnuts are roasted than it is when they are boiled. Having managed our chestnuts, we now proceed a step further, and attempt what are known sometimes as creamed walnuts, sometimes as caramel walnuts, sometimes as American walnuts. Kiln-dried walnuts would be the best for the purpose; but if these cannot be had, the kernels must be at least thoroughly dry. Pick the walnuts from the shell, divide them into halves, and keep the halves as whole as possible. Boil the sugar and water as before, until a fine silky hair hangs from the end of a fork that is dipped into it. Of course, do not stir it after the sugar has melted. Watch it closely, and in a second or two try it by dropping half a teaspoonful into a little cold water. If it can be taken from the bottom in a ball lift it from the fire and set it in a dry place (not in water that is, or on the sink, but in an airy place) to cool. Do not stir it or shake it whilst it cools, and try its condition by dipping the tip of the finger into it. It should look like thick clear syrup, and have only a sort of skin on the top. Stir it with a spoon for a few minutes. It will gradually begin to look milky, and will grow thicker, until it looks almost like lard. When it is so stiff that it can no longer be stirred with a spoon, put the hands to it, and knead it as one would knead dough, until it is a smooth compact mass. If it grains, or looks as if it were turning to sugar again, it has been boiled too long, and must have water added to it and be boiled all over again. If it does not thicken as described, but remains liquid, it has not been boiled long enough, and should be set on the fire again. If it is as it should be, it is what is called fondant, or French icing, and can be used for many purposes. Also, if pressed into a jar and covered with oiled paper it will remain good for weeks.

We must suppose, however, that we do not want to keep it but to use it for the walnuts. In this case we take a piece of the fondant about the size of an almond and work and press it with the hands till it is a sort of oval roll, and then press two halved walnuts firmly in on each side and show a little of the paste between the halved nuts. Afterwards put them where they can dry till the cream is quite firm. If preferred, the paste can be used for what is known as fondant icing. Doubtless girls have often seen at the confectioners cakes made of Genoese paste, and coated with icing of various colours which added greatly to their appearance. This coating was simply fondant. We may put three separate tablespoonfuls of the fondant in three cups, set these one at a time in a saucepan of boiling water, and keep stirring until it runs. If the fondant were melted

without being stirred, it would simply return to syrup; stirring it, however, causes it to remain creamy. When melted we can put either a few drops of cochineal to it to make it pink, a little saffron water to make it yellow, or a little melted unsweetened chocolate to make chocolate icing. The addition of strawberry juice and cochineal would produce strawberry icing; the addition of raspberry juice and cochineal would make raspberry icing; of grated orange peel and juice, orange icing; lemon peel and juice, lemon icing; liqueur of any sort, liqueur icing; and white icing by leaving the fondant unchanged. A handsome dish of iced cakes may, of course, be made by colouring the cakes differently, but in this case the various colours would need to be finished off one at a time, one colour being disposed of before the other was melted, otherwise the fondant would stiffen, and so cease to be workable.

To melt the fondant we simply put a little in a cup, set it in a saucepan of boiling water over the fire, and stir it till it looks like cream. If we did not stir it would return to syrup. To use the fondant as icing we simply take the melted sugar and pour it over the cakes, so that it covers their surface entirely. If it stiffens while we are at work, we dip a knife in boiling water and make it smooth by means of the knife. If it is not stiff we can simply move the cakes slantwise backwards and forwards to let the cream run over the surface.

Nuts daintily prepared according to the method described will keep well if put into a closely-covered box where the air cannot get to them. When to be presented to friends they should be put into a fancy box made of paper or stiff cardboard, and tied with China ribbon. When packed in an open box each nut should be placed in a little envelope of white paper, and this will keep them from sticking together.

It is very much to be hoped that girls who try to make these sweeties will not be discouraged if they do not succeed perfectly the first thing. As already stated, sweeties are not difficult to make; but also they are not easy. If they were they would not be so expensive to buy. Of the two sorts I think the walnuts are the easier, because the syrup of the marrons gets out of condition so speedily, and we have to be so very quick with them. A little practice, however, soon conquers difficulties. Of the girls I know who have experimented in these sweeties, the one who was the most successful carried on her operations in her own bedroom with a spirit-lamp and a small saucepan. She said that when she was not quite sure of herself she could get on best when no one was watching her. I fancy other girls have the same feeling.

There are a good many very sensible individuals who have a great objection to sweeties of every sort. They say that sweeties bring on toothache and produce indigestion, and that to spend money upon them is wasteful. Yet we invariably find that young folks like sweeties. When they have a little money to spare, and can reconcile it with their consciences to indulge, they are almost sure to possess themselves of a packet of dainty morsels, and these are reserved for private consumption or handed round amongst friends, according to the disposition of the owner.

The sensible individuals are quite right in their opinion, however. Common sweeties are very harmful; and it would be difficult to calculate the mischief they do. They not only injure the teeth and disturb digestion, but they destroy the taste for plain wholesome food, and make those who are in the habit of eating them fastidious and unhealthy. Their unwholesomeness is, however, very largely increased by their impurity. Manufacturers are now so skilful that, when they lack principle, there is no knowing what they will do, and

individuals who trust to them never know what they swallow. Here is a remark taken from the *South Kensington Science Handbook on Food*, which contains a little information concerning the flavourers used for cheap confectionery, which throws light on the subject so far as sweeties are concerned :—

"There are now known many artificial products, chiefly the so-called compound ethers, which resemble very closely indeed in taste and smell the natural flavours of certain fruits. The so-called essence of jargonelle pears is a spirituous solution of the acetate of amyl; it is employed in flavouring confectionery, especially pear drops. Unfortunately it is used too freely, and is seldom sufficiently pure for this purpose. Apple oil is chiefly valerate of amyl, pine-apple oil is butyrate of ethyl and butyrate of propyl, and grape or cognac oil is a mixture of several compound artificial ethers. Many other flavourers of similar character have been artificially prepared. They are much used by the makers of cheap confectionery."

To know that chemicals of this description enter into the composition of sweeties does not make us long for them. When consuming them we consume we know not what. If we could procure sweeties that were absolutely pure we should probably find that they were tolerably harmless, and so we might gratify our taste with impunity. Pure sugar, pure natural products, cannot be particularly hurtful. Also, it is very certain that pure sweeties are in the market. The only objection to them is that they are generally costly. If we could obtain pure sweeties without paying such high prices for them, it would indeed be agreeable. The advantage belonging to the dainties we have been talking about is that they are not only harmless, but cheap. They cost very little though they are so delicious, and all they want are care and patience. The probability is that they never will be low in price because they call for so much attention, and so far as I know they cannot be made by machinery. Care and patience, however, and perseverance also, *must* be bestowed upon them.

Some time ago an American writer named Mrs. Helen Alice Nitsch, now unfortunately no longer living, devoted a good deal of attention to the subject of candy making. It was through reading what she had to say that I first began to take an interest in them. This Mrs. Nitsch was, however, besides being a clever cook, a very good woman, and she had a great desire to help women to help themselves. She had a notion that girls might make dainties of this sort and of other sorts, such as jams, pickles, and home-made cakes, not merely for pleasure but for profit, and she induced a good many women to manufacture dainties and sell them for a fair price in their own neighbourhood. One wonders whether it would be possible for English girls who want a little pocket money to do the same thing. At any rate, it is very certain that there are a good many housekeepers who very much prefer home-made dainties to what are known as "bought dainties." If girls could arrange to make goods of this kind at home in a thoroughly superior way, and get a sale for them, they might earn money very comfortably. At the present time there is no accomplishment known that is more universally appreciated and more useful than skill in cookery, and girls who are possessed of it never need be at a loss at least for employment. By simply using their fingers they may always make themselves useful wherever they are; and if, in addition, they could earn a little hard cash should the need for it arise, surely they need not object. The arrangement of the detail of business of this kind must, however, be made by girls themselves. The suggestions given here are intended only to put them in the way of doing the work.

PHYLLIS BROWNE.

WHATEVER the season, sweetmeats, especially high-class confections, are always in favour, most girls finding them delectable when sitting over the fire as when resting in a hammock.

I purpose telling the readers of the "G.O.P." therefore some delightful recipes which I guarantee will not only be reasonable in price, but will look professional enough to enable you to refill any empty bonbon boxes you may possess as acceptable presents for your girl friends. But you must be very careful to follow my instructions most minutely, for like most handiwork it is the attention to details that ensures success. As space forbids I can only give the two following dainties as examples of what may be accomplished at home. They are Marrons glaces and Marzipane varieties.

Marrons Glaces.—For these take one quart of chestnuts, and after removing the outer skin cover with water, boil gently till soft thirty minutes to one hour, depending upon the kind of chestnuts. The Italian chestnut is the best for keeping its shape. Peel very carefully and put into a pan with any broken pieces there may be on the top.

Make a syrup of one pound of sugar and a quarter of a pint of water, boil briskly for five minutes or until it threads; by which I mean the syrup will form a tiny thread on dipping the finger and thumb in cold water and then into the syrup. Let this cool and then pour over the nuts and leave for thirty-six hours in a warm place, or longer if more convenient. Lift the nuts out and drain. Now another syrup must be made of one pound of sugar, a quarter of a pint of water, and one pinch of cream of tartar. Boil quickly for seven minutes; this time the thread must be thicker, and if registered by the thermometer it would be 250°. Take off the fire and place the nuts in carefully, and merely bring to the boil. Stir the syrup most gently and then lift out and drain them. When dry they are ready.

Little paper cases make them look more dainty; they can be got at any large stationer's.

A few hints on making syrup I think are necessary here before going to the next recipe. The first point to attend to is the saucepan, which should be perfectly clean and of strong enough material to prevent the syrup being likely to burn, and for this reason enamelled saucepans are not to be recommended. Then care must be taken not to let the syrup grain, which is the technical term for syrup crystallising again. A clean paint-brush or piece of rag dipped in water to wipe the sides of the pan. Skim carefully. Boil quickly, and do not stir, as stirring causes graining. For those who can afford a thermometer I should strongly advise its purchase; it simplifies the process of boiling syrup as it is much more accurate.

Marzipane Varieties.—Marzipane is made in various ways, but the recipe I intend giving is one that may be depended upon and will give satisfaction. One and a half pounds of almonds, two pounds of sugar, four eggs (whites only), half a saltspoon of cream of tartar, half a pint of water.

Make a syrup of the sugar, water and cream of tartar, boil for seven minutes in the same way as for marrons glaces. Stir in at once the ground almonds; if these be prepared at home the flavour is improved; those already prepared cost 1s. 4d. per pound, and answer very well. In either case add a few drops of almond essence and one teaspoonful of orange-flower water. Now put in the eggs, without beating; these must be stirred in off the fire and then returned to cook them slightly. You will find the quantities given make a large amount of marzipane; it may be considerably reduced, say to one-fourth, if desired. After the mixture is made, turn out on to a very large meat dish or marble slab (which is better) and work it with a wooden

spoon until it is cool enough to knead with the hands. When worked enough it should look and be of the consistency of a nice dough. The next thing is to divide the marzipane in three or four portions. Colour and flavour each differently—cochineal, coffee, vegetable sap green are all suitable, and one portion may be left its natural colour. Work the colours in most thoroughly, as a streaky appearance would spoil the whole effect. To make diamonds—take a piece of each of the colours and roll out about a quarter of an inch, damp each slightly with a little white of egg and place on top of each other. Rice paper can be bought quite reasonably at any good confectioner's. A small sheet of this damped and placed both at the top and bottom of the square of marzipane makes a professional finish to the diamonds. Leave an hour or two till quite dry, then with a sharp knife cut into slices half an inch wide and cut crosswise into diamonds. I must only give suggestions for several other varieties. Farced fruits, for example, farced being the term used to express stuffed; we will take French plums as an instance. Cut the plum carefully down the middle and remove the stone; cut a piece of marzipane about as large as a nut, roll in the palms of the hands till smooth and oblong, place right inside to show a little of the marzipane only. Cherries, raisins, etc., are all done in this way.

Another way to use the marzipane. Detach a piece of it as large as a filbert and roll again between the palms till smooth, and stick half a walnut on each side, or the walnut may be completely covered with the marzipane. Almonds may be used in the same way. Do not forget that all these goodies look much nicer if placed in small paper cases. Also when arranging them in rows with a little fold of white paper between each row. These do not by any means exhaust the sweets that can be made at home with profit and without undue labour.

SOME NOVEL METHODS OF USING STRAWBERRIES.

EW people know how very deliciously the flavours of chocolate and strawberries combine; here are a few inexpensive recipes, which are generally highly appreciated.

Strawberry Baskets.—Make a light cake batter with a quarter of a pound of flour, three ounces of castor sugar, two ounces of butter, two eggs, and half a teaspoonful of baking-powder; half fill little dariole moulds with it, and bake in a brisk oven. When cold scoop out the centre of each little cake, and put aside the crumb that is scooped out; now ice the outside of the cake lightly with chocolate icing, and fill the centre with hulled strawberries. Pile whipped and sweetened cream on them, and make a handle for the basket of a strip of angelica dipped in the chocolate icing. The pieces of crumb that were scooped out of the little cakes may be

lightly browned in a cool oven, and they are then delicious to serve with strawberries and cream.

Milk Puddings.—Any remains of cold milk puddings may be used thus: Lay some mashed and sweetened strawberries in a glass dish, over this put a deep layer of the milk pudding with which a few halved strawberries have been mixed. Pour a good custard over the top, or whipped cream may be used instead.

Strawberry Custard Tartlet.—Line a tartlet-tin with paste, fill it with a nice sweet custard, and here and there drop in a strawberry which has been hulled and dipped in sugar; bake the custard in the ordinary way.

Strawberry Blancmange.—Make a blancmange in the usual way, and when it is just on the point of setting pour into a mould, and drop into the mixture about half a pint of hulled strawberries, making them settle on different parts of the blancmange. When quite set turn it out, and garnish with strawberries and their leaves.

Chocolate Mousse, with Strawberries.—Prepare some chocolate mousse by dissolving a quarter of a pound of chocolate (Menier's is best) in two tablespoonfuls of hot water, stirring it over a gentle fire until a smooth paste is obtained; it should be of the consistency of thick cream; now lightly mix in a quarter of a pint of whipped and sweetened cream. Take some little custard glasses, and in each of these place crushed strawberries, sweetened and mixed with a little cream, to half fill the glasses; fill them up with the chocolate mousse, piling it up as high as possible.

Strawberry Icing.—This is very dainty for covering cakes; take six ounces of sifted icing-sugar and mix it with three tablespoonfuls of strawberry juice; stir this over the fire in a pan until just warm, and then pour over the cake. A cake iced with this icing is delicious if sliced evenly, and each slice spread with strawberries, crushed, sweetened, and mixed with a little cream; the cake is then built up again to its original form—of course this latter must be done before the icing is put on. ONE WHO KNOWS.

Apple Cream.—Take the pulp of one dozen large baked apples, and bruise smoothly with a spoon. Add the whites of two eggs well beaten up, and add powdered sugar by degrees until sweet enough, also a little brandy. It must be well beaten for a considerable time.

To Preserve Oranges.—Take the fairest and finest oranges you can get. If Seville oranges, grate them and steep them in cold water for three days, changing the water twice a day. Then put them down to boil in water, and lay a board on them to keep them down ; and as the water wastes, fill it up again with boiling water. This must be repeated until the oranges are soft enough for a wheaten straw to go through them. Then take them up, put them into a cloth, and lay them by till the next day. Then cut a small hole in the middle of each orange and carefully scrape out the seeds. Weigh the oranges and put them into white sugar, one pound to each pound of fruit, and enough water to wet it, in a preserving pan. Set it over the fire, skim it well, and when clear, put in the oranges. Let them boil until they look clear, and then put into glasses.

Orange Jelly.—Take the juice of ten China oranges and two lemons, a little lemon-peel, one quart of water, six ounces of sugar, two ounces of isinglass dissolved in a small quantity of water. Boil altogether and strain into shapes. A small quantity of saffron improves the colour.

Two Receipts for Cheese-cakes.—No. 1. Half a pound of sweet almonds, one ounce of bitter, blanched and pounded not too fine, yolks of five eggs well-beaten, three-quarters of a pound of white pounded sugar. These ingredients must not be mixed until just going into the oven. Half-an-hour bakes them. This quantity makes twenty small cheese-cakes. The paste round them should be thin and not very rich. No. 2. Blanch and pound finely four ounces of sweet almonds and a few bitter with a spoonful of water. Then add four ounces of pounded sugar, a spoonful of cream, the whites of two and the yolk of one egg well-beaten. Mix quickly and bake in a pretty warm oven about a quarter-of-an-hour. Cover the patty pans with light pastry, and don't fill them too full, as the almonds rise very much.

Prune Shape.—Stone one pound of prunes, blanch the kernels and boil them with the fruit, a little water, and two or three spoonfuls of port-wine, half-an-ounce of dissolved isinglass, and a table-spoonful of brown sugar. Put it into a shape, and when cold turn it out. A mould with a false centre answers best. Fill the centre with good whipped cream.

Irish Rock.—Blanch one pound of sweet almonds, one ounce of bitter. Pick out a few sweet almonds and cut them like straws. Pound all the rest in a mortar with one spoonful of brandy, four ounces of loaf sugar pounded and sifted, and half-a-pound of salt butter well-washed. Pound all together until the mass looks very white, and set it in a cool place to stiffen. Then dip two table-spoonfuls into cold water, and with them form the paste as much like eggs as possible. Place the eggs as high on a dish as possible, putting a small saucer *turned up* under the napkin, ornament with the cut almonds some green sweetmeats and a spray of myrtle. It is a very pretty dish.

SOME DAINTY SWEETS FOR SUMMER-TIME.

OUR young housekeepers will, we feel sure, delight in trying our suggestions for summer dishes, for when the fruits come in, when eggs are cheap, and cream plentiful, every amateur feels tempted in some degree to try what can be evolved from such delectable material. We may not actually invent

GATEAU STE. CÉLESTINE.

new things in cookery, but an imaginative mind can invariably evolve some new thing when there is an inclination to do so, and though there may be nothing specially new in the accompanying illustrations, the dishes have at least the merit of being tried and proven; they are not mere fanciful creations of the brain.

The first is a dish of dry meringues under a new form and name ; if left single they are known as *Little Loves,* but if joined together with cream or jelly between, they become *Egg Kisses.* You can have them either way.

To make them, beat until quite stiff the whites of three

"LITTLE LOVES" OR "EGG KISSES."

eggs, then lightly stir in a quarter of a pound of crushed icing-sugar and a few drops of any flavouring liked, either vanilla, almond or lemon. Divide the mixture into separate bowls and colour one portion pink by adding half a teaspoonful of cochineal. Sprinkle some sheets of white paper thickly with fine sugar, then drop teaspoonfuls of the meringue on these, keeping the colours apart; slip the sheets on to the oven shelves. The heat may be moderate at first for a few minutes in order to raise the meringues and make them crisp, but afterwards the oven door should be left open and the heat turned off. As soon as they are firm enough to handle, slip them on to clean papers with a sharp knife, and when quite cold store in tins. They must not be allowed to change colour in the oven.

The next is a cake which we have christened *Sainte Céles-*

LEMON TRIFLE.

FROTHED FRUIT SYLLABUBS.

out of the tin on to clean paper, and when cool split the cake and spread the lower half with a layer of currant jelly and whipped cream, replace the other half and cover with more jelly, then pile more whipped cream on **the top** making a ring border round the cake of ratafias. This is rather a nice cake, as may be imagined, and both these first dishes are suitable for afternoon tea. In place of jelly, ripe strawberries or raspberries could be used, adding plenty of sugar, and it should be borne in mind when whipping cream that it is made lighter as well as more economical by adding the whites of one or two eggs previously whisked to a froth thereto. Do not put much sugar with the cream.

The central illustration of our page represents *Frothed Fruit Syllabus*; the kind of fruit of course will vary according to what is in season. We can use pink rhubarb, green gooseberries, cherries, strawberries, raspberries, currants, red, white and black, plums, blackberries, etc. Make a syrup of sugar and water boiled together, half a pound of sugar and half a pint of water, then cook the fruit in this until it is soft and juicy. (It will be a better colour done this way than if stewed.) If there are skins and stones, rub the fruit through a colander, but the soft kinds will not need this. Half fill the glasses with fruit and syrup, then add a little thick cream to what remains and fill the glasses to three parts, on the top of all place a large spoonful of white of egg whisked stiff with sugar—this represents the "froth." Keep these glasses standing in a very cold place, on ice if possible, until required. They form a refreshing sweet to eat with biscuits for a light supper.

tine; it is after the pattern of the *Gateau St. Honoré* which some of our readers may have seen and tasted abroad.

The foundation of this is the ordinary jelly-cake mixture, namely, butter and sugar creamed together, a teacupful of each, the yolks of two eggs worked in with a little milk, then two teacupfuls of self-raising flour. Pour this mixture into a round baking-tin about two inches in depth, which has been well buttered inside and sprinkled with sugar. Bake in a moderately quick oven for forty minutes. Slip

SWISS CHARLOTTE.

Our fourth dish is a *Lemon Trifle*. Fill up the hollow of the glass dish and pile in pyramidal form with sponge fingers and soft biscuits. Next make a lemon cream by boiling together half a pint of water, a quarter of a pound of lump sugar, and the grated rind of a fresh lemon; stir in this the beaten yolks of three eggs, and an ounce of butter, also a dessertspoonful of cornflour wet with the juice of the lemon; bring all to the boil once more. Let this cool before pouring it over the cakes, and when all are quite cold, whip the whites of the eggs with three spoonfuls of sugar, and a teacupful of fresh cream, then pile this on the top. Decorate with a border of yellow flowers placed singly round the edge of the trifle.

The last illustration gives us a somewhat more substantial kind of pudding, but it is both simple and effective.

First of all, butter well the inside of a plain round mould, and line it with slices of Swiss roll cut about half an inch thick. Fit these in neatly, placing one slice at the bottom and also putting broken bits and a few ratafia biscuits in the middle hollow; next prepare a custard, using two fresh eggs and about a pint of boiling milk, adding as much sweetening and flavouring as seems desirable. Stir in this half an ounce of gelatine that has been previously soaked in cold water, and let this dissolve before pouring the custard into the mould. Take care, too, in doing this that the slices of roll are not lifted out of place, as the beauty of the pudding depends on these. Cover the mould with a buttered paper, then steam for an hour, and when quite cold, turn out and decorate with a little bright jelly on the top and a few macaroons.

Let cold sweets be really cold in summer-time; one way of cooling dishes when ice is not obtainable is to turn an earthen flower-pot upside down, standing it in a dish of water, and to set moulds or plates on this. It makes a very fair refrigerator.

L. H. YATES.

"CANDIES."

By the Author of "We Wives," etc.

EVER since an enterprising brother, intent on scientific research, found that a lump of sugar applied to the flame of a candle resulted in beads of crimson colour, candy-making has been a favourite pastime of ours. "Candle-beads," pretty as they look, are apt to taste of tallow and smoke. Sugared candies of other sorts are, or ought to be, free from such drawbacks.

Our "popped-corn parties" (*vide* THE GIRL'S OWN PAPER for April, 1896) could assemble all the year round if approved of. But our "candy club" only met at stated seasons. It was as a law of the Medes and Persians that butter-scotch (for instance) should only be made when the first blizzard powdered our wide prairie land with soft fleeces of snow. That raspberry-rock should be baked only when bluff and shoulder-ridge were pink with the wild cane. That "cream-toffee" and "honey-ball" should only make their appearance when a cow came into the dairy for the first time, or a hive of wild bees were rifled of their store.

If any reader of THE GIRL'S OWN PAPER is inclined to follow our family pattern and start a candy club, I would advise some such rules to be made. Sweets are apt to cloy when too often indulged in, and cookies are sometimes cross (at least they are in America). Of course the club should always provide sugar, fruit, and tins. Mothers, generally, do not grudge other flavourings and fire.

Most likely when this paper appears, every garden in "Eū-rope" will be rich in raspberries, or have just laid by a store of the seedy jam or crimson syrup. So I will begin by telling you how our candy club made

Raspberry Rock.—To every pound of lump sugar or refined molasses we allowed three-quarters of a teacupful of cold water. We boiled it until the syrup thickened, and "beads" of heat broke out on the surface. Very careful we were to keep stirring all the time, especially when the candy began to "crack."

We tried if it was done enough by dropping a little into a cup of cold water. When a "snap" followed and the droppings looked crisp and crinkly, we removed the pan from the fire and stirred in one of two things, either three dessertspoonfuls of jam boiled, with a little water, and run through a sieve, or as much raspberry acid. I will tell, at the end of this paper, how to make this acid. But, as our candy is popping and cracking, we must finish it up first. On the deal-table we always had some well-buttered plates. After stirring in the flavouring (and adding a few drops of cochineal, if needed, to improve the colour), we filled each with the hot syrup. It cooled slowly, and after a few minutes its face had to be scored with a knife, in diamonds or squares. The rock is too hard to break when cold, except with a sledge-hammer, unless this is done.

Some of the candy we used to "pull" into twists and true lovers'-knots. This is fascinating work, the feel of the soft, yielding, smooth stuff between one's fingers being especially delightful to a child, whilst well-boiled candy can take such pretty shapes!

The syrup or acid for this rock is made as follows:—It can be used as a delightful summer drink mixed with plain cold water. But it is (a brother's expression comes in here) "scrumptious," if added to a tumbler of "fizz," either soda-water or lemonade.

Take twelve pounds of raspberries. Put them into a pan, and pour over them two quarts of cold water, previously acidulated with five ounces of tartaric acid. Let all remain undisturbed for twenty-four hours, then strain through a flannel jelly-bag or piece of fine muslin, taking care not to bruise the fruit.

To each pint of this clear crimson liquid, add one pound and a half of finely-powdered sugar. Stir frequently. When quite dissolved, and after removing any scum that may have risen, bottle the syrup and store in a dry place.

This acid requires no boiling and will keep for a couple of years if required. It can be made from ripe strawberries in the same way, but, to my taste, the latter fruit is too luscious and the syrup lacks just the *soupçon* of tartness necessary.

Cream Toffee.—This is just a variation of the ordinary butter-scotch. To every pound of brown sugar, or molasses, we allowed a pint of thick cream. When the sugar boiled we stirred in the yellow, leathery stuff, instead of using mother's freshly-churned butter.

It was all boiled together until it "snapped," then turned into fanciful buttered tins and left till cold. Cream toffee is crisper and "shorter" than the ordinary stuff, but not quite as rich.

Butter Candy, heralded in, as it was, by the first snowstorm, was perhaps our favourite sweetmeat. It meant the beginning of stoves and hickory fires and winter sleighing. It meant the approach of long evenings spent in the pine-panelled kitchen busy with book or brush or plane. It meant earlier to bed and later to rise. It meant home lessons instead of school marms. So it was altogether suggestive of cosiness and cuddling and crooning and a great many other "C's"!

To make this, we always took half and half of butter and sugar. The browner the sugar the better the candy. It had to be boiled until clear and transparent, then poured into buttered paper. Some roughly chopped almonds sprinkled on it turned butter-scotch into almond candy. Or desiccated cocoanut strewn on its face masked it into cocoanut candy.

It was always stored in wide-mouthed bottles with tin tops. How long it lasted depended on how much we made, and on how many of the young fry were at home.

For "honey balls" we took half as much honey as butter and of course no sugar. We boiled until the "beads" appeared as in raspberry rock. When nearly cold, instead of "pulling" the honey candy, we rolled it into balls and set it aside to dry.

I think our candy club had one advantage many readers of this paper may fail to appreciate. Of course we had failures. Sugar "catches" easily, and burnt molasses is an abomination. But to our door sometimes came alarming looking squaws robed in buffalo and fringed with beads. On their backs always—we never saw a squaw unaccompanied in this manner—were one or two brown-faced, black-eyed, soft-skinned "papooses." What better way of hiding our failures (at the same time of propitiating the brave) than presenting a potful of "candy" to the dear things. They do not mind smoke, or tallow, or burn! A papoose with a cold potato in one hand and a bunch of burnt cream toffee in the other, is a sight to remember. And are there no wild Red Indians on the London streets? Whenever you fail in your candies call in the next little *gamin* that passes and see!

HOW TO MAKE AMERICAN CANDIES.

GIRLS who live in London, or any large town where American sweets are easily obtainable, will hardly care to take the trouble to make them. But many of our readers live in the country and remote places where these delicious sweets are never seen, and they may not object to trying their hands at the work.

These candies are so very pretty as well as excellent that they will come in very acceptably for dessert, be useful when you want to make a small birthday present, and be very nice for yourselves if you possess what is commonly called "a sweet tooth."

Yet another—no, two good reasons for learning to make them!

The American lady who taught me how these candies were made told me that, on one occasion, she had to take a stall at a bazaar, and it occurred to her to make quantities of these candies. This she did, putting them up into pretty little receptacles, and they sold capitally, a very good sum being realised by them.

There is a hint worth having for the next country bazaar at which you have to hold a stall, or at least to which you must contribute, and when you learn how quickly and easily the candies are made, I daresay you will use your knowledge practically. Then the next reason —one that will appeal to many girls who "wish to make a little money." If you live in the country where, as I say, these sweets are uncommon if ever seen, why not make them to sell? The more you make, the greater the profit. And, roughly speaking, if you sell the candies at three shillings a pound, which is quite a fair price, you will probably find that they have not cost you more than half that sum in materials. It would be worth trying, would it not? Now for directions.

The Foundation.—There is one foundation substance for American candies upon which changes are rung in the way of colouring, flavouring, and the mixing with it of nuts, etc., or the addition to it of fruit, nuts, etc. It is very important that this foundation— which, for the sake of clearness, I shall allude to throughout as the dough—should be well and carefully made, for the excellence of your candies much depends upon it.

You must procure some icing or confectioner's sugar, which is very much finer than castor sugar, and it is absolutely necessary that it should be quite fresh. If it is lumpy it is not fit to work with and you will not make good "dough." Break the white of an egg in one glass, and put an equal quantity of water into another. Put this into a basin and stir it with your sugar until of a dough-like consistency. The proportion of white of egg and water is two to each pound of sugar.

The next thing you require is a perfectly clean pastry-board or marble slab. If you like it, you can scrub a marble-topped wash-stand and use that. Many girls will be pleased to find by the way that they can make all these candies without a fire. A spirit-lamp for melting the chocolate is necessary if you have no fire, but that is all. Place a bit of dough on your slab and work it with your hands, using the sugar as if it were flour.

Candy Cherries.—Cut off a piece of your dough and make it into a thin long roll about half an inch wide. Take a sharp knife and divide it into small pieces. Take these pieces and roll them in your hands until they are like marbles. Those you want for chocolate creams you place aside to harden, but for cherries, etc., you use the marbles, as I shall call them, while they are soft. Get some glazed or crystallised cherries, slit them— without dividing them quite—and take out the stone. Press a small marble into the place where the stone was.

Cream Almonds.—Blanch your almonds, and cover them with dough. If you want to roughen the sugar up a little you can do so with a fork.

Walnuts.—Get the very best English walnuts, and, when shelled, do not remove the fine skin that is over them. Cut them carefully in half. If you have some that are broken do not use the bits for cream walnuts, as only perfect halves are of any use. Lay them aside and I will tell you later on how to use them. Now take two halves of your walnuts and put one on each side of a marble. Press together, and in so doing you will notice that the sugar comes out all round between the halves. Leave them to harden.

Cream Dates.—The dates must be fresh, and when procured slit down one side and the stone removed as in the case of the cherries. Put a marble into the place which was occupied by the stone, and, after pressing together, leave to harden.

Nougât.—Take your broken pieces of walnut and chop them up finely, adding almonds, pistachio nuts, and Brazil nuts. When all well chopped up small together stir these into some of the dough, this being best done in a basin, and it should be mixed up very thoroughly. When this is done place your dough on the slab and make it into long thin strips. Then cut it into pieces with a sharp knife.

Tricoloured Candy.—Take three pieces of dough—yellow, brown and red. (The colouring I shall describe later). Make each piece into a long, thin, narrow strip, and then lay the strips when on the board one over the other. This must be done very neatly, and, when completed, the edges smoothed off with a sharp knife. Cut into squares and leave it to harden. The squares can be about an inch square.

Crystallising.—This can be done to the almonds, cream walnuts, cherries and dates. Get some crystallised sugar and put some into a plate. Then put the cherries or whatever you want to crystallise into the plate, cover with another and shake it all up between the two plates. You can also take each cherry, etc., and simply press it down at the edge on crystallised sugar. Needless to say this must be done at once before the dough has begun to harden.

Colouring.—Colouring the dough adds to the effect of the candies, and sometimes, as with orange, you colour and flavour at one and the same time. All colouring must be done while the dough is in the basin. Colour one lump and put it aside, then another. Mix a lump with chopped nuts and also put

aside, and cut and use all these varieties while moist. For orange colouring add a very little grated orange peel and a little of the juice to the dough. Chocolate colouring, which flavours as well, is done with grated chocolate or cocoa powder.

Flavouring.—The flavouring of the dough is done in the basin. As will have been seen, orange (or lemon) colour and flavour at the same time as does chocolate. Grated cocoanut makes a variety in flavour. Pounded almonds mixed in with the dough are delicious.

You can make your marbles, of course, plain white and somewhat tasteless by leaving the dough as it is, or else you can make your marbles coloured, or containing chopped almonds, grated cocoanut or nougât.

Chocolate Creams.—Some readers may like to make these, so I will give you full directions. But they can be so easily obtained and are not so essentially American that probably they will not find such great favour as the others.

Rock chocolate, which has no sugar whatever in it, is necessary, and you must be most careful that you get it perfectly fresh. Break your chocolate into a cup and place it on top of a kettle filled with boiling water and which is kept boiling until the chocolate melts. This you can do on the most ordinary spirit-lamp. Do not stir this at all.

When the chocolate is completely melted, place your cup on the table and drop into the chocolate one hard marble at a table. Please note the adjective, for the dough marbles must be left quite to harden—which takes some hours before you cover them with chocolate. And if you use nougât or coloured marbles, or those flavoured with cocoanut, etc., make them into marbles while soft, but do not use for covering with chocolate until quite hard.

The way you take your marble out of the liquid chocolate is with two silver forks. You can drain the ball by passing it from one fork to the other. A better plan even than the forks is to make yourself a little wire spoon. Any wire will answer the purpose very well.

Every now and then you must place your cup over the boiling water which should be kept boiling for the purpose. Place your chocolate creams to dry on waxed paper, which you can easily get at any confectioner's. You can cover some of your nougât with chocolate, treating it exactly as you did the chocolate creams.

Lightness of touch and general daintiness are of the very greatest importance in the making of all these candies. If, in using a spirit-lamp, you find you cannot place your cup easily over the kettle, then use a saucepan. Put hot water in it, and place the cup containing chocolate in that *bain marie* fashion.

In packing candies to send by post, you should use fine paper shavings or waxed paper.

If you could but have seen the little basket full of candies my American friend gave me of her own making, you would feel tempted to try what you could do, and no doubt succeed quite as well.

SHORTBREAD.

Put one pound and a quarter of butter in a pan, and then add one pound of loaf sugar dust ; mix them well together, and then add four eggs ; mix well in as before, then add two pounds of flour, then roll the dough out, and cut them to the size you want them ; put a piece of peel on the top.

MADEIRA CAKES.

Put one pound of eggs in a pan, and add one pound of loaf sugar dust ; beat all together with a whisk till it gets a little thick, then add one pound of flour ; mix it in lightly with your hand ; add one or two drops of essence of lemon ; put white paper round, and bottom of the tins or hoops, then lay one or two pieces of peel and a few currants at the bottom.

TEA MILK SCONES.

Take two pounds of flour, add five ounces of butter ; rub it in as small as possible, then add half ounce of carbonate of soda and quarter of an ounce of tartaric acid ; rub them well in the flour, then quarter of a pound of loaf sugar dust, and quarter of a pound of currants ; rub them in as before, add about half a pint of milk ; then mix it, roll the dough out and fold it over two or three times, and then cut them to the size you want them.

JUBILEE POUND CAKE.

Take two pounds and a quarter of flour, then add half a pound of butter ; rub it in the flour very fine, add also one ounce of carbonate of soda and half an ounce of tartaric acid ; rub them in the flour as fine as possible, then add one pound of sugar and two pounds of currants, and rub them in the flour as before, and two ounces of mixed peel ; then add a pint and a half of milk and eight eggs, two or three drops of essence of lemon ; mix them.

LARDED TEA CAKES.

Take one pound of flour, six ounces of lard ; rub it well in the flour, then add two ounces of loaf sugar dust ; mix it in as before, then half a pint of milk ; make it into a dough, then roll it out and fold it three or four times, and cut them to the size you would like them.

FOREIGN CAKES AND SWEETS.

SUDELTORTE.

Ingredients.—Half a pound of butter, two eggs, half a pound of powdered sugar, half a pound of almonds, half a pound of flour.

Stir up all the above ingredients together, not forgetting to melt the butter and pound the almonds. Pour into a well-buttered tin and bake in a hot oven.

ZWETCHGENKUCHEN (*Plum or Greengage Cake*).

Ingredients.—Two pounds of blue plums or greengages, a quarter of a pound of sugar, cinnamon, two ounces of butter, ingredients for butter or dripping pastry crust.

Make a pastry of either dripping, butter or merely bread dough. Spread this out on a large tin. Halve and stone the plums. Place these as near to one another as possible on the crust. Strew over them breadcrumbs, cinnamon and sugar. Cut up some tiny lumps of butter and lay them on top. Bake in a warm oven.

P.S.—Like the apple cake, this plum cake may be made from simple bread dough, the plums laid on top and a cream of eggs and milk strewn over when it is half done.

PASTA NEAPOLITANA (*Neapolitan Cakes*).

Ingredients.—A quarter of a pound each of sugar, blanched almonds, butter and flour, two eggs, half a pound of icing sugar, half a cupful of preserved cherries, jam.

Rub the butter into the flour, pound the almonds and add to the flour, then mix in the two yolks of eggs. Roll out the paste, cut it in rounds, bake till light brown on a buttered tin. When the cakes are cold spread each with jam, place on top of each other. Beat the icing sugar and whites of eggs together. Ice the cake and decorate it with the preserved cherries.

KARTOFFEL TORTE (*Potato Tart*).

Ingredients.—Half a pound of sugar, six eggs, cinnamon, lemon peel, and half a pound of potatoes.

Mix the eggs and sugar well together, add, by degrees, the crushed potatoes with a flavouring of cinnamon and finely-shredded lemon peel. Pour the mixture into a form which must be first well buttered, and bake in a moderate oven.

PUDDING AL' ITALIANA.

Ingredients.—A quarter of a pound of Osborne biscuits, two ounces of macaroons, two ounces of candied peel, one ounce of sultanas, one ounce of blanched almonds, eight eggs, half a pint of cream (or milk), a small glass of rum. Powder up the biscuits, chop the peel, almonds and sultanas very fine, and mix with three whole eggs, five yolks, the cream and rum. Pour the mixture into a tin which must be buttered and lined with paper. Cook in a " bain marie " for about three-quarters of an hour.

PASTICCI DI RISOTTO (*a favourite Italian sweet*).

Ingredients.—A quarter of a pound of powdered sugar, half a pound of rice, a quart of milk, vanilla flavouring, egg and breadcrumbs, boiling lard.

Cook the rice, with the milk and sugar, over a gentle fire, and before it is quite done pour in some drops of vanilla. As soon as the milk has dried into the rice, retire from the fire and set it to cool. Form into round balls, cover with yolk of egg and breadcrumbs, and fry in boiling fat until of a nice brown colour.

Serve hot in a doyley with an accompaniment of fruit jelly or syrup. Any remains of rice may be used up in this way.

FOREIGN CAKES AND SWEETS.

ALTHOUGH no foreign country comes anywhere near England in its variety and perfection of cake and pudding-making, there are still some Continental recipes which I feel sure would prove a welcome change and addition to many an English table. Now that the fruit season is in full sway, it has occurred to me that some of the delicious fresh fruit cakes of Switzerland and Germany would be acceptable to those of our girls who superintend their own cooking and who are invariably pleased with novelties, especially if such novelties be cheap, simple and good.

The following recipes will, I trust, find favour with many a bonnie housewife.

KÄSE KUCHEN (*Cheese Cake*).

Ingredients.—Bread dough, or butter or dripping crust, half a pound of cheese, a breakfastcupful of cream or milk, two eggs if cream is used, three eggs if milk is employed, two ounces of butter, pepper and salt.

Cover a large open tin with bread dough, or butter or dripping crust. Cut the cheese up into dice or scrape it. Beat the eggs into the cream or milk, add the cheese, and pepper and salt to taste. Pour this mixture over the dough, add some small lumps of butter on top, and bake in a moderate oven. Any sort of old pieces of cheese may be used up in this way. The cake must be served steaming hot.

APFEL KUCHEN (*Apple Cake*).

Ingredients.—One pound of flour, half a pound of butter, two pounds of apples, sugar, cinnamon, and two ounces of almonds.

Make a nice rich butter piecrust with the butter and flour. Spread this out on a large buttered tin. Peel the apples and cut them into quarters (if very large, into eight pieces), lay them on the dough as near to each other as possible. Strew over them sugar, a little cinnamon, some finely-chopped almonds, and three or four little lumps of butter. Bake in a quick oven.

P.S.—It may be interesting to "Our Girls" who bake their own bread, to know that a delicious apple cake may be made by using the same dough as that used for bread. In Switzerland it is the custom to take round to the baker a dish full of cut-up apples and a couple of eggs mixed in a quarter of a pint of milk. For the small sum of threepence the baker strews a large pan with bread dough, places the apples, sugar and custard on top, and sends us in a steaming Apfel Kuchen.

ZWIEBELN KUCHEN (*Onion Cake*).

Ingredients.—Two Spanish onions, two eggs, a breakfastcupful of milk or cream, salt and pepper to taste, bread dough.

Although this and the following recipe does not come strictly under the title of a sweet, it is yet such a simple and tasty dessert dish that I need no apology for inserting it. Shred up the onions very fine and fry them in butter until of a light brown colour. Have ready a large open tin covered with bread dough or dripping crust, smear this entirely over with the onions, which must have been allowed to cool, and over all pour the cream and beaten-up eggs, with some occasional small lumps of butter on top. Bake in a moderate oven and serve hot.

HIMBEER KUCHEN (*Raspberry Cake*).

Ingredients.—One pound of raspberries, a quarter of a pound of sugar, a quarter of a pound of butter, two ounces of almonds, two ounces of flour, four yolks of eggs, and also the four whites. Butter crust.

Cook the raspberries and sugar together for about a quarter of an hour. Stir into this a quarter of a pound of butter, two ounces of finely-chopped almonds, two ounces more of sugar, two ounces of flour, the four yolks of the eggs, and finally the four whites beaten to a stiff froth. Place this mixture on a tin covered with butter crust and bake in a hot oven.

KIRSCHEN KUCHEN (*Cherry Cake*).

Ingredients.—Two pounds of stoned cherries, two gills of cream, four eggs, two ounces of almonds, two ounces of sugar, cinnamon, butter crust.

Take a large tin and cover rather thickly with butter crust. Lay the cherries closely together over this and strew over a handful of powdered sugar. Mix the cream, eggs, two ounces of pounded almonds, two ounces of powdered sugar, and a teaspoonful of cinnamon, pour over the cherries and bake the cake in a hot oven.

This cake is sufficient for eight persons. The crust should be made with half a pound of flour and a quarter of a pound of butter, a dripping or plain bread dough can also be used.

P.S.—To stone cherries attach a hairpin to a little bit of wood, then draw out the stone with the top of the hairpin. This is more practical than any of the machines sold for the purpose, and should not be forgotten when the plum and cherry jam season commences.

PREUSZISCHER ZIMMTKUCHEN (*Cinnamon Cake*).

Ingredients.—Half a pound of almonds, half a pound of powdered sugar, one egg, ten tablespoonfuls of sour cream, cinnamon, peel of a lemon, butter crust. Pound the almonds and add all the other ingredients, chop up the lemon peel and mix all well together.

Lay this mass on a tin over which a good butter crust has been arranged, and bake in a moderate oven.

MANDELSPECK KUCHEN (*Almond Cake*).

Ingredients.—Half a pound of butter, half a pound of sugar, two ounces of almonds, juice and peel of half a lemon, four whole eggs, and two extra yolks, butter crust.

Mix the butter, sugar, almonds, lemon peel and juice, four whole eggs and two yolks together, until a thick paste is the result. Strew this mixture over a butter crust, cover with a very thin crust, and strew over white of egg and sugar. Cook in a moderate oven.

JOHANNISBEERKUCHEN (*Red-Currant Cake*).

Ingredients.—One pound and a half of currants, half a pound of sugar, breadcrumbs, cream, and butter or dripping crust.

Cook the currants and sugar together with a little water. When there is scarcely any juice left, turn out the fruit to get cold. Over the butter crust, which must be placed on a tin, put a plentiful supply of breadcrumbs moistened with cream or milk. Cover with the currants and bake in a hot oven.

SPECK KUCHEN (*Ham Cake*).

Ingredients.—Four tablespoonfuls of flour, four eggs, two handfuls of bacon cut into small square pieces, and some finely cut up onion. Bread dough.

Cover a tin with the same dough as used for bread-making. Take four tablespoonfuls of flour and a little salt and stir up in milk, beat up the four eggs into this mixture with the cut up bacon, and two tablespoonfuls of minced green onion. Put this mixture over the dough, cut up on top some small pieces of butter and bake until of a light brown colour.

BRAUNE TORTE.

Ingredients.—Two yolks of eggs, half a pound of powdered sugar, half a pound of flour, peel of one lemon, two ounces of almonds, one teaspoonful of cinnamon, a quarter of a pound of butter, three whites of eggs.

Stir the sugar into the egg-yolks for at least ten minutes, add the finely-shredded peel of the lemon, flour, almonds, butter (which must be melted), and lastly the egg-whites, which must have been beaten to a stiff froth. Place on a well-buttered tin, cover with powdered sugar and bake in a moderate oven.

MANNHEIMER KUCHEN (*Mannheim Cake*).

Ingredients.—Two pounds of apples, ingredients for an ordinary butter crust, a quarter of a pound of macaroons, a quarter of a pound of sugar, yolks of four eggs, a pint of cream or milk.

Cut up the apples in quarters, peel them and lay them on a tin which must first be thickly covered with a good butter pastry. Strew over the sugar and cook in a moderate oven until half done. Over this mass add the macaroons, sugar, yolks of eggs, which must have been pounded up and well mixed together, and the cream (or milk). See that the apples are thoroughly covered with the mixture, and finish baking. Serve hot to table.

PANA ITALIANA (*Italian Cream*).

Ingredients.—One pint of cream or milk, one ounce of gelatine, the yolks of four eggs, one lemon.

Put the cream or milk to boil with the lemon rind and sugar to taste. When the milk is well flavoured by the lemon, strain it and add the beaten yolks of eggs. Place this mixture in a jug, and the jug in a saucepan of boiling water, stir until it thickens, but on no account let it boil. Take off the fire, stir into it the melted gelatine and juice of the lemon, beat well, fill a mould, and put to cool. When set turn out on a dish and garnish with stewed fruit or coloured jelly.

TWO BLACKBERRY PUDDINGS.

Lay in a pie-dish slices of bread as for a bread and butter pudding, but without the butter. Boil some blackberries with either damsons or bullaces, about half and half of each, and sufficient sugar to sweeten them; when hot, pour over and between the slices of bread. Let it stand the night, or at least five or six hours; turn it out into a glass dish (it will have acquired consistency), and before serving throw over it a custard made with one egg and thickened with cornflour.

The second pudding I would mention is made thus:—Butter the outside of a pound jar, place it in a buttered tin or pie-dish.

Pour into the pie-dish batter, and bake it. When ready to serve extract the jar, and into the cavity pour about a pint of blackberries and damsons sweetened and stewed.

In the matter of a preserve, I would remark, that I think blackberries boiled with common white bullaces make a far better preserve than with apples—I have tried both.—*Mab.*

STAFFORDSHIRE SHORTCAKE.

Beat a quarter of a pound of butter to a cream in a basin, add a quarter of a pound of castor sugar and two eggs; mix all together, then add four ounces of almonds, blanched and chopped small, one ounce of angelica and two of candied cherries, also chopped finely; add sufficient flour to make a fairly stiff dough; turn on to a board, roll out a quarter of an inch thick, cut into squares and diamonds, pinch the edges; bake in a rather quick oven to a pale brown tinge.

TINNED FRUITS.

A Medical Officer of Health and Public Analyst says that "it is practically impossible to preserve fruits with acid juices in tins without the acid acting to a greater or less extent upon the metal, and there are instances on record in which such foods have caused serious illness. Acid fruits should never be preserved in anything but glass or porcelain vessels."

HOME-MADE ICES.

E have all heard of the little girl who, when asked how she had enjoyed herself at a juvenile party to which she was invited, replied: "Oh, it was a beautiful party! There were two kinds of jam!" One fancies that grown-up girls experience the sort of gratification expressed by this child when they attend entertainments at which ices are provided. The mere sight of an ice makes them decide that the festival which it adorns is very high-class, and that the hostess on this occasion has been exceptionally liberal, and has specially exerted herself to make her friends have a good time.

When ices or ice puddings are seen in modest households, the explanation usually is that they have been sent ready-made from the confectioner's, securely packed in broken ice, to be taken out when wanted. How much more delightful the girls of the family would consider it if they could make the ices at home.

Also, the cost of utensils having been defrayed, how much more economical the home produce would be. An ice pudding, bought at a good confectioner's, would probably cost seven or eight shillings; and this means that for a great many people it would be unattainable, while of the many who might afford it, a large proportion would regard it as an extravagance. Made at home, however, an ice pudding might cost pretty well what the maker likes. When all is said and done, an ice pudding is only a good well-flavoured custard pudding, mixed with dried fruits and frozen, and there is nothing very costly in this.

Of course the difficulty in connection with ices is that in order to make them one must have certain appliances. It is impossible, for example, to make an ice in a saucepan over the fire. Yet the correct utensils required for the purpose are seldom within the reach of individuals of modest means.

Undoubtedly there are clever people in the world, who have plenty of time on their hands, and a capacity for taking pains, who can make ices in small quantities by simply putting the material to be frozen into a canister, surrounding this with ice and salt, then turning it about and stirring it from time to time until it is frozen. Thus, an individual who once very long ago was a girl much given to making experiments in cookery, can well recollect retiring with one of her sisters into an arbour in the home garden when snow was thick on the ground, with a tin containing milk, and rolling this about in ice and salt until it was a solid mass. The refrigerating process took a long time, and the operators were stiff with cold before it was ready, but the milk when it did freeze was most delightful, and was considered a dainty most suitable for the season. The objection, however, to this rough and ready method is that it is very tedious, and life is short; also, that it is so apt to turn out a failure. The lid of the canister must fit very closely, and the canister itself must be thoroughly well made, for if only a small quantity of the salt water gets into the pudding, not only will the custard freeze less readily, but it will also melt more quickly when turned out; while if salt water to taste gets into the pudding, the flavour will be spoilt. These drawbacks being discovered, we generally find that busy folks seldom persevere very long in making ice without proper utensils. They make the experiment to prove to themselves that they can do it, and then they either dispense with ice altogether, or contrive to get either a machine or a freezing-pot, and an ice-pail. Thus provided, their difficulties are ended.

When girls have made up their minds that they will commence ice-making at home, they must first of all decide whether they will invest in the primitive apparatus—that is, an ice-pail, a pewter freezing-pot with its cover, and a spatula—or whether they will procure an ice-machine. Probably their first idea will be that the ice-pail and freezer will be the less expensive of the two; but if they act on this supposition, the chances are that when they have bought everything that is required, and supplied all their needs, they will find that they have paid very nearly as much as would have purchased a small ice-machine; yet the latter would be much the more convenient. It will easily be understood that to be of any real use an ice-pail must be strong and well-made. Francatelli thus describes it: "It should be made of oak, with iron hoops; there should be a hole placed about an inch and a half from the bottom of the tub to let off the ice water at will; and there should be another hole placed at about four inches from the edge of the tub, to let off the rising water as the ice melts. Wooden spigots are usually kept in these holes to prevent the ice water from wasting. These tubs should be painted both inside and out, not merely for appearance sake, but also on account of the rust which necessarily would collect on the hoops, and soil everything approaching them. The tub must be large enough to admit of a space of at least two inches intervening between the inside of the tub and the freezer to receive the rough ice in the circular cavity thus formed." It is very evident that a pail answering this description could not be had for nothing; while even if we resolved to get something less perfect, we must at least have a stout well-made pail, with a hole in it near the bottom stopped with a cork to carry off the water which would collect as the ice melted. Then there is the freezer, which even if small will cost about half a sovereign; while the expense of the supply of ice has always to be considered. A good ice machine needs a smaller quantity of ice than is necessary to surround the freezer in a large pail.

It will greatly assist girls to decide what appliances should be purchased for making ices if they obtain a clear idea of what it is that they propose to do. Ices, then, are simply pleasantly-flavoured liquid preparations which have been frozen till firm by being subjected to the requisite degree of cold. When made of cream, or when cream enters into them, they are "ice cream"; when made of fruit juice and water, or of water flavoured in any agreeable way, they are water ices. Sometimes these frozen preparations are made in the form of a large mould—then they are ice puddings; sometimes they are served in a heap; sometimes they are put into small moulds and served in a shape; and sometimes they are put into cups or glasses. But in every case they are merely pleasantly-prepared liquids which have been frozen.

It is not at all unlikely that of people who have never made ices a good many (if they ever think of the subject at all) think that in order to freeze a preparation in this way it is necessary only to mix the ingredients properly, put them into a mould or pot, then surround them with ice, and leave them till solid. This idea is, however, altogether a mistake. For one thing, ice alone would never freeze anything; ice and salt are needed. For another, if a composition were placed where it could freeze it would simply in time become solid ice, quite unmanageable for serving at table. If taken up before being solid it would be harder near the sides of the mould than in the middle, whereas a perfectly-made ice is smooth, and of the same consistency all the way through. To produce this condition it is necessary to stir the ice and scrape it from the sides into the centre, and to move the freezing pot round and round during congelation, so that the contents may get equally frozen.

With the old-fashioned apparatus—the ice-pail and freezer—an ice-pudding of moderate size would need to be worked and churned for very nearly an hour; with a good ice-machine the business could be accomplished in a few minutes: the saving of time alone, therefore, is a consideration. If we remember also that in all ice-machines it has been the aim of the inventor to make the process as easy as possible for the operator, we shall see that a machine saves labour as well as time. If it can be procured, therefore, an ice-machine is decidedly to be preferred to an ice-pail and freezer.

There are at present a great many ice-machines from which a purchaser may make choice. It would scarcely be correct to say that all are of equal merit, although it is undoubtedly the case that a girl who bought a machine recommended by a respectable dealer would not run very much risk of making a mistake. Almost all the machines which have made a reputation have their special advantages, and the individuals who speak most highly of them are those who own them, have become accustomed to them, and learnt how to manage them. Each machine has of course to be managed differently; but the makers always send full directions for use with the apparatus, so that there is no difficulty. In all machines, however, the theory to be carried out is very much the same, so that if we understand one machine thoroughly we are not very much at a loss how to work all. Therefore I shall describe at length the method of procedure which has to be followed in a machine which is, in my opinion, as easily managed, as convenient, and as economical as any that could be selected by those who wish to make ice in small quantities. This is the American Freezer, a little ice-making machine sold by the Atmospheric Churn Company, whose head offices are at 119, New Bond Street, London, and whose goods could probably be obtained if ordered of any respectable ironmonger.

The American Freezer has been on view, and shown in practical operation, at several of the great Exhibitions which have been usual of late years. The price of the smallest size is two guineas complete. It consists of a little tub, the ends of which are moveable, though they can be screwed on quite tightly. The tub is hung in a stand, and it is made to revolve round and round with a regular movement, so that the mixture to be frozen is turned from one end of the freezer to the other, and thus it is frozen equally all through. A mould to receive the ice is put in at one end. This when filled is securely fastened, and the ice and salt are put in the other side, which is also fastened, so that there is no danger of the salt getting into the preparation, and the machine is then slowly revolved at the rate of not more than fifty revolutions per minute for five minutes. The machine is now opened, and the ice is scraped from the sides into the centre, and pressed together to make it quite compact, even, and solid. The end is again closed and the tub is revolved for another minute, after which the remainder of the ice is thrown out, and in its place is put cold water. This will loosen the ice from the mould, and make it turn out more readily. The ice is now ready for use. If not wanted at once, it can be put in a basin containing ice, and thus it will be kept from melting. Of course we must set it in a cool place, free from draught, and cover it with an old blanket or an old carpet, to protect it from the heat. Blankets and all woollen materials, as girls well know, are employed to maintain the temperature. We put them on ourselves to keep in the heat of our bodies; we put them on ices to keep in their cold.

An advantage belonging to the ice-machine to which reference has been made (and it belongs also to several other machines) is that it can be worked not only with ice and salt but with freezing mixtures. Concerning these a word or two needs to be said. First, there is no freezing mixture in the world (so far as I know) that is worthy to be compared with ice and salt. A mixture of ice and salt does its work more quickly; it is more reliable, more convenient and altogether to be preferred to any other. At the same time there are places and circumstances where ice cannot be obtained, and then it is most satisfactory to have freezing powders. The method of procedure with powders and the ice-machine would be very much the same as with ice and salt, with the difference that the machine would have to be turned a few minutes longer. If we were going to use freezing powders instead of ice and salt in using the American Freezer, for instance, we should fill the mould with the preparation to be frozen, and fasten up the end; then put into the other end the requisite quantity of the freezing mixture, and its proper allowance of water. If after a few minutes we found that the preparation did not freeze, the freezing materials would have to be thrown out and a second charge introduced. It would be of no use to keep on turning the machine longer, because after ten or fifteen minutes we may reasonably conclude that the power of the mixture would be exhausted. A second charge will, however, generally attain the desired end.

When ice and salt are used for freezing there should be provided two parts of ice for one part of salt. The ice should be broken up into pieces about the size of a hazel nut, and mixed very thoroughly with the salt. The easiest way of breaking a quantity of ice is to put it into a sack and beat it till small with a mallet. It should not be broken until just before it is wanted, and it should be well mixed with the salt immediately. Attention to these details has a great deal to do with success in making ices.

Freezing mixtures are to be bought ready for use, or they may be made at home. The following are the best with which a learned chemist, whom I know, it acquainted.

FREEZING MIXTURES.

1 (*Best of all*). 2 parts powdered ice, 1 part salt.

2. 4 parts sulphate of soda, 2½ parts chloride of ammonium, 2½ parts sulphate of potash, 18 parts water.

3. 12 parts pounded ice, 5 parts salt, 5 parts nitrate of ammonia.

4. Equal parts of chloride of ammonia and nitrate of potash. More than twice the amount of water.

5. 1 part nitrate of ammonia, 1 part carbonate of soda, 1 part water.

6. 2 parts ammonic nitrate, 2 parts ammonic chloride, 3 parts water.

Freezing mixtures of the sort described ought not to cost much; but their price is very variable, according to the locality in which they are bought. A peculiarity with regard to nearly all of them is, that after being mixed with water and used, they can be reconstituted by being put into a shallow glazed pan, and set in the oven or on the top of a closed stove until the water has evaporated, when they can be crushed with a rolling pin, and kept to be used again and again. The length of time needed to reconstitute them depends upon the quantity of water which has to be evaporated. A couple of pints of water would take perhaps two or three hours. The mixture when ready would have to be kept in a dry place. It is most important that a freezing powder should be kept dry.

Having done what we can to make our freezing apparatus right, we now come to the mixture to be frozen. Some time ago an individual who had devoted a good part of his life to the manufacture of ices, was asked what was the secret of success in this branch of work. He replied: "The secret of success in making ices is—do not put in too much sugar!" There was a good deal of truth in this remark, because it is the case that too much sugar renders freezing difficult. At the same time, too little sugar spoils the taste of the preparation, and also causes it to be hard and lumpy. Thus Francatelli says: "Great attention should be paid to avoid overcharging your ices with sugar, for in that state they would be too rich and ropy, and are difficult to freeze; but in such cases the composition may be instantly rectified by adding a little fruit juice, or even water. While, however, it is essential to avoid the error of adding an excess of sugar in the confection of ices, it is of equal importance that you should not fall into the other extreme. The fear of not being right must not mislead you into actually doing wrong, for when ices are prepared with an insufficient quantity of sugar they are poor, and are certain to be very imperfect, and hardly worth being sent to table."

Yet, although the amount of sugar is important, it is not easy to say what proportion should be used in every case, because this depends upon the nature of the ingredients to be sweetened. In recipes for making ices we constantly read "sweeten to taste," or "the amount of sugar must be determined by taste," or "experience only will teach the degree of sweetness required." These instructions sound very vague, but they are quite correct, because it is not possible to say what quantity should be used in every instance. It is to be noted, however, that sugar boiled to syrup is much to be preferred to plain sugar for this purpose; it amalgamates with the other ingredients better; and it is a great thing in making ices to have the ingredients thoroughly mixed before they are put into the freezer. An excellent syrup can be made by boiling a pound of sugar for twenty minutes with a pint of water. For convenience' sake. girls might make a quantity of this beforehand, and when cold bottle it and keep it for use.

Water Fruit Ices should be made always with the juice of fresh fruit. If the fruit is of a sort which yields its juice readily, it will need only to be bruised and rubbed through a sieve. The juice will flow more freely if a little sugar be sprinkled over it, or if a little water be poured over it. If it is of a hard sort it must be boiled to pulp, and the juice drained off. On an average we might expect that half a pint of juice would have to be mixed with a pint of syrup. Flavour and colour would have to be added if required.

Cream Fruit Ices can be made either with fresh fruit or jam. When jam is used the jam should be mixed, or even simmered, with a little water before being rubbed through the sieve. To improve the fruity flavour a little lemon-juice should be added. The amount of cream used would depend upon permission. Occasionally a custard made of eggs and milk is substituted for cream in making "Cream" Fruit Ices. Excellent ice creams may be made without fruit juice by mixing cream, milk, and syrup, then flavouring the preparation with coffee, chocolate, cinnamon, almonds, vanilla, tea, and similar flavourers.

It is probable that from the above suggestions girls might make any number of ice creams. For safety's sake, however, a few exact recipes may be given.

Nesselrode Pudding has been pronounced "the most perfect and the most insidious of puddings." It was invented many years ago by Monie, cook to the famous Count von Nesselrode, the Russian statesman and diplomatist. History tells us that, when Carême, who was the most celebrated cook of the century, heard of it, he was nearly beside himself with envy. This recipe is taken from Gouffé, who says he had it direct from his old friend Monie:—"Peel forty fine Italian chestnuts; blanch them in boiling water to remove the second skin, and put them in a stewpan with one quart of syrup registering 16°, and a stick of vanilla. Simmer gently until the chestnuts are done, drain, and rub them through a hair sieve. Mix in a stewpan eight yolks of eggs and half a pound of pounded sugar; add one quart of boiled cream and stir over the fire without boiling until the egg begins to thicken; mix in the chestnut purée and one gill of Maraschino, and strain the whole through a tammy cloth into a basin. Set a freezing-pot in the ice. Wash and dry a quarter of a pound of currants, and boil them up in some syrup registering 30°. Stone a quarter of a pound of raisins, cut them in halves, and boil them in syrup in the same way. Pour the chestnut cream in the freezing-pot, work it with the spatula until it is partly frozen, add three gills of whipped double cream, continue working until the cream is frozen, and mix in the prepared fruit, previously drained. Put the ice in a dome-shaped ice mould, close it, and spread some butter on the opening to prevent any salt or water penetrating inside; imbed the mould in ice, and let it remain there for two hours.

Make the sauce as follows: Put three gills of boiled cream in a stewpan with eight yolks of eggs and a quarter of a pound of pounded sugar. Stir over the fire without boiling till the egg begins to thicken: take off the fire and stir for three minutes more. Strain the custard through a tammy cloth, and add half a gill of Maraschino. Put the sauce on the ice till it is very cold without freezing. Turn the pudding out of a mould on to a napkin on a dish, and serve with the sauce in a boat."

Superior though this pudding may be, it is not likely that many girls will make it, although it is to be noted that the quantities given would make a very large pudding, and that a pudding a quarter the size obtained by dividing the quantities by four would give a pudding large enough for ten or twelve persons, because no one partakes freely of ice pudding; it is the kind of food of which we are accustomed to say that a little goes a long way. However, here is a more modest recipe, more likely to be acceptable to people of moderate ideas.

Ice Pudding.—Pour half a pint of boiling milk upon the yolks of two eggs; put the preparation into a double saucepan or into a jug set in a saucepan of water, and stir it till it thickens. Strain, and add two ounces of sugar and a flavouring of vanilla, lemon, ratafia, noyeau, or Maraschino, and half a pint of whipped cream. Freeze the pudding till it is like a thick batter; then add two ounces of any dried fruits, such as glacé cherries, or pine-apple, or preserved ginger cut small, and two ounces of stale sponge cake soaked in cream. Work the half-frozen mixture smoothly together, and press and shake it to make it compact; then freeze it again until firm enough to turn out, and put it into rough ice till wanted. When about to dish an ice pudding, recollect that the mould should be dipped for a minute into cold water to loosen the ice, and that the pudding should be put upon a napkin, or even upon a round of white paper rather than upon the dish itself, because it will not then be likely to melt so quickly.

Strawberry Ice Cream.—Hull a pound of ripe strawberries; sprinkle a quarter of a pound of powdered sugar over them, and rub them through a sieve. Mix with the purée its measure of cream, whipped; and freeze.

Pine-Apple Water Ice.—Take a small tinned pine-apple (or a fresh one if obtainable), cut it up, and pound it well with half a pound of sugar. Pour over it a pint of water and simmer gently for a few minutes, then let it stand for a while and strain off the juice. Freeze in the usual way. If liked, a few slices of preserved pine-apple may be added when frozen.

Coffee Ice Cream.—Make half a pint of very strong clear coffee, mix in half a pint of cream, sweeten, and freeze.

Brown Bread Ice.—Put into a bowl eight ounces of brown bread crumbs, fine and dry. Add six ounces sifted sugar, a wineglassful of curaçoa, and a pint of double cream, whipped. Mix and freeze.

Vanilla Ice Cream.—Make a custard with the yolks of four eggs and a pint of milk. Sweeten with two ounces of sugar, flavour with vanilla, and strain. When cold, mix and freeze.

Chocolate Ice Cream.—Melt four ounces of chocolate in half a pint of hot water. Sweeten, add a pint of cream, and freeze.

Orange Water Ice.—Take the raspings of three oranges, the juice of four oranges, half a pint of water, the juice of two or three lemons, and one pint of syrup. Mix, strain, and freeze.

There is one little detail which has not been mentioned, and which should not be forgotten. The freezer should on no account be filled with the mixture to be frozen. There should always be abundance of room left for it to be stirred round and round. Unless this point receives attention the cream cannot be smoothly frozen throughout.

One advantage of having an apparatus for making ice is that by its aid girls can manufacture a small quantity of perfectly pure ice for table use in hot weather, and for invalids. We all know that ice is a great luxury; yet of late years many warnings have been uttered against it, because it is said to be so frequently made of water that is not all it should be, and which may lead to typhoid. If we make ice under our own roof we can at least be sure of its quality, and we could have it well filtered, or even boiled and allowed to go cold before being frozen. This small quantity once made we might keep for hours by simply wrapping it first in paper and then in flannel, putting it in a tub, and setting it in a cool place out of a draught. When wanted, we could most easily break pieces off for serving by placing upon it the point of a darning-needle and tapping the other end of the needle with any light instrument. To see the way in which ice cracks and separates under the point of a needle is a most interesting experiment. Let us hope that during the summer the experiment will be tried by many girls upon ice which they have themselves frozen.

PHYLLIS BROWNE.

I THINK to most young folks the sweetstuff made by themselves at home tastes indescribably better than that which comes from what Scotch children call a " sweetie " shop. It has, at any rate, the merit of being more wholesome. With this idea I have written out some successful recipes, which have been duly tried and approved of by an appreciative circle of girl friends, and I think, if you carefully follow them, you also will be pleased with the results.

My first shall be for that time-honoured favourite, *Toffee*. Take one pound of brown sugar, two ounces of butter, and half a teacupful of cream or milk. Put these materials into a nice clean pan, and boil, without stirring, for twenty minutes. At the end of that time find out if it is sufficiently boiled, by dropping a little into cold water, when, if it "sets," the mixture should be poured into a buttered dish or tin. The addition of five or six drops of essence of vanilla, just before it is poured out, is a great improvement.

Toffee Balls are made by taking a little of the toffee off the buttered dish before it gets too cold, and rolling small pieces tightly into balls in your fingers. When you have thus shaped the balls, roll them about on a cold plate until they are perfectly hard and cold.

If you want to have *Almond Toffee*, blanch four ounces of almonds, split them into strips, and throw them into the toffee just before it is dished, omitting the vanilla flavouring. To blanch the almonds, throw them into a basin of slightly salted boiling water, and leave them to soak for two or three minutes. Then pour off the water, and you will find the skins slip off between your fingers. Drop each almond into clear cold water, then strain and lay them in a shallow dish to dry slowly in front of the fire before using.

Everton Toffee.—For this, half a pound of golden syrup, half a pound of Demerara sugar, lemon juice to taste, and from five to six ounces of butter are required. Mix carefully the sugar and syrup, and then add the butter in little bits, stirring slowly till it is all thoroughly mixed. Then cease stirring, or the toffee will "sugar," let it boil gently till a tiny bit thrown into cold water sets. If everything is satisfactory it will be beautifully crisp, and the whole should then be poured into a tin pre-

viously well rubbed with sweet oil or butter. When it is half cold, mark it into squares.

Butter Scotch.—Put into a very clean pan one pound and a half of soft sugar, two ounces of butter, half a teaspoonful of cream of tartar, and half a teacupful of cold water. Let the whole boil for about ten minutes without stirring, then dip a spoon in cold water, pop it into the pan, and back again with its contents into cold water, when if the mixture hardens it will do. You may add, if you like, a little powdered ginger or vanilla essence just before pouring it out. Mark it into neat squares when it cools a little.

Marzipan.—Procure half a pound of almonds, two ounces of bitter almonds, and half a pound of sugar. Blanch the almonds and pound them in a mortar; clarify and cook the sugar slightly, then remove it from the fire and stir into it the almonds. Warm all together, stirring well, and taking the greatest care that it doesn't burn. When it is cooked enough (that is, when it won't adhere to the fingers), pour it out on a board sprinkled with sugar. As soon as it is cool cut it into tiny fancy shapes, stars, rings, and fingers; and, if you are anxious to make it a very "swell" goody, decorate it with preserved cherries or other dried fruits.

Chocolate Creams.—Take one pound of loaf sugar, put it into a saucepan, and pour some good milk or thin cream over it, as much as the sugar will absorb. Let the latter dissolve, then boil it gently for a time, until when you drop a little into cold water it candies. Do not boil it too long, or, in place of smoothly creaming, the sugar will go into minute sand-like grains. Be most careful, too, that it doesn't stick to the pan, but do not stir it till it is taken off, when it must be continually stirred until it creams. Then beat until cool, when it has to be rolled into little balls, which form the inner cream of the sweetmeat. Now put half a pound of vanilla chocolate into a jar, and place over a saucepan of boiling water to dissolve; when melted, dip the creams into it, and place them on a buttered paper to get cool.

Cocoa-nut Tablet.—Get a small fresh cocoa-nut, open one of the holes at the top, and pour out the milk into a cup; crack the shell, take out the kernel, and pare all the skin from it, then grate about half of the kernel. Dissolve half a pound of loaf sugar in a large cupful of cold

water, and when it is dissolved put it on a clear moderate fire, without flame or smoke, to boil; a little of the cocoa-nut milk may be added. Allow it to boil for five or six minutes, carefully removing every particle of scum that rises, when the sugar should look like a thick white cream; then add the grated cocoa-nut, and let it boil for a few minutes longer, stirring it continuously from the bottom with a wooden spoon to prevent it catching. Try if it is ready by pouring a teaspoonful into a cup of cold water, when if you can gather a little soft lump at the bottom of the cup, it is sufficiently boiled. Remove it from the fire, pour it out upon a buttered plate, or sheet of clean, common note-paper previously laid in front of the fire to warm. When it is thoroughly set, but not quite cold, cut it into neatly shaped blocks. If you would like the tablet to be pink, add some drops of cochineal to the syrup while boiling, stirring to see the required tint.

Barley Sugar.—For this you require one pound and a half of fine loaf sugar broken into very small lumps and boiled over the fire in a pint of water. Keep on skimming it carefully till it looks like glue, and becomes so brittle when dropped into cold water that it snaps. Now add the juice of a lemon, and a few drops of essence of lemon, and boil the sugar up once. Stand the pan in a basin of cold water till the contents have somewhat cooled, when they may be poured out upon a shallow buttered tin; to prevent the sweetmeat spreading too much, draw it together with a knife. When it has cooled sufficiently to be handled, cut it into small pieces, and roll them into round sticks, which you can twist a little so as to make them look more like the barley sugar one buys in shops. All that remains to be done is to sift sugar lightly over the sticks when they have become perfectly cold and hard.

Fig Rock.—For this take one cupful of sugar, three-quarters of a cupful of water, and a quarter of a teaspoonful of cream of tartar. Boil till the mixture becomes an amber colour, but do not stir during the process; add the cream of tartar just before taking from the fire. Wash the figs, split them in half, and lay them flatly on a dish, pour the mixture over them, and let it stand till cold.

EDITH A. BRODIE.

USEFUL HINTS.

Rhubarb Meringue Tart.—Have the rhubarb ready cooked and cold ; it should be cut into inch lengths and cooked in sugar that the colour may be kept bright, add a drop or two of cochineal when the fruit is cool, if not sufficiently red.

Cover a flat tartlet tin with a sheet of puff or good short paste, crimp the edge and bake carefully to keep it from rising in the centre. When cool slip it on to a dish, place the rhubarb with a little of the juice in the middle, and heap upon it a meringue of the whites of two eggs beaten up with castor sugar, a drop of lemon juice and a tablespoonful of cream.

Green Gooseberry Tart is excellent if made in a similar way to the above, cooking bottled gooseberries beforehand with sugar and

covering the crust with them afterwards. In place of the meringue a thick custard made with the yolks of two eggs, a teaspoonful of cornflour and half a pint of sweetened milk, will be found preferable.

Cherry or raspberry tart may also be made after the same plan, and a custard made with custard powder goes exceedingly well with these, as its slight flavour of almond accords with the natural flavour of the fruits.

Chocolate Baisers.—Place the following in a mortar: Eight ounces of sugar, two ounces of chocolate which has been softened in the oven, two whites of egg. This must be pounded together for quite half an hour, until it is the thickness of jam, and must not on any account be so liquid as to run. Make with

this paste small round heaps on a baking-tin, which you have previously waxed. Bake in a moderate oven until done through.

Cheese Toasts.—Take the yolk of a hard-boiled egg, pound it with the same quantity of fresh butter and double the quantity of any crumbly kind of cheese, add salt and cayenne pepper. Cut some neat squares of thin toast, spread the mixture on them about the eighth of an inch thick, put the toasts in a dutch-oven before the fire to brown a little, and serve hot.

Small Tea-Cakes.—Two teacupsful of flour, one teacupful of ground rice, a pinch of salt, half a teacupful of soft sugar, three ounces of butter, two eggs, the grated rind of a fresh lemon, and a very little milk.

CREAM AND APRICOT TEA.

A MEAL of these colours is much easier to prepare in the fruit season than in spring or winter, for although we are not going to tie ourselves down to apricots and cream only, still they must enter largely into the factors of the meal; nevertheless, we will give suggestions that will make a cream and apricot tea possible at all seasons of the year, and a "cake tea" lends itself most accommodatingly to this arrangement of colour at all seasons.

You can arrange this meal either for a sit-down table tea or a stand-up buffet tea; in either case remember that the decorations, like those for breakfast, must not be too elaborate, but they must be very daintily prepared. We will begin with the table-cloth, which should be of fine cream linen, embroidered with apricot silk; a handsome arabesque border above the hem will be a very suitable pattern, and it should be repeated in a square or oblong for the centre. Or you may have a border of drawn thread-work, sewn with apricot silk. Fringe the linen all round, and make a double-knotted heading. In this case it will be better to have a loose centre, drawn and fringed to match. The pattern should be fairly open, and would look well lined with apricot silk or satin ribbon. Of course, whichever style you choose, your little serviettes must be worked to match. Tea serviettes differ from others, as they are only used for laying across the lap to prevent crumbs and drops of tea falling on the dress. They should be about eight inches wide and eighteen inches long, hemmed neatly at each side, and embroidered and fringed at the ends only. If you ornament them with drawn work, you need not line it with ribbon, but there should be just a suspicion of apricot silk embroidery between the rows of drawing, and you may embroider your crest or monogram at one corner. Fold them plainly, and lay one on each plate.

For table decoration you must be guided by the season; a light-looking plant in a silver or cream-china jar would be suitable for the centre. A well-trained thunbergia, with its fragile cream or apricot blossoms, or a well-grown begonia, either double or single, of the required shades of colour would look well, and you may have glasses of cream and apricot flowers lightly arranged with ferns round the centre and at the corners, but do not introduce flowers of any other colour. Your tea-service should be apricot and cream china, but if you have not that mixture, plain cream may be used; but if you are the fortunate possessor of an old Spode apricot-and-gold service, your scheme of colour will be perfect. Your tea equipage should be of silver, for a brass or copper kettle would upset the whole tone of your table; of the two, copper would not be quite so bad as brass. We will place our fruit on the table next, for tea without fruit would be like dinner without vegetables; and although I am going to allow you a few dishes of fruit, I must advise you to save enough for a fruit-salad, to be served in a cream-china bowl. In separate dishes you may have, of course, apricots, white raspberries, bananas with the rind taken off, oranges, peeled, and the white taken off, divided into quarters and covered with sifted sugar, apricot-fleshed melon, cut in quarters, and any other fruit attainable of the right shade of colour. The salad may be a mixture of any of the above fruits, cut in pieces and slightly mashed; pineapple also may be added, and ripe pears, sweetened with sifted white sugar; add a little grated nutmeg, and, if possible, a small handful of freshly-picked cowslip flowers. We miss a great deal of pleasure by not making more culinary use of flowers;

many of them are most wholesome and fragrant, and give a delicious flavour. A rich thick cream must be added to form salad. And now for the eatables. Bread and butter, daintily rolled, will be quite suitable; small glasses or shells of marmalade and apricot jam placed about the table will also give the right tone of colour, and you may have marmalade sandwiches; hot scones will be a better colour than any other hot tea-cake. You may also have shortbread, which is a nice cream colour; make them round, about the size of the top of a tumbler, pinch them round the edge and ornament them thus: Boil two or three large carrots till quite tender; then put a little of the water into a stewpan, with the juice of one lemon, four ounces of sifted white sugar, and a teaspoonful of powdered ginger. Boil to a thick syrup. Slice the carrots into rounds; then cut them to one size with an ornamental round tin-cutter. Boil them in the syrup for a quarter of an hour or more; take them out, and while hot roll them in a nice apricot-coloured coarse sparkling sugar, and place one on the middle of each cake. Don't scorn this carrot preserve because it is only a vegetable; carrots are far too much slighted by the English. They are wholesome, easy to obtain, and can be cooked in a great variety of ways, besides being served only with boiled mutton.

As all tea confectionery can be made to assume the shades of apricot and cream with very little trouble, we need not particularise every item of the menu, but give a few general directions; the first of which is: Do not bake anything too much. Keep all your buns and cakes a light colour, and for icing use a *little* coffee to take off the dead whiteness; and to make it apricot, put some of the yolk of the egg with the white, and a few drops of essence of cochineal to make it the required shade. We will give you a recipe for apricot cake, which is very good: Six ounces of butter worked to a cream, the grated rind of half a lemon, six ounces of white sifted sugar. Work this mixture ten minutes more, to look creamy; then add the yolks of four eggs and ten ounces of Vienna flour. Stir the mixture free from lumps, and then add the whites of the eggs, stiffly beaten, half an ounce of baking-powder, and six ounces of glacé apricots cut in pieces. Drop the fruit into the mixture as lightly as possible; put into a lined cake-tin, and bake one hour and three-quarters. When cold, ice the top with cream-coloured icing and ornament with glacé apricots, cut into leaves and small squares; a little candied lemon-peel may be used also if approved of, both for mixing in the cake and ornamenting it. Eclairs filled with cream will be very suitable for this tea, if lightly baked, and as an excellent recipe was given in this magazine, we need not repeat it. You may also have an orange cake, which is both pretty and good, and of a lovely apricot tint when properly made.

If you like to have some savoury sandwiches, make them thus: Boil two eggs hard. Shell them, and pound them to a paste in a marble mortar, with two ounces of butter, a little salt, a pinch of cayenne pepper, and a tablespoonful of anchovy sauce, which will make the mixture a good shade of apricot. Cut some bread-and-butter very thin, spread it with the mixture; lay another piece of bread-and-butter on the top, spread another layer of the mixture on the top of that, and so on, till you have three layers of the mixture. Then cut the crust off all round, and cut into strips about an inch wide. It is a little change from the ordinary sandwich.

Cassell's Family Magazine

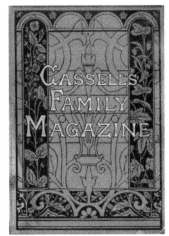

Another fine Victorian family magazine is *Cassell's Family Magazine.* It began as *Cassell's Family Paper*, but became *Cassell's Family Magazine* at the end of 1874 (hence its annuals began in December and concluded in November). In 1897 it became *Cassell's Magazine,* dropping the word "family" not only from its title but also from its purpose; in 1912, it became a fiction magazine.

Cassell's Family Paper was a general-interest publication. *Cassell's Family Magazine* clearly leaned more toward the lady of the house, with features on fashion, cooking, household care and décor, and such. It also had many general-interest pieces, and often addressed contemporary and social issues, though it did not become as involved in women's issues (such as work and education) as *The Girl's Own Paper.* Nor did it have quite the emphasis on religious and moral themes as the GOP, possibly because *Cassell's* was not a religious publisher per se.

In 1896, Max Pemberton took over as editor, and the magazine showed an immediate shift in direction. Pemberton's goal was to compete with *The Strand*, even publishing articles that were almost identical to pieces that had appeared in *The Strand.* The focus on family topics and women's interests all but disappeared (fashion articles dwindled from three to four pages per month to a page or two at most). Cooking articles, alas, also suffered.

Though cookery author Phillis Browne often contributed to *Cassell's Family Magazine,* she wrote about household issues rather than recipes. Cooking articles in the magazine varied from straightforward collections of recipes to wandering, first-person "Marge, do tell us how to cook a birthday supper!" pieces.

Like features in *The Girl's Own Paper*, however, the best cooking articles in *Cassell's Family Magazine* took a friendly and helpful tone, guiding the reader through the more intricate steps in creating a dish or an entire feast. This collection brings together all the magazine's articles on desserts and sweets from 1875-1896.

CAKES FOR THE FAMILY.

BY LIZZIE HERITAGE.

E will commence this paper with a few recipes for cakes to be eaten hot, and give first place to *Griddle Cakes*, which seem to be but little known here in England, except in the North, though they are easy enough to make in these days of close ranges and gas stoves, because the griddle should *not* be placed over a blazing fire. Those who have not a griddle may use an iron frying-pan, providing it is a thick one, and kept for the one purpose. Before baking the cakes, the griddle or pan should be allowed to get quite hot, then rubbed with a piece of fat pork, *just* enough to keep the batter from sticking, which for griddle cakes should be thin enough to *just* run when poured out on to the griddle. As flour varies, it is hardly possible to give the exact recipe ; on trial, if the first cake appears too stiff, add a little more milk, and after the batter is right, as many may be made at once as the pan will hold, allowing, of course, sufficient room for each spoonful to spread. When one side is brown, turn the cakes. Eat them hot, with butter.

Graham Griddle Cakes.—Half a pint of brown flour, half as much white ditto, a tea-spoonful of salt (a little sugar, if liked), an ounce of lard, melted in about three-quarters of a pint of buttermilk or sour milk, two eggs beaten light, and half a tea-spoonful of carbonate of soda dissolved in a table-spoonful of hot water. If no buttermilk can be had and fresh milk is used, cream of tartar must be added to the soda.

City Cream Cakes.—A pint of cream and a pint of milk, four eggs, salt, soda, and cream of tartar as usual ; flour to make a nice batter. These are a luxury.

Buttermilk Cakes without eggs are very nice. To a pint of buttermilk add a tea-spoonful of soda and salt, and nearly a pint of white flour.

Risen Griddle Cakes receive the addition of yeast, and should be mixed over-night. In the morning the butter or lard should be dissolved and stirred in.

Rice Cakes are a dainty, and must close our mention of griddle cakes. Half a cup of cold boiled rice, the same of corn meal, one egg, a bit of butter, salt, and sugar ; milk to make a rather thin batter. Grease the pan well, as these are apt to stick.

Dough Nuts seem better known in this country than Crullers are, and we give a very good recipe—as good as any we know of. One cup of sugar, two eggs, half a cup of sour milk, with half a tea-spoonful of soda dissolved in it, three ounces of butter, a pinch of salt, a tea-spoonful of ginger, cinnamon, and nutmeg mixed, and flour to make a soft dough. Cut into any shape preferred, or roll into tiny plaits, twists, and such-like. Fry in plenty of lard, and sift powdered sugar over while hot.

Crullers require some care in the frying, and, as will be seen, they are richer than dough nuts. Plenty of fat is required, very hot, then they will puff out and rise to the surface ; as soon as they are brown, the pan should be drawn a little from the fire, that they may be thoroughly cooked without being burnt. Rub half a pound of butter or lard to a cream, with half a pound of white sugar. Beat in four or five eggs and half a cup of milk ; then stir in flour enough to roll out as soft as you can without it being sticky. Roll into a sheet half an inch thick, and cut into rounds, or into strips, and tie in knots. Any spice or flavouring may be used, and baking powder, or soda and cream of tartar mixed with the flour, then fewer eggs will do.

A nice addition can always be made to any tea-table by setting on a dish of *jumbles*. They resemble short-bread in mode and taste, but are made small, in rings, leaves, and other shapes, not more than a third of an inch thick when baked. They should be *slowly* cooked to a pale brown, and be covered with sifted sugar before they are put into the oven.

Nut Jumbles may owe their name to walnuts or Brazil nuts ; the chopped kernels of either are very nice. Cocoa-nut, too, is excellent. Almond jumbles are as good as any. Beat together half a pound each of sugar and butter and three eggs ; add a quarter-pound of chopped almonds, and a little lemon-juice. Stir the flour lightly in, from half to three-quarters of a pound. Rose-water or orange-flower water is often used as a flavouring for these little cakes ; and a very superior kind are flavoured with a tea-spoonful of vanilla essence.

Seed Jumbles are a plainer kind, more suitable for children. The recipe is a quarter of a pound of lard, six ounces of sugar, two eggs, a quarter of a pint of milk, half an ounce of seeds, either caraway or pounded coriander, and nearly a pound of flour.

Molasses Cookies are nursery favourites, and very nice. Mix together, and warm, one cup of butter and two of molasses ; add a tea-spoonful of ground ginger and the same of nutmeg, and then, gradually, enough flour to make a stiff batter, firm enough for a spoon to stand in. Bake in greased small tins ; or the batter may be made stiff enough to mould with the hands into round cakes, which may be baked on a baking-sheet in a gentle oven.

Short Cookies.—Rub half a pound of lard or dripping into a pound of rice flour, add six ounces of brown sugar, one egg, and a table-spoonful of lemon-juice. Mix with a cup of warm milk into which a tea-spoonful of saleratus has been stirred. Saleratus is much used in America ; some prefer it to soda, though, if the latter is fresh and good, it may take its place.

Coffee Cake will, we think, prove a novelty, and it is worth a trial. It must be slowly baked in a tin lined with several sheets of paper, the one next the cake to be white and well buttered. Set a quart of flour in the oven until quite hot, then rub into it half a pound of butter, twelve ounces of sugar, four ounces of figs cut up, six ounces of stoned raisins, three ounces of mixed candied peel, and a good tea-spoonful of fresh baking powder. Then put in a quarter-pint of treacle, the same of cream or good milk, a tea-cupful of strong, clear coffee, and three eggs, yolks only. It will take two hours or more to bake properly, in a shallow tin.

Chocolate Cake is made similarly to the above; the best chocolate should be used, and made as if for drinking, as thick as custard. If the chocolate is very sweet, a little less sugar should be put into the cake. Both coffee and chocolate should be added cold. These two are great Yankee favourites.

Angel Cakes are indescribably light and good; they must, to be worth anything, be consumed while fresh. Beat the whites of six fresh eggs to a froth, add six ounces of white sugar and a tea-spoonful of vanilla flavouring. Stir lightly in four ounces and a half of white flour, well sifted and quite dry: in fact, it should be warm. Pour instantly into a tin (not more than half filling it), and at once transfer to a sound regular oven. When done, do not take the cake into a cool place until it is *quite* cold. Part of the mixture might be coloured pink and flavoured with rose essence; this would give *Rose Cake*. May we suggest that, in that case, some of the two, with coffee or chocolate cake, arranged in a silver basket, in alternate slices, would look and taste good.

Dessert Cake is made in perfection by American confectioners; there are several varieties, the most liked being a very rich one, with a selection of dried fruits, such as cherries, apricots, greengages, &c., cut up in it. We lately tasted one with crystallised pine-apple in small pieces, the cake being flavoured with pine-apple essence. The foundation resembles an English Madeira cake. An oval or square tin, rather shallow, is chiefly used for them.

Soda Cakes, white, light, and delicious, are the *rule* in America, but seem the *exception* here. We believe the chief reason to be this : English cooks frequently use soda alone, without acid. In America double the quantity of cream of tartar is added to the soda. It should be remembered that soda itself has no lightening property; acid must be added before effervescence can be obtained. If the cake is a plain one, in which the butter is rubbed into the flour, the acid may be mixed *with* the flour, then the fruit, sugar, &c., next the eggs, and the soda put in last of all, in the milk. In a rich cake, when the butter, eggs, and sugar are creamed, the flour, acid, and soda (all together) may be stirred in last thing. Soda cakes want a good oven; properly managed, few kinds are nicer.

Of *Sandwich Cakes*, or *Layer Cakes*, the variety is so great that we hardly know which to select. We will first impress upon our readers the necessity of a hot oven, and of putting the cakes into it at once. The tins should be round, about the size of a cheese-plate, and an inch in depth, never being more than half filled. Two are laid together to form the sandwich, first spread with jam, jelly, or lemon curd, corn-flour cream, chocolate cream, or, what is a great favourite, cocoa-nut cream. When the two cakes are turned out of the tins, the bottom of each must be spread; the tops, being browner, should be outside. To make the cake, beat hard together twelve ounces of sugar, four each of butter and lard, and five eggs. Then stir in a pound of flour, mixed with the third of an ounce of finely-powdered ammonia. Where the latter is discountenanced, soda and acid must take its place. *Cocoa-nut Cream* is made by grating the white part of a cocoa-nut, and adding half its weight of sugar, then mixing the two with the milk of the nut and the white of an egg, to bind it into a paste soft enough to spread easily. Some of the nut may be reserved, and sprinkled on the top of the cake. For the *Chocolate Cream*, boil together an ounce of grated chocolate and an ounce of corn-flour for a few minutes with a pint of milk. Sweeten, and flavour with vanilla essence.

Honey Apple Cake will sound to English readers somewhat odd, but those who try it once will be very likely to repeat it. Soak a cup of apple-chips for some hours; chop fine, and simmer for an hour in a cup of clear honey, stirring often. When cool, add a cup of sugar, half a cup of milk, half a cup of butter, a tea-spoonful of mixed cinnamon, nutmeg, and cloves, two eggs, a cup and a half of flour, and a heaped tea-spoonful of baking powder. Bake in a gentle oven, in a tin lined with buttered paper.

Our paper shall close with a delicacy seen on the tea-tables of most well-to-do American farmers—viz., *Fruit Shortcake*. Huckleberries are much liked; in this country blackberries or mulberries could be used in their stead, and nothing could be more delicious than Raspberry or Strawberry Shortcake. The recipe here given is rich enough for ordinary purposes, but of course more lard and butter can be used if liked. Sift and dry a pint of flour, rub into it two ounces of lard and two of butter, a little salt, a spoonful of baking powder, and half an ounce of white sugar. Mix to a nice paste with one egg and about a tea-cupful of rich milk. Roll into two round sheets, one thicker than the other; cover the thinner of the two thickly with the berries, well sweetened, lay the other over, and bake in a tin, just large enough to hold it, for about twenty minutes, until nicely browned. Strawberry Shortcake is usually made by laying the two pieces of crust one on the other, dividing when baked, then putting the fruit between in a thick layer. Have fully ripe berries, not too large; sweeten well, and slightly crush them; then press well on the top layer. These cakes are often eaten hot, with sugar and cream. When sour milk or cream is at hand, use it, in which case leave out the powder and put in soda.

TEA-TABLE DELICACIES FOR THE SUMMER SEASON.

BY P. H. DAVIS, AUTHOR OF "THE PRESERVING OF WHOLE FRUITS," ETC.

OME little time ago I contributed an article to the columns of CASSELL'S FAMILY MAGAZINE, explaining how fruit could be put to its best use during the time that it was plentiful. It is an easy step from fruit, which frequently appears upon the tea-table, to some of the many other things which might well accompany it. In summer one's appetite is likely to be jaded, and therefore something is required to coax it. This then must be my excuse for the present series of recipes.

Every one knows how fittingly blancmange and fruit combine, and as a rule it is taken for granted that cornflour is, or should be, the proper ingredient to make a blancmange. Cornflour will certainly produce a very excellent article, but I think that if a blancmange is required which will keep firm for a day or two, isinglass, or finely shredded gelatine, would be welcomed as a pleasing change. I therefore give such for my first recipe.

ISINGLASS BLANCMANGE.

Soak 2 oz. of isinglass in ½ pint of new milk, or if gelatine should be preferred, get that kind which is cut as finely as silken thread, and is nearly as colourless as water. If it should be considered desirable to add solid flavourings, such as spices or fresh lemon-peel, these must be added to the other 1½ pints of milk which will be required to complete the blancmange. Boil up the 1½ pints of milk which contain the flavouring, and whilst still scalding hot, pour it upon the first ½ pint of milk containing the gelatine. If essences are selected for flavouring they should now be added with 4 oz. of castor sugar, and the whole well stirred together; but if solid flavourings have been introduced, the whole of the mixture should now be strained through either a bag or a colander directly into a wetted mould of some pretty shape. Allow the contents of the mould to set, and if it is requisite to have the blancmange ready for the table in a very short time, stand the mould in a vessel of cold water in which a handful of rough salt has been thrown.

When the blancmange is required, dip the mould into hot water for a second or so, turn its contents out upon a glass dish, and decorate, according to taste, with fresh or preserved fruit.

Note.—Be perfectly sure that the interior of the mould is quite wet with cold water before attempting to pour the blancmange into it, but be equally careful that no quantity of water is left at the bottom of the mould, or it will form into small rivulets in the pattern and cause the resulting blancmange to have a "cockled" appearance when turned out.

ALMOND SHORTBREAD

is a very nice thing indeed for the tea-table in summer, and can be made quite simply. It is only requisite to use ordinary care in the manipulation of the ingredients, and to be watchful that the resulting cakes are not burnt or, in fact, baked to too deep a colour when in the oven. Allow these delicacies to come to the table of a fine golden-yellow colour, and as a *bonne-bouche* they will stand considerable criticism. Here then are the ingredients:—

> 1 lb. Ground sweet almonds,
> 8 oz. Castor sugar,
> 8 „ Sifted flour,
> 8 „ Good butter,
> The yolks of eight eggs,
> About eight drops of essence of ratafia.†

In the first place, see that the ground almonds are nice and fresh, for if they have the slightest taint or rancidity about them they are not at all suitable for the purpose. Having procured the almonds, mix them with the sifted flour and castor sugar, and then very, *very* carefully indeed, add a few drops of the ratafia, because too much of it would be positively obnoxious. Mix everything thoroughly and perfectly, so that the flavouring may be carried through and through the other dry ingredients. Make a space in the centre, and in this drop the yolks of the eggs, which have been examined as broken, one at a time, into a vessel. Then melt the butter, add that, and mix up the whole together until it is a nice, firm, stiff paste. This should now be rolled a great many times—in fact it cannot be rolled too frequently. When sufficiently rolled to appear like a strip of cream-coloured satin about a quarter of an inch thick, cut it into small squares with a sharp knife. Pinch up all the edges of each square, and in the centre of every cake lay the split half of a blanched almond. Now butter some baking-tins, lay the cakes upon them, and bake in a moderate oven to a fine pale yellow tint.

It will be found that this almond shortbread is a most delicious thing at all times, but more particularly when eaten in conjunction with fruit, because almonds and fruit always go well together, for the reason that the kernel of a fruit-stone is in nature something like an almond itself.

A DELICATE SPONGE CAKE.

Separate the yolks from the whites of ten eggs, and whisk the former to a light froth. Then gradually add to them 1 lb. of castor sugar, taking care to beat it up well until all the added sugar has been thoroughly mixed with the other ingredients. Now whisk the egg-whites to a very light but firm snow, and stir that into the batter and mix all thoroughly. Drop in a *small* teaspoonful † of essence of lemon, stir again and then sift in 1 lb. 2 oz. of nice, sweet, dry pastry flour, and

† These are open questions which must be left to (1) the taste of the person, and (2) the strength of the essence. No *definite* rule can be given.

whisk all up until perfectly blended. Now take some tins of any shape or size desired, wipe the insides out very carefully, and then grease them lightly with butter which has been previously creamed. Freely dust fine sugar over the butter, fill the tins three-parts full of the sponge cake; dust the tops rather heavily with sugar, and bake in a warm oven until the cakes are of a delicate yellow colour.

A Word of Caution.—As a rule, the housewife is so anxious to have her cake done before it *really* is baked, that by frequent opening and closing of the oven door she lowers the temperature of the oven, and causes the cake to fall in its tin, and thus become " sad." Here then is a word of advice:—First be certain that the oven is of the desired temperature, and supplied with sufficient fuel to maintain that temperature for the time it is expected the cake will require for baking. When the time has elapsed and it is thought the cake is ready, look at it and judge somewhat by its colour, but at the same time push well into the middle of the cake through one of the cracks in the top of it a good stiff straw. Remove the straw immediately, and if anything sticks to it, the cake is not yet done, but if the straw comes away quite clean the cake is finished.

ROSE BISCOTTINES.

These are indeed a novelty, and if properly made, are far superior to the world-famous Shrewsbury cakes. For five o'clock tea they are a decided innovation, and I claim for them the credit of being unique in every way because they are entirely of my own invention; and I sincerely hope those who would make these lovely little morsels to perfection will do me the credit of keeping exclusively to the proportions of the different ingredients I have given, and likewise will be careful that the biscottines are not over-baked, nor burnt in any way. Take—

1 lb. Fine dry pastry flour,
8 oz. Castor sugar,
8 „ Butter (fresh),
¼ „ Finely sifted biscuit powder,
A hock-glass-full of rose water,
Two eggs.

The flour and biscuit powder should be sifted together, and then the other ingredients well rubbed into them. The sugar should now be mixed thoroughly, and a space made in the centre of the lot, in which the eggs and rose water should be poured. Stir everything well together and produce a nice, firm, *stiff* paste. Roll this out into a sheet rather less than one-eighth of an inch thick, and then stamp the biscottines out of it with a small fluted-edged oval hand-cutter. Now lay these cakes on buttered baking-tins, put them in a warm oven, and keep them there till quite done.

By rolling the above dough out to only the thickness of stout note-paper, and baking the biscottines very lightly indeed—only about twenty seconds in a good hot oven—the result will be beautiful wafers to take with ices.

USEFUL HINTS.

Lafayette Cakes.—Into a warm bowl put six ounces of butter and six ounces of castor sugar, beat with a wooden spoon till light; break in one egg, beat, then put in a second egg, and beat well; mix into six ounces of fine flour one teaspoonful of baking-powder, add a little of the flour to the eggs, then break in a third egg, and sift in the remainder of the flour, beat all briskly for a few minutes, then put into a square, shallow, well-buttered tin, at once, and bake in a good oven from ten to fifteen minutes. Take out, lay on a sieve to cool, then with a sharp knife cut into cakes three or four inches long by about two broad, and lay them aside while you make the icing. I generally put several different kinds of icing on, as it gives more variety, and the cake itself is a good foundation for making a change. Sometimes you can cut the cakes in slices and put a thin spreading of jam between, and either leave them plain or put a plain sugar icing on them, or you can treat half of them so and merely put chocolate icing on the other half. Well, for the icing, supposing you want variety, take half a dozen of the little cakes and put jam in them, leaving the rest plain. Put into a bowl about half a pound of icing sugar, beat it free from all lumps, drop in some flavouring such as vanilla or pineapple, then add very carefully about a tablespoonful (or a little more) of warm water, beat smooth with the back of a spoon, then with the blade of a knife, previously dipped in boiling water; spread the top of each of the six cakes, lay on a sieve, hold in front of the fire a moment to set the icing, then let them cool. Into the half of the remaining icing drop some cochineal, just enough to make it a pretty pink, and ice half the plain cakes; then into the rest of the icing stir two tablespoonfuls of grated chocolate (it may be that you will require a little extra sugar), and a very little water, and ice the remaining cakes. A little practice only is required to make this icing. You will see by doing this that out of one baking you have actually three different tea-cakes. Only experience will teach you at first how much water is needed; very little does, as if made too thin it will not set. After mixing, if the bowl is held to the fire for a moment or two, it helps to make it spread smoothly and also to set. When icing, dip the knife frequently into a cup of boiling water; the wet blade puts it on much better.

Orange Cake.—Three eggs, their weight in butter, sugar, and flour. Beat butter and sugar to a light cream, add two eggs and half the flour, beating well, then add the grated rind of one orange, and half the juice; then put in the remainder of the flour, a small teaspoonful of baking-powder, and the third egg. Bake for half an hour.

Icing for Cake.—Six ounces of icing-sugar, and enough orange-juice to make it a thick cream. Pour it evenly over the cake while it is a little warm, and put it to set in a warm place. This is a most delicious cake. Another orange cake makes an equal bid for favour on account of its excellence. Six eggs, two cups of fine sugar, one scant cup of butter, one cup of milk, three good cupfuls of flour, three teaspoonfuls of baking-powder. Beat sugar and butter to a cream, add yolks and whites beaten separately, sift powder into flour, and add it lightly, and also a very little orange-juice. Bake in a round tin. When cold, cut the cake into three layers, and place the following icing between:—Grate the rind of one sweet orange, add it to the strained juice, and mix in enough icing-sugar to make a stiffish paste, and spread it evenly on the layers; pile upon each other, and ice over with more of the icing; make a little stiffer with extra sugar. Lemon used instead of orange is very good, and especially refreshing for summer.

German Cakes.—Half a pound of flour, quarter of a pound of castor-sugar, quarter of a pound of butter, a teaspoonful of baking-powder, one teaspoonful of lemon-essence, and one egg. Rub butter, sugar, and flour together till like bread-crumbs; add powder, essence, and egg well beaten. Work to a stiff paste with the hands, then divide into two pieces. Have a flat dinner-plate ready well buttered, roll out one-half of the paste to its size, lay it on, spread a thin layer of apricot or greengage-jam on it, then the other piece of paste rolled out. Trim the edges, pinch them up to keep in the jam, brush over the top with beaten egg, and sprinkle a handful of blanched and chopped almonds over it. Bake in a moderate oven for half-an-hour. When cold, cut into small squares or triangles.

DELICACIES FOR THE WINTER TEA-TABLE.

BY P. H. DAVIS.

 ARIETY is charming"—at least the old saying hath it thus— and as my writings on "Summer Tea - Table Delicacies" proved so acceptable, I continue the series by adding some seasonable articles when the days are colder, and the appetite demands something a little more substantial than in summer. I diverge widely from the beaten track by including only those novelties which I do not think have ever been published previously, and as all of them have been tested by myself, it may be accepted that they are reliable, and the recipes may be followed with confidence. I have only to repeat my request, which appeared in the June issue of CASSELL'S MAGAZINE, that those who would follow out my recipes will kindly do them the justice to use exactly the proportions given, and neither more nor less, because all the ingredients have been carefully adjusted with the object of preventing any failures.

I lead off with a very old-fashioned article indeed, which I have reconstructed and improved almost beyond recognition, and if it is served warm with a nice sweet sauce, it will be quite a novelty to-day; although, by-the-by, it may also be served cold with boiled custard, and I am certain will then be equally well appreciated. I will call it an

APPLE MOULD.

Commence by removing the peels and cores from some nice juicy apples, but do not cut up the fruit too small. Take the pieces of apple and put them into a stew-pan, with the peel of a fresh lemon and sufficient white sugar to suit the palate. Just cover them with water, stand them at the side of the fire, and then let them slowly simmer until they become a pulp. Remove the stew-pan from the fire, and, after taking out the lemon-peel, beat the apple pulp until it is perfectly smooth, when allow it to get cold. Now beat up two eggs until they froth, and amalgamate this with the apple pulp, and follow by the addition of two ounces of melted fresh butter and the same weight of stale crumbs of white bread. Whisk everything together until thoroughly mixed.

Take a mould of any pattern, prepare the inside of it by smearing it with creamed butter, and dredge that over thickly with more bread-crumbs. Into this pour the apple mixture, sprinkle the top over very thickly with bread-crumbs once again, and then bake in a moderate oven. Turn it out of the mould carefully, and serve either hot or cold, as directed above.

If other spices or flavourings are approved, they may be added to the apple mixture when it is quite cold, and just before it is put into the mould.

I recently took a summer trip to the Continent, and in the course of my rambles stayed in Belgium for a few days. There I met the very best sample of novel gingerbread that I had ever come across, and after some investigation I evolved a recipe for it, which I now append :—

ORANGE GINGERBREAD.

1¼ lbs. flour ; 8 oz. treacle ; 6 oz. brown sugar; 4 oz. butter ; 4 oz. finely chopped candied orange-peel ; 1 oz. baking powder ; 2 eggs ; 10 or 12 drops aniseed flavouring.

Method.-- Sift the baking powder and flour together ; make a bay in the centre, into which put the sugar and orange-peel ; add the treacle, and then melt the butter and pour that in. Add the slight flavouring of aniseed. Whisk the eggs, and pour them into the central hollow ; then mix all together in the bay, and work all up to a dough. Break it into small pieces, and place them in well-buttered pans. Sprinkle some caraway seeds over the tops, and bake in a warm oven. When baked, dredge some fine sugar over them, after having lightly brushed the tops with whipped whites of eggs.

Germany has many peculiarities which, I think, might readily be introduced into the *cuisine* of this kingdom, and from amongst other varied toothsome delicacies of the Fatherland I select for my present paper a recipe of an original

GERMAN NEW YEAR CAKE.

1 lb. flour ; 12 oz. castor sugar ; 8 oz. butter ; 4 oz. sultanas (washed and dried) ; 4 oz. mixed drained candied peel (cut small) ; 5 eggs ; a small teaspoonful of essence of lemon.

Method.—Beat the sugar and butter to a light cream in a warm pan. Whisk the eggs to a very light froth, and stir them into the cream. Add the essence of lemon, the sultanas, and peel, and then lightly stir in the flour. Turn the mixture into a baking tin which has been lined with buttered paper, and bake it in a moderate oven.

When it has become partly cooled, cover the top and sides with a thin icing, made with fine castor sugar and hot water, and coloured pink with a little liquid cochineal.

I add another German recipe, which I think will be welcomed at this time of the year, and I am certain it will prove itself to be a novelty of no mean order. Certainly it deserves attention, and the results of experiments which I have made with the recipe have been so highly satisfactory that the desire to include it is irresistible.

POTATO BUNS.

1 lb. flour ; 8 oz. boiled potatoes (carefully peeled and mashed) ; 8 oz. castor sugar ; 8 oz. butter ; 6 oz.

currants (picked, washed, and dried); 1 oz. dried yeast; 1 egg; half-pint of milk; a pinch of salt.

Method.—Rub the butter into the flour, and make a space in the centre. Add in the sugar and currants. Make half the milk lukewarm, and dissolve the yeast in it, and pour that into the bay. Stir the rest of the milk into the potatoes, and put that into the bay likewise. Beat the egg, and add that in also. Drop in a pinch of salt, stir all together, and mix everything up to a dough. Cover it over with a cloth, and let it lie for half an hour. Then break it into small pieces, mould them round, place them on buttered tins, and when they have swelled to twice their size, bake them in a sharp oven. While hot, wash them over with egg to glaze them.

Having given a New Year cake, it naturally follows that a recipe for an inexpensive and easily made Christmas cake is in order, and I therefore append it, although I have simplified the recipe as far as possible, and that with the main idea of producing an excellent result at a moderate cost. I have only to ask that my readers will kindly use the proportions given, and not deviate from them in any way.

CHRISTMAS CAKE.

1½ lbs. flour; 1 lb. castor sugar; 1 lb. butter; 1 lb. sultanas (washed and dried); 1 lb. currants (washed, picked, and dried); 12 oz. mixed drained candied peel (cut fine); 9 eggs; fruit flavouring of any kind—lemon, orange, raspberry, pineapple, &c.—quantity to taste.

Method.—Proceed exactly as for "German New Year Cake," but remember that this cake will require more soaking in the oven. Try if it is done by the old method of pushing a thin splint of dry wood into

the centre, and if that comes out dry the cake is done; if wet, and the cake sticks to the splint, it requires more soaking. When it is covered with icing, stick a few small fancy sugar ornaments about it, and put some fancy frilled coloured papers round the sides.

I conclude the present paper with a recipe for an article which has gained great favour in Switzerland and the north of Italy—say the Tyrol district—and I am satisfied that the result will commend itself to those who prefer to depart from the beaten track, and desire a thorough novelty for the tea-table. I have rarely met with any simple combination of ingredients which produces so excellent a result if carefully manipulated, and therefore I have every confidence in hinting that those who follow the recipe will be perfectly satisfied with the experiment.

CHOCOLATE TEA-CAKES.

8 oz. flour; 6 oz. castor sugar; 6 oz. butter; 4 oz. ground chocolate; 4 eggs; half-teaspoonful vanilla flavouring.

Method.—Beat the butter to a cream in a warm pan, add in the sugar, and beat both well. Whisk the eggs to a light froth, and stir them into the cream. Add a slight flavouring of vanilla, then lightly mix in the flour and chocolate. With a spoon drop the mixture on buttered flat tins, each cake the size of a large chestnut. Dust some fine sugar over them, and bake them in a warm oven.

Note.—If chocolate is not available, the same result may be obtained by substituting for it *two* ounces of perfectly pure cocoa powder, and then adding two ounces of extra sugar and a dozen more drops of vanilla flavouring. Chocolate is only cocoa, sugar, and vanilla flavouring, and therefore can easily be produced.

EVERY-DAY PUDDINGS, AND HOW TO MAKE THEM.

THESE hints, as the title implies, will be of the most homely kind, setting forth rules and principles for the guidance of those who are anxious to do simple things in the right way, and present a variety of puddings at their tables; for, be it remembered, variety is not only pleasant to the palate, but necessary for health.

Farinaceous Puddings, although the simplest, are

unquestionably, as a rule, improperly made and cooked; and as they are so nourishing and delicious when the right mode is followed, we will give them first place. Now, when cooking any kind of food, we are nine-tenths of the way on the road to success if we understand both the composition of the food and the effect of heat upon it, *i.e.*, the amount of heat required for its conversion from the raw to the cooked state.

First, then, the composition of the "food stuffs," or "cereals," all of which may be classed as farinaceous, viz., sago, tapioca, hominy, rice, semolina, pearl-barley, crushed wheat, &c. ; in a word, they are *starchy* foods, although the proportion varies—in some there is more than seventy per cent. of starch, for the perfect cooking of which a long time is required to enable the little cells to swell and burst; hence the absurdity of cooking them in a quick oven.

Everything of a starchy nature swells in cooking, so plenty of room must be allowed, and the proportion of rice, &c., should not be more than two ounces for each pint of milk used in the pudding; the dish should not be more than three-parts filled. What happens if the dish *is* quite full, the oven too hot, and too much grain, as we may term it, used? Just this : in a very short time the milk will be soaked up, so the grain cannot swell as it should, and some will have boiled over in the oven ; the result being a hard, indigestible, quarter-cooked mess, instead of, at less cost, a rich, creamy, nourishing pudding. Try the following method for any kind referred to above:—Wash well, in several waters, four ounces of the grain, put it in a dish well greased, with two ounces of sugar, a pinch of salt, and a quart of milk ; stir up and, if the flavour is liked, grate a little nutmeg on the surface, and bake from two to three hours in a *very slow oven.* Coarse oatmeal makes an excellent pudding of this kind ; children will enjoy it baked *minus* sugar, and served with warm treacle.

It is well to stir the contents of the dish a few times during the first part of the cooking. Some may say, "*How* slow should the oven be?" We mean that the milk should only just simmer, the very tiniest bubbles only appearing on the surface; indeed, after the pudding has reached simmering-point in the oven, the cooking may often be finished on the top of a range, or the hob of an open grate.

Some of our readers will exclaim, "No eggs!" and others will assert that the pudding cannot be made without them ; though, as a matter of fact, they are not required in an every-day pudding, and nothing is more indigestible than a long-baked egg. Those who insist upon adding them will be wise to make the pudding by cooking the milk and grain separately in a saucepan until nearly done, then adding the eggs when the mixture has cooled, and baking the pudding just long enough to set and brown the surface.

A Baked Custard.—How often is this seen watery at the bottom, and full of holes, rough-looking all through! There are many causes, the chief being excess of sugar, imperfect mixing, stale eggs, and too hot an oven. Really good milk should be used, and the pudding moved as little and as gently as possible ; the oven must be gentle, and a smooth custard will be the result. A very light pudding for an invalid is a *steamed custard;* two eggs, rather less than half a pint of milk, and a teaspoonful of white sugar should be thoroughly beaten, poured into a buttered basin, covered with a buttered paper, and steamed in a saucepan of gently-boiling water coming half-way up the basin for thirty to forty minutes. A *savoury*

custard is similarly made, *cold beef-tea* taking the place of the milk and sugar ; this is very enjoyable when cold, and furnishes a nice change.

Batter Puddings need careful mixing to insure freedom from lumps ; they are improved by standing some hours before cooking, and further improved by the addition of the whites of the eggs, separately beaten, at the last minute. Baking powder, too, should always be put in the instant before the batter is poured into the dish or basin ready for cooking, or it is useless. Very good proportions for "*Yorkshire Pudding*" batter are two eggs, a pint of milk, and six ounces of flour. Steamed or boiled puddings should be rather stiffer than baked ones, as the moisture evaporates to a greater extent in the dry heat of an oven than when they are cooked by steam. In separating eggs, yolks from whites, care must be taken to avoid any intermixture of yolk and white, as the former contains oil, and would prevent the latter being stiffly beaten. A current of air facilitates the beating ; so does a pinch of salt—it gives body ; the eggs *must* be fresh.

With regard to *Suet Puddings* of all kinds, *i.e.*, all puddings containing suet, they must, to be digestible and nourishing, be well cooked ; the suet should be first skinned and shredded, before chopping, and the finer it is chopped the better ; this is an operation very carelessly performed as a rule.

Beef suet makes the richer, but mutton suet the lighter puddings.

Bread-crumbs form a good addition, even to an ordinary rolly-poly ; if to each half-pound of flour two ounces of bread-crumbs be added, a lightness and delicacy unobtainable without them are a certain result, and the pudding is more wholesome. Steamed puddings are lighter than boiled ones, and there are other advantages ; viz., no cloth is needed, a piece of greased paper taking its place, and it matters not about the basin being full, as there is no fear of the water getting into the pudding if care is taken to set it in a saucepan with boiling water half-way up the basin, replenishing it from time to time with more boiling water ; keep the lid on, and allow at least half as long again as the same pudding would take to boil. Little puddings can be steamed nicely in an ordinary potato-steamer.

When liquids and semi-liquids—such, for instance, as a combination of milk, eggs, and marmalade—are added to puddings, they should be beaten together before putting them with the dry ingredients (imperfect mixing of the materials being a common cause of failure in turning out), and the mould or basin must be well greased with fat free from salt ; clarified dripping is preferable to salt butter—so often used for culinary purposes—as the latter would cause them to stick.

All whose digestions are imperfect will do well to avoid currants ; in the majority of cases sultana raisins can take their place ; besides, they are less trouble to clean, and really nourishing, while currants are not ; and every housewife knows how troublesome they are to wash, dry, and pick *properly*. In grating lemons, only the yellow part should be used—the white pith is bitter; or, if chopped peel is preferred, a little sugar will assist the process, as it moistens and so keeps the peel in a mass; in chopping it for forcemeat, salt, instead of sugar, helps in just the same way.

Bread Puddings, the very name of which is a hated sound in some houses, may be made really nice, and in a variety of ways, with but little more trouble than is required to prepare the uninviting heavy mess so often seen. For the basis, the thing to avoid is lumpiness; just soak the bread (crust or crumb) in water until soft, then squeeze it as dry as possible, and pass it through a cullender, or beat out the lumps with a fork; this may then be converted into many kinds for which fresh bread-crumbs often form the foundation—such as fig, treacle, lemon, date, &c. &c. —always remembering that it must be made stiffer; it will yield moisture during the cooking, whereas a pudding made of dry bread requires added moisture. With the Editor's permission we will give, on a future occasion, some recipes for puddings of this kind that, we promise, will give satisfaction to the juveniles, and mothers shall have no cause to complain of the cost.

Bread-and-Butter Puddings.—How often one meets with some such recipe as this :—" Fill a dish with bread and butter, pour over a custard of eggs, milk," &c. If you *fill* the dish with bread and butter, how can there be room for the custard, and the subsequent swelling during the baking? Try this method :— Supposing your pie-dish holds a quart, just half fill it with bread and butter, each slice sprinkled with sultana raisins, candied peel cut very small, or grated lemon-rind, and, if the flavour is liked, a little spice. Beat up nearly a pint of milk with two eggs and sugar to taste, about two ounces; pour this over the pudding, letting it soak awhile; put a few pieces more butter on the top, and cover with an old dish or something which fits, until it is about half baked—in a moderate oven—then remove the cover, and let it brown nicely, but it should not be hard; turn out, dredge with castor sugar, and pour a little plain custard or cream round it. This is very different from one made in the way above referred to, which is often as hard as the driest dry toast. For children, a pudding made without any butter, except to grease the dish, will be quite rich enough, and a little marmalade is very nice as a substitute for candied peel.

We will just refer to the old-fashioned plan, even now sometimes recommended, of boiling puddings in a cloth. A moment's reflection will convince any one of the absurdity of this; it is impossible in the case, say, of a plum pudding, to avoid losing some of the goodness, as the colour of the water plainly shows after boiling; and the flavour suffers equally. It may be well to point out that tin is a better con-ductor of heat than earthenware; a pudding in a tin mould holding a quart would be done in a fourth less time than one in a basin of the same capacity, crock being a bad conductor of heat; that is why pastry baked on plates is not so good as when tin patty-pans are used, as pastry needs a quick oven. For this reason, also, tins for Yorkshire puddings should not only be greased, but made hot after well greasing before the mixture is poured in; it will then rise better.

May we point out that perfect cleanliness is a desideratum? So are good and pure ingredients; of groceries generally, it may certainly be said "the best are the cheapest." Colourings, essences, and the like are plentiful enough of good quality, bearing the name of the maker; no good firm is ashamed of its name, and there is no need to purchase low-priced inferior goods of this kind, which are, in some cases, absolutely injurious. We find that, in the present instance, we have no space for actual recipes (save three with which we close our hints); later on we hope to give some. Meanwhile we would urge our readers to endeavour to master the principles of pudding-making, which will enable them the better to understand any recipes they may meet with; and when failures arise, as they sometimes will, in spite of the greatest care, they will the more readily grasp the cause, and so prevent the recurrence of the disappointment.

Nursery Pudding.—Measure half a pint of soaked bread, beaten as above directed; add one tablespoonful of cornflour, first mixed with half a pint of milk and boiled for a few minutes. Beat the whole until cool, then stir in one egg, spread a little jam at the bottom of a greased pie-dish, pour in the bread mixture, and bake in a moderate oven for half an hour. Alternate layers of the jam and bread mixture make a still nicer pudding, in which case call it "*Jam Sandwich Pudding.*"

Treacle Pudding.—This is exceptionally wholesome and a general favourite. Mix together four ounces each of bread-crumbs, fine oatmeal, and chopped suet; add two ounces of candied peel cut small, two ounces of flour, half a teaspoonful of mixed spice, a pinch of salt, and two eggs beaten up with half a pound of treacle. Mix thoroughly, put it in a well-greased basin, and steam it for *at least* three hours. Figs, dates, or raisins can be added by way of variety.

Combination Rolly-poly.—Roll out some suet crust, and spread it with the following mixture :—Half a pound each of figs, prunes, and dates cut small; the same of sultana raisins, brown sugar, and chopped apples, with a little spice to flavour; this will not all be needed for one pudding, but can be kept in a jar for use; the fruit is, of course, to be stoned. Roll up and boil from two to three hours according to size.

LIZZIE HERITAGE.

LMONDS are very moderate in price just now, and the desiccated cocoa-nut, which plays so prominent a part in hosts of dainties, is lower than ever. Those recipes enumerated below are therefore within the reach of almost everyone. Their digestibility is another matter; though it is certain that many who find nuts indigestible when only half masticated may partake of them without fear when finely ground ; and as this is the condition to which they are brought before they enter into the composition of the dishes, my qualms of conscience are somewhat quieted. Some of these sweets are quite simple, and not very costly when prepared at home, though expensive to buy ; and so I feel sure that when a dainty out of the common is wanted, they will be appreciated.

Almost everybody knows and likes the almond paste, which forms all too small a part of bride cake, and nearly all like good chocolate ; these combined, produce a real delicacy, that may crop up in all sorts of dishes. The combination is a very agreeable one, but careful mixing must be insisted on. Don't spoil the ship for the proverbial " ha'porth o' tar," but get the best chocolate your means allow.

Almond and Chocolate Paste.

Take half a pound of almonds; the Valencias answer for all cooking purposes as well as the more costly Jordans ; they should be blanched by bringing them to the boil over the fire in a little pan of water, then rubbing the skins off in a clean cloth. Here are two useful hints in this connection : always put the almonds on in cold water, and always rinse them in cold water before rubbing them in the cloth. Then chop them very small on a clean board ; any "foreign flavour" would ruin the delicacy of your dishes. The finer the better. Have ready in a basin an ounce and a half of fresh butter : the freshest of fresh, I should have said ; the same weight of pounded sugar and a few drops of vanilla essence ; the amount to use depends on the goodness of the chocolate : the more highly flavoured it is with the ever popular vanilla, the greater the chances of success. These are now to be worked to a smooth paste with the back of a wooden spoon ; the almonds and the yolk of a large egg being added, a little at a time. Just a shake of grated chocolate must go in from time to time ; an ounce will do, but some will like nearly double the quantity, then a little more egg yolk and butter will be wanted. Nothing short of a very velvet-like paste should satisfy you, and it cannot be prepared in five minutes. The best possible results are obtained when the almonds are pounded with a few drops of rose or orange-flower water instead of being chopped. I would also call the attention of busy people to the ground almonds sold in tins ; these are, however, mixed with sugar, which must be borne in mind, or the dish may turn out too sweet to be pleasant.

The uses of this ? They are many ; here are just a few. Imagine a cake of any light kind, such as Madeira ; place a layer of the paste on the top, making it level with a rolling-pin and rounding the sides neatly : points too seldom borne in mind, and which in themselves, if omitted, are enough to stamp the cake as the work of a novice. Then, if an expert in the use of an icing-bag and pipe, take a little coloured icing, and form any design ; or finish off simply by sifting coloured sugar over the top. Would you attain still higher success? Then get some good chocolate fondants, and put them over in a pattern, sticking them on with a morsel of icing sugar, and raw white of egg beaten to a paste. Cream fondants are used in just the same way. A delightful addition to the " cake basket " is made by slicing a cake, and "sandwiching" some of the above paste in between the slices, and then cutting it up after pressing well together again.

Then all sorts of fancy shapes may be produced if some cutters are handy, and the cake trimmings will come in for biscuits if stamped with yet smaller cutters. I ought to say that there are lots of people who would like the paste better minus butter, and there is no reason whatever why their whim should not be indulged. Tastes vary, too, much as to sugar ; it might be doubled in the foregoing recipe before the mixture would satisfy some ; the thing to bear in mind in adding extra sugar is that less moisture in the shape of egg and butter is necessary.

Almond Aigrettes.

These are sure to enhance one's reputation, for they are of such all-round utility that they can be as well served for tea as luncheon or dinner, and hot as well as cold. They are made by blending a gill of tepid water, a tablespoonful of salad oil, an egg, a teaspoonful of castor sugar, three ounces and a half of flour, an ounce of ground or chopped almonds, and a few drops of essence of almonds. There is a right way, and the mixing is troublesome if it is not followed. The flour, oil, yolk of egg, and water are to be beaten to a smooth batter ; the almonds and sugar follow, and the mass must be beaten for a few minutes, or the puffiness that should belong to the aigrettes will be lacking. The stiffly-beaten white of the egg goes in lightly at the end, and the mixture is put in well-greased patty-pans in little heaps, two forks being used ; they should be half-filled only, and the oven must be hot. They are soon baked, and must be served in a light pile, with plenty of sugar over, for it will be noticed that but little goes in the batter. These may be fried, but there must be lots of fat of good heat, and from the pan to the table is the motto; more flour will be wanted, about half as much again but the batter should be tested; it is stiff enough when it retains its shape in the fat and emerges brown and puffy. Drain on a hot cloth or paper. Almond essence is condemned wholesale by some people, but it is to be had free from poisonous properties and of guaranteed wholesomeness by the makers.

Almond Orange Cake.

This is simply delicious, as a trial will prove. The materials should be all in readiness, and here they are. Seven ounces each of chopped sweet almonds and fine castor sugar, an ounce of candied orange-peel chopped small, the grated peel of half a fresh orange, a quarter of a pound of butter, the same of fine flour, the same weight of rice-flour or potato-flour (but not *ground rice*), some orange marmalade, and yolks of eggs. The almonds and sugar are first to be blended with the white of an egg, then added to the other materials : enough yolks of eggs being added, one at a time, to make paste that can be rolled out on a board. The mass should look like rich shortbread. It is cut in rounds of four inches in diameter and half an inch thick, and baked in a very slow oven. The marmalade is spread over before serving, and some chopped almonds, that have been baked to a golden brown in the oven, are shaken over. These *may* be dispensed with, but the cake suffers. If for storing for a time, one good-sized thick cake can be made. Now for some very dainty

Dessert Biscuits.

Some of the last mixture should be rolled out as thinly as it is possible to roll it without breaking ; the addition of a few drops of yellow colouring does much to add to the rich appearance. Then cut in a number of fancy shapes, and bake as slowly and carefully as possible ; do not remove from the tins until cold. They may be sugared over, or served as they are, or piped with coloured icing. To convert them into fruit biscuits, place on half a cherry, or raisin, or strips of candied citron-peel, or little squares of candied fruit, as pine-apple, or ginger, or anything to taste. In the latter two cases, the baking is finished, and the fruit stuck on with icing sugar ; in the other cases the fruit may be baked. Other biscuits that mix well with these are prepared by taking portions of the "almond and chocolate paste," and moulding into tiny birds'-nests ; the circumference of a florin is the maximum size, and they may be smaller. Put in some coloured or white comfits to imitate eggs, and dry them on the plate-rack ; they should not be baked. Very pretty little cakes, which are really cakes or biscuits, according to size, are

Dominoes.

Again the "almond and chocolate paste" is brought into use, but it is so excellent that there is no fear of tiring of it readily. The paste must be rolled out in a thin sheet ; the size is a matter of taste ; but the *proportions* of an ordinary domino should be observed. Then the decoration must be of a kind to imitate dominoes. The icing used may be white or coloured, and a very small pipe is essential. A more effective way is to go all over first with a pale-coloured icing, and put the dots on in white. These are extremely pretty for festive occasions, and really little trouble to those who have mastered the art of icing.

Here is a delicious dish that somewhat resembles the cakes of the same kind that are popular in Germany ; and, by the way, it is a great deal less trouble than one would suppose after reading the directions.

The "filling" is the feature, and it should be prepared while the cake foundation is baking, that both may be ready together.

Walnut Cake.

Six ounces of flour, five of butter, a tablespoonful each of sugar and chopped almonds, the yolk of a hard boiled egg and that of a raw one, and two tablespoonfuls of skinned and chopped walnuts, form the materials for the cake ; they are to be mixed with a light hand, just as for short pastry, and the less water used, the better. The dryness of the flour and the care exercised in the sifting, no less than the goodness of the butter, must receive attention. The tin for baking should be round, and the size of a dinner-plate, and *must* have a turned-up edge. These tins are called "sandwich pans," as a rule, and cost about sixpence each ; they are useful for many purposes. After the paste is laid in, the bottom should be pricked, and the oven must be moderate, as the cake should not be dark in colour.

Now for the "filling." First put in a stewpan the yolks of three eggs, half a gill each of milk and cream, and three ounces of sugar, and stir over the fire until thick, but the boiling point is not to be reached. Then, off the fire, beat in the whites of the eggs and a quarter of a pound of chopped walnuts. This is to be put in the cake, the top made smooth and returned to the oven to set. All sorts of flavourings are added to nut cakes in the land where they are an institution. Spice is often used, but we advise that strict moderation be the motto ; one does not want a nut cake to taste of spice and nothing more. If served hot, no garnish is needed ; but in the cold condition, all sorts of dried fruits are suitable, or a dust of pink sugar is enough. A teaspoonful of chopped pistachios will give the dish a more highly finished appearance. Pistachios are expensive, but it is astonishing what a lot of ground a small quantity will cover in the chopped state, and how completely the dish is transformed.

Here are some biscuits that, for want of a better name, I call

Tip-Tops.

These are very good, and I assure you that they will keep any length of time, if allowed. Seven ounces of butter and five of golden syrup are first to be warmed together ; five ounces of lump sugar to be rasped on the rind of a fresh orange, crushed to powder, and added with half-a-teaspoonful of the best mixed spice that can be bought: that at two shillings a pound is really cheaper than spice at a shilling; nothing more certainly spoils anything than poor spice. Next put in a couple of ounces each of candied citron-, lemon- and orange-peel, very finely chopped: trouble in this direction is well bestowed; finally, two ounces of grated cocoa-nut and the same weight of walnuts or almonds, as most convenient, go in, with half a

pound of pastry-flour and a quarter of a pound of corn-flour.

The mixture is then to be set aside to blend in a bowl, covered with a cloth, for a few hours; it will take no harm if left all night. When ready to bake, shake in as much more flour as will make it stiff enough to roll out and cut in shapes—fingers, or any other—then put it in a gentle oven, and remove when brown and crisp. Remember that everything containing treacle requires steady heat and watchfulness.

DEBORAH PLATTER.

MORE ABOUT PUDDINGS.

WE will ask those who are desirous of learning "more about puddings" to read over the paper on "Every-day Puddings" which appeared recently in this Magazine.* As we here assume that the directions given, and rules laid down therein, will be followed by all who attempt to carry out these recipes, we shall thus save much repetition in the present paper.

We are mindful of our promise to give some further hints on puddings suitable for the nursery. Perhaps one of the best is *Albany Pudding;* this is a mixture of coarse oatmeal, crushed wheat, brown bread-crumbs, brown flour, and suet, two ounces of each; four ounces of treacle, and four ounces each of figs and prunes (stoned) cut up finely; one egg and enough milk (*about* a quarter of a pint) to make a stiff mixture are added to the above. This pudding should be steamed for three or four hours, or boiled a proportionate time, and served with hot treacle poured round it. Many mothers have proved the difficulty of inducing their children to eat porridge of any kind; they will do well to serve the ingredients in the form of a pudding such as the foregoing, the combination of cereals and fruit furnishing a most wholesome diet.

It is to be regretted that comparatively few people (vegetarians excepted) are acquainted with crushed wheat, for it is excellent for a variety of purposes, and suits many people better than oatmeal, being less heating to the blood.

Prunes and figs, as well as dates, may be introduced into many kinds of puddings with good results (being

* See Page 70

equal to raisins, and far superior to currants, which—we will repeat—should never be given to children); they are also excellent stewed and served with farinaceous puddings, or with boiled rice or macaroni; for it should be borne in mind that if starchy foods are partaken of frequently, fruit is necessary to counteract their constipating tendency. A favourite remedy for this complaint with a surgeon who is well versed in hygienic diet is a dish of stewed raisins; these should be stoned, and left to soak for some hours in a little water previous to stewing, until they are well swollen and soft; no sugar is to be added, but lemon-juice is recommended, and, to derive full benefit, stale wholemeal or malt bread should be eaten with them.

To return, however, to puddings: another, suitable alike for children and adults who cannot indulge in heavier varieties, is thus made:—Spread some thin slices of brown or white bread, or stale sponge-cake, with jam; make them into sandwiches, and then cut into small dice—there should be enough to fill a half-pint measure; put them lightly into a buttered basin, then pour over an egg and half a pint of warm milk beaten well together. Steam this for an hour (see previous directions for steaming). Marmalade may be used instead of jam, and any flavouring added to the milk.

A passing word about spice: this should never be added to puddings for invalids suffering from a cough, sore-throat, or allied ailments, as the smallest quantity often proves very irritating.

Empress Pudding is old-fashioned, but popular. Four ounces of well-washed rice are first to be simmered in a quart of milk, until the grain is soft and the milk absorbed; when cooled a little, a couple of eggs, with sugar and flavouring to taste, are beaten in, and the mixture put into a greased pie-dish, in layers, with jam between each, and baked a pale brown in a moderate oven. The substitution of other cereals for the rice, as well as of stewed fruit (apples are suitable), suggests itself; and those who do not possess that convenient utensil a "double saucepan" will be glad to know of a simple way of cooking rice and other grain, which obviates the frequent stirring required when it is "steeped" in an open saucepan. Just put the rice and milk in a tin canister, with a tight-fitting lid; set it in a saucepan with boiling water three-fourths up the tin; cover, and keep the water boiling fast until the grain is cooked. If no canister is handy, a mould or cake-tin will do, covered with a plate or a greased paper twisted tightly round. Our reason for preferring tin to crock is due to the fact that tin is a good conductor of heat. In either case, room must be left for the grain to swell, and a little butter will hasten the cooking.

Carrots form a valuable addition to many puddings, raw ones being superior in point of flavour to boiled ones, but they should be grated to pulp. *Devonshire Cheesecakes* owe their basis to grated carrots, to which an egg or two, currants, spice, and cream, with enough grated sponge-cake to give sufficient "body," are added; the mixture is baked in shallow pie-dishes lined with pastry. With richer varieties of these cheesecakes, some butter and other accessories are added, but the plainest are excellent, and have the merit of being cheap.

To plain plum-puddings, such as are known as "vegetable plum-puddings," carrots can always be added: they impart lightness as well as flavour, but as they yield moisture during the cooking, the mixture should be rather stiffer than usual, otherwise the pudding, if a boiled one, may break in the turning out. A small quantity of caramel (burnt sugar) improves the colour and appearance of this class of puddings.

Turning our attention to apples, we are confronted by a host of dishes sufficient to fill a volume, this wholesome fruit being justly and equally popular in all counties.

Apple Charlotte is made by stewing some apples, peeled, cored, and quartered, to a pulp, with sugar sufficient to sweeten pleasantly; the juice and grated rind of a lemon, and an ounce of butter, should then be added to each pound of apples; this must be well boiled, as the *marmalade* should be rather stiff; the tin or dish should be well buttered, and lined with thin slices of bread, buttered on both sides; then the apple mixture and more bread and butter alternately added until full, bread and butter forming the top layer. In lining the tin, the slices should overlap each other somewhat; sometimes they are cut into fingers, if they will more readily fit the tin. The *Charlotte* should be baked to a nice brown. A still more homely one is made of bread and butter as before, but with uncooked apples, over each layer of which, sugar, with spice or lemon-rind and juice, is sprinkled. There is yet another way of making it, if a good share of apples is desired: that is, to put a slice of bread at the bottom of a tin mould, and to line the sides, then fill up with the apple mixture; another slice of bread to cover the top finishes it. Bake as before.

Apple Amber owes its excellence chiefly to long cooking: the ingredients are a pound of apples chopped finely as for mincemeat, half a pound of bread-crumbs, one ounce of flour, three ounces of suet, the grated peel of a lemon, and a dash of nutmeg or cinnamon, two eggs, and three ounces of sugar. It is better to have this pudding *under* rather than *over* sweet, as sweet sauce or castor sugar can be served with it. It needs four hours to boil, or six to steam; the appearance and flavour are totally different if cooked for a matter of a couple of hours only. This resembles the pudding of olden times known as *Paradise* or *Mother Eve's Pudding*, only that currants are added thereto. In superior cookery, apples, after being stewed to pulp for puddings, sauce, &c., are passed through a hair sieve, and when this is omitted, care should be taken that no lumps are left in, and the mass should be well beaten.

Another pudding which can hardly be cooked too much is *Fig Pudding;* one of the undermentioned weight needs six hours to steam, or four to boil, *at the very least*, and the nicest we ever tasted, made from this recipe, was cooked for eight hours. First, slice and cut up ten ounces of *good* figs—poor ones are quite useless; mix them, on a board, with six ounces each of well-chopped suet and bread-crumbs, four ounces of brown sugar, and three ounces of flour; mix with the hand, then, with a sharp knife, chop the whole mass, turn it into a basin, add the grated half of a small nutmeg and two eggs, beaten with four table-spoonfuls of milk, and mix *thoroughly;* then put it into a well-buttered basin or mould, which it will quite fill, if it is to be boiled. A very suitable sauce to serve with this is thus made: —Dissolve an ounce and a half of butter in a stewpan, and stir in an ounce of flour until smooth; add, by degrees, half a pint of milk, stirring all the time; boil up well, and put in a table-spoonful of castor sugar and the grated rind of a lemon, or a few drops of essence of lemons. This sauce can also be served with batter, marmalade, and lemon, as well as many other kinds of puddings. Water can be used instead of milk, in which case more butter is required; the addition of lemon-juice is a pleasant one, and if a clearer sauce is liked, corn-flour or arrowroot can take the place of flour, but either should be mixed with a little cold water before adding it to the dissolved butter.

An authority on culinary matters recommends, for good plum-puddings, the outer fat of roast beef to be chopped and mixed with the suet; he says it is excellent. If for plum-puddings, why not for others to which suet is added? And if the outer fat of cooked meat, why not the inner? Those whose families are averse to fat meat may be glad to take the hint, and use up some of it in this way.

Here is a cheap, but excellent, pudding for the juveniles. Rub three ounces of clarified dripping (or shred it in cold weather) into half a pound of flour until as fine as bread-crumbs, add half a tea-spoonful of mixed spice and a good pinch of carbonate of soda; mix with an egg, half a tea-cupful of milk, and half a pound of golden syrup, all previously beaten up together. Steam for three hours, and turn out carefully.

Treacle Roly-poly is generally a failure, owing to the boiling out of the syrup; plenty of bread-crumbs mixed with the treacle are needed to obviate this, but it is better to make the pudding in a basin, lining it with the crust, and filling up with treacle and crust alternately, having crust at the top, just as for a fruit pudding. The syrup may be spiced or flavoured with lemon-rind. A very superior golden syrup (clear and of nice colour) is now sold in tins: a great improvement on the dark-coloured—often far from clean—treacle of years ago.

We have previously spoken of the use of sago as a substitute for eggs in plain puddings; here is a case in point : viz., a homely variety of *Snowdon Pudding.*

Line a greased basin with stoned raisins, the cut side to be pressed to the basin, and fill up with the following mixture :—three ounces of bread-crumbs, an ounce each of flour and small sago, two ounces each of moist sugar and suet, a table-spoonful of jam, and a quarter of a pint of milk. Boil for two hours. In *Snowdon Pudding* proper less sago is used, because eggs are added.

There are many other puddings we would refer to if space allowed, but we trust that those already treated will prove useful. On a future occasion we hope to mention some of the richer kinds in a chapter devoted to " Superior Sweets." LIZZIE HERITAGE.

DIVERS WAYS OF COOKING APPLES.

"FAMILIARITY," it has been said, "breeds contempt." More often than not, such contempt is unjust, arising, not from the worthlessness of the object with which we fancy ourselves familiar, but from our ignorance of its latent qualities and characteristics. It is unlikely that a fruit so useful to us as the apple will ever be altogether despised, yet I doubt whether every housekeeper appreciates it as much as it deserves, or is aware of the variety of forms in which it may be presented.

The apple has been known among us since the time of the Romans' invasion of our island, and was justly esteemed by them on account of its wholesome qualities. That is probably why it was amongst the fruits offered to the goddess of medicine. Claudius Albinus is said to have eaten a bushel of apples at each meal ! If this was meant as an act of piety, I think his faith in the goddess must have been gigantic, and cannot help feeling that the consequences must have been disastrous, both morally and physically ; yet, although I do not recommend such a wholesale consumption of the fruit to my readers, I believe that apples, in one or other of the many forms in which it is possible to present them, would be a desirable and wholesome addition to our daily meals, especially at a time of year when fruit is scarce. Acting upon this conviction, I have gathered the following recipes from various reliable sources.

Apple Trifle.—Take a dozen large and good cooking apples. Pare and core them. Stew the cores and parings in half a pint of water, keeping as many of the pips as possible in the cores. Add to the liquor thus produced the grated rind and juice of two lemons, and a tea-cupful of brown sugar ; now add the apples and stew in this syrup, taking care that it does not burn. Cut into three slices of equal thickness, a six-penny Madeira cake, place a slice in a deep glass dish, pour over it a wine-glassful of brandy ; spread thickly over it a layer of the pulped apples ; repeat the process till the two remaining slices of cake are used, leaving the top slice without a layer of apple. Arrange the rest of the apple around the base of the cake. Now beat thoroughly the yolks of two eggs, to which add half a pint of milk and half a pint of cream ; sweeten with white sugar ; put it over the fire, stirring it until it is just upon the boil ; now pour it over the apples ; chop two ounces of sweet blanched almonds, strew over the custard, and lay upon the whole a fine whip of cream, made some hours previously ; arrange spoonfuls of red-currant jelly round the base of the trifle ; dye with cochineal a little crushed white sugar, strew over the top, and serve.

Pippin Tarts.—Take three large Seville oranges, peel them very thinly, boil the peel until it becomes soft, then chop it small; then pare and core four dozen small golden pippins, boil with only enough water to cover them; when nearly done, add a pound and a half of brown sugar, the chopped peel and juice of the oranges; boil all together till smooth, and allow it to cool; line your patty-pans with thin paste, fill up each with the fruit, bake for ten minutes or a quarter of an hour in a brisk oven. These tarts are equally good cold or hot.

Marmalade de Pommes.—Peel some golden pippins, core them and cut them into very thin slices, put them into an earthenware or stone jar; place the jar in a saucepan of boiling water; to every pound of apples add three-quarters of a pound of loaf-sugar, and a small half-tea-spoonful of powdered cinnamon; put the saucepan over a moderate fire; frequently shake the contents of the jar, but on no account stir with a spoon; when the marmalade looks smooth and clear put it into preserving-pots, and allow it to cool before tying down tightly.

Pommes Glacées.—Pare the apples; boil them in water; drain well; put in a wide-mouthed jar or deep dish; get ready a syrup of boiling sugar, pour it over, and let them remain in it a day and a night. Remove the syrup, boil it up; again throw it over the apples; repeat this process four times in four days. Now take out the apples, and dip them into a fresh syrup, boiled until it snaps; lay them upon sheets of paper in a dry place. This makes a very nice dessert-dish.

Apple Pudding à la Mode.—Take half a dozen large apples, peel, core, and cut them into quarters; steam or bake in a covered dish until they are quite soft; mash them to a pulp; add the grated rind and juice of a lemon; beat up the yolks of four and the whites of two eggs; add a quarter of a pound of butter just melted over the fire; mix the whole smoothly together; line a dish with a light puff paste, bake twenty minutes, and serve.

Apple Chocolate.—In a quart of new milk boil a pound of scraped French chocolate, and six ounces of white sugar; allow it to cool; beat the yolks of six eggs and the whites of two, add gradually to the warm but not boiling chocolate, stirring well all the time; have ready a deep dish in which you have placed a couple of pounds of pulped apple, sweetened to taste and flavoured with cinnamon; pour the chocolate gently over it, and place the dish over a saucepan of boiling water. When the cream is firmly set, sift over it some finely-powdered sugar, and glaze with a salamander or red-hot shovel. This preparation is not only delicious, but also very wholesome, as the apple acts as a corrective to the richness of the chocolate.

Pommes à la Duchesse.—Take a dozen small apples, peel, core, and steam them until quite soft. Pulp them, mix smoothly with two well-beaten eggs, a gill of cream, some powdered white sugar, and bread-crumbs enough to form them into small cakes; lay them in a pan of boiling butter, and when nicely browned take them up. As soon as they are cold, squeeze some lemon-juice over them, lay on each a spoonful of thick cream, sprinkle with powdered sugar, and serve.

Pudding à la Rachel.—Take a pound of bread-crumbs, a pound of finely-chopped apples, half a pound of finely-chopped mutton suet, a pound of grocer's currants, a flat tea-spoonful of powdered cinnamon or nutmeg, but not both, the rind of one lemon grated, the juice of two, and four eggs well beaten. Mix all together, put it into a well-buttered pudding-mould, place some well-buttered cooking-paper on the top, and boil four hours. Care must be taken that the water does not come within three inches of the top of the mould, and that the saucepan be kept well covered. Serve the pudding with wine sauce.

Pommes à la Frangipane.—Take some Ribstone pippins, pare, and bake them till they are thoroughly tender, then pulp them into a deep dish. Now mix with four well-beaten eggs, four small table-spoonfuls of flour, dilute with a quart of sufficiently sweetened new milk, add six macaroons, powdered finely, and a gill of orange-flower water. Place this mixture upon the fire, and as it thickens stir it well; pour it over the apples. Bake in a moderately heated oven for half an hour, dust over with white sugar, and serve.

Besides several other sweets prepared with apples, they can be used in the preparation of seasoning for game, salads, and savoury dishes.

THE PRINCIPLES OF PASTRY-MAKING.
BY A PROFESSIONAL TEACHER OF COOKERY.

MANY people are reluctantly compelled to own that they have never in their lives made pastry which they were not ashamed to present at table, and, as a rule, they are unable to account for their failures, the causes of which might usually be briefly summed up thus:—

1. An insufficiently heated oven.
2. Excessive moisture in the mixing.
3. Heavy or superfluous handling, or sometimes the two combined.
4. Hard rolling; and—

5. Carelessness in the selection of the ingredients, which are too often of an inferior quality.

A humorist has said that "railway grease is all very well in its place," but it does not improve pies and puddings; and we feel that we cannot do better than begin with a few general hints that would-be pastry-makers will do well to bear in mind, whatever the kind or degree of richness of the pastry desired.

1. Have everything perfectly clean, and as cool as possible, and commence operations as far from the fire as convenient; in hot weather the cellar is the most suitable place.

2. Have everything in readiness before commencing, not forgetting the oven, which must be well heated.

3. Take care that the flour is perfectly dry and free from lumps; to insure this, pass it through a sieve just before using it, and when baking-powder is added, sieve that also.

4. See that the fat, whether butter, lard, or clarified dripping, is quite free from taint of any kind, or the least suspicion of mouldiness or rancidity.

5. If it be inconvenient to bake the pastry as soon as made, it must be kept in a cool place.

6. In rolling, the less flour used the better. Some cooks work in so much that it detracts considerably from the richness of the pastry.

7. After baking, leave the pastry (if not required for table at once) in the place where it was baked; if taken while hot into a cellar or larder, the sudden rush of cold air will tend to make it heavy.

These hints might be multiplied to an almost unlimited extent, but for the present they will suffice; experience will teach much, and a few facts thoroughly grasped at the outset are of far greater value to beginners than a number only half mastered.

A special note as to the baking:—Much might be said if space allowed, but one thing is certain: many a batch of pastry has been ruined in the oven, and it seems very difficult sometimes to hit the happy medium between "cinders and rawness." A cold oven will spoil any pastry, as the fat will run out, hence it is impoverished, and the starch grains in the flour will not cook properly; if the crust is "flaky," instead of a delicious crispness there will be toughness, and if "short crust," instead of being crumbly and almost melting in the mouth, it will prove leathery and most indigestible.

The less frequently the oven-door is opened the better; those with a small glass pane inserted are very useful; and the door should be closed very gently; if banged, as it too often is, the pastry cannot fail to be soddened, for this reason :—hot air, that in the oven, is light, hence the rising of the crust; cold air is heavier than hot, hence the sinking. Supposing, though, a good-sized pie, with a tolerably thick crust, has to be baked: it must first be put in the hottest part to make it rise, and prevent the loss of fat previously referred to, then transferred to the cooler part to finish the baking; smaller articles may generally be baked at the same temperature throughout.

With reference to the various kinds of pastry, it is certain that to explain thoroughly the mode of making *Puff Pastry* alone would occupy several pages; indeed, if half a dozen good cooks were making it together, each would carry out many individual ideas in the manipulation of the ingredients, while the ways of folding are multitudinous. There are, however, two golden rules:—

1. Always keep the edges even; and—

2. Take care that the fat does not work through during the rolling, and stick to the board.

Good results will be obtained if the following directions are carried out :—Take a pound of flour, a pound of butter (or half lard will do, in which case it must be blended with the butter before commencing), the yolk of one egg, a table-spoonful of lemon-juice, a pinch of salt, and some cold water; the exact quantity of this last requisite cannot be stated, as the weather, the consistency of the butter, and the quality of the flour, all prevent this, for, as experienced people know, the better the flour the more moisture it will absorb. Before commencing, read over the general hints, then put into a bowl, or on the board, the flour and salt, and rub two ounces of the butter into it, then make a hollow in the centre, into which must be put the beaten yolk, lemon-juice, and a little water, and the whole formed with the tips of the fingers into a paste as stiff as the butter was at commencing : that is, the paste and the butter should be as nearly as possible of the same consistence. It should then be worked into a smooth ball, and rolled out into a square sheet of equal thickness all over. The butter should be freed from all superfluous moisture by squeezing it in a clean cloth, and if at all salt it will need washing in several waters first; then spread it all over the sheet, and fold the edges together in the centre; again fold, making four layers one on the other; turn it round, roll out, then fold in three. It must be left in a cool place for ten or fifteen minutes, then rolled, and again folded; repeat this until it has been folded and rolled seven times, when it is ready for use. If it cannot be left to cool between every roll, it *will* do with three or four coolings in all. We have given this mode as a comparatively simple one for beginners, and will give, as a substitute, a recipe for *Rough Puff Pastry;* it is made in less time, and is nearly equal to the foregoing, if very lightly handled.

The materials are :—A pound of flour, a pinch of salt, half a tea-spoonful of baking-powder, six ounces each of lard and butter blended, cold water, and a tea-spoonful of lemon-juice. All the dry ingredients are to be well mixed, and the lard and butter broken up into them in pieces the size of a walnut; then sufficient water added, together with the lemon-juice, to make a rather stiff crust, which should be rolled out straight and even into a long narrow sheet—as long as possible without breaking; it may then be folded up like a roly-poly pudding, and after turning round, rolling out, and folding again four times in all, it is ready for baking.

This is very suitable for meat-pies, patties, rolls, &c., and in a good oven will rise considerably. We may here remind our readers that the best glaze for savoury pies is a mixture of beaten egg (yolk and white) and milk. Yolk of egg alone is often used, but it is very liable to burn in the oven. We may just instance *Flaky Pastry* as a homely variety of Puff Pastry; it is made in the same way, but only half the quantity of fat is used, and a good pinch of baking-powder should be put into the flour.

Short Crust is unquestionably the most generally met with; besides having the merit of digestibility, it is also more readily prepared; indeed, after the ingredients are ready to hand, to cover a pie with short crust is the work of a few minutes only.

A short crust good enough for ordinary use may be made by putting a pound of flour and a tea-spoonful of baking-powder into a basin, and rubbing in, until fine as bread-crumbs, six ounces of lard or clarified dripping; if required for tarts, fruit pies, &c., a tea-spoonful of castor sugar may be put in. Sufficient cold water to make this into a stiff paste, and one roll out to size required, and it is finished; it needs no folding or cooling; and beginners must remember that if "self-raising flour" is used, no baking-powder is needed.

A very delicious *Short Crust* is thus made :—A pound of flour, which should be a mixture of Hungarian and superfine, or pastry flour alone; five ounces each of lard and butter, or all butter; a little sugar, the yolk of an egg, a few drops of lemon-juice, and suffi-cient cold water; mix as above directed; this should be dredged with castor sugar after baking, or, if pre-ferred, it may be lightly sprinkled with cold water, or brushed with the white of an egg, and dredged with

sugar *before* baking, though it will eat harder if the latter mode be adopted; indeed, this kind of glazing is more suitable for puffs, &c., made with flaky or rough puff pastry.

A last word about *Suet Crust*, which is, in many instances, the most carelessly prepared of all, and this fact is the more regrettable when we consider how very suitable and valuable a diet it is for use in cold weather, and how digestible it *may* be made with very little more trouble than is taken in preparing the indigestible mess one sometimes sees.

For a nice "Family Crust" mix together fourteen ounces of flour, two ounces of bread-crumbs, a tea-spoonful of baking-powder, a little salt, and six ounces of suet, first skinned, then shredded, and lastly chopped as finely as it can be; for this a sharp knife and a well-floured board are essential. After mixing the dry ingredients, enough cold water must be added to make a stiff crust, the stiffer the lighter; it must be well boiled whatever the kind of pudding it is used for.

USEFUL HINTS.

Peel Cake is very good indeed. For it, put into a warm basin one pound of fine granulated or castor sugar and a heavy three quarters of a pound of butter, and beat both to a light white cream with a wooden spoon; half an hour's beating should be about right. Have half a pound of orange peel, half a pound of lemon peel, and half a pound of citron peel, cut it into shreds; into one and a half pounds of flour sift two heaped teaspoonfuls of baking powder. Add a little of the peel and flour to the butter and sugar, beat, then break in two eggs and beat briskly, then add more flour and peel, mix and put in other two eggs, and so on till you have added twelve eggs and all the peel and flour. Beat all well for five minutes or so, then pour into a well-buttered and paper-lined tin and bake in a steady oven till done. About an hour should bake it, but by trying it with a skewer you can judge best. Be sure and put a paper on the top. I find in baking the larger cakes that require some time in the oven, it is always best to put a paper on the top at the first, and also that a stout piece of brown paper sprinkled with water keeps from burning much longer than any other kind.

Spice Cake.—This is a much nicer cake than the ordinary ginger-bread, and the only difficulty with it is that it requires careful baking to prevent it getting burnt. All things, cakes and biscuits with syrup or treacle burn much more readily, and it is wiser to put a double layer of paper in lining the tin, and the same on the top. For this cake you require three quarters of a pound of flour of rice, quarter of a pound of ground rice, half a pound of flour, three quarters of a pound of butter, one pound of sugar, nine eggs, one and a half pounds of golden syrup, one ounce of ground ginger, one ounce of ground cinna-mon, and half or three quarters of a nutmeg, grated. Beat eggs and sugar till light, add butter beaten separately to a cream, add spices, ground rice and flour of rice by degrees, some

of the syrup and the flour with two teaspoon-fuls of baking powder sifted in, and the remainder of the flour and syrup. Mix all well together for at least a quarter of an hour, then pour into a square tin or into two smaller ones. This cake requires about an hour and a half to bake, and the oven good but not too hot.

Rice Cake.—Beat one pound of butter to a cream, whisk one dozen eggs to a cream with one pound of castor sugar, stir in a quarter of a pound of ground rice, three quarters of a pound of flour of rice and a good half pound of Austrian flour; next add the beaten butter, a little flavouring, and two and a half teaspoon-fuls of baking powder; beat for half-an-hour and bake in moderated oven for an hour. This quantity makes a large cake.

The above cakes all depend for success on plenty of beating, it makes them so much lighter.

Almond Cakes.—Mix together a quarter of a pound of ground rice and half a pound of flour; rub in three ounces of butter, three ounces of castor sugar, one teacupful of ground sweet almonds, a little salt, a heaped teaspoonful of baking-powder. Mix with two eggs beaten light, and bake as for the lemon-cakes.

Chocolate Cake.—One cup of sugar, two eggs, two cups of flour, one teaspoonful of cream of tartar, half a teaspoonful of baking soda, two tablespoonfuls of butter melted. Beat eggs and sugar till very light, add the butter, then sift in the flour and tartar and add the soda dissolved in a little milk. Bake in two layers. When baked put the following cream between the layers. A large cup of milk, put it in a pan, and when boiling stir in the beaten yolks of two eggs, one teacupful of fine sugar, and six tablespoonfuls of grated chocolate; mix well together. Boil till stiff, and when cool add some vanilla essence, and

spread the mixture between layers. On the top of the cake put icing made with well-beaten white of one egg, three-quarters of a cupful of icing sugar, and three tablespoonfuls of grated chocolate; spread smoothly with a knife dipped in hot water.

Lemon Teacakes.—Rub into three-quarters of a pound of flour three ounces each of lard and butter; add six ounces of moist sugar, the grated rind of a lemon, a little of the juice, and a heaped teaspoonful of baking-powder. Mix into a moderately stiff paste, with two well-beaten eggs, divide into rocky cakes, place on a buttered tin, and bake in a brisk oven for twenty minutes.

Sponge Fingers.—Half a pound of sifted sugar, four eggs, yolks and whites beaten sepa-rately, quarter of a pound of flour, the juice of one lemon, and half the grated rind. Beat egg-yolks and sugar till light, add alternately whites stiffly beaten, and flour, and lastly the lemon-juice and rind. Rub out on buttered-paper in long, narrow "fingers" not too near each other. If they run, beat the sponge-mixture hard for a little longer. Bake in a quick oven to a pale-brown. These fingers are nice, for a change, put in pairs and dipped in chocolate-icing, or else plain icing, and then rolled in desiccated cocoanut.

Welsh Cheese Cakes.—Have ready some tartlet tins lined with pastry made with half a pound of flour rubbed with a quarter of a pound of butter, a tablespoonful of sugar, and enough cold water to make a paste. Fill the cases with mixture made of the weight of one egg in butter, sugar, flour, and half a tea-spoonful of baking-powder. Beat butter and sugar together, add beaten egg, flour and powder. Into each lined tin put a very little jam of any kind, then a spoonful of the cake mixture, and bake in a pretty quick oven for half an hour. This quantity makes about eighteen cakes.

HOW TO MAKE PASTRY.

BY THE AUTHOR OF "COMMON-SENSE HOUSEKEEPING."

THE making of pastry is one of the pleasantest parts of a cook's work. Young ladies, who would never dream perhaps of preparing a stew or a soup, are delighted to go into the kitchen to make pies or tarts. The result of this amateur cookery is not always felicitous, though failure is scarcely ever the result of carelessness. And seeing that the work stands so high in popular favour, I hope a few hints as to the best way of setting about it will not be unwelcome.

There is one element of success in the production of good pastry that we must on no account imagine we can dispense with, and that is—practice. Close attention to the best written instructions that could be given, would not be certain to insure success to a novice in the art of pastry-making. It is quite possible that good pastry might be made on a first attempt, but it would by no means follow that the result of a second or third trial would be like unto it. We want to be able to make pastry so that we are sure of success every time, and need not regard the affair as a matter of chance, the pies sometimes "coming out" right, oftener wrong. For this we must "have our hands in" for the business; so only can we acquire the lightness and dexterity that is necessary to success.

There are two kinds of pastry used for making pies and tarts, namely, puff paste and short crust. Also, there is what is called hot-water paste, for raised pies, but into this I am afraid my space will not permit me to go.

Puff paste and short paste are entirely different from each other. In short paste the butter, lard, or dripping that is used for shortening is mixed with the flour, kneaded into it, and so made a part of it. In puff paste the butter and the flour (made into a paste to begin with) are kept separate, and laid one over the other in leaves or flakes, something like meat and bread is in sandwiches; the pastry is rolled again and again to make these flakes thinner and thinner, and the skill of the cook is directed towards their being kept quite apart.

Thus it will be seen that the processes of making these two varieties of paste are dissimilar, and therefore before we begin to make pies we must decide which kind we intend to patronise.

The choice made must depend upon our requirements and our tastes. I suppose few will agree with me when I say that for domestic use my own predilection is in favour of short crust. Puff paste is much the more difficult to make of the two, it is also the more indigestible. It needs to be made with a large proportion of butter, a pound to a pound of flour, cooks say, while practical people seldom attempt to make it with less than twelve ounces of butter to a pound of flour. The consequence is, the pastry is rich, and likely to cause derangement of the stomach. We all know that if we have to consult a doctor upon any difficulties of digestion he is sure to say, first thing, "No pastry." It is puff paste that is thus objectionable. Good plain pastry, although not suited to the dyspeptic, constitutes very wholesome, appetising food for ordinary mortals.

The superiority of puff paste lies in its appearance. No one can deny that it *looks* most delicious. Pies or patties made of light puff pastry, brightly browned in baking, and filled with savoury or sweet preparations, are most tempting to the eye. But, like many other things of the same kind, their qualities are not equal to their charms.

Opinions differ, however, all the world over, and the majority of people will most likely decide that puff paste is to be preferred to any other kind, and especially for articles that seem properly to call for it, such as meat pies, vol-au-vents, patties, and tartlets. Let us, therefore, see how it is made.

We shall need for our purpose ¼ lb. of Vienna flour, ¼ lb. of sweet butter, and six or eight drops of lemon-juice; also a marble pastry slab. If this cannot be obtained, a good-sized slate may be used instead; what is wanted being something that will keep the pastry *cool* whilst it is being rolled. With the same object, coolness, the hands should be washed in hot water a minute or two before commencing operations, and the pastry should be made in a cold place.

If the weather be warm, a little ice will also be needed. Sometimes the yolk of an egg is used and it helps to make the paste elastic, but as it is much easier to make the paste in cold than in warm weather, we may well dispense with this in winter time. The ice will be used as a resting-place for the pastry between the turns.

The flour should be thoroughly dried, then sifted, in order to free it from lumps. It must not, however, be put to the fire just before being used. The butter, too, should be well pressed in a cloth to free it from moisture. If the weather be cold, and the butter be very hard, it should be worked a little, in order to make it of the consistency of paste.

All being now ready, we first put the flour on a slab; we then make a hole in the middle, and put into it a very small pinch of salt, and the lemon-juice. We then add water, a very little at a time, and mix flour, water, and lemon-juice together till we have a smooth but not stiff paste. The consistency of this paste has a great deal to do with the excellence of our pastry. It should be the same as that of the butter, for we want to roll the two together, and if the butter be either harder or softer than the paste it cannot be rolled successfully.

We now sprinkle a very small quantity of flour on the slab (if much flour is taken the paste will be mottled) and roll and knead the paste with our hands, for ten minutes or more, till it feels something like dough. The kneading will make it workable, but we must remember that a few minutes after kneading must elapse before the butter is put with it, or the paste will not be cool.

Everything being now prepared, we roll the paste out quite straight, and one way, and lay the butter on one half of it, covering it over quite evenly with the other half, and pressing the edges of the paste together with the fingers, in order to enclose it securely. We now flatten the paste with the rolling pin, and *roll*, not *push* it, to a long straight piece. We must be careful to roll it straight, or the flakes will rise in a slanting direction, and we must not let the butter break through its envelope. If by any mischance it does break through, the place must be mended at once with a little piece of paste. If a crackling sound is heard during the rolling, or if air bubbles are found, the paste is likely to be light.

When the paste is rolled once, it must be folded in three and put upon ice, or aside in a cool place, for a quarter of an hour. The rolling and folding constitute what is called a *turn*. The pastry must have seven turns, with a quarter of an hour's rest between each two. It should always be laid on the board with the rough edges towards the cook, and it should be handled as little as possible. Pastry thus made will puff up to five, six, or even seven times its original height. A light, even, cool touch is required for making it, and it should be remembered that the paste is to be kept dry and the butter cold. Unless these points are attended to, the sandwiched flakes will intermingle, and the pastry be spoiled. If we wish to use the paste for fruit pies or tartlets, we might add a spoonful of sifted white sugar to the flour.

When the method described above is considered either too troublesome or too expensive, a simpler recipe for making puff paste may be followed with very satisfactory results. The pastry thus produced will not rise so high as true puff paste, but it will be very good. Put half a pound of flour on a board, and *break* (not rub) the butter into it with the fingers; or, if this cannot easily be done, chop the butter into the flour with a knife. Mix the pastry with water and a few drops of lemon-juice, and remember that it must not be too stiff, or it will not be light. Give it three good rolls, and after each roll double it in two, and turn the rough edges of the pastry to the front. It will be necessary to lightly flour both the rolling-pin and the board, or the pastry will stick. Pastry thus made is known among cooks as Rough Puff; but it is so good that, if it is *rough*, no one need desire to have it smooth. If preferred, good firm lard, or even home-made dripping, may be used instead of butter, the same method being followed in either case.

Flaky crust, too, is easily made, and is very good for pies and tarts. For this put half a pound of flour into a bowl with a small pinch of salt, half a tea-spoonful of baking-powder, and half a tea-spoonful of fine white sugar. Mix these ingredients thoroughly, then make into a stiff paste by stirring in the white of one egg whisked to a stiff froth and mixed with a little cold water. Take now half the weight of flour in butter or clarified dripping, or a mixture of the two, and divide it into two portions. Roll the pastry out one way till it is a quarter of an inch thick, spread one portion of the butter upon it, dredge flour over, fold it in three, and turn it round with the rough edges to the front. Roll it out again, spread the rest of the butter on it, dredge flour over once more, and roll it again to the thickness required for use. Pastry thus made is excellent for meat pies.

Short crust, on the contrary, is specially suited for fruit pies. I have already said that in this kind of pastry the butter or dripping is kneaded into the flour, and so becomes a part of it. It should be rubbed in thoroughly, no lumps being left; indeed the rubbing should be continued till the flour looks like fine oatmeal all through. The pastry may be rich or plain. It may be made either of butter, lard, or good dripping. For my own part, for superior short crust I prefer equal parts of good lard and sweet butter to anything else, and for plain pastry good dripping will be found excellent: indeed, in every case good beef dripping is always to be preferred to inferior butter. A little baking-powder helps to make plain pastry light, and it also renders it more digestible.

This baking-powder may be bought ready-made of the grocer, but it is more satisfactorily made at home. To make it, take an equal *bulk* (not weight) of tartaric acid, carbonate of soda, and either ground rice or corn-flour: mix thoroughly, and rub the mixture through a wire sieve.

One secret of making short crust light is to roll it only once, and to handle it as little as possible. Superior pastry will be improved by the addition of the yolk of an egg and two or three drops of lemon-juice. It is generally understood that, for the best crust, equal quantities of butter and flour should be taken; but very excellent pastry indeed may be made with half the weight of butter to that of flour, and good plain pastry may be made with six ounces of butter or clarified dripping and a tea-spoonful of baking-powder to one pound of flour. For meat pies it is really undesirable that a large proportion of butter should be used.

The baking of pastry has a great deal to do with its excellence. The oven must be hot, but not fierce. If too hot, the pastry would stiffen before it had time to rise; if too cool, the fat in the pastry would melt before the starchy grains in the flour had burst, and this would make the pastry heavy. One way of testing the heat of an oven is to put a piece of stale crumb of bread in it: if in five minutes the bread has become a bright brown colour, the oven is hot enough for pastry.

Small articles, such as tartlets and patties, may be put into the hotter part of the oven at once, and left till they are sufficiently baked. Larger articles, such as pies, must be put in the hotter part till they have risen and the crust is light, then be removed into the cooler part, to allow the meat as well as the pastry to be cooked through. With pies of any size, it is always well to lay a sheet of paper over the pastry as soon as it has risen, to keep it from scorching, and then to let it bake gently, that the contents of the pie may be tender. And above all things we must never forget that "the oven will not look after itself."

PHILLIS BROWNE.

HOME-MADE ICES.

 WILL commence by stating that this paper is intended for the sole use of amateurs; by which I mean those who not only have never made an "ice" in their lives, but who, perhaps, have never entertained the idea that they could make one; and to such I will endeavour to prove that it is a simple matter to manipulate a score; indeed, so far as suggesting variety is concerned, my difficulty will be to know where to stop. It would be useless to speak here of the professional system of making ices, because the "freezer" and "spatula" are not in the possession of ordinary people, neither could time be given to the process, which is tedious, whereas in following out the "blocking" system the ices are, in a great measure, independent of attention.

The necessary utensils—which ought to be found in every house—are a bucket, or small tub, or pan, of earthenware or zinc, and a tin mould, having a close-fitting lid. Any size or shape will do, so that it is water-tight, and the lid really fits; if at all loose, a piece of stout calico should be laid over the top of the mould before the lid is put on. I know of nothing that will answer the purpose better than a "Devonshire cream" tin, which is a plain round canister, but having loops of tin on the lid and canister too, it can be securely tied down; besides, as the cream is sent in them to all parts of the country, they are of better make than the ordinary tins, containing mustard, coffee, &c., which, as a rule, will not hold water. A cake tin, or jelly mould, will answer your purpose, but the rim must be plain—a fluted one will not do—to fit which any tinman would make a lid for a few pence.

For a mould that holds a quart or thereabouts, you will need from fifteen to twenty pounds of ice, according to the weather and the nature of your preparation. In winter time it may probably be collected from your own tubs and pails; but if you buy it at a fishmonger's, ask for "table ice," and you'll get the right thing. Don't have that in which fish has been packed. Presuming, therefore, that you have to purchase it, it will cost but about a penny a pound, and as a quart mould would be sufficient for a dozen people, the extra expense (taking into consideration that the dish is a real treat) is not much. More than half the weight of ice would, however, be required to freeze a pint; so it is cheaper in proportion to make the larger quantity, as for two quarts not more than twenty-four to twenty-six pounds would be needed. I am giving the maximum amount when the weather is really hot, and the recipes are, in most cases, for one quart, and can easily be reduced or increased at pleasure by the reader.

Now for the process, which, besides being simpler than that of "freezing" proper, referred to at the commencement, is cheaper as well, though I do not claim that ices "blocked"—though they are equally delicious and refreshing—are so smooth; this is owing to their not having been worked with the "spatula" at intervals during the "freezing."

First cover the bottom of the tub or pan with ice, broken up into pieces the size of an egg, and mixed with common salt. Next set the mould in, and entirely surround it with more broken ice, until the top is reached; then spread another layer of ice and salt—of which a pound or more will be wanted altogether—all over the top of the mould. You see now the necessity for a tight-fitting lid. Set it in a cold place until required. In cool weather it will probably be firm in two hours, but in hot it may require four, or six, so some of the ice must be reserved and added, with salt, the water being drained off from the first supply as it melts; for unless the mould be kept well covered, the mixture will not be uniformly frozen.

I will give instructions for making both cream and water ices, though I think you will probably be more successful with the former, which should be, as their name implies, made from cream; though perhaps few will go to that expense (except those who are fortunate enough to have the run of a dairy); and very good ices may be made with equal parts of milk and cream, or even less of the latter, in some cases, where eggs are used.

Fruit Creams, such as *Raspberry, Strawberry, Cherry, Blackberry, Plum, Peach, Apricot, Currant,* &c., are sure to find favour, and all that is necessary in most cases, providing the fruit be ripe, is to rub it through a coarse hair-sieve into the milk and cream, sweeten to taste, and it is ready for blocking. If a sieve is not at hand, the fruit must be squeezed in a cloth and the juice extracted that way. The juice of currants is best drawn off as for jelly, and all fruits not ripe enough to "sieve" easily should first be simmered with the sugar for a few minutes. Three quarters or a pound of fruit, according to quality, and six or eight ounces of sugar, to taste, will be required. A small quantity of lemon-juice will improve most kinds, and those made from stone fruit are further improved by the addition of a few drops of almond essence, or the kernels blanched and pounded, or finely chopped.

Jam can be used instead of fresh fruit in winter time, and added, as before, but in a rather larger proportion. The lemon-juice must not be omitted. Tinned or bottled fruit, by leaving out some of the syrup, may take the place of jam. If the latter happens to be dry or too stiff—sometimes the case with bought preserves—the jar should be set into a saucepan of water, which must be kept boiling until the jam is soft enough to mix with a little of the milk warmed; this will facilitate the "rubbing through" part of the business very much. Any ices for which red fruit is used should be coloured with a few drops of cochineal; otherwise they will have a "muddy" look

Pine-apple Cream is worthy a trial, and the tinned fruit answers even better than fresh, as it is rich and syrupy. If whole or sliced pine is used, it should be simmered in its own syrup with more sugar until tender enough to rub through the sieve, but "grated pine" can be just mixed with the milk and cream; it requires no cooking.

For *Cocoa-nut Cream*—very nice—use about half a large nut, or one small one, and avoid making it too sweet, or it is sickly. Add a grate of nutmeg if the flavour is liked.

The following kinds need a custard foundation, because, unlike the fruit creams, they have no "body," so they need the addition of eggs. Three or four, yolks only, should be used to a pint and a quarter of milk, and half a pint of cream; but if the latter is unobtainable, five or six will be wanted. Make the custard in the usual way by thickening the milk and eggs over the fire in a jug set into a saucepan of boiling water, and when cool add the cream, well beaten, and the flavouring, which may be maraschino, curaçoa, or any other liqueur.

Vanilla Cream is a general favourite. Use the pod if you can get it, and simmer it in the milk; if not, essence will answer.

One table-spoonful of lemon-juice with two of ginger syrup and a couple of ounces of preserved ginger makes *Ginger Cream;* and two ounces or more of sweet almonds, with a few bitter ones, blanched and pounded, is nicer than essence for *Almond Cream.*

For *Orange* or *Lemon Cream* the rinds should be grated, or thinly peeled, and simmered with sugar in the milk, and the juice and cream added when quite cold. The rinds and juice of three or four will probably be wanted, but as fruit varies so much at different seasons of the year it is impossible to say accurately; and the custard must not be poor, or the juice will make it thin. Orange cream is far nicer if a lemon is used as well.

Chocolate Cream is made by mixing with the custard four or six ounces of good cake chocolate, boiled separately in a little milk; vanilla essence—just a dash—will improve this, and it is also necessary for *Coffee Cream,* made in the proportion of half a pint of *very strong clear coffee* to a pint and a half of custard.

I will now pass on to water ices, though I have by no means exhausted my list, yet sufficient variety has doubtless been suggested for the majority of people.

Now here there is greater restriction as to kinds; for only what I may term sharp flavours—such as *Currant, Raspberry, Lemon,* and *Orange*—are really nice, though others are often served. First, a syrup must be made by boiling together, in the proportion of a pound to a pint, loaf-sugar and water for fifteen minutes or so until thick; then the fruit can be added in the same manner as for cream, or if not quite ripe it can be simmered in the syrup and "sieved" as before. In recommending tinned or bottled fruit for cream ices, I said leave out some of the syrup or juice, but in the case of water ices it can *all* be added. The rinds of oranges or lemons must be boiled in the syrup, but the juice will retain a fresher flavour if added off the fire. The reason for making the syrup instead of adding sugar and water is plain; for it is obvious that solidity must be given in some way, so as to make the mixture a good consistence. The exact proportion of fruit and syrup cannot well be given, so I deemed it better to give the correct mode of making the syrup, the basis of all water ices. So if, for instance, a pint be made, the fruit can be mixed in sufficient quantity to suit the palate.

Currants, black, white, or red, will make a delicious ice. Equal parts of the juice and syrup will be about right.

Lime-juice, too—the genuine unsweetened—about half a tumbler to the quart, will make a refreshing ice for those who like its peculiar flavour. It is generally much cheaper than the "syrups" or "cordials;" so is pure lemon-juice, which answers equally well.

I may mention that *Jellies, Blancmanges, Creams,* &c., made in the ordinary way with gelatine or isinglass, are often "blocked," which not only renders them more grateful to the palate, but hastens the setting when time is an object. They, it is hardly necessary to say, need not remain in the ice for more than an hour or two, so only a small quantity would be wanted. If put in—for extra convenience—while warm, the mould must be set in without the lid, care being taken to make it firm, and not to allow the ice and salt to come quite to the edge of the mould.

Many kinds of puddings "iced" in this way would furnish a treat at a nominal cost, but they are best put into the ice when cold, and the lid secured, just as for the ices.

Summer Pudding, mentioned in " Picnic Dainties," would be as welcome as any, or one made of alternate layers of sponge-cake, ratafias, and macaroons, each layer covered with boiled custard.

Pine-apple Pudding is a delicious preparation. Arrange the fruit—first cooked in the syrup—and thin slices of cake, or bread, in the mould, filling up with custard and syrup alternately.

The following I can recommend as good and economical. Simmer four ounces of Carolina rice in a pint of milk until cooked, and beat in three or four eggs with sufficient sugar just before removing it from the fire ; and when cool, stir in a quarter-pint of cream, or it *may* be dispensed with. Fill up a mould with this mixture and layers of jam, raspberry, currant, or strawberry ; or marmalade gives variety. If plum or apricot jam is used, mix an ounce or two of pounded almonds with the rice. If tinned fruit is used instead of jam, the fruit *only* can be put into the mould, and the syrup, also set in the ice, served with the pudding. If preferred, the rice may be blocked separately, with a fruit compôte, or whipped cream, as an accompaniment;

and ground rice or, better still, rice-flour may be used.

A very delicious *Pudding Sauce* is made by mixing a quarter-pint of cream with a table-spoonful of red currant jam, a few drops of vanilla essence, and a tea-spoonful of brandy, or with apricot jam and a glass of sherry.

Cocoa-nut Custard Pudding is a Yankee favourite. Boil a grated nut in a pint and a half of milk, add two eggs and a little cream, and pour it over two ounces of grated bread. A grate of nutmeg or pinch of cinnamon is sometimes added.

The foundation for any others into which eggs enter that fancy may dictate to the reader, must be thickened over the fire to cook the eggs.

To turn out all the kinds of ices, jellies, and blanc-manges, dip the mould quickly for a second into hot water, and as quickly dry it with a cloth, and slip the contents into the dish.

In conclusion, I will just say that in making ices on a large scale it is well to provide two kinds, which, being often eaten together, should blend well in flavour. Vanilla Cream with Raspberry, Currant, or Cherry, either cream or water, and Strawberry Cream with Lemon or Orange water are safe combinations. Vanilla and Chocolate Cream, or Coffee Cream, eat well together ; so do Apricot and Almond Cream.

But be the kind whatever it may, I think that those who make a trial when " our boys" happen to be at home for the holidays, will not run short of helpers, either in the concoction or the consumption of their ices.

LIZZIE HERITAGE.

HOME-MADE SWEETMEATS.

BY PHILLIS BROWNE, AUTHOR OF " COMMON-SENSE HOUSEKEEPING."

SUPPOSE that there are not many grown-up people who have not, at least once during the period of youthful days, indulged in the supreme delight of " boiling toffee." We can all remember doing it: first laying our plans, then persuading the cook to admit us into the kitchen, then obtaining possession of the requisite saucepan and ingredients, and after a time, when the house was filled with a scent suggestive of a sugar refinery in flames, producing a compound burnt and sticky and horrible, which yet was " sucked " with appreciative gusto, and presented in minute portions to intimate friends as a conclusive and valuable proof of esteem and regard.

We have grown wiser since those days, and have come to understand that confectionery is one of the fine arts, and is not to be taken up and practised at a moment's notice. Perhaps we have been favoured with a view of French sweetmeats, and have seen the chocolate creams and liqueur bon-bons, the flavoured tablets, the almond and pistachio soufflés, the Psyche's kisses, and the brochettes of dried fruits, the brilliant rosolios and imitation fruits, the bouchées and the prâlines of Parisian manufacture. These have affected us much as a picture by Millais would, or a sculptured figure by Woolner, or a brilliant pianoforte performance by Rubinstein. We acknowledge the beauty of the performance and the wonderful genius which it displays, but we feel that it is something quite beyond us, and that if we were to attempt to imitate it we should be sure to fail most ignominiously, and, more than that, our good materials would be wasted and destroyed.

It must be confessed that when a good confectioner is at hand, ordinary people, who only require his elegant fanciful trifles in small quantities and at uncertain intervals, will find it more economical and more satisfactory, as well as more convenient, to buy what is wanted ready-made, rather than to attempt to make the things at home. Still there are a few simple sweetmeats which do not present so many difficulties as the rest, and these may be attempted without fear of failure. They will be very useful for dessert and supper dishes, as well as for treats for the children; making them will afford a pleasant variety to the ordinary business of the kitchen; and they will be sure to be appreciated.

And first for our old friend the toffee. To make this 1 lb. of very finely powdered sugar should be procured; the kind which is called by confectioners castor sugar is the best for the purpose. This should be put into a perfectly clean saucepan with a teacupful of cold water, and placed on the fire till it is dissolved. Then 4 oz. of fresh butter, which has been beaten in a bowl with the hands or with a wooden spoon till it looks like cream, should be stirred into the syrup, and the mixture should be kept stirred until it will "set"—that is, until a little dropped into cold water becomes at once crisp and hard. It will be necessary to try the toffee frequently, as it quickly passes from the "done" to the burnt stage; just before it is ready five or six drops of the essence of lemon should be added to it. The preparation should be poured upon an oiled or buttered tin and left till cold, when it can be easily removed and broken up into convenient pieces. If liked, it can, when it begins to set, be marked in squares, into which it can afterwards be broken. Four oz. of blanched almonds, which have been split into strips, can be thrown into the toffee instead of the lemon flavouring, if preferred; thus almond toffee will be produced.

Barley sugar is another sweetmeat that may, with a little practice, be successfully made. It is a great favourite with children, and when quite pure is very wholesome; and, of course, there need be no anxiety about the purity of home-made barley sugar. For this, 1½ lbs. of fine loaf-sugar should be broken into small lumps, and boiled over the fire with a pint of water. It should be skimmed carefully till it looks like glue, and when dropped into cold water becomes brittle and will snap. The juice of a lemon and six drops of essence of lemon should now be added, the sugar boiled up just once, and then the bottom of the pan should be placed in cold water till the first heat has subsided. The preparation should then be poured upon a marble slab which has been slightly smeared with butter. It will, of course, spread out, but it should be drawn together with a knife, and kept as much as possible in a lump.

As soon as it is cool enough to handle, pieces about the size of an egg may be cut off, rolled to the form of round sticks, and twisted slightly, as barley sugar usually is bought. These should be put on an oiled sheet and left till they are cold and stiff, when sugar should be sifted lightly over them. They should be stored either in tin canisters or closely stoppered glass jars, and kept in a dry place.

Burnt almonds, properly called prâlines, are delicious and favourite sweetmeats, and they are not particularly difficult to make. For these it will be necessary to have any quantity of good Jordan almonds, say half a pound. These should be rubbed in a clean cloth and shaken in a sieve, to free them from dust and broken fragments, then put before the fire to get slightly warmed; three-quarters of a pound of sugar should now be boiled with half a pint of water, till the surface looks like large pearls or globules, when a few drops of prepared cochineal, a few drops of vanilla, or any other suitable essence, and the almonds should be thrown in, and all stirred gently together with a wooden spoon, to detach the sugar both from the bottom and sides of the saucepan. The almonds should be kept from sticking to the bottom of the pan, and should be thoroughly turned over and over, so that they may be well coated, or, as it is called, "charged" with sugar. As soon as they give out a crackling noise the pan should be removed from the fire and still gently stirred, until the sugar has the appearance of being grained almost like sand, when almonds, sugar, and all should be turned upon a wire sieve and covered with paper for five minutes.

At the end of that time the almonds should be picked out, and the grained sugar put again into the sugar boiler with just enough water to dissolve it, and when it is again boiled to the point it had before reached, the almonds should be thrown in again, and stirred again until they have received another coating, being careful only to keep them entirely separate. The operation may be repeated a third, and even a fourth time, when they will probably be double their original size and are done. It is to be expected that a little additional sugar flavouring and colouring will have to be added before they are finished. They ought to have a rugged uneven surface, to be of a light pink colour, and to be crisp and hard when bitten in half. They may either be used as they are or wrapped in fancy papers.

If it is wished to impart a glazed appearance to burnt almonds, they should, when prepared, be dropped into a little thickly dissolved gum-arabic, boiling hot, and stirred lightly till they are covered with the gum, then turned on a sieve to dry.

Cocoa-nut rock, that favourite with the youngsters, may also be managed with comparative ease. For this it will be necessary to procure the ingredients in the proportion of 1 lb. of cocoa-nut to 1 lb. of loaf-sugar, a half-pint of milk, and the whites of two eggs. Grate the cocoa-nut and boil it in the milk with the sugar until the syrup seems to be about to become solid sugar, then add the well-whisked whites of the eggs and beat all thoroughly. Have a Yorkshire pudding tin already buttered, spread the mixture in this about three-quarters of an inch thick, and put it in the oven to dry. The oven must be of a gentle heat, and the door had better be left open while the rock is in it. Cut the preparation into squares and store in a dry place.

Preserved fruit is such an indispensable article when sweet dishes of various kinds are to be prepared, that the skilful housekeeper will be very certain to prepare a good store of jam and jelly when fruit is in season. Yet it must be confessed that the practice of preserving fruit is becoming more and more uncommon, especially in large towns. Our grandmothers would be horrified could they see how their degenerate daughters buy jam instead of making it. This is the more to be regretted because bought jam, however good it may really be, cannot for one moment be compared with good home-made jam, made from freshly gathered fruit, boiled with refined sugar, and stored in a dry well-ventilated closet.

And if it is becoming more and more uncommon to boil jam at home, it is still more unusual for housekeepers to bottle fresh fruit. The process of jam-making is very generally understood. Very few people would think of boiling fruit that was broken, or that had been gathered in wet weather, and it is almost universally acknowledged that the best sugar is the most economical for making jam. The trouble and fatigue of the work is the real reason why fruit is not so extensively boiled at home as it was once upon a time; not because housekeepers do not know how to set about it. But this cannot be said about bottling fruit. The process is a very simple one, and it involves comparatively little trouble. It requires only that great attention should be paid to small details, for if these are neglected, failure will certainly be the consequence. Then bottled fruit is most delicious. In it the original flavour of the fruit is preserved better than it is either in jams, jellies, or fruit-paste. It furnishes a convenient and excellent delicacy for winter use. Pies and tarts made with it afford a pleasant variety to those made with jam; and last, but not least, the fruit prepared at home will cost about one-third less than that which is bought at the shops.

It is true that the bottles take up a good deal of room, and where space is limited this is a disadvantage; but if this difficulty can be got over, the thrifty and economical housekeeper will find it well worth her while to make the bottling of fresh fruit one of the methods by which she lays up stores for her household.

MAKING TOFFEE

In order to do this it will be necessary that she should have the fruit, some tall wide-mouthed glass bottles, corks to fit them tightly, string or wire to fasten them down, bottle-wax or a little beeswax to cover the corks, and a stock-pot or some other large vessel of sufficient size and depth to hold the bottles.

The fruit must be fresh, sound, and not over-ripe; and it must have been gathered in the morning and in dry weather. The stalks must be picked without bruising the fruit, and any that are at all blemished must be rejected. The bottles must be perfectly sound, without crack or flaw of any kind, and they 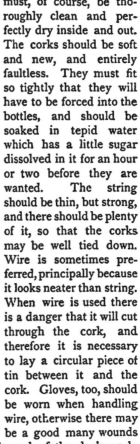 should be of equal thickness throughout. They must, of course, be thoroughly clean and perfectly dry inside and out. The corks should be soft and new, and entirely faultless. They must fit so tightly that they will have to be forced into the bottles, and should be soaked in tepid water which has a little sugar dissolved in it for an hour or two before they are wanted. The string should be thin, but strong, and there should be plenty of it, so that the corks may be well tied down. Wire is sometimes preferred, principally because it looks neater than string. When wire is used there is a danger that it will cut through the cork, and therefore it is necessary to lay a circular piece of tin between it and the cork. Gloves, too, should be worn when handling wire, otherwise there may be a good many wounds and bruises to deplore at the end of the day's work. Bottle-wax may be bought of any oil and colour shop. It should be melted in an earthenware pipkin, and beeswax stirred with it in the proportion of an ounce of beeswax to a pound of bottle-wax. When buying bottle-wax it must be remembered that green wax is poisonous, and should not be used for fear of accidents. The other colours are harmless.

When all is ready, put the fruit into the bottles and shake it down till it is closely packed, but not in any danger of being bruised. Fill up the bottles with a thin clear syrup, cork them tightly, and tie them down securely. Put a wisp of hay round each one to keep the bottles from knocking against each other, place them standing upright side by side in the vessel, and pour cold water round them nearly up to their necks. Lay a wet cloth upon them, put on the lid over this, and put the pan on the fire. Let the water come to a boil, draw the saucepan back and let it boil gently for a few minutes, then lift the pan quite off the fire and leave the bottles untouched till they are cold.

When ready to be taken out they should be lifted up carefully and the corks examined. If, as is very probable, any of the corks have burst out or become loose, they must be re-corked and tied down again. The nozzle of each bottle must then be dipped into the melted wax, which should, however, have been allowed to cool a little, or it may crack the glass. The bottle should be turned about gently so that the wax may run all round the cork, and when all are finished the bottles may be placed in a cool cellar.

The time that the water should be allowed to boil must depend upon the nature and size of the fruit. Currants, raspberries, strawberries, and ripe gooseberries require about eight minutes' gentle ebullition ; cherries and apricots must have twelve minutes ; while for green gooseberries and the larger stone fruits, such as greengages and peaches, a quarter of an hour will not be too much. To make the syrup with which the bottles are to be filled, put a quart of water and a dessert-spoonful of the white of egg with every three pounds of loaf-sugar. Whisk all together in a sugar-boiler over the fire, and let the syrup boil gently for five minutes. Throw a table-spoonful of cold water into it once or twice while it is boiling. Strain it through a napkin, and when cold it is ready for use.

Very agreeable sweetmeats may be made by preparing compôtes of fresh fruit. Compôtes are simply fruit stewed in a thin syrup and intended for immediate use. The fruit should simmer gently in the syrup until it is tender but unbroken ; the syrup should be perfectly transparent, and should be poured over the fruit when cold. These preparations are delicate in flavour and very wholesome. They are very refreshing too, and are much more economical than tarts and puddings. They will not keep very long, indeed the quantity of sugar which they contain is not sufficient to preserve them in good condition for many days ; but they can be kept in a cool larder for a day or two, and even longer if they are gently boiled up a second time.

Compôtes may be made of all kinds of fruit—apples, pears, rhubarb, cherries, strawberries, raspberries, currants, plums, apricots, peaches, pomegranates, green figs, pineapples, melons, cucumbers, chestnuts, green walnuts, oranges, lemons, barberries, crab-apples, cranberries, prunes, and grapes. They can be dished in various ways, but they should always be both neat and elegant. The ordinary way of serving them is to put the drained fruit into a compôtier, or glass dish, a few minutes before it is wanted, and to pour the syrup over it. Sometimes a thin circular sheet of clear colourless jelly is slipped over after they are dished and garnished, and this greatly increases their brilliancy. Round fruits are usually arranged with one piece in the centre and the rest round it in a circle.

The surface may be decorated with ornamental shapes cut out from angelica, coloured jellies, preserved cucumbers, the red peel of apples, orange and lemon rind, chopped pistachio kernels, &c. ; or, if preferred, pastry stamped out into fanciful shapes ; or plainly boiled rice or macaroni may be employed both as a garnish and an accompaniment.

The quantity of sugar used for the syrup must depend upon the nature of the fruit ; it must be remembered that the sweetness should not overpower the flavour of the fruit or destroy its agreeable acidity. In a cold or wet season more sugar will be needed than in a warm dry one. For the majority of fruits a syrup made by simmering 5 oz. of sugar with half a pint of water for ten minutes will be sufficient for 1 lb. of fruit. The finest loaf-sugar should be used for the purpose, and it should be broken into small lumps, not crushed to powder. If powdered sugar were used the syrup would be less brilliant.

USEFUL HINTS.

SALLY LUNNS.

Put a pint of warm water into a quart jug ; add two ounces of German yeast, break it up into the water ; add also a tablespoonful of flour, and the same of sugar. Mix them well together. Put the jug in a warm place. When the ferment is risen and just going down again it will be ready. In the meanwhile put two pounds of flour in a basin, rub six ounces of butter into it, also six ounces of sugar, including what you put in the ferment ; then pour the ferment into the basin ; add one egg. Mix them into a dough, and leave it in the basin for about forty minutes, then place a few small hoops, according to the size you want them, on a flat tin ; mould them in pieces that will half fill the hoops, then let them prove nearly to the top of the hoops, and bake them.

A GOOD SODA CAKE.

Take two pounds of flour, one ounce of carbonate of soda, rub it in the flour, also ten ounces of butter ; then add one pound of loaf dust and one pound of currants and a little mixed peel ; then make it into a dough by adding one pint of milk and six eggs.

DUNDEE MINCE CAKE.

Make first a plain paste ; take half pound flour, add three ounces of butter, rub it in the flour and make it into a dough by adding about a teacup of water, roll it out and fold it over twice ; then roll it out and put it on a flat tin ; spread some mincemeat all over it, about half an inch thick. Then make some cake dough as follows :—Take four ounces of butter, add four ounces of loaf dust, beat them well together with the hand, add two eggs, mix them in, also add half pound flour. Spread this dough all over the mincemeat about the same thickness as the mincemeat. When the cake is baked and cold, make a little white icing, as follows—Take one white of an egg, add four ounces of loaf fine sugar (this sugar must be as fine as flour) ; beat them well together with a whisk until it gets thick, and then spread it all over the cake thinly. When the icing is dry, cut the cake across each way so as to make square blocks suitable for the table.

VICTORIA SPONGE.

Mix two eggs, three tablespoonfuls of white moist sugar, two teaspoonfuls of baking powder, three tablespoonfuls of flour. Add a piece of butter size of a walnut previously melted, mix well together ; divide in equal parts, bake on two dinner plates well buttered, in a moderate oven. When cold spread a layer of jam, and fold together. Cost, fourpence ; time to make and bake, twenty minutes.

ALMOND ROCK CAKES.

Take two pounds of flour, rub six ounces of butter into it ; add also twelve ounces of loaf dust and one pound of currants and a little peel, with one ounce of almonds, chopped up. Add three-quarters of an ounce of carbonate of soda and half an ounce of tartaric acid ; then half a pint of milk with six eggs, and three drops of essence of almonds. Mix it, and make it into a dough ; get a table fork and fork pieces out about the size of a small egg, place them on a tin or paper, and put them in the oven.

DAINTY ORANGE DISHES.

THE fruit under consideration needs no recommendation. Much might be said in its favour, and little or nothing against it. Amongst other advantages, its appearance, cheapness, and wholesomeness may be specially named. The people who find oranges disagreeable are in the minority; and although in a few cases the peculiar acid found in the tribe of fruits of which the orange, lemon, and lime are familiar types, causes discomfort, for the most part, "golden pills of health," as a well-known surgeon has christened oranges, is a well-deserved title.

Such dishes as "orange jelly," "orange sponge," and others of a like nature, are not enumerated here, being pretty well known; my object is to introduce a few less familiar dishes, which will be found economical and delicious. Here is a dish that is pretty enough to put on the table at a wedding-breakfast, and simple enough for the birthday tea of a four-year-old child, being far less hurtful than the indigestible fruit cakes one often sees on such occasions. Not that fruit cakes are of a necessity unwholesome; I am speaking relatively.

Orange Cake

Take a plain sponge cake, of a pound weight and not less than two days old. This may be bought of a confectioner or made from any reliable recipe. A very good one is to allow as much sugar as the eggs used weigh in the shells, and two-thirds the weight in fine flour; say, six ounces each of the first-named and four ounces of flour. The flavouring should be the grated rind of an orange or a few drops of essence, or the two mixed.

Then proceed as follows :—Cut the cake in slices—a sharp knife, please—and let the layers be even in thickness; then squeeze the juice of an orange and sweeten it a little; spread each piece with a thin coating of good, genuine orange marmalade, and moisten with the juice, then build the cake up to its old form. Now for a mixture to coat your cake. This is simplicity itself.

Two more oranges will be wanted; the rinds are to be grated with that of a lemon—it is wonderful, by the way, what a difference the addition of a lemon makes to all sorts of orange dishes; then add all the juice—strained, let me remind you, for a single pip will make it bitter. Then put in water to make the whole up to half a pint; add a tablespoonful each of sugar and marmalade and a little orange essence, and thicken with a generous tablespoonful of corn-flour, smoothly mixed with some of the liquid. The boiling-up does want care, easy as it is to avoid lumps, and as soon as the mixture does boil, remove the pan to a cooler part of the stove and let it simmer a minute; but do not cease the stirring, and use a wooden spoon. Then, when cool, spread the top of the cake smoothly, using a palette-knife.

The dome part only is to be coated, the sides being left uncovered. For the finishing touches, chop up a morsel of any green dried fruit and shake over the top, then cut a few strips of the same—there is nothing better or cheaper than angelica—and with a wooden skewer make some holes round the cake, and put in the strips to form a pattern. Or, in place of fruit, some fondants may be used; green and yellow mixed are the most effective, and they should be fastened on with a little icing sugar, mixed to a stiff paste with the white of a raw egg.

Those used to icing cakes will know how to set about this task. A last reminder: Serve this in thin slices from top to bottom, that all may get some of the top coating, which is the making of the cake. For the sake of appearance, dish it on a green paper or on a white one with a garniture of green leaves.

Orange Pudding.

This ought to be called a soufflé, for it is too light for an ordinary pudding; but some are alarmed at the mention of a soufflé, which is often supposed to be too much of a mystery for ordinary cooks, so to encourage a trial of it I have given it a homely name. It sounds a good deal more extravagant than it is. The materials should be all to hand; they are four eggs, two ounces of the finest rice-cream, two and a half to three ounces of castor sugar, four oranges, half an ounce of butter or a dash of cream, a little orange essence, and half a pint of milk. The mode is simple, but involves care; those who possess a copper or steel pan, as bright as hands can make it, should use it; a burnt pan will ruin the dish. The rice-flour is to be mixed with some of the cold milk, and it *must* be smooth; the rest of the milk is to be boiled with the sugar and butter, and stirred to the rice, and then boiled up; remove the pan, and add by degrees the grated rinds of all the fruit, and the juice of half the number, together with the pulp, which must be freed from any trace of white, and should be rubbed through a coarse hair seive; but which may, if more convenient, be scooped out with a spoon. A hint that will perhaps bring a smile to the face of the experienced cook is to wipe the fruit with a cloth before grating it, and to remove the grater before the white is reached. How many puddings and cakes have been made bitter for lack of this precaution!

The milk cannot be too good and fresh for all dishes containing fruit. Now put in the yolks of the eggs, one at a time, without previously beating them, and give a good vigorous beat between each addition. The mass by this time should be smooth and rich-looking. The whites of eggs are the final addition. Some of my readers are new ones, without doubt, and many may be novices in the culinary art; if of the latter class, they have it in their power to completely spoil this pudding. But we will pass over the wrong way and detail the right.

Put the whites on a large plate with the tiniest pinch of salt—I am assuming that in breaking the eggs no trace of yolk got mixed in the white—then beat (in a current of air) with a knife, until the mass is so stiff that, when the plate is reversed, the eggs show no tendency to drop. A simpler way to some is to put the eggs in a jar and beat with an egg-whisk. The fresher the eggs the firmer the froth; do not try to beat stale ones in this fashion, for it cannot be done.

Now transfer the snowy mixture to the pan with a few light strokes, so as to incorporate the whole without any more beating. Remember you have now filled the pudding mixture with a number of air bubbles, which with the heat of the oven will expand, and bring about the lightness that is the feature of this dainty. The dish for baking should be deep and well-buttered, and the oven should be what is known as "sound and steady," without being fierce enough to burn the top.

It should be firm to the touch, and a delicate brown when done. This is good without sauce, but better with; and here is a famous one, as nice with hosts of other puddings as with this particular one.

Orange Sauce.

Melt in a stewpan two ounces of fresh butter, and take care to skim away any scum; then stir in two ounces of fine dry flour, a little at a time. The precaution of sifting should not be forgotten; stir and add the juice of two oranges left over from the pudding, and enough water to make about half a pint of liquid; when this boils add sugar to taste and a little of the clear part of some orange marmalade, quite free from any chips—say a tablespoonful—then put in a few drops of yellow colouring.

Remove the pan and add another ounce of butter, a bit at a time, stirring it well in, and do not let it taste the fire again. The use of a quarter of a pint of whipped cream will be better liked by some, but the sauce loses in heat what it gains in richness. Another way is to use a little cream only with about half an ounce of butter.

In all these ways the sauce may be recommended. When a fuller orange zest is liked, a few drops of orange essence may go in. A mixture of orange and vanilla essence is thought to be better than anything else by some cooks; the blending of the two flavours is certainly very pleasant, but the vanilla must be good, and not used in excess: that is, the dish must not actually taste of vanilla, but owing to its variable strength the precise amount to use can only be determined by the cook.

The sauce and pudding must be so timed that neither waits for the other, and no time is to be lost in sending them to table.

Orange Butter.

This is easy to make. Take two hard-boiled eggs and put in a mortar with an ounce of butter, a tablespoonful of thick cream, an ounce of blanched chopped almonds, two ounces of sugar, the grated rind of an orange, and a little colouring; then pound all and moisten with orange juice until a softish paste is formed. Sometimes a mixture of orange-flower water and orange juice is preferred, but the first mode is the cheaper and better liked, as a rule. The whole should be sieved.

Lemons and oranges can be thus blended, and the exact amount of sugar regulated by taste. Set by in the coldest part of the house until the time comes for using—best of all, set on ice. As to the uses, they are very numerous. Serve with biscuits or thin bread and butter, or make sandwiches by putting the "butter" on one slice of bread and a morsel of honey or nice preserve on the other: sweet sandwiches are now quite a feature at afternoon teas. With many puddings, both hot and cold, instead of sauces of the ordinary kind, this butter is acceptable: and a particularly good dish is made by cutting up a sponge or Madeira cake into little blocks—triangular, for instance—and spreading one side with the butter and covering it with Devonshire or any other thick cream.

I have seen this made so stiff, by using more egg yolks, that it can be moulded into little pyramids, but then there is not a chance of working in so much of the juice, and the taste is not nearly so nice. The deficiency is then made up by an extra supply of grated rind.

Tangerine Creams.

This is one of the best dishes on my list. The peel is to be taken off and the fruit cut up in thin slices, and put on to boil with half its weight in crushed lump sugar. Then to every half-pound of sugar used allow half a pint of water and the juice of a lemon—bearing in mind these proportions, any quantity can be made. The whole should boil—about ten minutes should suffice—then add an ounce of sheet gelatine, stirring until it is quite melted, for every half-pint of water. When on the point of setting, take some tiny glass dishes, rather deep, or some of the little fire-proof china cases of any fancy shape, and three-parts fill them.

When quite cool, pile on the top some stiffly-whipped cream that has been sweetened and nicely-flavoured with orange rind or essence. The mixture *may* be poured in one large dish, and finished off in the same manner, but it is not intended to be moulded and turned out; it should be served from the dish into which it is poured.

For a more elaborate sweet, some green fruit or coloured sugar can be used for garnishing the cream; or lumps of orange jelly can be put about it. I can recommend a variation that entails but a trifle more trouble and expense. Reduce the water to half, and when the pan is taken from the fire add some good orange jelly that has been just melted, and if this is stiff and the weather cool, very little gelatine need be added, for the precise consistence is a matter of taste. Then again, you may pour a good orange-flavoured custard over instead of cream, or cream can go over the custard. In all these ways I venture to say that it will be a case of " Cut and come again." Jaffa oranges can be used instead of tangerines.

Orange Trifle.

This is a dish for festive occasions, and no one need be alarmed at a request for more from the juvenile members of the family. Some ordinary penny sponge cakes are to be sliced into a deep glass dish, and moistened with orange jelly that is tepid and just beginning to set. When the slices have formed a layer nearly an inch thick, a thick plain custard should go over; one made from corn-flour answers admirably, but it should be coloured a little and be well-flavoured with orange rind.

Then have a compôte of oranges, made by dividing the fruit in its natural sections and removing the pips, and stewing the fruit in a thin syrup of sugar and water until done. The syrup should be reduced and thickened by further boiling after the fruit has been taken up. This must be cold before it is laid on the custard, and that should be cold; if either be warm, a messy dish is a sure result. There must be only enough syrup to coat and moisten the fruit. Now take some whipped cream and some lumps of orange jelly; the latter may be made by pouring the jelly into a tin or deep dish, and cutting in squares when cold.

Use these for garnishing, putting some jelly and cream alternately, covering all but the centre; to be explicit, make a ring of the garnish. The centre should be highest, some more of the stewed fruit being piled up at the last. The colder this is served the nicer; and those who will look over the preceding hints and recipes will see a number of ways of varying it when tired of it in its present form.

ORNAMENTAL CHOCOLATE DISHES

OR one person who takes chocolate as a beverage, perhaps a dozen eat it as a confection. The explanation of this is not far to seek. Nothing that comes under the head of sweets is more temptingly displayed in our shop windows ; while every day brings us novelties, either as chocolates pure and simple, or blended with other delightful confections, but all so cunningly fashioned and flavoured as to appeal equally to the artistic eye and the refined palate. How much some of these dainties would be missed in the dessert course of the modern dinner !

The dishes here given should appeal to chocolate eaters generally. They are original, wholesome, and less costly than many sweets of the more familiar sorts. Where no special kind of chocolate is named, it is assumed that a reliable brand will be selected. Never make experiments with low-priced stuff. And a rule that should never be deviated from is to buy no chocolate that has been exposed in a sunny window and lost both flavour and colour. The original brightness should be looked for, particularly for ornamental dishes.

Are you yet acquainted with those little dainties known as "Chocolat aux Noisettes"? If not, a treat awaits you. There *may* be more than one maker of chocolate under this name; I know but one. The exquisite little creams are of melting softness, and of such a delicate tint as to blend with almost anything in the way of coloured sugars, icings, or confections. In fact, they are quite distinct from the dark brown usually associated with chocolate. Then, owing to their size, that of a hazel nut, they can be adapted to the decoration of cakes of all shapes and sizes.

Meringues à la Suchard.

The fashion of the moment is for flowers of pink and mauve blended ; fawn and mauve are also appreciated ; the meringues combine these colours, and are as delightful to eat as to look at. The meringue cases may be bought of a confectioner or home-made, so that they are even in size and a good shape ; they should be all white, or rather of the delicate tint which passes as white. The fresher they are the better, that the crispness be not lost.

To prepare them for table, some of the little chocolates above referred to will be wanted, as well as a supply of crystallised violets and rose petals, and a "filling." First take each half meringue and spread the outside very thinly with a white icing, made by mixing the white of an egg with enough sifted icing sugar to form a smooth paste. Be very careful that the edges are not smudged ; before the icing dries, commence the pleasant task of garnishing. Start at the edges, as by so doing any spare icing gets worked up to the top, whereas, by reversing the order of procedure, it would run over at the edges and spoil the appearance.

What about pattern ? This may be left to the individual. No two halves need be just alike ; the idea is to blend the three colours artistically. In some, the edges may be of the chocolate, and the pink and mauve kept for the tops ; in others, this may be reversed. Stripes and irregular spots are other simple modes.

As to the filling, whipped cream with sugar and vanilla flavouring almost everyone knows and likes, and it is not readily dethroned. But change is ever welcome. Try the cream with a morsel of preserved ginger, chopped, and a little of the syrup, with, if you like, vanilla or grated lemon rind ; the amalgamation of these flavours is most satisfactory, and ginger seems to possess the power of reducing the richness of cream or custard preparations somewhat. Those to whom ginger is not acceptable may be inclined to make trial of cream flavoured with good essence of rose and coloured the faintest pink. I say good essence, for bad ones are an utter abomination. The service of these meringues is as usual, so far as putting the halves together goes; but place them in a single layer only, on a flat dish, garnished with natural green leaves, and nothing is prettier than ferns. Never be satisfied with artificial substitutes for the real thing. Some, in the modern craze for paper decoration, appear to ignore Nature altogether.

Chocolate Jellied Cake.

This is of so decorative a character as to be quite an acquisition to the supper-table, and it will stand the heat of a room for some hours without suffering in appearance—more than can be said for many sweets. A round sponge or Madeira cake is wanted (a Madeira for choice); cut out the middle, leaving a wall an inch thick. The portion removed is to be soaked in a little hot jelly, holes being first made in the cake. One of the best of the tablet jellies will answer admirably for this, but a little extra flavouring is often the making of it; and as brilliancy is not essential, a few drops of any essence may be used.

The outer surface of the cake is then to be coated with an icing made as under, and put on with a palette knife dipped from time to time in cold water. Here are the proportions; the quantities may have to be doubled for a large cake: One ounce of chocolate, very good, hard, and flavoured well with vanilla; half a pound of finely-sifted, good quality icing sugar; six tablespoonfuls of hot water; and if spice be not disliked, a dash of ground cinnamon, or cloves. The grated chocolate and water are to be mixed and stirred to the boil in a small bright stewpan, and the sugar added off the fire; a rapid stir, and it is ready. The soaked portion is now to be restored to its original position, and the cake set on the dish for serving. The brightest of glass is called for here.

Finally, surround the cake with a ring of jelly, the deepest yellow at your command; it should be chopped on a sheet of slightly-damped, stout white paper. Here and there put a few pieces of crystallised oranges, both green and gold; and for the top of the cake cut some of the same fruit into spikes and stick them in, after making good-sized holes with a skewer. A whole orange should be reserved for the top. Another way of finishing off may be noted: that is to cut the top off entirely and coat the cake with more chopped jelly and fruit as directed for the base.

The effect of such dishes as these, where the rest of the sweets are pale in colour, is very good. With reference to the soaked portion of the cake, it may be useful to add that fruit syrups serve as well as jelly for soaking; the surplus syrup from many kinds of canned or bottled fruit may be instanced. A little gelatine must be added.

Apple and Chocolate Trifle.

"Chocolate with apples," someone will exclaim; "what a strange mixture!" The answer is that the combination is very agreeable, and there are any number of more costly trifles that do not look or taste as nice as this, and it has the added merit of wholesomeness. A large, deep glass dish is wanted. First, a thick layer of apple pulp should be sandwiched between two layers of thinly-sliced bread or cake and put at the bottom. To make the pulp, stew some pared and cored apples in lemon-juice and sugar and beat or sieve it; anyway, see that it is smooth. The flavouring may be spice or vanilla, or lemon-peel can be added. If the cake be soaked in some melted apple jelly, a great improvement is effected. But here is a cheap substitute: Stew the parings with the cores and pips in a little water for some time, then strain off and add sugar and reduce to a thick syrup by quick boiling. Next in order comes a layer of macaroons, softened in the above way.

And now for a custard. First, a pint of milk and cream, mixed in such proportions as can be afforded; very little cream, remember, serves for a plain dish, and imparts the smoothness which no substitute *does* impart. Two ounces of grated chocolate, three or four ounces of sugar, a heaping teaspoonful of ratafia powder (made by sieving some crushed ratafias), the yolks of four and the whites of two eggs, are the remaining materials. The chocolate and some of the hot milk are to be mixed and boiled up; all the rest must be added, and the whole thickened in the orthodox custard fashion over the fire, viz., without boiling. This must go over the cake while hot, and be set by to get *stone cold*. When ice is available, spread a baking-tin or an old tray with a layer crushed small, and set the dish on it. Failing this, use cold water and plenty of salt in a shallow vessel, renewing the mixture as it becomes warm.

For the top garnish, endless ways could be given. One consists of pale pink jelly, maraschino, or vanilla, in blocks or chopped. Either way, the custard should show between; and, by the way, the colour of the custard is preferably deepened by the aid of a few drops of brown colouring. Or use a plain custard, adding a little gelatine to set it, pour it on a flat dish, and cut in pretty shapes with a fancy cutter. Some may be tinted a pale green and a leaf cutter used; this enhances the appearance, and the extra cost and trouble are not worth consideration. The ways of using the shapes are as varied as leaf decorations for open jam tarts; no two people will place them exactly alike. In addition, a morsel of angelica is quite a boon, especially if only a yellow custard be at hand. And yet another mode. Some of the apples may be stewed in quarters and a border formed of them. They want careful treatment, and firm apples should be selected to avoid breaking. A pile may be put in the centre, and for a plain dish will pass muster.

To cheapen the trifle, so as to make it suitable for a children's party, use a greater amount of bread and dispense with the macaroons, add a layer of plain custard, such as cornflour, before putting on the chocolate, and dust over with "hundreds and thousands," or crushed pink sugar candy. There are few children who dislike apples, and fewer still who would turn away from chocolate.

Cherry Roll with Chocolate Icing.

This is our old friend "Swiss roll" with a new face. The well-known foundation of equal weights of flour, sugar, butter, and eggs cannot well be improved upon. Supposing from four to six ounces of each to be used, incorporate with them about a quarter of a pound of glacé cherries, cut in quarters, and enough pink colouring to give a *decided* pink tinge. If too little be used, the cake will look *muddy* when done, and imperfect mixing will result in *streakiness*. These two hints are worth attention when colouring cakes of any description.

Assuming this to be carefully baked as usual on a flat tin, it must be spread with all speed and rolled while warm. You cannot roll it if allowed to get cold, for there will be cracks all over it. But what about the "spreading"? A choice is at your service, but something yellow is required. Lemon or orange curd, marmalades of the same fruits, magnum bonum or apricot jam, all good, and not much of either, must be used, or the cake will be not only rich, but sickly. When quite cold, finish off with the icing given for the jellied cake, and served in slices overlapping each other straight down a dish. The combined pink, yellow, and brown blend very harmoniously. It may be served hot, in the pudding course; this is worth remembering by way of a change, and, given a good oven, it does not take long to make either. In this case, the chocolate custard of the apple trifle comes in handy, and it should just coat the roll. Round it, if time permits, a hot custard, coloured pink, and flavoured with cherry syrup, may be poured; or the syrup from bottled cherries, heated, will be found delicious.

The mixture given for the roll is a good one for hosts of small cakes baked in moulds of fancy shapes. They may be decorated on the tops after baking with cherries or other pink fruits, and small fancy chocolates of various kinds; or yellow colouring and fruits of the same hue may be put in the mixture, and the same fruits used with chocolate outside. With the latter, some of the tiny silver sweets sold by confectioners may be used with certain success, for gold and silver with brown, though not very common, is most effective. DEBORAH PLATTER.

AFTERNOON TEA.

 HIS pleasant meal has now become an institution, and hostesses vie with each other in furnishing their tables with dainties pleasant alike to both eye and palate; and in presenting to our readers the following suggestions, we are catering for those who, from any cause, are unable to give a dinner or supper party, but do not find it difficult to entertain their friends at a nice meal in the form of tea.

A word, in passing, as to "the cup that cheers." Be it remembered that tea is not a *decoction*, but an *in-fusion*—therefore, if it stands more than four or five minutes the tannin will be extracted; in which case, no matter how light in kind the edibles may be, indigestion will surely claim some of the party for its own.

Fancy Bread and *Cakes* are certain to be required, and in commencing we will, assuming that at most tea-tables there are some who dare not partake of rich cakes, give a recipe for a *Diet Cake*, than which, if properly made and baked, there are none more wholesome, and few nicer; but, as the method is different from that known as "creaming," as well as from the still better-known one of "rubbing in" the lard or butter, we must ask for special attention. The materials are :—three eggs, three ounces of castor sugar, four ounces of sifted flour, an ounce of fresh butter, a level teaspoonful of grated ginger, and the same quantity of fresh lemon-rind, also grated. Now for the mode. Put the yolks of the eggs into a bowl with the sugar, set the bowl over a saucepan of hot water (nearly boiling), and whisk the mixture until thick ; then stir in gradually the dry ingredients and the butter, which must be melted just sufficiently to reduce it from a solid to a liquid, but by gentle heat only. Last of all stir in (do not beat) the whites of the eggs, just beaten to a stiff froth. Have ready a tin, lined bottom and sides with buttered paper, pour in the mixture, which should only half fill it, and bake at once in what is known as a "steady oven :" that is, a moderate one, the temperature being even, as nearly as possible, from first to last. When a wooden skewer will leave the centre of the cake quite clean, and it feels firm top and bottom, it is done. It should be a pale brown only. The directions for this are necessarily minute, but once learned, an ingenious cook may make many varieties in the same way. Ground carraway or coriander seeds, as well as that pleasant spice, Jamaica pepper, commonly called allspice, may be substituted entirely, or in part, for the ginger in the foregoing recipe, as they all have the merit of being wholesome: indeed, they aid digestion.

Shortbread is generally liked, though usually made too rich for most people. The recipes which follow will produce real dainties, although of a plainer kind than is often met with. To avoid repetition, we may say that they all need slow baking, as the shortbread ought to be pale, although thoroughly done ; if cut small into any shapes preferred, they can be handed round as "biscuits," and will keep well if stored in tins in a dry place.

For *Oaten Shortcake.*—Put into a bowl half a pound of fine oatmeal, with enough boiling milk to form a stiff paste ; cover, and leave it for a few hours, then add half a pound of flour, two ounces of corn-flour, six ounces of castor sugar, and six ounces of butter, just liquefied by gentle heat ; work the whole into a smooth mass with the hand, then roll it out for use on a floured board. It may be shaped into ovals or rounds, and decorated according to fancy with candied peel in strips, cut-up dried fruits, coarsely crushed sugar, or carraway comfits. The edges should be pinched with the thumb and finger, this being a distinguishing feature of shortbread. It will probably be noted that this mode is not the usual one, the butter being often simply rubbed into the flour ; the fact is, oatmeal requires a long time to cook, and the preliminary soaking in the milk enables the starch cells to swell, thus rendering it more digestible.

Another variety, known as *Royal Shortbread*, is thus made :—Equal weights of flour, arrowroot, sugar, and butter are required—say four ounces of each—the yolk of an egg, two ounces each of dried cherries, almonds, and candied peel, all cut very small, and a pinch of salt. The butter is first rubbed into the arrowroot and flour, just as in making short pastry, then the fruits are put in, and lastly the sugar and egg, the whole being well worked as before. This is very delicious ; it should be ornamented with chopped almonds and fruits.

Cocoa-nut Fingers are enjoyable, and as the nut, grated and dried, may now be had of grocers, there is every facility for indulging in them. The ingredients are eight ounces of flour, three ounces each of sugar and butter, rubbed together ; one ounce of cocoa-nut, and two table-spoonfuls of cream, in which the nut should soak awhile before being added to the other ingredients. The fingers should be three inches long, and rather more than half an inch wide.

German Honey Cakes are very easy to make, and a decided novelty ; it is probable, however, that they will be too highly spiced for most English people, although the cakes we tasted, made exactly as described, were very good. Six ounces of honey and two ounces of butter are to be just warmed together previous to mixing with six ounces of flour, half a tea-spoonful of ground cloves and nutmeg mixed, the same of chopped lemon-peel and carbonate of soda ; this is covered with a cloth, and left all night, then rolled out thinly, and cut into fancy shapes. These require a very gentle oven, as does anything containing honey or treacle. A word of explanation is here necessary. We have, in previous papers, stated that the addition of carbonate of soda to cakes, &c., is useless unless it is combined with an acid. In ordinary cases this is true, but cakes or puddings into which treacle has entered are an exception, as an element of both is what we may briefly describe as a "natural acid," which, in combination with soda, creates effervescence.

Chestnut Pyramids will meet with the approval of all lovers of the nut in other forms ; and when making forcemeat or sauce from chestnuts, there will be a good opportunity for a trial baking. Three ounces of chestnuts (previously baked or boiled, and carefully freed from the husk) are to be pounded while hot with two ounces of flour, two eggs, one ounce each of butter and sugar, and a few drops of vanilla essence—the last-named to be added when the mass has cooked somewhat, otherwise a good deal of the flavour will be lost. Place these in small rocky heaps, the size of a walnut, on a greased baking-sheet ; brush them over with beaten egg, and bake in a rather brisk oven. They should be allowed to cool on a sieve, as should small cakes generally, and never taken into cold air immediately. We now pass on to a couple of recipes which, if carried out, will enable our readers to set before their guests something new in the bread and butter line. Both are best if baked a couple of days before cutting up, and are equally good cut into thicker slices, and toasted and buttered in the same way as the well-known "Sally Lunns."

Hungarian Tea Loaf deserves first place. A pound and a quarter of Hungarian flour, two ounces of white sugar, and half a teaspoonful of salt are to be mixed in a large bowl ; in another bowl, half a pint of warm milk (in which three ounces of butter have been melted) is added to the yolks of two eggs, the white of one, and two table-spoonfuls of fresh barm. With this mixture the ingredients in the large pan must be made into dough with the hand, and left to rise for a couple of hours, then put into a tin—well greased, and plenty of room left for rising. The heat of the oven should be quickest at the first, and allowed to subside during the baking. As soon as the loaf is taken from the oven, brush it over with the white of an egg, beaten up with a table-spoonful of castor sugar; sprinkle it with chopped almonds, then return it to the oven to set, and lightly brown the surface. Dried yeast, half an ounce, may take the place of fresh barm; it should be "creamed" as described in our article on "Home-made Bread."

Scotch Roll is less expensive than the above; ordinary flour, a pound and a half, is used for it, the other ingredients being two ounces each of lard and sugar, one egg, three ounces of sultana raisins, three-quarters of a pint of tepid milk and water mixed, and fresh or dried barm as above : the mode is also the same, but no tin is required, the dough being made into a roll or twist. When baked, brush it over with a table-spoonful of milk and a lump of sugar warmed together.

We will conclude this paper with a few hints on quickly-made *Fancy Bread*, and our readers will remember that expedition is necessary to insure lightness; indeed, only quick workers will be wise in attempting this pleasant task.

Under the above heading we may class *Dough Nuts*. A very inexpensive recipe is the following :— Rub an ounce of butter into a pound of flour, add an ounce of sugar, two teaspoonfuls of *good* baking powder, a pinch of salt, and, if liked, a few currants. Mix this to a very stiff paste with an egg and a little milk—as little as possible. Divide into sixteen or eighteen parts, form them into small balls, then make a hole right through each with the finger, to form a ring. These are now ready for frying, or, to be accurate, for *boiling*

in fat : the latter being sufficient in quantity to cover them, and quite hot when they are put in. A few minutes will cook them, and after draining them from the fat, and dredging with sugar, pile them lightly on a dish, and serve hot or cold. The reason the hole is made is that the hot fat may reach the centre, otherwise it would not be sufficiently cooked by the time the outside was done. In cooking they puff up, and the hole closes. These may also be made in fancy shapes—little knots, plaits, &c.

Milk Rolls are similarly made to the above, except that the milk should be tepid, and no egg is required; about three-quarters of a pint of milk will be sufficient for a pound and a half of flour; they may be made small, or the dough rolled out to the thickness of an ordinary rolling-pin, and "gashed" at intervals of two inches. When baked, break where gashed. If brushed over with beaten egg or milk previous to baking, the appearance is improved; egg gives the richer colour, but is more likely to burn. Or they may be brushed after baking; a very good "wash" is the milk and sugar one previously referred to; or milk with a morsel of butter may be used instead for rolls which are intended to be eaten with meat, in which case, of course, no sugar should be used in making them.

Another pretty-looking tea-cake is made by rolling up the dough (made as above) like a roll pudding; this is cut into slices, and baked what we may call sideways : the flat side, that is, being laid on the tin. The rolling should be loosely done, but the outer edge must be brushed with beaten egg, and lightly pressed down, or the cakes will open too much in baking. Glaze them, and sift sugar over before serving.

Scones are perhaps too well known to need a detailed recipe, but we may say that an egg improves them considerably—one to each pound of flour; and the latter, for superior scones, should be at least half Hungarian or pastry flour.

LIZZIE HERITAGE.

NEW PUDDINGS.

BY A. G. PAYNE, AUTHOR OF "CHOICE DISHES," ETC.

ROBABLY all people will admit that there is a charm in novelty. Educated persons feel this want more than those who are uneducated; and within certain limits a change of diet is advisable, not only for the well-being of the body, but for that portion of the body which we may term brain, and which is so intimately connected with our thoughts that we hesitate to call it body.

In most households it will be found that the general thought is to settle down into a course of routine, and

if we are not careful, we allow our cook to degenerate from being an *artiste* who ought to be able to play from sight, into an organ-grinder who can only play a certain number of tunes.

There are perhaps few parts of the dinner more open to change than that known as sweets. Of late years this portion of the dinner has received greater attention in consequence of the enormous increase in the number of those who have given up the habit of taking any kind of alcoholic stimulant with their meals. The amount of saving and the additional happiness that have ensued in consequence throughout the country generally have been enormous ; and all medical men are agreed on one point, and that is that those who take no stimulant have a desire for some substitute in the shape of sweets.

Housekeepers should be very careful in watching a change in the price of provisions. In some parts of the country butter varies in price from eight-pence a pound to one-and-eightpence. The same change is noticeable in fresh eggs. One of the ingredients in making plum-pudding is sultana raisins, which have lately so greatly increased in price. Where economy is a duty, why do not housekeepers help the universal law of supply and demand which keeps the world in its balance, by avoiding purchasing expensive commodities which are not necessaries but simple luxuries, and endeavour to supply their place by a cheaper substitute ?

To be practical, we will endeavour to describe how to make two or three new puddings, which, while being very nice, shall at the same time be much cheaper than the ordinary run of puddings. We do not refer to the plainest kinds of puddings, such as rice and suet, but to what may be called the better class of puddings, such as Christmas pudding. This is, as we have shown, now dearer than ever owing to the increase in the price of the materials of which it is composed ; and these sudden advances in price are very apt to be overlooked, especially by young house-keepers.

Try the following simple recipe :—Take a quarter of a pound of suet, a quarter of a pound of flour, and a quarter of a pound of Porto Rico sugar. Chop the suet very finely. Inexperienced cooks may take a hint even in this simple operation. After chopping the suet finely as you think, if you place it in a basin and shake the basin, the big lumps will come to the top. Now take a pound of dates, and stone them and cut them up into small pieces. There is no occasion to chop the dates as finely as you did the suet. Mix all the ingredients in a basin, and add a quarter of a nutmeg, grated. Moisten the whole with only suf-ficient water to make the ingredients adhere. The reason of adding this small quantity of water is that, when the pudding is exposed to heat by steaming, the suet melts, and consequently the pudding becomes more moist. But first we must describe how to cook the pudding. The ingredients should be placed in a basin, which should be slightly buttered, in order to ensure the pudding turning out without breaking. The basin should be tied over with a cloth, and the pudding should be steamed in the ordinary way for about four hours. In private houses, where there is no regular steamer like those attached to big hotels and re-staurants, this can de done by placing the basin in a saucepan half full of boiling water, keeping the water boiling with the lid on for the time specified.

It will be observed that, among the ingredients, we have said that the sugar should be what is known as Porto Rico. This sugar is darker, stronger, and *sweeter* than most sugars. As it is the cheapest kind of sugar sold, it is particularly economical. It is only suitable for puddings like the one we are describing,

that contain fruit. It would also do to sweeten coffee or cocoa ; it would be very unsuited to sweeten tea, and it is equally unsuited for any kind of custard, or custard pudding. But to return to our pudding.

The pudding should be turned out on to a dish just as is an ordinary Christmas pudding. It is very nice plain, but a little sweet sauce poured over it would by some people be thought an improvement. It is exceedingly like good, rich Christmas pudding, both in appearance and flavour, and might easily be mistaken for one. The whole cost of the pudding we have mentioned, and which is amply sufficient for six persons, would be less than fivepence.

Another very nice and even cheaper pudding still can be made from dates as follows :—Take a pound of dates, stone them, cut them up and place them in a small saucepan, and let them stew gently, using about an ounce of butter, adding as before a quarter of a pound of this coarse brown sugar. It is best to let these stew very gently from one to two hours. Next take a tea-cupful of rice and boil this in sufficient water to be absorbed when it is finished. This would be about two breakfast-cupfuls. Wash the rice thoroughly, grease the bottom of the saucepan with a tiny piece of butter to prevent the rice sticking, and let the rice boil quickly for ten minutes, adding, as we have said, two breakfast-cupfuls of water to a tea-cupful of rice. You can put the rice into hot water at starting, but take care that it boils for quite ten or eleven minutes. Now move the saucepan to the side of the fire, and let it stand for about twenty minutes or half an hour, at the end of which time it will be found that the rice has swollen and absorbed the whole of the water. There is nothing like economy in little things. The reason we did this is that we do not waste the water in which the rice is boiled. It is as wrong in principle to throw away the water in which we have boiled our rice as to throw away that in which we have boiled a nice fresh piece of silverside of beef. Turn the whole of the rice out on to a dish, and with a spoon smooth it neatly round the outside, at the same time making a sort of well in the middle. In fact we are making a rice border. The well in the middle must be made large, but only just sufficiently large to receive the stewed dates. These dates are poured into the middle, piled up slightly, and the dish sent to table. The dates should be of the consistency of thick jam. It will be seen that we have not recommended any flavouring to the dates. We can, however, add a little nutmeg, and it may perhaps be an improvement to add the juice of half a lemon, but it is by no means essential. Still, if you have half a lemon by you, getting stale, it would be a good opportunity of using it up. This is a very cheap pudding, and looks very pretty, the brown dates reposing, so to speak, in a white nest. Should we have this pudding on some special occasion, we can ornament it as follows, and when ornamented its appearance is such that it might be served as a sweet at the wedding breakfast of a princess.

While the rice is cooking, after it has been placed by the side of the fireplace, take out a tea-spoonful and absorb the moisture with a cloth, and then separate the grains of rice one from another with a fork on a plate, and dry these grains by putting the plate in the oven for about a minute. Take half of these grains and put them in a saucer with two or three drops of cochineal, and shake them about till you make them pink. Don't soak them in cochineal and make them too dark, but roll them backwards and forwards on a pink saucer till each grain becomes a bright pink. It would be best to colour rather more than half the tea-spoonful pink, as we shall want rather more pink than white. Next, before sending the dish to table, and after piling up the stewed dates in the middle of the dish as much as possible (and for this purpose we must take care not to make the well in the rice too deep) sprinkle a few of the white grains of rice on the dark brown dates. We can next take a very few pink grains and sprinkle them on the top between the white.

Remember that we do not want the grains of rice sprinkled too thickly or too closely together; if they are an inch apart they will be quite near enough. Next take the remainder of the pink grains of rice and sprinkle them, keeping them the same distance apart, about an inch, over the white rice border. This makes the dish look extremely pretty, and a little cut lemon might be placed on the edge of the dish, but this is not necessary.

If by chance you have any angelica in the house, you can sprinkle a few specks of green on the white rice as well as the pink. The little pink and green spots on the white look extremely pretty. Any kind of green crystallised fruit does for the purpose as well as angelica, as long as it is a fairly bright green; and the quantity required is so very small that the cost may be said to be nothing. There is a great satisfaction, in sending a pretty dish to table, in thinking that no money has been *wasted* on it.

A very nice pudding, and which will be found to be a novelty, can be made from bananas. Bananas are sometimes sold in London as cheap as six a penny, but, at any rate, they can generally be bought four a penny when they look very black and stale. Many persons will not buy them when they are black, because they think they are bad. Such, however, is not the case. Of course they are not equal in flavour to a ripe banana picked from the tree abroad, but bananas, like pineapples, have to be picked before they are ripe, and then allowed to ripen afterwards; otherwise we could not have them in this country at all. Take six bananas, and peel them and beat them to a smooth pulp in a basin with a spoon; or, better still, rub them through a wire sieve. Add two table-spoonfuls of white powdered sugar. Next beat up four eggs very thoroughly and add these to the mixture. Now take a pint of milk and boil it, and after it has boiled add the milk gradually to the mixture, and keep stirring. Pour the whole into a hot pie-dish, and bake in the oven till the pudding is set. As soon as it is set, take it out and let it get cold. When it is quite cold, cut it right round the edge with a very thin knife and turn it out on to a dish; of course an oval silver dish is best. Take a preserved cherry and place it on the top in the centre, and cut four little spikes out of green angelica and place them round the cherry. This makes a very pretty dish, and it is a mistake to think that it is expensive because we have made it look pretty. If we always have by us in the house, say, a quarter of a pound of dried cherries and a quarter of a pound of angelica, we shall always be able to have pretty-looking dishes at a very small cost. Dried cherries cost sixteenpence a pound. Fourpennyworth would last a very long time indeed if we only used one for every pudding. Angelica is still cheaper, but fourpennyworth of that would probably last as long as fourpennyworth of cherries.

An ordinary custard pudding, instead of being sent to table in a pie-dish, can likewise be turned out and ornamented; and if the custard pudding is a little watery, as is often the case, a few drops of cochineal can be added to the water that runs into the dish, which makes it look like a pretty pink sauce.

Of course it is not necessary to turn the pudding out, as it can be sent to table in the dish. And it will be seen that this banana pudding costs no more than an ordinary custard pudding beyond the addition of the bananas. It can also be sent to table hot in the dish, but it is nicer cold, as when hot there is a scented flavour about it. Still, it is worth trying both ways.

Charlotte Russe.

Apples à la Parisienne.

Fruit Pudding.

Jelly of 2 Colors.

Christmas Plum Pudding

Lemon Cream.

PASTRY—AT HOME AND ABROAD.

BY A PRACTICAL COOK AND CONFECTIONER.

WE will state at the outset that in the present paper the term "pastry" is to be understood in a very elastic sense, as we shall include many pretty little dishes suitable for dinner and supper parties, suggesting only those that will taste as good as they look. Many readers have, no doubt, at some time in their lives, cast a longing glance at a beautiful-looking combination of glittering jelly, whipped cream, and bright-coloured sweetmeats, &c., and ventured on a taste, maybe to leave the greater portion, after shudderingly exclaiming, "What a mess!"

Our aim shall therefore be to show that sweets *can* be made pretty enough to form part of the table decoration (and in some cases, regarded in this light alone, they are a necessity), as well as pleasant to the palates of all, with the exception of those who avoid sweets of any kind. In some instances our space will only admit of suggestions, though these are often as great a help to a quick, practical cook as a number of cut-and-dried recipes would be.

We must assume, necessarily, that the art of making puff pastry is understood by all who venture upon the concoction of sweets of a superior kind. Were we to attempt *that* description, it would take up the whole of our space. Perhaps it would astonish readers to watch a good German confectioner making pastry. After working out perhaps a dozen recipes, from all the odds and ends he will produce the most dainty little dishes with astonishing rapidity. Nothing comes amiss to him. Out of an apparently useless pile of cuttings of pastry, remnants of jellies, and preserved fruits, and a few spoonfuls of whipped cream or meringue mixture, he will turn out tiny dainties of all shapes, utilising the scraps to the last bit.

When something really pretty is desired, nothing is more useful as a foundation than some "almond paste"; if made at home, it is not expensive, as a little goes a long way, while it is so delicious that almost everybody will appreciate it. A pound and a half each of sweet almonds, pounded, and fine white sugar, with half an ounce of bitter almonds, also pounded, mixed with the whites of four or five eggs, will make a "paste" of about the right consistency, and bitter enough for most palates. A yellow paste is obtained by using the yolks of the eggs instead of the whites.

Most confectioners sell this—as it is used in making wedding-cake—so when only a very little is wanted it will be as cheap to buy it. The addition of a few drops of *vegetable* colouring is quite harmless, and will increase its utility when wanted chiefly for ornamenting other dishes. Some American cooks add a flavouring of rose or orange-flower water; either may be recommended as a decided improvement.

Cocoa-nut Paste is delicious made in the same way, but with a rather smaller proportion of sugar. The nut must be grated on a perfectly clean grater, and in mixing it white of egg only used, as the paste should be snow-white. Orange or lemon essence is most suitable as a flavouring for this. Other kinds of nuts are also used abroad, walnuts and Brazil nuts being especially suitable; the latter make a very nice paste. Any of the above can be substituted for puff paste for tartlets, darioles, &c.; tiny patty-pans or dariole moulds should be lined with the paste, rolled as thin as possible, then put into a gentle oven until firm and crisp, but kept quite pale. They may be filled with preserves, jellies—both clear and opaque—fruit compôtes, whipped cream, or *blanc-mange* mixture. The last-named may be of many flavours and colours, and should be poured in just before it sets; the whipped cream, too, may be coloured; and a spot here and there on a tartlet filled with anything of a contrasting colour has a pretty effect. A meringue of white of egg, beaten to a stiff froth, mixed with an ounce of crushed sugar to each white, can be utilised in precisely the same manner.

Fancy shapes in great variety can be readily produced: for instance, tiny balls the size, say, of a nutmeg, hollowed with the thumb, then filled with large sugar-plums, white and coloured; or pistachio nut comfits. The latter are pale green, and very nice. These little nests should be laid on a baking-sheet, covered with white paper, and baked as directed above *before* filling. By cutting out a ring, then filling it with thin strips of the pastry, "bundles of sticks" are obtained, while small cones, imitation flowers, fruit, leaves, and stars are some of the simplest devices of nut paste. Any may be decorated, before baking, by means of almonds or roughly-pounded sugar—white, green, or pink; or, after baking, with preserves, candied fruits, or whipped cream; in the latter case care is necessary in the dishing-up.

To make *Almond Sandwiches*, roll out a sheet of almond paste, and cover it thinly with icing (as used for wedding-cake), mixed soft enough to spread easily; then sprinkle it over with anything pretty—pink sugar candy, crushed, tiny bits of chopped fruit, or anything handy—then leave it until set, when it may be cut with a sharp knife into diamonds, triangles, &c., and either mixed in a dish with fancy biscuits, or used as a garnish for other sweet dishes. These need not be baked, but just dried on the plate-rack or top of a cool range. In the above, or any recipe where bitter almonds are mentioned, they may be dispensed with if a few ratafias, finely crushed, are substituted. We have dwelt at some length on nut pastes because, when once the mode is understood, they are so useful in the hands of an ingenious person.

We saw lately a dish of little cakes called *Steeples;* and the mode was very easy. Some sponge-cakes had been baked in tins six inches high, and as large round as a penny. When cold, these were cut into slices half an inch thick, and made by alternating a slice of cake with one of almond paste, some pink, some green, until the desired height of three inches was obtained ; the tops were coated with clear jelly whipped to a froth. These would be nice for a supper party, and equally good at "high tea."

Another convenient way of serving cake is to cut out as many kinds as are available—one at least should be a rich fruit-cake ; the rest may be seed, sponge, or any other plain sort—then to pile them with Devonshire cream between each slice, and cut them into fingers or squares. It is astonishing what an improvement in the appearance of a table may be effected by a few minutes spent in this way.

Vol-au-vent cases are universal abroad, and when filled with a variety of fruit compôtes the effect is very good ; and we are inclined to the opinion that they are general favourites. Skill and experience are necessary to produce good results in this line when large ones are made, but the small ones are comparatively easy, and the necessary oval cutters can be had in all sizes.

Savoury Vol-au-vents are equally popular on the Continent, and quite as common as *patties* are in England, and when filled with a nice mince of ham and chicken, lobster, salad, oysters, &c., and prettily garnished, they present a very appetising appearance.

A really artistic dish, which can be made large or small, as required, owes its foundation to puff pastry, baked in thin square sheets, first sprinkled with sugar. Each sheet should be one inch less on each side than the one beneath it : for instance, in a large *Leaf Tourte à la Française* the bottom sheet may be seven inches square, and the top one three inches. Each must be laid on the preceding one in a contrary direction : that is, for the corners to come in the centre of each side, and the said corners must be turned up—previous to baking, of course. Need we say that few sweets afford greater opportunity for ornamentation than these? The corners and sides may be garnished with almost anything in the way of jelly, roughly chopped or cut out in patterns ; cream, coloured, and dotted here and there ; almond pastry ; icing sugar ; candied or fresh fruit ; any good fondants of nice shapes being also suitable. A simpler kind may be made by just covering the edges with jam of several sorts, and coating the top layer with whipped cream. Pistachio nuts are much used as a garnish, but they are too expensive for general use ; and chopped almonds, or any other nuts, may be tinted with a little vegetable green colouring, and will answer equally well.

Venetian, or *Venice Cakes,* are real delicacies. They are usually served in a round or oval form, but on the same principle as the foregoing—viz., one above another, from large to small, leaving a margin of half an inch or more between each. They are often made, however, of an equal size. The foundation, or crust, is prepared as follows :—Into a pound of the finest white flour (half of which should be Hungarian) rub half a pound of fresh butter until very fine ; add six ounces of pounded sweet almonds and half an ounce of bitter ones, fourteen ounces of powdered lump sugar, and a pinch of salt ; make into a *firm* mass with the yolks of three eggs ; if small, four may be necessary. Roll out to the fourth of an inch in thickness, brush over with the white of an egg, sprinkle with sugar, crushed, and bake in a gentle oven to a delicate brown. The several layers—for a large cake —should be piled up while warm, and spread with apricot jam or marmalade, and another kind, of a contrasting colour, alternately. The smaller ones look tempting with just a little stiff preserve, such as damson or plum cheese, in the middle, and dished in a circle, one overlapping the other ; but when thin jam is used this is not practicable.

Another effective shape is to pinch up the rounds—which should be cut with a crimped cutter—into tiny baskets, with a strip across the top, fastened on with a dash of white of egg, to form the handle. These must be filled with a dry biscuit or bit of bread to retain their shape during the baking. They may then be filled according to fancy, custard and cream, of course, being included.

The same pastry rolled into the shape of an egg, and baked as directed, makes a nice dish if each one, on being taken from the oven, is dipped into white of egg, then into crushed sugar of various colours, and left to dry. Many people would venture to try one, who would carefully avoid richer sweets.

Grated chocolate, and chocolate icing, must not be omitted in our list of articles wherewith to decorate sweets, but it should be of the very best quality, with the true vanilla flavour. *Chocolate Meringues* are delicious, and a little brown colouring can be added with advantage, so far as appearance goes, as, of course, sufficient chocolate cannot be added to the sugar to make them a decided brown.

Boston Cream Cakes, or *Puffs,* as they are sometimes termed, must close our remarks. They sound extravagant, so many eggs being used, but in reality are not so, as a little of the batter goes a long way, for being light, it rises considerably. We have tasted them in England, but not in such perfection as those of the States. To make them, put half a pint of water into a saucepan, add four ounces of butter, and bring slowly to the boil ; then stir in gradually half a pound of flour, beating well. Let it boil a couple of minutes, then turn out until cool, when the yolks of six eggs should be beaten in, and finally the whites, whisked to a stiff froth. This must be dropped from a dessert-spoon upon sheets of greased paper, laid upon a tin in a *hot* oven. When baked, slit one side with a sharp knife, and fill with corn-flour *blanc-mange* mixture, made in the usual way, but with extra sugar, as, it will be noted, there is none in the batter for the cakes themselves. A little butter is an improvement, and few flavourings can hope to rival vanilla. These are only nice while quite fresh, but in that state are certain of a warm reception, and form a delicious accompaniment to fruit at high tea.

IT has been said by an authority, that throughout Austria the puddings have reached the summit of perfection; the same may be said of the sweets generally, many of which are of such a nature that they are as acceptable at one meal as another, and serve the purpose of a pudding or a cake. Cleanliness is a leading feature, and one reads again and again, in directions for the making of delicate dishes, that the hand should not be used where it can possibly be avoided. The use of porcelain utensils in the form of rolling-pins, pastry cutters and the like, has much to recommend it. Such articles are kept cleaner than when made of wood, while the material equals marble in its coolness.

Tyroler Zelten.—This is a dish that would be certain of a welcome, though very cheap, and there are many ways of sending it to table. It is first-rate with a simple sweet sauce, as a pudding ; and, with butter, it may go in either hot or cold for tea. Those who bake at home would do well to try it, for any nice light yeast dough will form the foundation. Supposing a pound and a half of dough, take about half a pound of the following materials, mixed : raisins, currants, figs, and almonds, the latter in small quantity only ; then season well with cinnamon, or any spice to taste, and add some grated lemon peel. All the fruits should be finely divided, and the mixing should be very thorough. This is sometimes baked as a cake, or it may be rolled and baked as a pudding. When done, a shiny surface is secured by a sprinkling of sugar, and the use of the salamander, for appearances are by no means forgotten in Austria, and many simple dishes are raised from the commonplace to the high class by care in the finishing touches.

Lemon Chandeau. —This sauce is so good with almost every sort of sweet that it deserves to become a standing dish in any household, and we need scarcely say that it is delicious with the above dish. The materials are a couple of good lemons, water, four eggs, and four ounces of sugar, and it is to the method rather than the cost that the success is due. Watch an Austrian cook peel those lemons, and you might almost read through the rind ; certainly you will find it as yellow on the inner as the outer side, but only the rind of one will be put in the above sauce. The juice is carefully strained, for pips would spoil it ; it is then left to blend with water, to make half-a-pint, in a covered vessel for some time. The yolks of eggs go next, and the whole is whisked over the fire, and carefully watched that it does not boil. Those who know how to make chocolate by the process termed " milling " will have no difficulty in making this sauce. This is ready for serving in the hot state, but as a cold sauce there is a further treat in store. The sauce is beaten until cool, then the whites of the eggs are put

in, and what a mass of sauce these materials make ; but the eggs must be fresh, and let none cease beating the whites until they are stiff enough to bear the weight of a raw egg.

There seems, at first glance, nothing to warrant the excellence of a dish called *Dampfnudeln*, for the ingredients are homely enough for use in any kitchen ; but when one considers the perfection of the flour of the country, and the care taken in sieving it, combined with the energy that is thrown into the kneading of the dough, one begins to understand the delicious lightness of these dainties. A pint of flour will make a good number ; to it should be put a pinch of salt, and a dash of sugar, about an ounce ; the less sugar, the lighter the dough ; this fact is undeniable. An ounce of the freshest of dried yeast, if one may use such a term, is next added, with enough lukewarm milk to make a leaven ; then a couple of ounces of butter and two eggs must be added, with as much more milk as is needed, and the whole left to rise, when, after the final kneading, the dough is cut into lumps, which emerge from the oven not unlike the penny sponge cakes with which we are all familiar, but *so* puffed up and *so* brown ; and are not these perfections due mostly to the glowing heat of the oven, and the freedom from the *peeps* that a too-anxious English cook will often take during the baking process? We think so. When served with a sweet sauce, as they often are, and they are just as delicious with jam, the sugar may be left out altogether. The salamander, or its substitute, an old shovel, gives the last touch to these.

Here is a very peculiar pudding ; only a sort of roly-poly made from apples. Are you tired of apple puddings as usually met with ? If so, try this, and you will not shelve it afterwards. The foundation is a plain sheet of pastry, but mixed with lukewarm water instead of cold, and strewn with bread crumbs that have been fried in butter to a dainty crispness. The next layer is composed of apples in slices, raisins and currants, and the indispensable cinnamon—a spice much favoured by the Austrians. This is then rolled and baked, and served with dissolved butter poured over it generally, but we venture to recommend a nice sweet sauce, served apart, as the more enjoyable. Those who will take the trouble to fry a few more crumbs to sprinkle on the outside when the pudding is dished, will probably agree with us that the taste and appearance are improved ; but this is an English innovation.

Next on our list comes a pudding that, judging from the materials, is only a batter pudding of the ordinary sort, except that there is a good proportion of eggs in it ; but we will not pass it over, it is so good as to be more like a soufflé, but to eat it in perfection the flour of the country must be used for it, and a fire-proof china dish is required for the baking. A quarter of a pound of flour, half-a-pint of milk, an ounce of sugar, a saltspoonful of salt, and five eggs. These are the materials ; it is the blending that does most to bring about perfection. After beating the flour and milk until as smooth as cream, the yolks of eggs are put in, with the sugar and salt, and the mixture left awhile. Then the whites are added in the same frothy condition above referred to, and there is art in the way in which they are mixed in ; a few strokes of the whisk only, *no beating*, to make them fall again ; and not a moment is lost in pouring this delicious batter into the dish, in which a couple of ounces of butter have been heated.

The sight of this makes one hungry, for it equals an omelette in appearance. It may be noted that no flavouring is mentioned in connection with this dish ; there are, however, many suitable ones. Amongst the most delicious are vanilla sugar, orange flower water, rose water, or any essence of good quality ; but it must be remembered that when a liquid of the nature of either of these waters is employed the milk should be proportionately reduced. We may be pardoned for reminding the reader that butter *is* butter in Austria ; no concoction that would be considered unfit for table would find a place in such a pudding as this, and the eggs would be really fresh.

A dish that will commend itself to the juvenile members of the family is an *Auflauf*, made from jam. This is nothing more or less than a meringue mixture, mixed with jam, of which apricot is favourite. For the whites of four eggs, the same number of tablespoonfuls of white sugar, and about the same, or a trifle less, of jam would be used. The mixing takes some time, a little of each being put in the bowl and whisked well. When all are used up the mass is piled on a dish, and a goodly pile it makes ; then baked, or we might say dried, in the oven, so slow is it, until a pale brown. It is eaten hot or cold ; in the latter form it is a good dish for a children's party, eaten of course in moderation.

Speaking of the children reminds us of a dainty *Snow Cake*. Butter, sugar, and flour, in equal weights, are wanted for this, and for twelve ounces of the mixture the whites of four eggs ; the best flavouring for it is grated lemon peel. The ordinary method of creaming the butter and sugar is followed, the flour is sifted in by slow degrees, and most carefully blended (you will not find an Austrian cook beating it), the eggs, beaten to a snowy pile, are put in with the same light touch, and when baked with care there are few more delicious cakes than this. Those who would like a novel pudding should try this hot, with the lemon sauce above ; the combination is first-rate, and in this case we advise that the sauce be poured over the cake, to soak it a little. A cake similar to the above is composed of equal parts of corn flour and wheaten flour. Another owes its goodness to a mixture of potato flour and wheaten flour ; by the latter we refer to the fine flour of Austria.

Here is an old friend, with a very new face, in the shape of *Potato Pudding*. In some cases there may not be much in a name, but those who may try this will own that there is a good deal in method. But the mixing ! We dare not venture to give this in the original, for who can give the hour demanded for the blending of the materials ? Well, we have found it so excellent when made in less than half the time that we make no apology for the deviation. The materials are a quarter of a pound of mashed potatoes, the same weight of sugar, and four whole eggs, with the yolks of four more for a first-class pudding ; but the four alone will bring about very good results if the potatoes be increased by an ounce, and a tablespoonful or two of milk be put in. The dryness of the potatoes is of primary importance, and if they are not sieved the pudding will be but a poor substitute for the original. The best way to make this is to whisk the ingredients until they resemble a thick custard, or thin batter. The flavouring is a matter for the individual, and so is the sauce ; a very good one is made from thin melted butter, with a nice jam or fruit jelly mixed in, or some fruit syrup is just as good. The mould should be thickly buttered, and coated with bread crumbs ; and the oven should be gentle.

A sweet famed through Austria is made from a mixture of chocolate, bread crumbs, sugar, eggs, almonds and spice. The peculiarity consists in the unpeeled condition of the almonds. We must say that, having tried this in both forms, we give the preference, both on the ground of flavour and digestion, to the peeled almonds of every-day life. A very nice sweet of this sort is to be had from four eggs, to two ounces each of the other materials ; but many will increase the sugar to four ounces, and the varieties of spices that are used are many. Cinnamon with nutmeg is a favourite, but we prefer the old combination of vanilla and almonds, which perhaps many have never tried, for one would hardly think that the result would be good ; but it is, in our opinion. This wants careful baking.

Cherry Cake must close our list, and it is an excellent illustration of a cake and pudding in one. About a pint of bread crumbs will form the basis of a good-sized one, and to them should be added half their weight of fine sugar, three eggs, the chopped peel of half a lemon, and a generous handful of ripe cherries, the darker and juicier the better. For this, half an hour's beating is demanded, and at the last the whites of two more eggs should go in. The custom of adding some of the eggs at the end, and with the whites separately whisked, is almost universal, and those who are inclined to begrudge the trouble, or think there is " nothing in it," a term we have often heard, should note the difference in size and lightness of a pudding so made, and one to which the eggs are added in the ordinary manner. This is baked in a buttered mould lined with bread crumbs, and served hot or cold, and with sauce or without. This principle, we may say in conclusion, may be carried out with other fruit as well as cherries. We have an idea that damsons would yield a delicious dish of this sort ; and we are sure that any fruit juice, boiled to a syrup with sugar, and served as sauce, will recommend itself.

SIMPLE SOUFFLÉS.

WHAT is a soufflé? or, rather, what should it be? A very light pudding, either sweet or savoury, steamed or baked. There are writers on the *cuisine* who assert that no one can learn to make a soufflé by reading, and that a practical lesson is the only thing to ensure success.

I think otherwise. I yield to no one in my belief in the value of practical training for any sort of work; but I am of opinion that any person of average intelligence who can make a pudding worthy the name should be able to concoct an eatable soufflé (not, perhaps, a first-rate one) although she had never watched the operation. Why? Just because certain principles underlie the art of the making of soufflés, and if these are committed to memory, the rest should be plain sailing.

There are people who have what is termed a "heavy hand"; there are others who are above paying attention to details; neither of these ought to attempt the task under consideration, as they would be sure to fail.

No mention is made in this paper of the elaborate cold savouries now served as soufflés, and I will confine myself to the humblest of the class of dainties that bear the name. If the first venture should turn out too much of a failure to set on the dinner-table, the chances are that it will be consumed secretly, if not openly. Let all beginners in the culinary art take comfort in the thought that there was a time in the history of the greatest of French *chefs* when the boiling of a potato was beset with difficulties, and that perfection is the child of experience. But to our dishes. First, the

General Rules for Guidance.

The flour, or any other farinaceous substance that may form the foundation, must be dry, free from lumps, and carefully sifted. Eggs should be fresh and separated, so that not a particle of the yolk gets mixed in the whites. The latter must be beaten so stiffly that the egg should not fall from the plate when turned upside down. During the beating a pinch of salt will facilitate the stiffness, and there should be a current of air.

The person beating should stand near an open window or door. However hard the mixture may be beaten *before* the whites of egg are introduced, there must be nothing more than thorough *mixing* after. For a *steamed* soufflé, the water should simmer regularly the whole time; for a *baked* one, the heat should be great enough to fetch it up without burning; and the smaller the dish, the quicker the heat all through.

From the oven to the table should be the work of a moment; and better keep the eater waiting five minutes for the soufflé than reverse the order, even by half the time. The serviette* to pin round the tin should be quite ready and well warmed by the time the soufflé is done.

Now we are a little way on the road to success. A last general hint: the most scrupulous cleanliness is absolutely needful; the least taint in saucepan or baking-tin spells failure.

A soufflé-tin proper is to be bought of any good ironmonger; one about three and a half inches in depth and four and a half in diameter will be found a handy size; but the beginner may use a bright new cake-tin, either oval or round: I say new, because one that has been burnt and scraped will not do—the soufflé would stick; and after use it should be wiped out while hot with a clean coarse cloth. Failures will happen, and any burnt part *must* be scraped away; but avoid this as much as possible. Then to grease the tin: no salt should be in the butter used, and it is best melted and brushed thoroughly into every part; the soufflé will stick to any unbuttered portion. Then pin a strip of thick paper, also buttered, round the tin, to come a few inches above, because the soufflé should rise a good deal. This is best pinned at the join and tied round the tin; it is then doubly secure. For a *steamed* soufflé, put on a saucepan of water, and when it boils, set the tin in; the water should come an inch or two round it, and must not touch the paper; a sheet of paper should be buttered on the top side and laid over before the lid goes on. The soufflé should rise gradually, and when done, must be firm to the touch. The one below will take about twenty minutes, or a trifle more. It is called

Vanilla Soufflé.

I have given this first place partly because it is very easy, and partly because those who can make this may make a dozen more by altering the flavouring. It is literally a dozen dishes in one. There is no harm in

---

* This is to be put round the tin or dish in which the *baking*-tin is slipped.

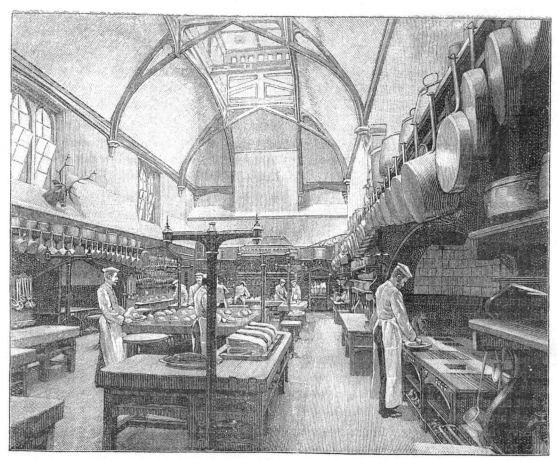

THE QUEEN'S KITCHEN, WINDSOR CASTLE.
(*From a photograph by H. N. King, Shepherd's Bush.*)

trying one's prentice hand with even half the quantities given below.

An ounce of flour, an ounce of butter, three-quarters of an ounce of castor sugar, a quarter of a pint of milk, about half a teaspoonful of vanilla essence, and four eggs* are required. The mode is as follows :—Take a little saucepan and melt the butter by gentle heat ; shake the flour in and stir to a smooth paste ; then, still stirring, add the milk ; let it boil up, not ceasing the stirring, and when it leaves the sides of the pan take it from the fire and sweeten it ; then put in the yolks of three eggs, one at a time, beating hard, but do not put the pan on the fire again ; the flavouring and four stiff whites go next (*see* the hints above). Should this turn out "tough," you may take it for granted that you have *over* cooked it. If *under* done, the sides will crack.

The turning-out needs a little "nerve." The soufflé must be gently slidden on to the dish. Don't be in a violent hurry, although

* For soufflés made with three or four eggs, omit one of the yolks, the whites generally exceed the yolks in this proportion.

speed is important. Cut the string and take the paper off, lift the tin up and slope it towards you, then turn it, that the edges of the soufflé may leave the tin ; and in turning it on to the dish, mind not to drop the tin, or its weight would crush the soufflé. If any sauce, pour it gently and neatly round without splashing.

Any good sweet pudding sauce does, but a very nice one is made by boiling a tablespoonful of raspberry jam in a gill of water for a minute ; a little colouring, a few lumps of sugar, and a squeeze of lemon-juice will be wanted : or, in place of lemon-juice, a heaping teaspoonful of good marmalade. The sugar and water should boil to a syrup before the rest of the materials are added ; and in straining the sauce, remember to make the strainer very hot. Apricot jam in place of raspberry is only one of the dozens of variations, and a little thin melted butter sweetened with red currant or black currant jelly can be recommended.

The amount of sugar in the soufflé itself is small, for much would reduce the lightness ; for this reason a sweet sauce is called for.

Now conjure up some other flavourings for the soufflé proper; and when dealing with spices, let me remind you that essences often give a better flavour than ground spices, without injuring the colour.

Cassia, nutmeg, mace, ginger, cinnamon, and many others, are almost certain to be liked, but always adapt the sauce to the dish. For example: if flavouring the soufflé with ginger, it will at once occur to you that the syrup from some preserved ginger, with a little of the fruit, if you like, in tiny dice, forms a fitting adjunct to the sauce.

Lemon Soufflé.

This will take about forty minutes' steaming. The ingredients are an ounce and a half each of sugar and butter, the same of arrowroot or corn-flour, four eggs, a lemon, and half a pint of milk. The lemon must be wiped and peeled, and the peel infused in the milk for a time on a warm corner of the stove. When well-flavoured, the milk is strained off, and the materials blended in the way I have detailed above. Another way, which I recommend to those who do not begrudge a little extra trouble, is to rasp the rind of the fruit on the lumps of sugar, and then to crush it, and add as before.

Of course, essence of lemon might be used, but the dish is not so good in any respect. A little good custard, flavoured with fresh lemon-rind, goes well as sauce with this. Should you have no arrowroot or corn-flour handy, use a couple of ounces of pastry-flour; the larger quantity is owing to the difference in the amount of starch. Of arrowroot less is needed, by reason of its starchiness; this should be borne in mind always in making variations of this sort.

Orange Soufflé.

This needs a little less sugar than the lemon soufflé. The rind of a small orange should be used in addition to that of half a lemon; otherwise, proceed as above. A good sauce is composed of the juice of an orange and half a lemon, some sugar, and a little orange marmalade, boiled to a thin syrup.

Cherry Soufflé.

This is a dish that is very popular in Germany. The term *auflauf*, the German word for soufflé, is applied to dishes of very peculiar kinds, many of which are of a very substantial nature so far as the foundation goes; in such cases a large number of eggs have to be used to produce the lightness of a really good soufflé; and some are troublesome to prepare. The following is one of the simplest: the foundation is nothing more than a carefully-made batter, and all sorts of stone fruit may be used in the same way, the spice being regulated according to taste. Too much sugar, however tart the fruit, must be guarded against; a little extra sweetness in the sauce should be relied on to make up any deficiency.

Take an ounce of fine flour, the same of potato-flour, half a pint of milk, two ounces of butter, three eggs, a saltspoonful or so of powdered cinnamon, two or three ounces of sugar, and half a pound of ripe black cherries. The flour and milk are blended and stirred over the fire to the boil, and cooked until smooth, then removed and stirred until half cold. The butter is beaten to a cream and added with the yolks of the eggs, and the beating can hardly be too hard; the sugar and spice go next, and then the whites of the eggs, prepared as detailed above; here the yolks and whites are equal; at the same time, an extra white always means increased lightness. The fruit is put in just before baking, and if not put in the oven at once it will sink. A good heat is wanted at starting, but after, a slightly reduced temperature is desirable. This may be simplified by using an ounce more flour and an egg less, and a smaller amount of fruit; the dish will then be found good.

Sugar alone may be sent to table, or sugar and cream, or a sauce of the melted butter type, with sugar and a little syrup—that from bottled cherries comes in handy; but for the best dishes some cherry syrup is used, drawn from the fruit as for making jelly, and it is much improved by mixing a little currant juice with it.

Apple Soufflé.

When apples are cheap, this is quite a low-priced, though high-class dish, in the matter of taste and appearance. There are hosts of ways of preparing the apples for the base, but not one beats the simple one of baking them in their skins.

Supposing, then, half a pint of pulp be handy, free from core and skin, of course: let it cool, then beat it up until white and foamy with white sugar and a little spice; the grated peel of a lemon is a good flavouring, or some like almond essence; then add half a pint of batter, prepared as for the cherry soufflé given above, but with the yolk of one egg only, and the whites of two. Butter is optional—from an ounce to two or three would be used by many cooks, or cream would replace it. It wants a moderate oven, and should be dredged with sugar.

Space fails to tell of the number of soufflés of the *savoury* order, but with the Editor's permission, they shall have attention later.

DEBORAH PLATTER.

CONFECTIONERY AT HOME.

BY CATHERINE OWEN.

IT would surprise careful English mothers to see the quantity of candy consumed by the average American child, and yet by far the largest consumers are young ladies —although older ones plead guilty to a "sweet tooth," nor are the stronger sex far behind in the weakness—in fact, the Americans are a candy-eating people, and by "candy" they understand everything in the way of confectionery, from Everton toffee to chocolate creams. Confectioners' shops are everywhere, and from the splendour of their fitting-up one may judge how remunerative and well patronised their business is. Young lovers take a box of French candy to their lady-loves, as an Englishman would a bouquet (although the bouquet will not be forgotten by the American lover), and many husbands make a point of taking a regular supply home. Candy is thus a considerable item of expenditure among all classes above the rank of working people. A pound of fine candy costs from seventy-five cents (three shillings) to a dollar (four shillings) according to the store at which it is bought.

As American women excel in making preserves, and attain a proficiency in the art of making delicate cakes, only equalled out of America by professed pastrycooks, it is somewhat surprising that they have never turned their artistic hands to the elaboration of anything more *recherché* than molasses candy in the way of confectionery. Yet to make fine French candies requires no more patience, and is as satisfactory in its results as many of the so-called artistic *distractions* of the present day, it is more cleanly than modelling in clay, and not less so than pottery work. Although many English women are less of sweetmeat-eaters than their American cousins, pure and beautiful candies are indispensable at children's entertainments, and by many ladies of Continental tastes a *bonbonière* is by no means despised. I will therefore give some instructions in the art, beginning with the simplest form of French candy, called *fondant*.

It is generally supposed that special utensils are necessary to make fancy candies, and the ordinary directions in a work on confectionery bewilder you with the names of articles to be used, but perfect results can be obtained with a small enamelled or brass saucepan, and a silver spoon and fork.

Fondant.—Take two pounds of the *best* loaf-sugar, put it in the enamelled saucepan with just enough water to wet it through, and set it on a clear fire; let it boil ten minutes, removing any scum that may rise; then take two smooth sticks, dip one in, and if on touching it with the other a thread forms, take your candy from the fire quickly, have a basin of very cold water ready, and drop a little candy in it from the end of the stick; if, after you have given it time to cool, it does not form a soft ball between thumb and finger, it is not yet boiled enough; return it to the fire, and boil a minute or two longer, trying it frequently. If, however, the candy on being dropped into the water has at all a brittle feeling, it is boiled too much; then add a table-spoonful of water and put it on to boil again till you reach the right point of firmness without brittleness. This may require a little experimenting with, but once the experience is gained the chief difficulty in making creamy candies is overcome. When your sugar is boiled to the right point, set it aside to cool; if it is quite right, when cooling a thin jelly-like skin will form over it, but it may happen that a sugary coating like thin ice may cover it, which I will term *granulating*. If, however, the candy is only granulated on the top, and the bottom of the saucepan is quite smooth, you can skim off the thin sugar cake, and then take a spoon and stir, and beat the candy till it looks creamy and begins to get firm. If boiled enough it will look like lard by the time it is cold. When it is in this state, lay it aside; it is ready to use for many purposes. If, however, it is not firm you must repeat the process, that is to say, boil the sugar up once again, leave it on the fire (without more stirring than necessary to melt all parts alike) till it is quite clear, then again put to cool, and beat when half cold as before.

Your fondant made, provide yourself with blanched almonds, oil of lemon, extract of vanilla, pistachio-nuts, some *prepared* cochineal, strong infusion of Spanish saffron, a few walnuts taken in halves from the shell, some chocolate, a little fine rum, and Curaçao, Maraschino, noyeau—anything, in fact, for flavouring that may be convenient, or preferred. To try the effect of your work, now take a piece of the fondant, divide it into as many parts as you have flavours, drop (with *great care*, as too strong a flavour is disagreeable) a little lemon on one piece, a little raspberry syrup (very strong this must be, or your candy will be too wet) on another, a drop or two of vanilla on another, rum for another; with the lemon you can also put enough strong decoction of saffron to tint it a pale primrose, enough cochineal on the raspberry for a pink. Then take each piece and work it like a piece of bread-dough till thoroughly mixed; if colour or flavour is not satisfactory, add more; here your own taste must decide, many mixtures of flavours being excellent, such as lemon, lemon and ginger, bitter almonds and lemon; and lemon is always improved by a tiny speck of tartaric acid. Your pieces all worked up, break off little bits, and make into little eggs or balls, or grooved cones ; examine the forms of fine French candies, which are nearly all formed by hand, and imitate them. This, with the mixing and arranging of colours, is the artistic part of confectionery. If you make some of your pink balls as large as a damson, take a blanched almond, press it sideways in it, till it looks like a bursting fruit, just showing a kernel; these are handsome and may be made in all colours and flavours. You have now made raspberry creams, lemon creams, vanilla creams, and so on.

Panaché Fondant.—Take three pieces of your fondant, melt a little chocolate with as little water as possible by standing it in or over boiling water, when a smooth paste put it with one piece of fondant, work them together, adding a drop or two of vanilla ; when the flavour and colour suit you, lay it aside. With a second piece pound up some almonds or walnuts very fine ; if almonds, add one drop of bitter almond flavour; walnuts require nothing ; colour the fondant pink, and work nuts and candy together ; when well mixed and coloured a bright pink, lay this aside. The third piece is to remain white and needs only flavouring.

Divide the chocolate-coloured fondant in two equal parts, also the white, make each part into a ball, then with a small round phial bottle roll each piece on the back of a dish, just as you would a piece of paste, using the finest *powdered* sugar instead of flour, to prevent sticking ; roll the candy in the form of a strip an inch and a half wide, a quarter of an inch thick, and as long as your fondant allows; when you have the two white and two chocolate strips, take the pink, roll it as nearly the same width and length as the others as you can, but let it be at least *twice as thick*, then take one strip of chocolate, lay it on a piece of buttered paper, lay next a white strip upon it, fitting as neatly as possible, then the pink on that, then another white, and last of all the second chocolate ; now press them gently together, but not so as to put your panaché out of shape, and lay aside for an hour in a cool place.

When firm, take a sharp knife, give a sharp clean cut to the four sides to remove uneven surfaces, and you will then have a neat brick-shaped piece of candy before you ; now with the knife cut it neatly crosswise into little tricoloured slabs half an inch thick ; leave these a day to dry and harden, and pack away in rows in paper boxes for use.

Chocolate Creams.—Take a piece of fondant, flavour with vanilla, roll it into little balls the size of marbles, then take some grated chocolate—it must be finest French—let it get hot, then take the white of an egg well beaten, and mix both together; when the egg and chocolate form a smooth *thick* batter, dip each little ball in it from the end of a fork; if the white shows through, add more chocolate ; drop each on a piece of oiled paper, and set aside for twenty-four hours.

There is a new kind of candy lately introduced by fashionable candy makers in New York, and in most of the handsome stores. A confectioner stands at work in the window, showing the process of dipping the creams ; the skillet of hot creamed candy stands beside him, with an under-pan of boiling water to keep it just right. Walnut, almond, and every variety of candy are thus dipped now-a-days, and are much more delicious than the old-fashioned candies of solid sugar.

Orange and Lemon Creams.—Take an orange, carefully grate off the yellow part of the peel on to a plate, then you will have about a table-spoonful of the grated rind, squeeze on this the juice of half the orange, and the juice of half a lemon, or a tiny bit of tartaric acid ; then take enough finely *powdered* sugar to make the orange into a stiff paste, make it into little balls, and put for some hours to dry. Then take a piece of fondant, put it in a cup, and stand it in boiling water ; it will soon soften ; move it about till it is like thick cream, then dip each orange ball in it and drop it off on to oiled paper. If the cream is too thin to cover the inside colour, let it cool for a minute, warming it again if it gets too thick. Lemon creams are made in exactly the same way ; walnuts in halves should have this cream candy flavoured with vanilla, then be dipped and dropped from the end of the fork in the same way.

Roman Punch Drops.—Make some little balls of fondant, flavoured with lemon and a grain of tartaric acid, then melt some more fondant as for orange creams ; colour it pink and flavour it with rum, then dip each of your lemon-flavoured balls in it, and drop them from the end of the fork on to oiled paper. This dropped form of candy is very pretty and delicious, and may be made in infinite variety ; for instance, mix a little grated cocoanut, or chopped almonds, with fondant, make it into balls, flavour the outside cream as you choose, and dip them in it ; but in making a quantity of candy it is well to have some sorts that require less time, using the drop to ornament the whole.

To this end make fondant as before, take a piece the size of an egg, chop some almonds, work them into it as you would fruit into a cake, flavour it with vanilla, rose, lemon, or bitter almond, and have a case made of stiff paper about an inch wide and deep, and as long as your candy will fill, press it well in, to form it into a neat bar, and when you wish to use it take off the paper and cut it into small cubes with a sharp knife ; if the latter is wetted with spirits of wine it will cut more neatly.

To make these bars, the fondant must be very firm ; the best consistency is as hard when cold as winter butter ; should it by chance be so hard that it crumbles or you cannot work it, wet your hand once or twice with any spirit.

In your first efforts at making fondant you may find, instead of it being as smooth as butter, that it will have a slightly sugary texture. If you have the patience, before flavouring or colouring it, add two or three table-spoonfuls of water and boil it up, taking care you have put in enough liquid to thoroughly dissolve the sugar. To ascertain this take a little in a spoon when boiling ; if it is a smooth syrup it is right ; if gritty, or particles of candy still remain, add a little more water ; boil now till it will form a soft ball between the fingers as before directed. To save time you may pour off a little in a saucer, set it in a cold place, and when ready beat it with a spoon; if the result is smooth and gets firm as it cools, you may conclude the rest in the saucepan is right; if it is white and creamy, but not firm, boil it two or three minutes longer.

Many people do not object to the sugary texture, but I would advise getting the fondant once perfect. The failure to do so once or twice will only teach you the art of sugar-boiling better than a chapter of words, and you will see for yourself how it passes from one degree to another. A pinch of cream of tartar put with the sugar when boiling will tend to prevent granulation; but if the least bit too much is added, it will also make it very hard to cream.

In giving these directions I have endeavoured to be very clear, remembering my own difficulties in teaching myself from books. For this reason I will emphasise one or two things—always use the *best* white sugar; be very careful that flavouring, colouring, &c., are highly concentrated, as even a drop too much liquid will make your fondant run. When using chocolate get the best French *unsweetened*—your own candy supplies the sugar; and in making dipped candies take care your cream is thick enough to cover well, and not to run. If very hot it may be too thin; then stir a minute or two till it thickens, keeping it in boiling water all the time it is being used, or it will get hard at once; and when you put the fondant into the bowl to bring it to cream, stir it as it warms the whole time, or it will go back to syrup. In using a fork to dip, do not stick it into the article; drop your ball or nut into the candy, taking it out on the fork as if the latter were a spoon, rest it on the edge of the bowl a second to drain it, then neatly drop it on to the oiled paper. The cream candy should not run off on to the paper, leaving the inside bare; if it does, beat longer.

Lastly, when I say powdered sugar I mean such as you would use for cake-icing, as fine as flour.

A GOOD GRIDDLE CAKE.—The Scotch are quite famous for their excellent griddle cakes. The griddle is a similar pan to our frying-pan, with this difference—there is a handle over the top and the bottom is slightly thicker. For the cake the materials required are quite a pint of sour milk, two breakfastcupfuls of sifted flour, one teaspoonful of carbonate of soda, two teaspoonfuls of green treacle, and half a teaspoonful of salt. If the treacle is rather thick it can be made more liquid by putting it in a cup and standing it on the stove for two or three minutes; then mix it with the milk. Put the salt and flour in a baking bowl and mix them well. Make a hole in the middle and stir in the milk carefully, so there shall be no lumps. Beat it for five minutes and then add the soda dissolved in boiling water. Turn into the greased griddle and bake for about a quarter of an hour.

SODA CAKES.—Sift a teaspoonful of carbonate of soda into a pound of flour, put in a pinch of salt, and make it into a stiff dough with sour milk; divide into three portions, roll out and make each into a round cake an inch thick. Bake in a fairly hot oven, giving them ten minutes to rise, and bake one side, and then turn them over. When baked split each one, put on plenty of butter, and let them be eaten at once. These cakes suit dyspeptic persons who cannot eat a hot cake made with shortening. The following cakes are suitable for either breakfast or tea, and may be baked on a gas ring when the kitchen fire has been let out on a sultry day. If intended for breakfast it is a saving of time to mix up the batter over night, adding the soda in the morning.

CREAM CAKES are also baked on a griddle, but instead of being baked in one large cake the batter is baked a cupful at a time. The materials required are—a pint of slightly sour milk and same quantity of cream; four eggs, yolks and whites whipped separately; a teaspoonful of soda, a saltspoonful of salt, and sufficient flour to make a good batter.

Put about two cups of flour in a bowl, and mix it smoothly with the cream and milk (mixed together) into a batter, of course adding more flour if the batter is not thick enough; then stir in the eggs, and lastly the salt and soda, the latter dissolved in just sufficient hot water to cover it. Beat all well up three or four minutes before baking. As they are baked lay them in the folds of a clean cloth to keep hot; they are best then. There are many other recipes I might enumerate, but will close with the German dish that does not require much preparation. Let the milk stand in the jug or bowl until it is quite stiff and resembles a blancmange, then put it in rather a deep dish and let powdered sugar be eaten with it. This is delicious, if liked; but the taste for it is mostly an acquired one.

PIGEONS DE BORDEAUX À LA BOURGEOISE. —Procure as many Bordeaux pigeons as you require, and cut each one into four; have ready a saucepan with as much butter as you think necessary to brown them. When they are nicely browned lift them out gently, and fry one dozen small quenelles, which are very nice made of forcemeat and shaped with two teaspoons; when these are brown, take them out carefully so as not to break them, then rub into the butter one good heaped-up tablespoonful of flour, and let this fry till brown, then add not quite a pint of thin stock, or water will do, with the addition of a small quantity of Liebig's Extract. Stir till it boils, then add one wineglassful of port or sherry, and pepper and salt to taste. Now put in your pigeons, quenelles, and one dozen mushrooms and eight French olives which have been previously stoned, and let all stew gently for three-quarters of an hour. In a separate saucepan boil one dozen of carrots and turnips cut as near the shape of quenelles as possible, and serve the pigeons in the centre and the quenelles, mushrooms, carrots, turnips and olives placed alternately round with one dozen fried croûtons cut kite shape.

WE cannot help feeling that bread has first claim on our space. As a rule, there is so little variety on an ordinary table, be the meal what it may, and as the various kinds of flour can now be bought of grocers and at the vegetarian depôts in most large towns, there is but little excuse for the non-appearance of many kinds, at once cheap and nourishing. On a New York breakfast-table bread in every form, size, and colour, either hot or cold, is obtainable, as well as many other dainties which we hope to include in future articles. American housewives are skilful judges of flour, but it will suffice here—without entering into detail as to the various tests of quality—to advise our readers always to buy the best only, whether brown or white, and for whatever purpose it may be required. Equally important is the goodness of the yeast; a nice batch of bread is an impossibility if stale, sour yeast is used; and many Americans make their own, even when it is quite easy to obtain good brewers' yeast. Without recommending home-made in preference to brewers' (for, when really good, none is better), we give one or two recipes that may be useful, and are certainly reliable.

Newhaven Yeast.—Boil a handful of hops in a bag in a couple of quarts of water, with eight ounces of pared potatoes, until the latter break; then mash them up with an ounce of flour, three ounces of salt, and the same of brown sugar. Pour the boiling hop-water on this, and when lukewarm, add enough German or French yeast to ferment it well. Bottle when cold, and keep in a cool place.

Potato Yeast is made by mashing a dozen large boiled potatoes with a tea-cupful of flour and a tea-spoonful of salt, then mixing with dissolved German yeast to make a batter; this is best for immediate use, but may be bottled if kept very cool.

A good yeast, "self-working"—that is, without the addition of any other to excite fermentation—can be got by boiling two ounces of hops in a gallon of water for one hour; then, when lukewarm, remove the hops (which should be tied in muslin), and add the hop-liquor gradually to a pound of flour; beat in a table-spoonful of salt and half a pound of white sugar, and set away for a couple of days in a bowl covered with a cloth in a warm place. On the third day add the hop liquor to six or eight potatoes, boiled and mashed. Let it stand for twelve hours longer in a warm kitchen, then store in jars; cork well. This will keep three or four months in a cool cellar.

A very excellent and nutritious bread, which we recommend for general family use, is made with two-thirds Graham flour (what is called in England whole meal or brown flour) and one-third fine white.

To each quart a good tea-spoonful of salt should be added. As the English are not so fond of sweets as their American cousins, they will reduce the quantity of sugar and molasses sufficiently to suit their palates; therefore, instead of recommending a tea-cupful of treacle, mixed with the yeast, for each loaf of the bread, we think that quantity to *four* loaves will be more to their mind. This dough requires good yeast, and must be well kneaded, mixed soft, and thoroughly baked. A fierce oven will spoil it.

Boston Brown Bread.—Make this by substituting two parts Indian meal and one part rice flour for wheaten flour, adding, as well as yeast, a small quantity of soda or saleratus. It requires well kneading, and must rise for five hours at least, and after it is made into loaves they should rise an hour longer. Bake a four-pound loaf quite three hours; the oven *must* be slow.

Ordinary family bread from white flour is generally mixed with "sponge" made over-night. A very good recipe is as under:—Half a dozen potatoes boiled and mashed while hot, a quarter-pint of brewers' yeast, two ounces of white sugar, two ounces of lard, one tea-spoonful of soda, three cupfuls of flour (say a pint), one quart of warm water—that in which the potatoes were boiled. In mixing, add the soda last of all. Cover lightly in warm weather and tightly in winter. This quantity will make up from two to three quarts of flour—sufficient to bake at a time for a small family. The inexperienced in bread-making from sponge in place of yeast must remember that it requires to be twice kneaded: first when the sponge and flour are well amalgamated, then the most thorough kneading is necessary, and again after the dough has risen when ten minutes or so will suffice. Then, after putting into greased tins, or making into rolls and laying them in one large tin, again leave the dough near the fire for an hour previous to baking.

We must now mention a few kinds of fancy bread; they will perhaps be more welcome to the majority.

Rice Bread, very light and delicate for invalids, and a pleasant change from that usually made, requires that a tea-cupful of well-boiled rice be added to each quart of wheaten flour. When making the bread, put in with the yeast a little sugar and dissolved lard or butter. *Hominy Bread* is made the same way; take care that the hominy is well boiled. In each case put salt as usual.

Buttermilk Bread is a great delicacy, popular all through the United States. It is very easy to make, and particularly wholesome. Into each pint of buttermilk, made hot, stir flour to form a thick batter, add a couple of spoonfuls of yeast, and let it stand a few hours. Then stir in a tea-spoonful of soda, the same of salt, and a couple of ounces of dissolved butter, and work in enough flour to make a nice dough. Knead well, make into loaves, and let it rise until light.

Buttermilk Muffins have but to be tried to become a standing winter dish. Beat hard two eggs into a quart of buttermilk, stir in flour to make a thick batter, about a quart, and lastly, a tea-spoonful of salt and the same of soda. Bake in a hot oven in well-greased tins. Muffins of all kinds should only be cut just round the edge, then pulled open with the fingers.

Graham Muffins are more substantial and easy of digestion than those made with white flour. Mix into a smooth batter three cupfuls of Graham flour, one cupful of white ditto, one quart of milk, half-cupful of yeast, one tea-spoonful of salt, one ounce of sugar, and the same of lard dissolved in the milk. Set to rise over-night, and in the morning beat in an egg, and bake in a good oven for twenty minutes.

Cream Muffins are delicious; perhaps only those who keep cows will feel inclined to be extravagant enough to indulge in them. Beat six eggs, a pint of cream, and a pint of milk well together; add an ounce of lard and an ounce of butter, a tea-spoonful of salt, and a quart of flour *stirred in lightly.* Half fill the rings, and bake in a sound oven.

Rice Muffins.—Beat hard into a batter a cupful of rice—boiled—a pint of flour, two eggs, a little salt, an ounce of butter, and nearly a quart of milk. The harder you beat and the more quickly you bake, the better they will be.

French Rolls made thus are worth trying :—Set a sponge, by mixing a quart of flour, a cupful of yeast, and a quart of warm milk; when light, work in an egg, a tea-spoonful of salt, half as much soda dissolved in hot water, an ounce of sugar, and flour to make a soft dough. In two or three hours, shape into balls, and set them in a greased baking-tin. In half an hour's time, gash each one across with a knife. Brush over with milk, and bake in a good oven nearly half an hour.

Potato Scones are very good. Mash eight or ten boiled potatoes, mix with two ounces of sugar, half a pint of warm milk, a couple of table-spoonfuls of yeast, and enough flour to make a batter. Let this rise, then beat in enough flour to make it sufficiently stiff to roll out; again let it rise, then roll out half an inch thick; cut into rounds or squares, and bake. Butter the tops liberally.

Dough Crumpets are Boston favourites, and easily made. A pound of ordinary bread dough, white or brown, needs a half-cupful of white sugar, three ounces of butter, and three eggs, to be beaten hard into it. Bake in muffin-rings well buttered.

Lincoln Shortcake ought to become popular at high teas. Beat four ounces of lard and butter into cream, stir in a salt-spoonful of salt, and a good pinch of soda dissolved in just enough vinegar to cover it; then put in a pound of fine flour, dried and sifted. Mix with water or milk to a stiff paste, and roll out half an inch thick. Prick all over, and bake until brown. Split while hot, and butter plentifully.

We must not omit a couple of recipes for " hot biscuits," taking care to impress upon those who make note of them that in America the word " biscuit " is applied to what, in Great Britain, would perhaps be called buns, tea-cakes, or fancy rolls; and what *here* are called biscuits are known *there* as "crackers." Try, then, either of the following when you want to initiate yourself into the good graces of any one who has come to take tea.

Yeast Biscuits require a pint of milk, a half-cupful of lard and butter mixed, a half-quartern of yeast, a table-spoonful of sugar, a salt-spoonful of salt, and flour to make a soft dough. Mix all together six hours before tea-time, adding *half* the flour only—just enough to make a leaven ; cover with a cloth, and leave to rise. Make up with the remainder of the flour, roll out half an inch thick into round cakes, leave to rise in the baking-tin for twenty minutes near the fire, and lastly, bake in a hot oven for twenty minutes, or rather less. These will be beautifully light and sweet if properly mixed, and the oven really hot.

Soda Biscuits are equally good. Mix together a quart of *dry* white flour, a tea-spoonful of carbonate of soda, and two of cream of tartar; pass through a sieve to lighten, then rub in two ounces of lard and a little salt. Mix with milk quite soft, only stiff enough to handle without sticking to the fingers; roll it out on a floured board, then double it over and roll out again : this makes thin flakes. Cut and bake as for " yeast biscuits." Either may be eaten with or without butter, and brown flour used in place of white makes *Graham Biscuits.* Buttermilk, or sour milk, may take the place of sweet, in recipes where soda and cream of tartar are used, provided the tartar is *left out,* buttermilk or sour milk being sufficiently acid, only soda is necessary.

Our bread paper would be sadly incomplete if we failed to mention "corn-meal bread," a staple article of diet in some parts of the States, among the poorer classes chiefly, though any one would find a meal of it very satisfying during cold weather, and nearly all children like it. Indian meal should be bought in small quantities ; the lighter in colour makes the best bread.

Risen Corn Bread may be made in the ordinary way with yeast, using two-thirds corn and one-third wheaten flour, except that a little sugar improves it, and two ounces of lard or butter should be added to every quart of meal used. An easy way for a "test-loaf" without yeast is to beat three eggs hard with three cupfuls of milk, in which a piece of lard the size of an egg has been dissolved, then put in three cupfuls of Indian meal, one cupful of flour, one tea-spoonful of salt, six of sugar, one of soda, two of cream of tartar. Beat hard again, and bake in a well-buttered mould very steadily. Muffins or crumpets may be made as above, but a little thinner, more milk being required. Bake in rings or patty-pans.

The numerous family of griddle-cakes, as well as jumbles, crullers, dough-nuts, and the various kinds of richer cakes, are reserved for treatment in a future chapter.

HOW TO MAKE PLAIN CAKES.

BY THE AUTHOR OF "A YEAR'S COOKERY."

A LITTLE while ago I said that one of the pleasantest parts of a cook's work was the making of pastry; but most people will acknowledge that it is equally interesting to make cakes. There are very few of those interested in cookery who have not at one time or other tried their hands at this business, and sometimes after taking no end of pains the cake has come out heavy, or doughy, or burnt, and then what a disappointment it has been! I think, however, I can promise that those who will follow exactly the directions I am going to give now will succeed in making very good plain cakes, quite equal to "bought cakes," at a reasonable cost.

When once we have made up our minds to make a cake, the first thing we must think about is the oven. Every oven has an idiosyncrasy of its own. Wise men tell us that we conquer Nature only by obeying her; and in the same way we may say we get the most out of ovens only by studying their peculiarities, and falling in with their little ways. You understand your own oven; I do not—I only understand my own. Only I would advise you, whatever you do, to take such measures as will insure your having a good hot oven to bake your cakes in. If you cannot get that, leave the matter altogether, for very much of the excellence of a cake depends upon the baking.

What do we mean by a "good hot oven?" For my part, I mean an oven that feels glowingly hot when I put my hand into it for a minute. If the heat were such that I could not bear to keep my hand in, I should know the oven was too hot for my cakes, while if it were only pleasantly warm it would be too cool. This, however, is rather an uncertain way of deciding the question. The surest plan would be to have a thermometer let into the front of the oven, and we should know that we had the right heat for a moderate-sized cake when this rose to 240°. Thermometers, however, in ovens are not common, and so we must decide the matter in another way. Before putting the cake in the oven we may sprinkle a pinch of flour in the bottom of it. If in one minute this turns a bright golden brown the oven is of the right heat; if it turns black, it is too hot; if it does not brown, but is a dirty yellow colour, the oven is not hot enough.

One or two little points we must not forget. Small cakes require a quicker oven than do large ones. All cakes should be put into the hotter part of the oven first, and left until they rise. They should then be placed in the cooler part, and allowed to bake gently through. If they brown too quickly they should have a sheet of paper laid over them. When we cannot have a perfect oven, it is better to have one that is too hot rather than one that is too cool. It is always possible to put an extra baking sheet under the cake-tin, and to lay a sheet of paper over the top if it is browning too quickly, thus retarding the action of the heat; but an oven that is "slack" is certain to make our cake heavy. Before beginning to mix our cake we should have all our ingredients prepared and weighed out. Cakes that are made with baking powder or soda (and it is of this kind that I am speaking now) should be baked as quickly as possible after they are moistened. Besides, it saves time to get the things ready beforehand, then mix them all together. If we mix our butter and flour, then stop to clean and dry our currants, and put them in; clean our hands again to beat the eggs, then stop all the proceedings while we line the cake-tin with buttered paper, we shall take twice as long over the business as we have any occasion to do.

The following are the preparations required:—

Grease the inside of the cake-tin throughout with dripping or butter. This will be best done with the fingers. For a superior cake line the tin with paper that has been buttered all over. The tins must not be more than two-thirds filled with the mixture.

Weigh the currants or raisins, turn them over, and see that no stones have been accidentally left in them. If they are not already washed, it will be better now that we are at this stage of the proceedings to leave them unwashed, contenting ourselves with sprinkling flour upon them and rubbing them well between the folds of a soft cloth. This would be to avoid using them either damp or hot, and so run the risk of making our cakes heavy. It is always best to clean currants in quantities as soon as they come from the grocer. They should be washed in cold water (boiling water injures their flavour), drained, spread out a few at a time on a towel, and have a little flour sprinkled over them, then dried slowly at the mouth of a cool oven (quick drying also injures their flavour), and tied down in jars for use. Sultanas may be cleaned in the same way.

Remove the sugar from the inside of the candied peel, and cut it into very thin strips. The flavour will be imparted to the cake more effectually by preparing it thus, rather than by either chopping it or putting in large pieces. Mixed peel is the best for cakes. This consists of citron, which is green; orange, which is dark; and lemon, which is light-coloured.

When large raisins are used they should be stoned and chopped small. Sultana raisins are not nearly so full of flavour as the others.

Butter, if salt, should be washed in two or three waters before being used. Good dripping is excellent for plain cakes. It will be more easily mixed with the flour if it is not over-hard; therefore, it may be softened in cold weather by being put into a basin and surrounded with boiling water for awhile, then broken up with a knife. It must not be *hot* when put in, or the cake will be heavy. In making superior cakes the butter should be "creamed"—that is, it should be beaten in a bowl with the hand till it is of the consistency of very thick cream—and the flour, sugar, eggs, and currants should be beaten in by turns a little at a time. But in making plain cakes the dripping may be rubbed into the flour, and the dry ingredients mixed thoroughly before any liquid is stirred in.

What is called castor sugar is the best for cakes. When loaf sugar is used it should be pounded and sifted. Flour, too, should be of fine quality. Home-made baking powder is the best for making cakes; the recipe for making it was given in CASSELL'S FAMILY MAGAZINE for May, 1880, page 363, in the article on Pastry. [*See Page 81.*]

When fresh lemon-rind is used it should either be grated on a coarse grater, or cut off very thinly without any of the white, and chopped small. The white part of lemon-rind is very bitter, and not fit for use.

Eggs should always be broken one at a time in a cup before they are put together. This is for fear any of them should be bad. The specks also should be removed. In making superior cakes the whites and the yolks are beaten separately—the yolks are stirred in briskly, and the whites are simply dashed into the mixture at the last moment. In plain cakes, however, the eggs may be beaten together, and mixed with the milk.

Last of all, we should be careful to mix the cakes *stiffly*. This is a great secret in making plain cakes. The flour must, of course, be entirely moistened, and the liquid well mixed with the dry ingredients; but when it is remembered that the fat in the cake will melt, and the sugar be dissolved, it will be seen that an abundance of moisture is not required.

Now that we have all our materials together, I will give a few recipes. The first is for a very cheap cake, plain and wholesome, but good. Put a pound of flour into a bowl, and with it a pinch of salt, and a large heaped tea-spoonful of baking powder. Mix thoroughly. Rub in a quarter of a pound of good beef dripping, and add half a pound of currants picked and dried, a quarter of a pound of sugar, one ounce of candied peel thinly cut, and half a tea-spoonful of grated lemon-rind. Make into a stiff paste with milk, and bake in a good oven.

The next cake is a little richer, and better altogether. It also is a cheap cake. Many mothers find that currants are not good for their children. When this is the case sultanas may always be used instead, as they are in this recipe. Put ten ounces of flour into a bowl, and add a small pinch of salt and two tea-spoonfuls of baking powder. Rub in four ounces of butter or clarified dripping, and add two ounces of

moist sugar, four ounces of sultanas, an ounce of candied peel, a tea-spoonful of grated lemon-rind, one egg, and milk to make a stiff paste.

The next is a seed cake. Put a pound of flour with a pinch of salt into a bowl, and rub in six ounces of butter or dripping; add six ounces of sugar, a tea-spoonful of mixed spice, and a table-spoonful of caraway seeds. Put a tumblerful of milk into a basin with a tea-spoonful of carbonate of soda, and set it in the oven till the soda is dissolved. Let it cool, and when cool add a table-spoonful of vinegar. Stir the liquid into the mixture to make a stiff paste, and bake the cake.

A richer seed cake may be made thus:—Put ten ounces of flour into a bowl with a pinch of salt, and two even tea-spoonfuls of baking powder. Mix thoroughly, then rub in four ounces of butter or good dripping, and add two ounces of sugar and a tea-spoonful of caraway seeds. Beat an egg; mix with it two table-spoonfuls of milk, and make the mixture into a stiff paste with the liquid. Bake as before.

Corn-flour cake will suit those who do not care for either currants or seeds. Take six ounces of corn-flour, three ounces of castor sugar, three ounces of butter, one even tea-spoonful of baking powder, two eggs, and a spoonful of milk. Beat the butter to cream, put with it the sugar, eggs, and milk. Mix the corn-flour and baking powder, and add these gradually, beating the mixture briskly for some minutes. Add four or five drops of essence of almonds, and bake in a lined tin in a brisk oven.

The following also is a good but rather rich cake:—Put a pound of flour into a bowl, and mix with it a quarter of a salt-spoonful of salt, and three tea-spoonfuls of baking powder. Mix thoroughly. Rub in half a pound of butter, or a quarter of a pound of butter and a quarter of a pound of lard; and add half a pound of sugar, half a pound of raisins, half a pound of currants, two ounces of mixed peel, a quarter of a tea-spoonful of grated nutmeg, two eggs, and milk to make a stiff paste.

In order to tell when a cake is sufficiently baked, push the blade of a knife quite down to the bottom of it in the middle. If this comes out clean and dry the cake is done. If at all moist, it must be put back again in the cool part of the oven again to "soak;" otherwise it will taste doughy. As soon as a cake is taken from the oven it should be turned out of the tin and placed on its side, but leaning on something to keep it from breaking. If left in the tin till cold it may become heavy.

Before closing I should like to give two recipes— one for Rock Cakes, and the other for Soda Buns. They are very easy to make, are inexpensive, and at the same time so good that they are sure to give satisfaction. The ingredients should be mixed very stiffly, and the cakes or buns placed an inch and a half apart on a floured baking sheet, in little knobs about the size of a walnut, and baked in a brisk oven.

Rock Cakes.—Put a quarter of a pound of clarified dripping into a basin with half a tea-spoonful of baking powder. Beat the fat to cream, and work in gradually half a pound of flour. Add a quarter of a pound of currants, picked and dried, two ounces of moist sugar, two ounces of mixed peel finely cut, the rind of one lemon grated. Beat one egg, and mix with half a gill of milk, and stir these into the mixture.

Soda Buns.—Rub six ounces of butter into one pound of flour; add six ounces of white sugar, two ounces of mixed candied peel, finely shred. Put a quarter of a tea-spoonful of carbonate of soda into a table-spoonful of milk in a cup, and place this in the oven till the soda is dissolved. Let it cool, and put it with the flour, butter, and sugar. Drop in separately the yolks of four and the whites of two eggs, and mix thoroughly. Bake also in a brisk oven.

Many people consider cakes unwholesome. Very rich cake undoubtedly is so, but a small portion of good plain home-made cake cannot hurt any one who is in good health. Any mother who wishes to give her children a treat cannot do better than give them one of the simple cakes the recipes for which have been given, and if the youngsters are not pleased with it, all I can say is, they are differently constituted from the little people of my acquaintance.

PHILLIS BROWNE.

INEXPENSIVE JERSEY WONDERS.—To be eaten hot, never later than three days old. 1 lb. butter, 4 lb. flour, quarter pound of sugar, 1 egg, well beaten, with sufficient water to make all the ingredients (with a large teaspoonful of baking powder) into a paste. Knead it well, and roll out as you would for pastry, cut into portions three inches long and two broad, make two slits lengthways in each, and plait the three pieces down in a plait of three, so as to make a shape like a small French roll. Lay them when done on a flat dish ready for boiling. *Boiling.*—Put into a deep stewpan 1 lb. of fresh lard; when it boils drop into it four wonders; they will almost immediately rise to the surface. Turn them about with a steel fork until they are of a rich brown colour, take them out with a strainer on to dishes to dry. Be sure the lard boils again before you put in others, as if it bubbles at all it is a sign the lard does not boil, and the wonders will be spoilt.

CRYSTALLISED FRUIT.—To every pound of fruit allow 1 lb. of loaf sugar and a quarter pint of water. For this purpose the fruit must be used before it is quite ripe, and part of the stalk must be left on. Weigh the fruit, rejecting all that is in the least degree blemished, and put it into a lined saucepan with the sugar and water, which should have been previously boiled together to a rich syrup. Boil the fruit in this for ten minutes, remove it from the fire, and drain the fruit. The next day boil up the syrup and put in the fruit again, and let it simmer for three minutes, and drain the syrup away. Continue this process for five or six days, and the last time place the fruit, when drained, on a hair sieve, and put them in an oven or warm spot to dry. Keep them in a box, with paper between each layer, in a place free from damp.

QUICKLY-MADE AND SIMPLE PUFF PASTE. —Take 1 lb. of dry flour, rub into it 8 or 10 oz. of butter and lard, in thin flakes, placing them on a plate, until nearly all the shortening has been absorbed; mix a little water with the remaining flour, until it is a stiff paste; roll this out as thin as possible, arrange the flakes of butter and lard over it evenly, fold it up and roll it out; fold and roll till the pastry is thoroughly mixed; line your tins, put in mince, or preserve, cover, place in a quick oven, and in about ten minutes they will be of a delicate brown, and will rise to the twenty flakes, which is the ambition of most cooks to attain. The whole affair will be over in half-an-hour, if the artiste has a quick light hand.

RASPBERRY SANDWICHES.—Take one breakfast cup of flour, three-quarters of a breakfast cup of castor sugar, 3 large eggs, a pinch of salt, 1 teaspoonful of cream of tartar, half a teaspoonful of carbonate of soda. Mix the flour, sugar, salt, and cream of tartar together, beat the eggs up well and mix them in, pour a dessertspoonful of boiling water upon the soda, and add that to the mixture; after beating it all well together, spread thinly on well-buttered tins, and bake in a moderate oven. Cut up in slices and put layers of jam in between; sprinkle a little powdered sugar over the top.

MUD STAINS FROM FRENCH MERINO, TO REMOVE.—Dissolve a little carbonate of soda in water, and wipe the stains with it.

PAINT OR TAR FROM HANDS, TO REMOVE.—Rub the hands with a little butter or grease, and then wash with soap and water.

TO KEEP MOTHS FROM CLOTHES.—A few clippings of Russian leather laid in the drawers and boxes where the clothes are kept.

SPOONS FOR BOILED EGGS.—Cheap bone spoons are the best with which to eat eggs. Silver spoons become discoloured, owing to the sulphurous matter contained in the eggs. The quickest method of removing these stains from silver spoons is to rub them with salt between the thumb and finger.

HOW TO KEEP YOURSELF WARM.— Should there be insufficient clothing upon the bed, lay a sheet of brown paper, or newspaper, under the quilt. This will answer all the purposes of a good blanket, and without a heavy weight. A sheet of paper wrapped round the body under the jacket or mantle is a great comfort during a cold winter walk.

APPLE TANSY.—Pare some apples, cut into thin round slices, and fry in butter. Beat up half a dozen eggs in a quart of cream, and pour them upon the apples.

GINGER WINE.—Six gallons of water, and eighteen pounds of lump-sugar. Thin rinds of seven lemons and eight oranges, and eight ounces of ginger. Boil the whole for an hour, and cool. When lukewarm, add the juice of the oranges and lemons, and three pounds of raisins. Work with yeast, and put into the cask with half an ounce of isinglass. Bottle in six or eight weeks.

SENTIMENTAL COOKERY.

BY ARDERN HOLT.

IN the opinion of a celebrated French dramatist, "Sociability over a book or good eating doubles the gratification from either or both." This probably is the reason why so many anniversaries and so many events are commemorated by some one article of food. The most prominent example of this lies in cakes: hot-cross-buns, wedding, funeral, fair, Easter, and harvest cakes, occur to the mind at once.

The subject is an interesting one, and I am going to give you some of the details — some of the whys and the wherefores thereof. I will begin with the wedding-cake — a subject that never seems to pall. It is of very ancient origin : brides of old offered cakes to Diana, and the Confarreatio—the most ancient and solemn marriage ceremony of the Romans—was so called because the cake (*far*) was carried before the bride. In England, we came to the present perfection of wedding-cake by degrees. Cakes and buns superseded hard, dry biscuits, and were made of spice, currants, milk, sugar, and eggs in Elizabeth's time ; when some were thrown over the bride's head or put through her ring, and eaten for luck to inspire prophetic dreams ; like the dumb-cake or dreaming-cake of a later time. This cake was divided into three ; some was eaten by the young maidens, and some placed beneath their pillows, or in the foot of the left stocking, and thrown over the left shoulder while retiring to bed before twelve, the maidens walking backwards the while, in order that they might see their future husbands in their dreams. The small marriage-cakes of Elizabeth's reign became the rich mass of almond paste, plums, currants, citron, &c., in the hands of the French cooks brought over at the Restoration. Very curious customs appertain to bride-cake all the world over. In Yorkshire, a plateful is thrown from an upper window to be scrambled for ; in Liburnia, the bride throws a hard cake of coarse flour over the bridegroom's house,

and the higher she throws it the happier she will be. In Georgia and Circassia, the bride kicks over a plate of dough set for her, and scatters it all over the room ; and an old English custom was to raise a cake on a high pole, and the young man who first reached it was allowed to receive the bride and bridegroom on their arrival at their own home.

From gay to grave. In the North, a packet of flat sponge-cakes like saucers, with grated sugar on the top, often accompanies the invitation to a funeral, or the cakes are eaten on returning from church, or are sent with the subsequent hat-bands and gloves.

Fair-cakes are of all kinds, but gingerbread always plays an important part therein. I have a very pleasant remembrance of some we had as children in Yorkshire, which were not gingerbread ; they were square, made of pastry, the corners turned up, and filled in with currants, spice, and nutmeg. These served for two fairs, held within three weeks of each other ; it is hardly necessary to say that they ate better at the first. On similar occasions in the same county, we ate spiced ginger-cheese, pepper-cakes, and gingerbread loaf ; and for the 5th of November, Yorkshire parkin is prepared. Never lose a chance of eating this. Make it, if you can, as follows :—4 lbs. of good Yorkshire oatmeal, 4 lbs. of treacle, 1 lb. of soft sugar, 1 lb. of butter, 2 oz. of powdered ginger. Mix the treacle and butter well together, and, when melted before the fire, add the other ingredients, stir with a knife, but do not knead it, and bake in a cool oven, in tins, about two inches thick. Turn it out when cold.

The use of cakes in old days was almost universal at religious festivals. Egyptians, Babylonians, Samians, Greeks, and Romans, all had sacred bread and cakes. In England, there are St. Michael's bannocks for Michaelmas, and the carvis or seed-cake for Allhallows Eve. These used to be called Soul cakes, and were sent about to friends in Northamptonshire and other counties. Very probably the plan originated in a country custom of sending wheat-cakes when wheat-sowing was over ; these, plentifully besprinkled with carraways, were among the ploughman's perquisites ; and Allhallows Eve fell at the same season. In old days, in Shropshire, these Soul cakes were laid on the table in a high heap—like the shewbread. They, in a manner, remind one of the harvest-cakes, which every county, as far as I know, patronises, though the ingredients differ. I will, however, give you a simple and good recipe, which I am sure is worth making :—2 lbs. of flour, 3 tablespoonfuls of fresh yeast, ¼ lb. of currants, ¼ lb. of sugar, 2 eggs, a little spice,. and enough warm milk to make the mixture light. When it has risen sufficiently, work it into cakes of ¼ lb. each, bake in a cool oven for ten minutes, then brush over with milk and sugar.

For Christmas celebration there is no end to the good fare associated with the season : Yule-cakes, baby-cake, and the most delicious ginger and spiced cakes and loaves, which are sure to be offered you, in many parts of Yorkshire, and—last, not least—waffel cakes, which are thin, like the gauffre cakes sold at fairs.

This is how you make them :—¼ lb. of butter, 3 eggs, 2 table-spoonfuls of flour, a tea-cupful of milk, salt and nutmeg. Beat the butter to a cream, mix the yolks with it, add the flour by degrees, and pour on the cream ; beat the whites of the eggs into a froth, add them to the other ingredients before baking. Rub the waffel-irons with butter, pour in the batter, so that all the interstices are filled ; bake a light brown.

The following is a good North Country Yule-cake :— 1 lb. of sifted flour, a salt-spoonful of salt, ¼ oz. of German yeast, ¼ pint of tepid water. Stir in the flour with a wooden spoon, and let it stand in a warm place to rise, add ¼ lb. of butter beaten to a cream, ½ lb. moist sugar, a little grated nutmeg, ¾ lb. of currants, 4 oz. of candied peel, 2 beaten eggs. Mix well ; half fill a tin, bake in moderate oven for two hours. Turn it out of the oven to get cool.

Twelfth Night cake was, as far back as 1620, made of flour, ginger, honey, and pepper, one for every family ; portions were set apart and given away in alms. The maker thrust in a small coin at random when kneading it, or a bean, and a pea, and those who found them were constituted king and queen for the evening—a custom borrowed from the French *roi de la fève*. As time went on this has been enlarged upon; but the white sugared cake still survives.

There was an old custom in some places of placing the twelfth-cake on the horns of the oxen, with much ceremony. At St. Albans, Herts, on New Year's Day, curious buns in the shape of a woman were sold, and called Pope ladies. This reminds me of some curious cakes associated with Easter—viz., the Biddenham cakes, in commemoration of the Biddenham maidens, who were joined together at the hips and shoulders somewhat after the fashion of the Siamese twins. On Easter Sunday 1,000 rolls were for years given away to all strangers, with the effigies of these ladies upon them, dressed in the costume of Mary's reign, and showing that they possessed but one pair of arms between them. The money for this distribution was secured upon some twenty acres of land left by them for the purpose. The rolls were to be accompanied by cheese in proportion. Eggs, herb pudding, tansy-cakes, which were all given at Easter, had their origin in the fact that people poured into the churches for the Easter communion, many coming long distances. The hotels were filled, and the clergy and laity were refreshed after the service. Herb pudding was made of the tops of young nettles, docken leaves, and other early greenery, to be found in the hedges or specially cultivated for the purpose. During the Easter holidays young people played hand-ball for tansy-balls ; but why and wherefore has not been told us.

This is a good recipe for the ordinary Easter cake : —4 lbs. of flour, 2 lbs. of butter, 2 lbs. of sifted sugar, eight yolks and four whites of eggs, a tea-spoonful of sal-volatile, and cinnamon to taste. Mix 1 lb. of butter with the flour, add the sugar and spice ; melt the other pound of butter and mix it with the eggs, then all together, roll it out thin, cut the paste into good-sized rounds, put them on a floured tin, and bake in the oven.

St. David's Day was celebrated by taffy-cakes, and Lent by these same tansy-cakes, and the carling, simbling, and simnel-cake for Simmel or Mothering Sunday—viz., mid-Lent Sunday.

Harland, in his " Lancashire Legends," talks of—

" The good rounde sugarye
    Kinge of Cakes, a Burye Symnelle,
    It speaks of deareste familye tyes,
    From friende to friende in Lent it hyes ;
    To all good fellowshippe yᵗ cries,
    I'm a righte trewe Burye Simnelle."

It is made of 3 lbs. of flour, 1 lb. of butter, well rubbed into the flour, 3 lbs. of currants, 1 lb. of sugar, 3 oz. of ground cinnamon, 2 oz. of bitter, 2 oz. of sweet almonds, blanched and chopped, 3 oz. of candied lemon, four eggs, taking out two yolks, and some cooks add half a tea-cupful of barm. There are varieties in the recipe, but this a good one.

Pan-cakes are of very ancient origin, and were an offering by the pagan Saxons to the sun. Shrove Tuesday really means confession Tuesday—the day immediately before Ash Wednesday—when everybody was expected to obtain absolution, and, to remind them, a great bell was rung in every parish. This in time came to be called pancake bell, as it was the signal for the cook to put the pancake on the fire. Old writers describe them as made of wheaten flour, water, eggs, and spice, placed in a frying-pan with boiling suet. In some places the youths and maidens used to flit from house to house collecting the various requisites to make them. There is a superstition that some of the white of egg should be put into a glass of pure water and set near the window, where, the sun shining on it, it will foretell the future, for the white of egg floats about and takes some form—say a ship or a tent, foretelling a sailor's or a soldier's career, for example.

Hot-cross-buns, like most cakes eaten at religious seasons, were a sort of stay to the appetite till more substantial fare could be obtained. By some they are considered symbolic of the bread broken by our Lord Himself at the Last Supper, and of His death on Calvary. To break a Good Friday bun has always been considered a pledge of friendship, and a surety against disagreement, the act being accompanied by the words :—

" Half for you and half for me,
    Between us two goodwill shall be."

Hot-cross-buns were supposed to be endued with some peculiar sanctity, and were kept through the year for good luck, as a charm against fire, and a remedy for certain diseases.

THE complications of modern life are many. Our grandmothers had an easy time of it, when they did their shopping within half a mile from home, never visited anybody residing beyond a short driving distance, while our grandfathers took all their meal which ladies love beyond all others, might well carry us through the difficulties which beset us on those days when, starting off for a long spell of hard labour among West-end shops, or picture galleries, or a summer day's expedition, we feel we may be terribly

meals in a regular way, and business was far too leisurely to keep dinner waiting. The fates forbid that some new invention shall make it possible for us to "pop over" to Edinburgh or Paris, or shall compel us to offend our friends in those places by shirking their evening invitations !

A pleasant north country custom, the combination of substantial viands with the refreshment of that unpunctual for our six o'clock dinner, and that nothing would be so welcome to our jaded nerves as the aroma of the tea-pot ? Again, why should not the caterer for our comfort on long, pic-nicking summer days be relieved of such elaborate responsibilities of knives and forks and spoons, of potted meats and leaking jam-pots ? How much less burdensome—how much "nicer," to use that abused word which expresses so much—a few simple, cleanly sandwiches and lovely fresh fruits, and then a home-coming to a bountiful meal, where the very latest adventures of the holiday may be summed up and discussed.

It was in this dilemma, intent on proving ourselves considerate to the wants of one of these expeditionary parties, that some useful brownie at our household hearth whispered, "High tea!" And the moment the thought came we exclaimed, "The very thing!"

It would suit everybody. Mr. C. would find some substantial viands to sustain him. No formality could separate Dr. B. and Miss E., and we shall be all in the drawing-room by eight o'clock. Nobody will go away starved.

"High tea" is a meal which can be arranged quite fittingly in many rooms, where any attempt at a "dinner-party" would look pretentious and absurd. It will not overwhelm even the modest breakfast-parlour of a suburban villa. It will not embarrass the thrifty mistress of a single servant. Its dishes are not of huge proportions or superabundant heat, and there is a pleasant, sociable easiness about it, which encourages polite little attentions among the guests themselves, and does not too severely tax the domestic waiting powers.

It can be made the prettiest of all meals. A well-chosen tea-urn is a graceful object in itself, and tea-china is generally much prettier than dinner-services, unless the latter be very expensive. Tea and coffee should be always offered, and there should be abundance of milk on hand. Let the china be as varied as possible : if every article can be different from the others, so much the better : if not, arrange those similar in little groups. Three plates should be allotted to each visitor—viz., a small one for bread-and-butter, &c., a larger one for the savoury dishes, and another for the sweet ones. These two last can be set on the table or reserved on a sideboard, as convenience or taste may dictate. Take care that a sufficiency of knives, forks, and spoons are provided —which seems an unnecessary reminder ; but any informality of hospitality is too apt to degenerate into slovenliness, and servants want more direction and watching on these occasions than when they have harder and faster lines to guide them.

When possible, have a growing plant on the table, placed in a china pot or a pretty wicker fencing. This is the most pleasant decoration for an entertainment which must never be deprived of a sort of impromptu character. When flowers are difficult or costly to procure, a very pretty effect of colour may be made by a wise purchase and arrangement of fruit in a high epergne, the simpler in its form the better. Grapes and blushing apples are always refreshing to the eye, and can be had in winter. Remember to introduce no fruit, such as oranges, which would be unsuitable for eating with tea or coffee.

It must never be forgotten that high tea must offer some really substantial edibles. At the same time, there should be nothing difficult to serve or to partake. A cold fowl is always welcome, but it should be carved in readiness as should be some well-roasted and attractive-looking cold beef. But in addition to the cold dishes which must always figure at a meal instituted partly for the benefit of those who cannot be strictly punctual, there are one or two hot dishes which are very suitable for the more fortunate guests. Daintily minced and seasoned mutton, served up in a fencing of nicely mashed potatoes, will be found very acceptable to visitors coming from a distance, and really requiring a good meal. "Rissoles" are also deservedly popular. For these the best parts only of meat are chopped very finely ; a quarter of its weight of bread-crumbs is added, then an onion boiled to a tender pulp, the whole flavoured with pepper, salt, and beaten egg in fit proportion to the quantity of meat and bread-crumb. If the balls do not seem to bind, some flour may be added. An ounce of butter will serve for the frying of several of these rissoles, and they must be very carefully turned. If considered too dry without it, they may be served with gravy.

"Kidneys sautés" are another suitable dish. Choose them of a nice size, and cut them the round way into thin slices. Dip these into flour well mixed with pepper and salt, and fry them gently, allowing not more than a minute for each side. Pour over them a little gravy thickened with flour, and serve them very hot.

"Potato croquets" are often very popular, and will go well with the kidneys, or by themselves. They are one of the simplest and cheapest of dishes. Boil and carefully mash some excellent mealy potatoes. Add pepper and salt and beaten egg sufficient to make a stiff paste. Make this into nice-sized balls, roll them in bread-crumbs, with a little more egg ; boil some frying-fat, put the balls into the wire basket, and fry for a minute. They must be only of a light brown colour, and should be quite crisp on the outside.

For sweet dishes, open jam tarts are never out of place. In winter time take care to provide stewed pears or plums. If high tea is given in the days of strawberries, cherries, and currants, so much the better.

If one wants to indulge in a little "cookery," a chocolate *soufflé* is a nice dish, and not at all common ; but it ought not to be in the bill of fare unless cocoa or chocolate is served, as well as tea and coffee. To make this, mix two table-spoonfuls of flour with two of powdered loaf-sugar, two ounces of butter, and a quarter of a pint of milk. Stir this over the fire till it boils ; let it cool, and then stir in the yolks of four eggs and a quarter of an ounce of cocoa. Add the whites of eggs well beaten. Bake about forty-five minutes. Any other flavouring, such as vanilla, can be substituted for the cocoa.

"Marmalade pudding" is a variety among "mould" dishes, which introduces a flavour very suitable for a tea-table. This is made in the following proportions : —To one table-spoonful of marmalade, five ounces of bread-crumbs, two ounces of currants, one ounce of butter, two ounces of sugar. Melt the butter and mix it with the other ingredients, then add two eggs well beaten, and half a pint of milk. Butter a mould and pour the mixture into it, tie a cloth tightly over it, and boil it for an hour and a half.

It should not be forgotten that at high tea there should be plenty of nicely-sliced bread-and-butter, and two or three varieties of cake of the simpler and lighter kinds.

We feel quite sure that, as a form of hospitality, high tea might become thoroughly popular. It is a meal at least as adapted for the requirements and exigencies of rapid London as it is for the quiet moorlands of the North, where it is such an old-established favourite. It should be always a genuine meal, and not a mere ceremony; and yet it is the meal least likely to become the sole "entertainment," or to be anything but a genuine refreshment for that interchange of thought and kindliness which should be the true purpose of all social gatherings.

Glossary of Victorian Cooking Terms

While most of the instructions and ingredients listed in these pages will be easily understood by the modern cook, a few will set us to scratching our heads. Lacking modern electric or gas ovens, microwaves and other devices, for instance, Victorian cooks had utensils at their disposal that most of us have never seen or even heard of (such as the "salamander"). Measurements are often indicated by weight, or by units long since abandoned (e.g., the gill, the noggin and the drachm), or by even less helpful terms as "a sixpennyworth." (I can give you translations for gills and noggins, but I'm afraid determining what a "sixpennyworth" of an ingredient might mean today is beyond my capabilities!)

I'm sure I haven't covered every odd or unusual term in these pages, but this glossary should (I hope) cover most causes of potential confusion for the modern cook. Where appropriate, I've also indicated whether an item or ingredient is available today, and/or what to use as a modern substitute.

Unless otherwise noted, definitions in quotes are taken from Wikipedia. (Since most of these Wikipedia entries are British, I've simply retained the original spelling of the definitions.)

Angelica - There are many varieties of this herb, but the one referred to in Victorian recipes is Garden Angelica *(A. archangelica)*. "Crystallized strips of young angelica stems and midribs are green in colour and are sold as decorative and flavoursome cake decoration material." Roots and seeds of angelica have been used to flavor gin and various liqueurs, including Chartreuse. **Substitute:** Crystallized angelica as a culinary decoration no longer seems to be available. Since this was used primarily for decorative purposes, simply substitute some other form of decoration.

Auflauf - A German term; in British cooking it most often refers to a soufflé or baked pudding. In German it is more likely to refer to a casserole. (http://www.dict.cc/german-english/Auflauf.html) One recipe in this book describes Auflauf as a meringue.

Bain Marie - A "water bath"—basically a double-boiler, in which a lower pot contains water and the upper/inner pot contains food items, such as chocolate, that should not be cooked or melted over direct heat. **Available:** Yes; a search on this term will bring up both bain maries and double-boilers. **Substitute:** A double-boiler. If you do not have a double boiler, simply use a small saucepan resting within a larger pot containing water.

Barm - "Barm is the foam, or scum, formed on the top of liquor... when fermenting. It was used to leaven bread, or set up fermentation in a new batch of liquor. Barm... is sometimes used in English baking as a synonym for a natural leaven." **Substitute:** Yeast.

Biscuit - In British terminology a "biscuit" is what an American would refer to as either a cookie (if sweet) or a cracker. Conversely, an American "biscuit" would be referred to as a roll or bun or possibly a scone in Britain. These terms remain the same today; if you wish a "cookie" in Britain, ask for a biscuit!

Biscuit-powder - Unknown; possibly baking powder.

Castor or Caster sugar - "A very fine sugar in Britain and other Commonwealth countries, so-named because the grains are small enough to fit through a castor, a form of sieve. Commonly used in baking and mixed drinks, it is sold as 'superfine' sugar in the United States. Because of its fineness it dissolves more quickly than regular white sugar and is thus especially useful in meringues and cold liquids. Castor sugar can be prepared at home by grinding granulated sugar for a couple of minutes in a mortar or food processor. **Available:** Yes; sold in the US as "caster" sugar. **Substitute:** "Superfine" sugar.

Chartreuse - A dish made in a mold using pieces of meat, vegetables, or fruit in jelly. (Google definition.)

Cochineal - A red food coloring made from insects. **Substitute:** Red food coloring. (Cochineal dye is still available but not for food use.)

Compote - "Compote is a dessert originating from medieval Europe, made of whole or pieces of fruit in sugar syrup. Whole fruits are cooked in water with sugar and spices."

Corn-flour - Cornstarch.

Dariole - "A French term meaning a small, cylindrical mold. The word also refers to the dessert that is baked in the mold. Classically, the dessert is made by lining the mold with puff pastry, filling it with an almond cream and baking until golden brown."

Drachm (dram) - "The *fluid dram* is defined as ⅛ of a fluid ounce." When used as a measure of weight, a dram equals ¹⁄₁₆ ounce.

Dressed flour - A more finely milled flour than regular flour; defined by the size of the sieve through which it could pass. **Available:** No. **Substitute:** Cake flour.

Ebullition - "The act, process, or state of boiling or bubbling up" (Merriam-Webster).

Flummery - "A starch-based sweet soft dessert pudding known to have been popular in Britain and Ireland from the 17th to 19th centuries."

Fool - "A fool is an English dessert. Traditionally, fruit fool is made by folding pureed stewed fruit (classically gooseberries) into sweet custard. Modern fool recipes often skip the traditional custard and use whipped cream. Additionally, a flavouring agent like rose water may be added."

Gallipot - Originally a small earthenware jar or bowl used by apothecaries. Later this evolved into a small, shallow bowl, which might be earthenware or metal, usually with a rim around the edge. **Available:** Yes. **Substitute:** Any small, round, relatively shallow bowl.

Gâteau - Defined as a rich cake, typically one containing layers of cream or fruit. Victorian cooks, however, did not seem to use this term synonymously with "cake," so don't assume that a recipe for "gâteau" is in fact a cake recipe. In fact, some recipes use cake as an *ingredient* in gâteau—e.g., slices of cake layered and glazed with jam or marmalade.

Gill - "The gill is a unit of measurement for volume equal to a quarter of a pint."

Girdle - Griddle

Hock-Glass - A glass for white wine. Since a hock glass once was quite large, holding 1½ cups of wine, this was undoubtedly meant as a measurement. (http://www.ehow.com/facts_5292426_hock-wine-glass.html).

Hydrochloric acid - This might seem like a strange thing to add to one's cooking, but the Victorian housewife would undoubtedly have had it around the house for cleaning purposes. When mixed with baking soda it creates a bubbling, aerating action that is useful in making certain types of bread. Modern recipes for soda bread call for the use of baking soda and baking powder, which sounds like a better idea!

Isinglass - "A substance obtained from the dried swim bladders of fish [primarily sturgeon]. It is a form of collagen used mainly for the clarification or fining of beer. It can also be cooked into a paste for specialized gluing purposes... Before the inexpensive production of gelatin and other competitive products, isinglass was used in confectionery and desserts such as fruit jelly and blanc-mange." **Available:** Yes. **Substitute:** Plain gelatin.

Noggin - A noggin (or "small cup") is ⅙ of a gill (23.7 ml).

Ratafia/Ratifia biscuits - "Ratafia is a term used for two types of sweet alcoholic beverage, either a fortified wine or a fruit-based beverage. The latter type is a liqueur or cordial flavoured with lemon peel, herbs in various amounts (nutmeg, cinnamon, clove, mint, rosemary, anise, etc.) typically combined with sugar. It may also be prepared with peach or cherry kernels, bitter almonds, or other fruits, as many different varieties are made. The same name is given to a flavouring essence resembling bitter almonds, and also to a light biscuit." The correct spelling is "ratafia," though some recipes in this volume use "ratifia." **Available:** Yes. **Substitute:** Macaroons; Italian-style almond cookies (e.g., Amaretti).

Redded up - Cleared up, cleaned up.

Rennet - "A complex of enzymes produced in the stomachs of ruminant mammals which is used in the production of most cheeses. It can also be used to separate milk into solid curds used for cheese-making and liquid whey. **Available:** Yes; sold as "junket rennet tablets." And by the way, the recipe you'll find in the junket box for making plain "junket" is quite delicious!

Rissole - "Initially created in France, [this] is a small croquette, enclosed in pastry or rolled in breadcrumbs, usually baked or deep fried. It is filled with sweet or savory ingredients, most often minced meat or fish, and is served as an entrée, main course, dessert or side dish."

Rissolette - I haven't found a precise definition for this term, but assume it is a diminutive of "rissole."

Sago or Sego - The correct spelling is "sago," which is "a starch extracted from the spongy centre, or pith, of various tropical palm stems... Large quantities of sago are sent to Europe and North America for cooking purposes. It is traditionally cooked and eaten in various forms, such as rolled into balls, mixed with boiling water to form a paste, or as a pancake. Sago is often produced commercially in the form of 'pearls.' Sago pearls can be boiled with water or milk and sugar to make a sweet sago pudding. Sago pearls are similar in appearance to tapioca pearls and the two may be used interchangeably in some dishes. **Available:** Yes, generally as an ethnic food. **Substitute:** Tapioca pearls.

Salamander - A device used to grill, toast or brown the top of a dish. A salamander consisted of "an iron disc on a handle which is heated and placed over a dish to brown it... In the 18th century, a salamander was the tool of choice for toasting the top of a dish. It consisted of a thick plate of iron attached to the end of a long handle with two feet, or rests, arranged near the end (where the iron plate is) for propping the plate over the food to be browned." Some Victorian recipes note that a small shovel can be heated and used for the same purpose. **Available:** Yes – electric salamanders are available, primarily for use in commercial kitchens. **Substitute:** Today the same results are usually achieved with an overhead grill in one's oven, or in the case of making a crème brulee, a culinary blowtorch.

Saleratus - "The word *saleratus*, from Latin *sal æratus* meaning *aerated salt*, was widely used in the 19th century for both sodium bicarbonate and potassium bicarbonate." **Substitute:** Baking soda.

Tammy cloth - A light-weight worsted cloth generally used for bunting and ribbons; when pressed its surface had a high gloss. **Available:** No. **Substitute:** Unknown.

Tartaric Acid - "Tartaric acid is a white crystalline diprotic acid. This aldaric acid occurs naturally in many plants, particularly grapes, bananas, and tamarinds, is commonly combined with baking soda to function as a leavening agent in recipes, and is one of the main acids found in wine." **Substitute:** Cream of tartar.

Tire-Bouchon - Literally "corkscrew" in French. In the recipe on page 39, the pastry is wrapped around a stick to create the look of a corkscrew.

Treacle - While this is a familiar term to British readers, it's less well known to Americans. "Treacle is any uncrystallised syrup made during the refining of sugar. The most common forms of treacle are golden syrup, a pale variety, and a darker variety known as black treacle. Black treacle, or molasses, has a distinctively strong, slightly bitter flavour, and a richer colour than golden syrup. Golden syrup treacle is a common sweetener and condiment in British cookery, found in such dishes as treacle tart and treacle sponge pudding." **Available:** Yes; readily available in the UK; available in specialty cooking stores or online in the US. **Substitute:** Corn syrup for golden treacle, or molasses for black treacle.

Vienna flour - An extremely fine, highly milled flour. **Available:** No. **Substitute:** Superfine flour; in addition, consider sifting it or running it through a sieve before use.

Recipe Index by Title

Recipe Index by Category

For easy reference, this section lists recipes in the categories of **Breads, Cakes, Candies, Custards & Creams, Ices & Ice Cream, Pastry Basics, Puddings,** and **Savouries.**

Breads

Cakes & Tea-Cakes

Candy

Cookies & "Biscuits"

Custards & Creams

Ices & Ice Cream

Pastry-Making

Puddings

Savoury Dishes

If You Love Christmas, Thank a Victorian!

What do you love most about Christmas?
- The tree, with its lights and glittering baubles?
- Decking the halls with greens and holly?
- Filling the stockings and making the little ones' holiday dreams come true?
- Christmas cards that keep you connected with friends old and new?
- Christmas movies that rekindle the holiday spirit (with endless variations on "Scrooge"...)

Chances are, the traditions you love the most have their roots in the Victorian era. The Victorians didn't *invent* Christmas, but they certainly *redefined* it. They brought us the Christmas tree, Christmas cards, and a host of traditions that are a cherished part of our celebrations today. They even brought us our most beloved holiday icons - Santa and Scrooge - who still provide a means of expressing the Christmas spirit even to those who prefer not to celebrate a religious holiday.

A Victorian Christmas Treasury

Recipes, Reminiscences, Games, Decorations, Celebrations, Parties, Folklore, Stories, Poetry... and Much More!

Edited by Moira Allen

Wouldn't you love to be able to travel back in time to experience a genuine Victorian Christmas? Well, now you can! This book is your magical time travel guide to Christmas in Victorian times. It brings you never-before-anthologized articles, poems, stories and carols from dozens of Victorian magazines, from the 1840's to the turn of the century. You'll discover:

- Authentic Victorian recipes
- "New" ideas for Victorian decorating
- Victorian Christmas carols (some familiar, some you've probably never heard before)
- Glimpses into how Christmas was celebrated in the Victorian home (and elsewhere)
- Christmas traditions around the world
- Christmas history and folklore - including a look at London's pageants and Europe's "mystery plays"
- Christmas stories and poems that celebrate the Victorian season
- Plus exquisite Victorian holiday artwork!

It's a unique holiday collection you'll treasure for years to come!

Order it today from Amazon!
Find out more at www.VictorianVoices.net/books/Christmas.shtml

CPSIA information can be obtained
at www.ICGtesting.com
Printed in the USA
BVHW02s1114210118
505895BV00018B/506/P